COAST GUARD AIR STATION
HOUSTON

COAST GUARD AIR STATION
Puerto Rico
LES SAR FROGS
BORINQUEN

COAST GUARD AIR STATION
SITKA, ALASKA

U.S. COAST GUARD AIR STATION
SEARCH AND RESCUE
NORTH BEND, OREGON

USCG
AVIATION TECHNICAL
TRAINING CENTER
ELIZABETH CITY, N.C.

COAST GUARD AIR STATION
WASHINGTON

COAST GUARD AIR STATION
CAPE COD MASS

SEARCH and RESCUE
COAST GUARD AIR STATION
BROOKLYN

COAST GUARD AIR STATION
SEMPER PARATUS
BARBERS POINT HAWAII

U.S. COAST GUARD
SEARCH AND RESCUE
CGAS ELIZABETH CITY NC

SAN FRANCISCO
SEARCH AND RESCUE
UNITED STATES COAST GUARD AIR STATION
SERVING THE GOLDEN GATE DISTRICT

US COAST GUARD AIR STATION
CORPUS CHRISTI TEXAS

COAST GUARD AIR STATION
SAVANNAH
S.C.
GA.
FLA.

WITHDRAWN

UNITED STATES COAST GUARD
AVIATION TRAINING CENTER

A HISTORY OF
U.S. COAST GUARD
AVIATION

A HISTORY OF
U.S. COAST GUARD
AVIATION

ARTHUR PEARCY

Naval Institute Press

Published and distributed in the United States of America and
Canada by the Naval Institute Press, Annapolis, Maryland 21402.

Library of Congress Catalog Card No. 88-62578

ISBN 0-87021-261-3

This edition is authorized for sale only in the United States and its
territories and possessions, and Canada.

Printed in Singapore.

Contents

Foreword

Arthur Pearcy, author and aviation historian, has created a fascinating blend of facts, photographs and stories which combine to make a thoroughly entertaining history of Coast Guard Aviation. He takes us on an authentic trip through the excitement, danger and romance of flight, sharing the achievements and adventure of those who pioneered aviation in our Service, and those who struggled to bring it to its present level of excellence.

The course of aviation in general has not run smoothly. So too, the Coast Guard's aviation experience had early start-up problems, lacking financial support from Congress to sustain their initial flying efforts. But our aviators persevered. They were men of vision who couldn't fly very high or fast or far, but they saw the great potential for aircraft surveillance over water, to improve our search and rescue, law enforcement and other maritime missions along the coast. From the first days, when the Coast Guard was financed and formed to develop techniques through trial and error with a variety of flying machines, the author traces our people and our aircraft through seven decades, leaving us with some thoughts about the future of aviation in the Coast Guard.

The book takes us from the early 'stick and wire' seaplane days, through the golden age of the thirties, and into the days of all metal fuselages, retractable landing gear, amphibians, radio improvements, shipboard operations off our cutters and the rapid expansion during World War II. We see the age of reciprocating engines begin to give way to turboprops in the late fifties with C-130 Hercules, followed by turbine engine helicopters in the sixties; the eighties bring sweptwing jets. Gone are the special sounds and smells of our old piston pounders with computers now in every cockpit; we fight the airborne drug smugglers with Falcons as all weather interceptors vectored by our own baby 'AWACS' (E2C Hawkeyes) and one of our young aviators is in astronaut training . . . The future is bright.

I believe this volume represents a truly significant contribution in our continuing search to improve the awareness and understanding of Coast Guard Aviation. All those magnificent people who have fixed and flown our aircraft deserve no less.

Rear Admiral Donald C Thompson USCG
Commander, Atlantic Area and Commander
United States Maritime Defense Zone Atlantic
United States Coast Guard
June 1988

Dedication

This book is dedicated to Gordon Sear Williams, my good friend for many years, who died on 25 June 1986. 'Gordy' served in the Coast Guard at Port Angeles air station and took many of the excellent photos used in this volume. He is seen here on the left, with his brother, George Harold 'Bud' Williams, at Port Angeles air station, Washington

I also dedicate this tribute to Coast Guard Aviation to all those intrepid USCG aviators who answered the call, but failed to return.

Acknowledgements

Firstly, my sincere and grateful thanks to all the many Coast Guard personnel who, over the past twenty years or more, have made me so welcome when visting the USCG air stations and facilities. On the brief visits to USCG HQ in Washington DC made prior to 1987, the Public Affairs personnel made me more than welcome and when the Public Affairs office invited me to spend some time in the archives, it was an opportunity not to be missed. The United States Coast Guard Historian, Robert L Scheina, aided my research into the archives and photo library, providing a wealth of advice, whilst the Chief, Media Relations Branch, Werner A Siems, ably assisted by the Assistant Chief, Nicholas G Sandifer, treated my many queries and requests for information with the utmost patience and understanding. The week I spent with them in the Spring of 1987 was more than productive, and my sincere thanks go to all those personnel who assisted me in any way.

Apart from all the official USCG assistance with this volume, the author would like to thank William T Larkins, who over many years has made available his large collection of memorabilia on USCG aviation, and granted access to his large private collection of USCG negatives. Peter M Bowers also put his large photo and negative collection at my disposal, as did Vic Seeley, both of Seattle, the latter now deeply involved in the new Museum of Flight. David W Menard at the USAF Museum located at Dayton, Ohio, also assisted with photos including those of the unique Le Page helicopter.

Hans Halberstadt of Presidio Press, San Francisco, assisted by ace photographer George Hall, published a beautiful and colourful paper-back tribute to the US Coast Guard. My sincere thanks to both of them for the material they provided.

The aircraft manufacturers who provide the hardware for the Coast Guard were more than co-operative, providing material and photographs as required. They include, Lois Lovisolo, Corporate Historian (Grumman Corporation): Joseph Dabney, News Bureau (Lockheed-Marietta): Fred C Lash, Manager, Media Relations Programme (Sikorsky Aircraft): Harry Gann, Manager, Aircraft Information (Douglas Aircraft Company); and Terry A Arnold, Manager, V-22 Communications (Bell Helicopter Textron). To other companies and agencies, too numerous to mention, my grateful thanks.

Peter Wells, a scientist involved in helicopter research, and an aviation buff, kindly volunteered to provide the three-view drawings of the early McDonnell projects, and Dustin W Carter, retired aero-engineer, provided plans for the US Coast Guard Sabreliner project. Photos and colour slides were obtained from two United Kingdom photo agencies: Military Aircraft Photos (MAP) under the guidance of friend Brian Pickering, and Aviation Photo News (APN) with Brian Stainer. John Gaffney, Public Affairs Officer at San Francisco air station kindly loaned his personal collection of USCG aircraft colour slides taken at various exotic locations.

My warmest thanks go to Vice Admiral D C (Deese) Thompson for writing the Foreword to his definitive history of US Coast Guard Aviation. Admiral Thompson, a highly respected aviator, acknowledged my request without hesitation.

Alastair Simpson, Director of Airlife Publishing Limited, has co-operated since the birth of the project. He has guided, encouraged and devoted a personal interest in this production. My wife Audrey, whose motto is 'If you cannot fight them, join them,' has proof read every word and has been a tower of strength. My grateful thanks for her continued patience and vigilance.

My sincere apologies and thanks to those I have not mentioned, but who contributed to this tribute to US Coast Guard Aviation, a vital part of the United States' oldest continuous sea-going military service.

Arthur Pearcy
Sharnbrook, Bedford
July 1988

Introduction

Currently within two years of its bicentennial celebrations, the United States Coast Guard is the fifth military arm of the USA, but under the jurisdiction of the US Department of Transportation. It is the smallest of the five, but yet the most active, especially in the field of Coast Guard Aviation which has been described as 'a way of life, not merely a job'.

It currently has a force of over 38,000 personnel on active duty, with nearly 1,000 officers and 3,000 enlisted ranks employed in aviation. Its reservists total nearly 19,000 and it has a unique membership of auxiliaries numbering nearly 40,000 nationwide. Retirees total over 24,000.

The Coast Guard *Air Operations Manual* tersely describes the mission of Coast Guard Aviation as being '. . . to provide operational and logistics support to Coast Guard mission areas'. However, a more pragmatic description of the mission is, '. . . to professionally meet the unexpected mission of greatest demand, while preserving the flexibility to accommodate anything less'. Today, the men and women of the Coast Guard adhere to the service's motto of being *Semper Paratus* (Always Ready) for professional response to aviation mission requirements, ranging from the monumental to the mundane, throughout the world. In so doing, these dedicated professionals support, maintain and operate over 170 aircraft, twenty-four hours a day throughout the year from twenty-seven Coast Guard air stations along the coastlines of the United States, including the Great Lakes, Alaska, Hawaii and Puerto Rico.

A red flag, hoisted over the camp occupied by Orville and Wilbur Wright on 17 December 1903 summoned the surfmen of the Kill Devil Hills Life Saving Station to the aid of the would-be inventors. So the US Coast Guard was introduced to aviation in 1903, these surfmen providing the Wright Brothers with added muscle during the pre-launch activities of that epic flight. Three surfmen helped carry the fragile biplane from the shelter of the sand dunes to the launch site at Kittyhawk in North Carolina. Surfman John T Daniels took the only photograph of the event using the Wrights' camera.

Early in 1915 the first practical steps toward a Coast Guard air arm occurred when Lieutenant Elmer Stone and Norman Hall conceived the idea of using aircraft for Coast Guard missions. With the backing of their commanding officer they approached the Curtiss Flying School at Newport News, Virginia, discussed their idea and were taken on experimental flights in the school's aircraft. A Curtiss F flying-boat was used for much of the experiment. In spite of the technological limitations of the aircraft, the experiment proved successful. As a result, in April 1916, Elmer Stone and five others were assigned to the Naval Aviation School at Pensacola, Florida, for pilot training. Norman Hall was sent to the Curtiss factory to study aeronautical engineering. Later in 1916, US Congress authorized the Coast Guard to establish ten air stations, but no money was appropriated and the efforts were stillborn.

A second false start for Coast Guard Aviation occurred in March 1920, when the Coast Guard's first air station was established at Morehead City, North Carolina, when the service took over the abandoned US Navy's air station and borrowed a few Curtiss HS.2L flying-boats, and possibly one or two Aeromarine Model 40s from the US Navy. The aircraft were particularly useful in locating those in distress and finding derelicts. Unfortunately, funds were not provided to support the operation and the station was closed on 1 July 1921.

Despite the early promise of aviation, the Coast Guard did not receive any money from the US Congress during and immediately following World War I. In 1925 Lieutenant Commander C G von Paulsen borrowed a Vought UO-1 seaplane from the US Navy. Operating from Squantum, Massachusetts, and later Ten Pound Island in Gloucester Harbor, he demonstrated the potential of aviation in combating the smuggling of whisky. Prohibition had become law in 1920 and soon its enforcement became the dominant mission of the Coast Guard. As a result, the US Congress appropriated $152,000 for five aircraft, the first to be owned by the service. Three Loening OL-5 amphibians and two Chance Vought UO-4s were purchased. The Coast Guard adopted a special colouring of its own for their new aircraft, a bright chrome yellow covering the entire wings and body. This colour was clearly visible at sea, and distinguished the Coast Guard aircraft clearly from those of the US Army Air Corps and the US Navy.

The first function of the new air arm was to locate derelicts and vessels in distress; secondarily, they acted as scouts and chastising agents in rum warfare. President Coolidge in his budget message to Congress gave intimation that he would ask for further resources for prohibition enforcement that year. The President told Congress that the activities of the Coast Guard 'should be enlarged and strengthened at the earliest date possible'. 'To this end,' the President added significantly, 'I propose to recommend to the Congress additional appropriations for the Coast Guard for the remainder of this fiscal year and for the next fiscal year.

'Every available resource of the Government will be employed for prohibition enforcement. The recommendations which I propose to make to the Congress are for the purpose of increasing this available force. Such reinforcement is needed. It should be provided.' The President's message was published in the *Washington Star* dated 17 December 1925.

By the late 1920s the search and rescue clientele had changed primarily from coastal sailors to ocean-going motor ships. Trade routes were moved further out to sea so that when the emergency arose, they were frequently far off the coast. In 1928 an aviation section was established at Coast Guard Headquarters under the command of Commander Norman Hall. It drew up specifications for a multi-mission aircraft which, given the technology of the day, could be met only by a large seaplane or amphibian. To aid distressed mariners, the Coast Guard developed the concept of the 'flying lifeboats'. This concept can still be recognized today as the Coast Guard Research & Development team attempt to design a specification for today's requirements.

The specification of those early pioneering days was based on an aircraft that could fly hundreds of miles, land in an open and frequently uninviting sea, and carry out a rescue. Seven aircraft were acquired, two Douglas RD-2 *Dolphins* modified to Coast Guard requirements, plus five General Aviation Flying Life Boat PJ-1s, these being specifically designed for the service. This fleet was involved in numerous rescues.

In 1934 Henry Morgenthau became the Secretary of the Treasury, the department responsible for the Coast Guard. He was an aviation enthusiast and supported its expansion within the Coast Guard. His enthusiasm for USCG aviation was important to its development. He obtained Public Works Administration funds for the purchase of new aircraft and additional air stations. By 1936 the Coast Guard had six air stations, two air detachments and forty-two aircraft.

Also during the 1930s, the marriage between the USCG cutter and aircraft took place. The 327-foot cutters each embarked a Grumman JF-2 *Duck* amphibian. These aircraft-equipped cutters were designed to patrol against opium smuggling off the west coast and fisheries violations in Alaskan waters, and to serve on plane guard duty in the Atlantic to protect the embryonic transcontinental commercial air service. With the introduction of the helicopter, its potential mating with the USCG cutter was soon recognized, a partnership retained today.

World War II accelerated the growth of aviation within all the US armed services, the Coast Guard being no exception. It played a critical role in the defence of Greenland. Prior to the entry of the United States into the conflict, the USCG cutter *Duane,* with a Curtiss SOC-4 *Seagull* on board, surveyed the coastline of Greenland for potential airfield sites during 1941. After the USA entered the war, USCG aircraft operated from cutters and located German weather stations in the frozen northern areas of Greenland. These stations were providing critical data to U-boats operating in the North Atlantic; the stations were captured by the Coast Guard. Aircraft of the USCG performed harrowing rescues, flying through snow storms and landing on the ice cap to pick up distressed Allied air crews who had crashed whilst attempting to ferry aircraft to Europe across the Atlantic. During the latter part of 1943, Patrol Bombing Squadron Six was activated in Greenland.

The Coast Guard was incorporated into the US Navy on 1 November 1941. By this time the USCG was seriously interested in developing the helicopter for search and rescue work. Lieutenant Commander William Kossler had represented the Coast Guard on an inter-agency board formed in 1938 for the evaluation of experimental aircraft, including the helicopter. In early 1943 the USCG was tasked with developing the helicopter for anti-submarine warfare. Sikorsky HNS-1 and HOS-1 helicopters were ordered and pilot training began at Brooklyn air station, New York. It was Coast Guard personnel who trained British pilots to undertake a joint British-American helicopter trial on board the merchant ship *Daghestan.* In fact, during World War II all Allied helicopter pilots were trained by the USCG at Brooklyn air station. The *Daghestan,* fitted with a landing deck and carrying two HNS-1 helicopters, crossed the Atlantic in convoy during November 1943.

Additional helicopter evaluation tests were carried out on the USCG cutter *Cobb.* This old coastal passenger ship had been converted into the world's first helicopter carrier. On 29 June 1944 Commander Frank Erickson made the first landing on its deck in Long Island Sound. As the war progressed and the U-boat threat moved deeper into the North Atlantic and then abated, the service re-orientated its helicopter research from anti-submarine warfare to search and rescue. Credit must go to Commander Erickson for pioneering this new invention, developing much of the rescue equipment himself and carrying out the first ever life saving flight. He maintained a close link with the helicopter manufacturer Sikorsky. Any student of helicopter research will at once acknowledge the long line of search and rescue helicopters supplied to the Coast Guard by the Sikorsky company.

During 1943 an Air Sea Rescue Squadron was formed at San Diego air station in California. The primary impetus for this was the increasing number of offshore crashes, mostly by student pilots. These resulted from the rapid expansion of military aircraft training during the war. Initially, the very successful and popular Consolidated PBY-5 *Catalina* assisted by high speed rescue craft were chosen, the success of these resulting in additional squadrons being formed. In December 1944 the Office of Air Sea Rescue was established at Coast Guard headquarters. By 1945 Air Sea Rescue was responsible for 165 aircraft and nine air stations. During that year alone it had responded to 686 aircraft crashes. After World War II the PBY-5 was supplemented and eventually replaced by the Martin PBM-5G *Mariner.*

The post war years brought an explosion in the number of recreational boats and created a new search and rescue clientele for the Coast Guard. Today there are an estimated forty million pleasure craft in use, especially at the weekends and holidays. The helicopter was and still is ideally suited for this mission. On shore during the off-season, USCG reservists and auxilaries attempt to educate the mass of boat owners in the art of seamanship, basic meteorology, care of equipment etc. The helicopter is able to react swiftly, being able to lift entire pleasure boat crews from imminent disaster, or in less trying circumstances, deliver de-watering pumps and fuel. Admittedly, during its early years the helicopter had a major handicap — the pilot required three hands in order to fly it. Today it is just the opposite, having an on-board mission computer that gives flight guidance and control and provides the pilot with his third hand. It was not long before USCG helicopters rescuing distressed mariners became a commonplace event around the US coastline.

Following World War II the responsibilities of Coast Guard fixed wing aviation also increased. During 1946 USCG aircraft were used for the first time on the International Ice Patrol, a practice that continues today, ably assisted by avionics including Side-looking Airborne Radar (SLAR). Since 1983 the patrol has used the Lockheed HC-130 *Hercules* as the primary reconnaissance tool. At the normal altitude of 8,000 feet the SLAR can cover a swath extending thirty-five miles on each side of the aircraft. Even so, the flight tracks are normally between 1,000 and 1,500 nautical miles long, involving some six to eight hours flight time.

During the 1950s the Coast Guard developed open-ocean ditching techniques that are still in use by commercial airliners today. These resulted mainly from experiments conducted by Captain Donald MacDiarmid, who in 1986 was enshrined in the US Naval Aviation Museum in Pensacola, Florida. In 1959 the Coast Guard took delivery of its Lockheed C-130 transport. Large, rugged and extremely reliable, this aircraft can cruise on two of its four engines thereby greatly extending its range. By the time the latest *Hercules* has been delivered, the USCG will have operated nearly fifty of this versatile workhorse, often referred to as the 'Jet-age Gooney Bird'.

During the Korean conflict, the Coast Guard established air detachments throughout the Pacific all involved in maintaining search and rescue patrols to safeguard the tens of thousands of United Nations troops that were being airlifted across the Pacific.

The ubiquitous helicopter is a primary rescue tool and will continue to be so into the foreseeable future. New models are already on order, including the Sikorsky *Rescue Hawk.* The Sikorsky HH-52A *Seaguard,* now replaced by the Aerospatiale HH-65A *Dolphin,* has rescued more persons in distress than any other helicopter in the world. In October 1980, the Sikorsky HH-3F *Pelican,* the service's current medium range helicopter, was the primary rescue vehicle when hundreds of individuals, mostly senior citizens, were plucked from bobbing lifeboats some 200 miles out in the Gulf of Alaska. This followed a fire on board the cruise liner *Prinsendam* and was one of the most successful maritime rescues in history.

While Coast Guard aircraft are most frequently recognized in support of the traditional peacetime role of Search &

Rescue, today's Coast Guard supports a myriad of mission responsibilities which spawn less publicized aviation employment. Evolving roles in Maritime Law Enforcement, Marine Environmental Protection, Polar and Domestic Ice Operations, and Aids to Navigation, each find benefit from employing Coast Guard aircraft. More recently the Coast Guard has become involved in Drug Interdiction. Today two Grumman E-2C *Hawkeye* surveillance aircraft, plus six HU-25A *Falcon* jets acting as interceptors, are being used in an effort against air smugglers in the world's drug traffic problem. The Coast Guard is also operating HH-3F *Pelicans* in a joint operation with the Bahamian Defense Force and Bahamian law enforcement personnel on an around-the-clock basis in the Bahamas.

The primary aircraft in the Coast Guard inventory are the HU-25A *Guardian,* the HC-130H *Hercules,* the HH-65A *Dolphin* and the HH-3F *Pelican.* During the mid-1980s, forty-one HU-25A medium range surveillance fan jets replaced the Grumman HU-16E *Albatross* and the Convair C-131A *Samaritan,* both prop driven aircraft. The *Guardian* is the service's first multi-mission jet. It is nearly twice as fast as any aircraft in the inventory and can get to the scene quickly to perform its role. Sixteen new HC-130H *Hercules* turboprop aircraft have joined the Coast Guard fleet and replaced earlier models. The primary missions of the 'Herky Birds' are long-range surveillance and transport. The Coast Guard is currently adding ninety-six short range HH-65A helicopters to its fleet, these having replaced the ageing HH-52A *Seaguard.* Primarily a search and rescue vehicle, the twin engine *Dolphins* operate up to 150 miles offshore and will fly comfortably at 150 knots for three hours.

Intent on continuing its superiority in aerial surveillance, the Coast Guard's Office of Research & Development is actively investigating the use of state-of-the-art remote-sensing equipment to improve its surveillance capabilities. 'Aireye' is the designation of an advanced surveillance system currently developed for HU-25A aircraft. It is a multisensor system that includes a side-looking airborne radar (SLAR), an infra-red/ultra-violet line scanner, an aerial reconnaissance camera, an active gated television (AGTV), and a control and display console. In conjunction with Northrop Corporation, the Coast Guard developed a prototype Forward-looking Infra-red (FLIR) Sensor that was installed on an HH-52A helicopter. The main function of FLIR is to form an infra-red image that can be received by the operator on a standard 525-line TV display. The USCG FLIR is designed specifically for the search and rescue mission. It will go a long way towards eliminating the obstacle of darkness for successful searches. In 1976, joint US and Canadian efforts demonstrated a search and rescue satellite-aided tracking system, designated SARSAT. The Coast Guard has carried out a number of tests assessing SARSAT's ability to detect and locate signals on the distress frequencies 121.5, 243 and 406 Mhz using emergency position-indicating radio beacons (EPIRBs) aboard ships and emergency locating transmitters (ELTs) in aircraft. If all the electronic sensors fail, the USCG Office of Research & Development has a unique system for use in helicopter searches. The project is called Sea Hunt, and both detection and processing are done in a pod under a helicopter. The sensors are common pigeons that have been trained to respond to the colours red, yellow and orange by the US Naval Ocean Systems Center. The Sea Hunt pod contains three trained pigeons, with overlapping fields of view, placed approximately at the ten, two and six o'clock positions. When a pigeon sees a red, yellow or orange object, it pecks on a key which closes a switch and illuminates an indicating light. Preliminary testing showed the pigeons could perform ocean searches better than the crew flying the helicopter.

Whether success is measured by technological advancements using state-of-the-art computer equipment or by an innovative research project using the keen eyesight of pigeons, the Coast Guard is 'on the step' in progress.

US budgetary constraints in the defence field often naturally affect the Coast Guard. Currently there is a possibility that the Chicago air station will close. Another recent change is that the USCG 12th Coast Guard District with HQ in San Francisco has been absorbed by the 11th Coast Guard District with HQ at Long Beach, California.

To assist those in distress and to patrol national waters, the Coast Guard flies nearly 200 aircraft from its twenty-seven air stations, large and small, throughout the continental United States, Hawaii, Alaska and Puerto Rico. The Coast Guard is the seventh largest naval air force in the world. Coast Guard Aviation, rotary and fixed wing, moves into the future proud of its past and confident of its future.

The expectation of 'flying to the limits of the envelope' under uncertain, and often adverse, conditions to save human life is a constant challenge to Coast Guard aviators. As a consequence, they must, and do, view their profession as a way of life — not merely a job.

CHAPTER ONE
The Beginning

The age of flight was just seven years old when President Woodrow Wilson, on 29 August 1916, signed into law an act establishing an 'Aerial Coast Patrol'. That was the beginning of over seventy years of Coast Guard aviation. However the history of US Coast Guard involvement in aviation extends back as far as 1900. In that year two men of the US Life-Saving Stations in the vicinity of Kitty Hawk, North Carolina, became involved in the experiments of a well-known pair of brothers whose normal occupation was manufacturing bicycles in Dayton, Ohio. Orville and Wilbur Wright were attracted to the Outer Banks of North Carolina by the flatness of the terrain and steadiness of the winds. Frequent shipwrecks had brought the Life Saving Service there some decades earlier. Out of this coincidence there developed a relationship which was to continue for several eventful years.

In 1902 the Wright brothers were using a glider, which they flew until 1903. The surfmen of the Kill Devil Hills Life-Saving Station, located a little over a mile from Kitty Hawk, provided logistic support for the Wrights and routinely assisted at the launching of the brothers' early experimental gliders. These included J T Daniels, Robert Westcott, Thomas Beachman, W S Dough, Uncle Benny O'Neal and A D Etheridge. These men, members of one of the agencies which were later combined to form the modern day US Coast Guard, were already a skilled ground crew when they were called upon to assist in the memorable events of 17 December 1903.

That first of many Coast Guard ground crews helped to launch on that memorable day the first-ever heavier-than-air powered flight. It was not many years later that the Coast Guard made efforts to acquire its own aviation resources. The Naval Deficiency Act of 1916 was a late mid-summer bill that authorized the Treasury Department to plan for some ten Coast Guard air stations along US coastal waters. Unfortunately this original act foundered by failing to appropriate the necessary funds to further its plans. Not long afterwards, the USA became involved in World War I, leaving the birth and any promise of Coast Guard aviation in limbo, delaying its operational introduction for several years.

The aviation facilities provided for in the Act of 1916 were modest. The air stations were to be sited along the Atlantic and Pacific coasts, the Great Lakes, and the Gulf of Mexico. The Coast Guard was authorized to train its aviators at the Naval Air Station at Pensacola, Florida. That arrangement still exists and hundreds of Coast Guard fliers have received their wings at this well-known US Navy facility. The first two Coast Guard graduates were Second Lieutenant Charles E Sugden and Third Lieutenant Elmer F Stone.

This historic photo is the only one depicting the first heavier-than-air machine. It was taken for the Wright Brothers, with their camera, by Coast Guardsman John T. Daniels, one of the crew of the nearby Kill Devil Hills Life Saving Station on that memorable day, 17 December 1903.
(USCG from Wright Brothers' Collection)

There is no doubt that Coast Guard aviation owes its beginning to two young officers, Second Lieutenant Norman B Hall who had professional training as a naval architect, and Third Lieutenant Elmer F Stone. Assigned to the cutter *Onondaga,* they convinced their commanding officer, Captain Benjamin M Chiswell, that what the Coast Guard needed was a flying surfboat. Fortunately their idea received his enthusiastic support. At that time, *Onondaga's* base was Hampton Roads, Virginia. Nearby, at Boat Harbor Point, Newport News, was one of the early flying schools operated by the Curtiss Aeroplane & Motor Co, principally for the purpose of training pilots for the Canadian service. Both Hall and Stone found an interested supporter in Captain Thomas A Baldwin, a pioneer balloonist and pilot, who was manager of the school. He thoroughly supported their views that the airplane could serve a useful purpose in locating derelicts, in beach patrol duties, in rescue work, and in the whole catalogue of other responsibilities charged to the Coast Guard. Baldwin arranged for the two officers to be flown on a number of experimental flights in a Curtiss 'F' flying boat, one of the first successful flying boats developed. There were no facilities for navigation, and it was not feasible to get out of sight of land in their under-powered craft, yet their range of observation and operation was so great in the air that the flights conclusively demonstrated the practicality of their ideas.

The Curtiss F- Boat, one of the first successful flying boats, was one of the earlier types of patrol aircraft flown by the Coast Guard. With no navigation facilities, it was suitable for flying only within sight of land. (USCG)

Captain Chiswell and his two young officers then set about selling aviation to Coast Guard officials. In the spring of 1916, when the *Onondaga* was visiting Washington DC, Captain Chiswell took the opportunity to entertain on board Glenn H Curtiss, famous pioneer airplane designer and manufacturer and a longtime government contractor, and Assistant Secretary of the Treasury, Byron R Newton. Newton as a young newspaper reporter had witnessed the first flight of the Wright brothers at Kitty Hawk. It is related that when he filed his first-hand account of that momentous occasion he was immediately fired from his job, his editor maintaining that only a drunkard would dream up a story about a successful flying machine. The idea which developed during the meeting aboard *Onondaga* is contained in an historic letter which Chiswell wrote to a Construction Corps officer named Hunniwell at Coast Guard headquarters.

The original idea to fit wings, powerplant, propeller and control surfaces to a standard Coast Guard surfboat proved impracticable. Thereupon Glenn Curtiss, the inventor and original developer of the flying boat, designed and built his 'life-boat' plane. This was a triplane flying boat with a short,

boat-like hull and with the control surfaces mounted high to the rear on tail booms. This idea of this hull with tail surfaces mounted aft on outriggers would be employed later by Curtiss and the US Navy aeronautical engineers in the design of the Navy's famous transAtlantic flying boats, NC-1, NC-2, NC-3 and NC-4. Twin four-bladed propellers mounted out in front of the wings were turned by a single engine mounted in the hull. Wings, control surfaces and propellers could be easily cast off. The hull could then proceed on the surface under its own power. Unfortunately, by the time this craft had been completed, the US was engaged in World War I and all further experiments were stopped.

In the meantime Coast Guard headquarters took an active official interest in the ideas of Captain Chiswell and Lieutenants Hall and Stone. Captain Charles A McAllister, Chief Engineer of the Coast Guard, drafted tentative legislation looking to the creation of an aviation section, and the commandant, Captain E P Bertholf, queried the Navy Department concerning the possibility of training Coast Guard officers as pilots. It was agreed that the US Navy would accept two Coast Guard officers for training at the newly-established Naval Air Station at Pensacola, and on 1 April 1916 Second Lieutenant Charles E Sugden and Third Lieutenant Elmer F Stone were ordered to proceed to that station. Second Lieutenant Norman B Hall, who with Captain Chiswell and Lieutenant Stone was responsible for the introduction of the aviation idea, by virtue of his education as a professional naval architect, was ordered on 28 October 1916 to the Curtiss Aeroplane & Motor Co factory at Hammondsport, New York, to study aircraft engineering and construction.

Concurrently, legislation promoted by the Aero Club of America and sanctioned by the Treasury Department was introduced into the Senate. This proposed legislation provided $1,500,000 for the establishment of an 'Aerial Coast Patrol', which was to operate as an auxiliary of the Coast Guard.

Almost simultaneously the proposed legislation previously worked up by Captain McAllister was revamped. When submitted, it received Congressional approval and was signed into law by the President on 29 August 1916. This legislation, a part of the Naval Appropriation Act of that year, provided for the ten Coast Guard air stations. Provision was made for the establishment of a Coast Guard aviation school and an aviation corps was authorized, which was to consist of ten line officers, five engineer officers, and forty enlisted mechanics. Implementing funds were not provided for and, in spite of repeated efforts, Congress refused to grant the money required to make the Act operative.

Authorization was obtained in the meantime to train an additional sixteen coastguardsmen at the Naval Air Station, Pensacola. Thus eighteen aviation pilots, an aviation engineering officer and an officer at Coast Guard headquarters, with the legend on the door, 'Inspector of Aviation', constituted the Coast Guard air section as the US entered World War I.

Coastguardsmen gave a very good account of themselves in that war, and the members of the aviation section were no exception, these being assigned to the US Navy's Aviation Division and ordered to naval air stations in the US and abroad. Lieutenant Charles E Sugden became commanding officer of the Naval Air Station, Ille Tudy, France, and was honored by the French Government with the award of the French Chevalier of the Legion of Honor. Another member of the Coast Guard commanded the Chatham Naval Air Station in Massachusetts. He piloted one of two Curtiss HS-1 seaplanes which bombed and machine-gunned a German U-boat off the coast of New England. Unfortunately the bombs failed to explode and the submarine escaped. The HS-1 seaplanes were the aircraft used by the US Naval forces in France, but participation was limited by the nature of the conflict and permitted little opportunity for action over the enemy lines or in actual combat.

With the end of World War I, the Coast Guard returned to the jurisdiction of the Treasury Department. In the unsettled times following the war, Coast Guard aviation was all but lost, no provision being made for it in any way. In fact, it seemed doubtful that it had any future at all. The dedicated souls in the Coast Guard who now wore the cherished wings of a naval aviator were more convinced than ever before of the contribution which the flying Coast Guard could make to the country in peace time. Then an event occurred which gave them hope.

A by-product of the war effort was the stimulus and potential to fly the Atlantic. In May 1919, four Navy Curtiss seaplanes, each crewed by five, began the great experiment. The three US Navy Curtiss built flying boats, NC-1, NC-3 and NC-4, took off on a flight across the Atlantic to Europe, via the Azores, to demonstrate the reliability and usefulness of big, patrol-type flying boats. The date was 16 May 1919. The pilot of the NC-4, the only one of the three flying boats to successfully complete the journey and the first airplane ever to fly the Atlantic, was Lieutenant Elmer F Stone of the Coast Guard, the only non-Navy man in any of the crews.

The successful crossing of the Atlantic by the NC-4 had far reaching effects. Among other things, it demonstrated the soundness of the big flying boat concept, proved the feasibility of long distance over-water flying and navigation, and did much to sell both the general public and the government on the worth of aviation. However, at least two more years passed before there was any Coast Guard aviation activity, and then it was extremely limited. In the meantime, Lieutenant Stone served at the Naval Aircraft Factory, located in the Philadelphia Navy Yard, Pennsylvania, where he was responsible for the power catapult which was used until the advent of World War II to launch aircraft from cruisers, battleships, and other vessels.

Fortunately the Coast Guard commandants have always made positive efforts to keep the concept alive. Typical was the action of Rear Admiral William R Reynolds, commandant in 1920, in obtaining six Curtiss HS-2L flying boats on loan from the Navy's Bureau of Aeronautics. This type remained the standard single-engine patrol and training flying-boat in the post-war years. These HS-2L flying boats were used in establishing the Coast Guard's first air station at Morehead City, North Carolina, opened on 24 March 1920. It had been a Naval Air Station which was now abandoned. No operating funds had been appropriated for the new station and it functioned on an experimental basis aimed at demonstrating the value of aviation in the performance of Coast Guard duties. Although these flights were a complete success, the government did not recognize them, or provide positive financial support. So, after some fifteen months of operations,

on 1 July 1921 the Morehead City station was closed. The aircraft, which may have included a few Aeromarine Model 40 flying-boats, also ex-Navy, were returned to the US Navy, then declared obsolete and destroyed. In spite of the strong representations made before Congress by Admiral Reynolds, the aviation programme was denied government blessing. It was not until four years later that there was any further aviation activity in the Coast Guard.

During the 1920s rum running became so flagrant that surface craft were unable to cope with it. Again it was decided to demonstrate the usefulness of Coast Guard aviation. This time the demonstration received official notice and action. Early in 1925 Lieutenant Commander C G von Paulson secured the assistance of Commandant Rear Admiral Frederick C Billard in obtaining the loan of a Vought UO-1 seaplane from the US Navy for a year. Operating from Squantum, Massachusetts, and later from Ten Pound Island in Gloucester Harbor, he demonstrated the potential of aviation in combatting the smuggling of whisky. Prohibition had become law in 1920 and soon its enforcement became the dominant mission of the Coast Guard.

In 1925 a schedule of daily patrol flights substantially curtailed liquor running in the area. As a sideline to the patrol flights, the staff at the base gave instruction to Coast Guard aviation students and performed a number of experiments in the use of radio communications between aircraft in flight and between aircraft and ship-ground stations. One of the most important achievements in this latter area was the development of the first loop-type radio direction finder.

Impressed by the activity of the air station at Ten Pound Island and plagued by the increasing operations of rum runners in other areas, Congress finally appropriated $152,000 for the purchase of five aircraft. These planes were the first the Coast Guard could claim as its own, all previous equipment having been borrowed from the US Navy. Three Loening OL-5 amphibians and two Chance Vought UO-4s were purchased. In 1926 an air station was opened at Cape May, New Jersey, the Navy again co-operating by making a portion of its air facility available to the Coast Guard. These new aircraft were flown from the air stations at Gloucester, Massachusetts, and Cape May until 1931 when they were replaced. Thus, Coast Guard aviation owed its first aircraft to the mission of law enforcement.

The Class of 1916 became the first USCG aviators. They are seen at NAS Pensacola on 22 March 1917 with their crewmen at the time of graduation. Of the eighteen in the photo, nine remained in the Coast Guard, three becoming Rear Admirals, one a Vice Admiral, whilst another won the Congressional Medal of Honor. The aircraft in the background is an early Curtiss N-9. (USCG via William T. Larkins)

COAST GUARD CUTTER

ONONDAGA

TREASURY DEPARTMENT

UNITED STATES COAST GUARD

Potomac River, April 18, 1916.

My dear Hunniwell:

    If practicable, please mail me as soon as con-
venient plans, specifications and blue prints of a type of motor
surfboat which you may regard as best adapted to the following:

    Mr. Glenn H. Curtiss, at luncheon with Mr. Newton on the
ONONDAGA last Sunday, suggested that it might be practicable to
convert a surfboat into a flying boat with wings and motor so arranged that they could be quickly eliminated when the boat light-
ed on the water and within a few minutes it would be, instead of
a flying boat, an ordinary motor surfboat.   If the lifeboat is
better adapted, send lifeboat.   He promised to think about it
and I am going to try to encourage him.

    If it is possible to perfect something of that kind I be-
lieve it would be the biggest find for the Coast Guard of the
century and might be the means of saving hundreds of lives.
Maybe if you could hear them say nonchalantly that they are now
building machines capable of lifting 20 tons, you would not be
quite so skeptical as I ~~believe~~ ~~know~~ you to be at present.

                Sincerely,

                [signature]

THIS LETTER CONTAINS THE GERM FROM WHICH COAST GUARD AVIATION SPRUNG.

This copy of the original letter written by Captain Chiswell to Construction
Corps officer Hunniwell at Coast Guard Headquarters, was discovered by the
author in the archives held today at USCG HQ in Washington DC. It contains
the first specification for a 'Flying Lifeboat' for use by the Coast Guard. (USCG)

RECOLLECTIONS OF EARLY COAST GUARD

By Captain William P Wishar[1]

Captain Wishar graduated from the Revenue School of Instruction in 1909. He completed flight training at Pensacola in 1920, graduating at the top of the class. Captain Parker, then head of aviation matters at Headquarters, wrote him: 'We are very gratified at the splendid showing made by Coast Guard officers on duty at Pensacola. The Commandant has noted that you and von Paulsen stood No 1 and No 2 in the class of 22 Navy, Coast Guard and Marine Corps officers, and it is his intention to let you know of his pleasure at learning this'. Shortly after completing flight training Captain Wishar commanded the first Coast Guard Station, at Morehead City, North Carolina.

Coast Guard's early years of aviation were hard struggling ones. It was a struggle to get money from Congress to start the new branch. Finally, planes, a station, equipment, trained personnel were obtained. In 1920, Coast Guard's first Air Station was in operation — all on a 'shoestring'. In 1922, this station had to be placed out of commission because funds were not obtainable from Congress for its continuance. Four or five years later, Coast Guard Aviation was restarted with not even a shoestring.

[1] US Coast Guard Academy Alumni Association Bulletin Vol XXXII No 1 (Jan-Feb 1970).

There were men of broad vision in the Coast Guard in those days (as indeed in these days). They saw the potential of aviation for more efficient Coast Guard work. They did all within their power to start an air arm for the Service. But why did the Coast Guard need an air arm? It has always been essentially a surface sea-going service. One of its most important duties has been assistance to vessels in distress.

For generations, a large proportion of US Atlantic coastal trade and trade with Caribbean areas was carried in three- and four-masted wooden schooners. They were designed and strongly built in New England shipyards, manned by experienced sailormen from 'Down East', born and bred to the sea. This trade had been developed years before the advent of the steamship. As the eastern seaboard and the Caribbean area developed, trade expanded. In spite of steam freighters becoming a factor in freight carrying business, the sailing schooner was still important in economical freight transportation. Of course, schooners were at the mercy of the wind, sea and current. Radio was not yet developed for general maritime use. There were little or no marine weather broadcasts or hurricane warnings. Celestial navigation was not used much by the grand old skippers of those sailing ships. It was said of them: 'They sailed by guess and by God', and they could smell their way in fog. If a storm or hurricane 'occurred', well, they just rode it out: many were sunk; some were dismasted or became derelicts; some were driven onto beaches or, mostly, onto treacherous shoals from Florida to New York. Because of this, the Coast Guard was constantly busy searching for and hauling-in derelicts, assisting vessels in distress, or ashore on shoals and beaches, blowing up menaces to navigation. A schooner ashore on a shoal with heavy waves pounding it and breaking it, is a most difficult thing to save by pulling off. Cutters I've been attached to have tried to haul off dozens without success. Heavy waves would smash into and break up a vessel. Being of wood, large pieces of the ship's side or its masts or other parts would float off and be carried by wind and wave into the ships' lanes, serious menaces. Most of these tragedies occurred in winter. So, 'Wintering Cruising Orders' became a yearly routine. Starting about the middle of November, cutters based at Atlantic and Gulf ports and with assigned cruising districts were ordered to proceed to sea, each one covering its district in search of vessels in trouble or for any menaces. They would leave port full-up with fuel, fresh water and provisions. Their orders were not to come back to port except to replenish supplies when they began to run low, or for some emergency. It was tough duty, this 'Winter Cruising'. When radio became more dependable and was carried on vessels, it became more practicable to have the cutters on ready-standby, prepared to leave port without delay upon receipt of information regarding a need for aid at sea. This was more efficient and economical, saved wear and tear on engines, ship and crew.

Coast Guard assistance to vessels in distress was not limited to wooden sailing ships. Beginning in the middle 1800s, freight and passenger ships began to be steam powered. They grew in numbers. They too were caught in storms, driven ashore on coasts and shores, caught on fire at sea, broke down, were in collision, or had other distress situations to which the Coast Guard cutters responded. There were few, if any, floating derelicts of steel, unless the cargo was of material which kept the hull afloat. But any ship in trouble at sea had to be searched for by a surface cutter, and vital time was lost searching. The sea is awfully large.

This then was the background of the need for Coast Guard aviation. An airplane, in weather that would allow it to fly and search, could cover enormously greater areas at sea than a cutter could. In times of unfavorable weather, of course, they could not fly. But the value of an aviation arm for the Coast Guard was recognized. The problem was to overcome the inertia of government and to get it started. But it *was started, was eliminated, was restarted, and has proved its value to our Country*. Hundreds of lives have been saved; seriously injured persons at sea flown to hospitals in time to save their lives; vessels saved by dropping them equipment, supplies, pumps; vessels in distress located for surface vessels to bring them assistance or tow them into port, and many other beneficial acts possible by air.

Commander Benjamin M Chiswell and Lieutenant Elmer F Stone and Norman B Hall, with the backing of the Commandant of the Coast Guard, E P Bertholf, were the officers whose foresight and efforts initiated Coast Guard Aviation. Chiswell had passed the age acceptance for flight training. Stone was sent to US Naval Air Station, Pensacola, Florida, for flight training and qualified as a heavier-than-air pilot. He became Coast Guard Aviator No 1. Some years later, Stone was chosen as 1st pilot of the Navy's flying-boat NC-4, with a co-pilot; Lieutenant Commander Albert C Read, US Navy, commanded and was navigator of the NC-4. This plane made the first trans-atlantic flight of a heavier-than-air craft, flying from Newfoundland to Lisbon, Portugal, in May

1919. Also, Stone, who had been loaned to the Navy as a test pilot, pioneered in the design and flight testing of power-catapults to launch planes into the air from the deck of a ship. Stone was a *great* flyer!

On 30 March 1920, Headquarters started a list of Coast Guard aviators. Elmer Stone, who was greatly responsible for the Coast Guard becoming involved with aviation, was designated CG Aviator #1. Only those officers actually engaged in flying at that time were put on the list, thus Donohue became CG Aviator #2 and Thrun became #3. Sugden, who had been on duty at the Academy, was reassigned aviation duty on 8 April 1920, and thus became CG Aviator #4. When Wishar and von Paulsen completed their training at Pensacola, they became CG Aviators #5 and #6. At this point the record shows that Coast Guard Aviator designations were extended to all the other Coast Guard officers who held Naval Aviator designations. Thus Parker, Coffin and Eaton became CG Aviators #7, #8 and #9.

We would have more opportunities to locate vessels in distress, derelicts, menaces to navigation, and vessels ashore on Diamond Shoals, Lookout Shoals and Frying Pan Shoals. Parker was in accord, and informed the Navy the Coast Guard would take the Navy's Morehead City Air Station.

During World War I, US Navy's heavier-than-air and lighter-than-air training was greatly expanded and was given mostly to Naval Reserve commissioned, warrant and enlisted personnel. Regular officers of the Navy, practically all graduates of the Naval Academy, trained and educated for surface fighting-ships, could not be spared for aviation training. They were needed to man the enormously expanded fleet of seagoing vessels. Ten months after the end of World War I (in September 1919), the Navy started its first post-war class of regular Navy, Marine and Coast Guard officers at Pensacola Air Station. Three Coast Guard officers were assigned to that flight class: Lieutenant Carl C

The Curtiss H-10 flying boat was one of the earliest aircraft borrowed by the Coast Guard for patrol, search and rescue experiments. This flying boat was used by Norman B Hall in developing aero-navigation systems in 1916. (USCG)

One of the six Curtiss HS-2L flying boats borrowed from the US Navy being worked on at the Coast Guard's first air station located at Morehead City, North Carolina, which was opened on 24 March 1920.
(USCG — National Archives No 26-G-20808)

No more designations were issued until August 1926, when Walter Anderson and Leonard Melka became CG Aviators #10 and #11.

Lieutenant Commander Stanley Parker had obtained his Lighter-Than-Air pilot 'wings' at Pensacola. He made what was then an outstanding record non-stop flight of a dirigible (called 'Blimp' for short) from New Jersey to Naval Air Station, Pensacola. He later headed Coast Guard Aviation at Headquarters, Washington DC, and initiated the first CG Air Station. While I was completing my torpedo-plane training, after heavier-than-air, free balloon and Blimp training, Parker, then handling matters connected with CG Aviation, contacted me and informed me I was to command this first Coast Guard Air Station. He asked my views as to which of two available surplus Navy Air Stations would be better for our Coast Guard aviation work: the one at Morehead City, North Carolina, or Key West, Florida. I gave him my ideas: that Key West would be a better-weather, less rugged Station; Coast Guard had to prove the worth of aviation as an adjunct to its duties. The rougher-weather Morehead City Station was closer to 'the graveyard of the Atlantic' (Cape Hatteras).

von Paulsen, Lieutenant Edward F Palmer and myself. Palmer was found to have a minor eye defect which the medical officers felt precluded flight training. However, he was retained for aviation-engineering training, and made many flights. Around the latter part of May 1920, this flight class completed its heavier-than-air training and each graduate received his coveted 'wings' as 'Naval Aviator'. Navy and Marine officers were detached and assigned to aviation billets.

Among the Navy officers of that flight class were Lieutenants Felix Stump, John Dale Price, and Ralph Davison. Each rose to high responsibilities and high rank in the Navy, with splendid battle records in World War II. Stump and Price rose to four star admirals, Davison to three star admiral. In the flight class which entered in the early part of 1920 was Lieutenant Arthur Radford, who became CNO (Chief, Naval Operations) and Chairman of the Joint Chiefs of Staff.

Lieutenant Command Parker's interest in lighter-than-air training led him to believe that dirigibles could be of great value in Coast Guard searches. So, von Paulsen and I were assigned to L-T-A training, and when we completed that we took the torpedo-plane training. We finished these courses the first part of November 1920. Von Paulsen went to the Army Air Force Field at Arcadia, Florida, for land plane flight training. I had been granted leave of absence, (to be married), so went on leave, was married 25 November.

One of the most heart-breaking episodes in World War I happened to Lieutenant P B Eaton, US Coast Guard. He was in command of the Navy Air Station at Chatham, Massachusetts. A report came in that a German submarine was surfaced at a location to the northeastward. Eaton regularly took patrol-flights as a pilot. He located the surfaced sub; many of its crew were on deck. Apparently, due to hazy weather, Eaton's plane had not been seen by the sub's men. Eaton made his approach, caught the submarine unaware, dropped two bombs; *one landed on the sub but did not explode, the other landed close to the sub's hull but did not explode!!!* The German crew thumbed their noses at the plane! Could this have been sabotage on bomb-mechanisms at the Air Station, known to the Germans? There was speculation to that effect, but, more probably faulty design. Who knows? I was shipmates with Eaton in 1925 on the famous old Coast Guard cutter *BEAR* in Bering Sea and the Arctic Ocean, and heard the story from him directly.

Lieutenant Commander C E Sugden, USCG, a pilot, had commanded a US Navy Patrol Base in France during World War I. He was assigned to command the Morehead City CG Air Station pending my return from leave of absence. I returned to the Station early in 1921. The complement of the Station was: Lieutenant Robert Donohue, Executive Officer and pilot, (he commanded a US Navy Air Station in Nova Scotia during World War I); Lieutenant Carl C von Paulsen, pilot; Lieutenant Edward F Palmer, engineering officer; Warrant Gunner C T Thrun, pilot and in charge of plane assembly; Warrant Machinist Walter S Anderson, pilot and engineering; Chief Petty Officer Leonard Melka, pilot; Warrant Carpenter Theodore Tobiason, carpenter and plane work; and about sixteen enlisted men. I was CO and pilot. It was a fine group of very able officers and men. I was justly proud of them.

The plane we had as our 'work horse' was the Navy HS-2L flying boat. It was a heavy plane; single engine (Liberty), pusher-type, open cockpit. It was staunchly built, could land in a fairly heavy sea when emergency demanded, and could take off in a moderate sea. It took off at a speed of 48 knots and flew at 55 knots, a leeway of 7 knots between flying speed and stalling speed. If she stalled, she went into a spin. No flyer that I've heard of ever pulled a fully manned and equipped HS-2L out of a spin. Everyone that spun crashed, killing all on board. It had to be constantly 'flown' while in the air. It carried a pilot, co-pilot, and in the 'bomber's' seat in the bow a combination observer and radio man. It was tiring to fly: constant pressure had to be maintained on the rudder-bar because of torque of the single propeller. I've come in from many a flight, and, upon landing, my right instep would be so painful it was difficult to walk.

Rare photo from a negative discovered by the author in USCG HQ archives, depicting the US Navy flying boat NC-4 which made the first trans-Atlantic flight in May 1919. This was eight years before Lindbergh's famous solo crossing. (USCG)

To prevent this, the Navy developed a heavy rubber cord attached to the left end of the rudder bar thence to the rear for about three feet where the end was secured. It was adjusted to equal the pressure needed on the other side of the rudder bar, while flying, to keep the plane straight. It was called a 'Bungee'. In a way, it was dangerous because, when the engine was cut for a landing glide, prop torque ceased, the Bungee caused left rudder, the plane turned without banking, was difficult to control, and would tend to go into a spin. The pilot had to remember this and press against the Bungee's pull on the rudder when he had cut his engine. Some pilots forgot. They never had the chance to forget again.

Flying boat designer Grover Loening presented this OL-5 photo to Secretary of the Treasury Andrew Mellon, whose department was responsible for the Coast Guard. It depicts OL-5 CG-1 delivered on 4 October 1926, which unfortunately crashed into the yacht *Whiz* in New London Harbor on 21 June 1930. (USCG)

Speaking of 'spinning' an H boat: Lieutenant Robert Donohue believed the HS-2L *could* be brought out of a spin. One day at the Morehead City Air Station, he had all removable gear and weights removed from an HS-2L, (such as anchor and anchor line, sea-anchor, mooring lines, water casks, emergency gas can, tools, etc), and with a moderate amount of gas and only himself in the plane, took off. I had not known of his intention. When he was in the air, someone told me he was going to try a spin. I would not have permitted it had I known. I discovered no preparations had been made for rescue in case of a crash. I raised merry old 'H', getting together wire-cutters, axes, fire-extinguishers, life-preservers, medical kit, etc, commandeering a fisherman's boat and otherwise preparing for what I feared would be a crash. Donohue climbed to about 3,500 feet then deliberately put the HS-2L into a spin as we watched helplessly — expecting a crash. He made four complete turns in his spin, then smoothly brought her out and landed just off the Station! He had proved that an HS-2L flying boat could be brought out of a spin. I didn't know whether he should have a court-martial for risking the plane and his life or be recommended for a medal for bravery beyond the call of duty. He retired as Rear Admiral.

One of the Curtiss HS-2L flying boats taken over from the US Navy by the Coast Guard and assigned to Morehead City, North Carolina, after World War I. (National Archives 80-C-1053768)

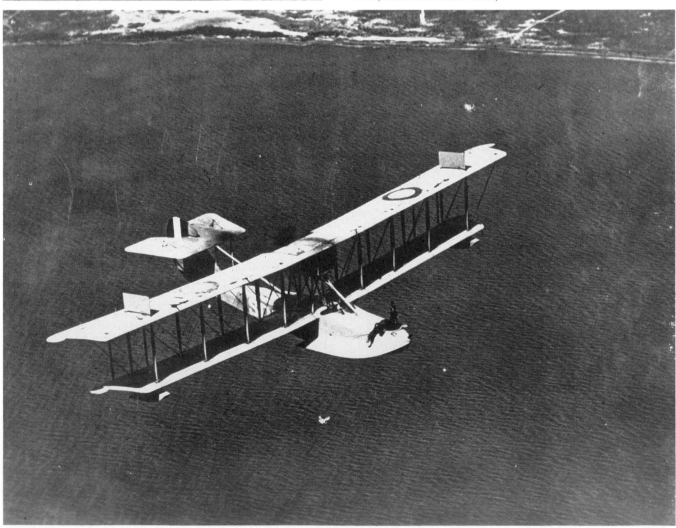

Four Naval Aircraft Factory N3N-3 training aircraft were acquired by the US Coast Guard in a trade with the US Navy for four Grumman JF-2 *Ducks* to assist the USCG pilot training programme. This preserved N3N-3 2582 is seen parked during a visit to Nut Tree Airport, California. (AP Photo Library)

Previous page: The US Coast Guard ensign came into being in 1799. Its concept is unique among US military services and 1989 marks the 190th Anniversary of its origin. It has flown over every continent and on every ocean in the world, and has fluttered in every conflict in which the USCG have been involved, including Vietnam. (USCG)

Grumman J2F-6 *Duck* BuNo 33581 indicating an ex US Navy aircraft, seen in US Coast Guard markings. Today veteran USCG such as this can be seen in the huge US Naval Aviation Museum located at Pensacola, Florida, in a section devoted to Coast Guard aviation. (AP Photo Library)

Right: A rare colour photo taken on 10 January 1944 showing a Consolidated PBY-5A *Catalina* of VPB-6 Squadron parked at its base at Narssaq, Greenland. It appears to be parked on PSP – pierced steel planking. (USCG)

Below: In wartime camouflage, this Port Angeles air station based Grumman JRF- *Goose* is seen in flight over the nearby Olympic Mountains in Washington State. The US Coast Guard operated twenty-seven of these rugged utility aircraft in many roles, equipping them with depth charges, mines and bombs. (USCG)

Martin P5M-1G *Marlin* 1296 from San Francisco air station seen on 28 August 1954 during 'Open House' celebrations. Seven served the US Coast Guard from 1956, going to the US Navy as trainers in 1961. (William T. Larkins)

Early post-war scene in the deep snow at Salem US Coast Guard air station in Massachusetts depicting a parked Martin PBM-5 *Mariner* flying boat with heaters connected to the Wright Cyclone engines in case it was needed in an emergency. (USCG)

A 'cache' of gasoline and oil in drums was set up in a shed at Kinnikeet on Pamlico Sound approximately half a mile north of Cape Hatteras. When starting on a search at sea in the vicinity of Cape Hatteras, it was imperative to have a full fuel tank: the cruising range was only four hours. We would fly from Morehead City Station the 75 miles to Kinnikeet and fill up with gas before taking off for the search.

HS-2L flying boat was equipped with a 'Venus' carburetor: the bowl and jets were of aluminium. There were many instances of engine stoppages without warning while flying. This necessitated overhauling the carburetor, thoroughly cleaning all parts, particularly the jets. Donohue had a stoppage at sea one time south of Lookout Shoals. He landed safely in the rough sea. After many tries, they got the engine restarted, but Donohue could not take off in the rough sea. He finally taxied many miles into the shelter of Lookout Bight, a safe harbor for winds from north to east. I had three engine stoppages while flying. The last occurred as I was return-ing to Kinnikeet from a search for a derelict reported south of Diamond Shoals Light-ship. It had been a cloudy day with strong easterly winds. The cloud layer kept lowering until, as we approached Cape Hatteras, it was perhaps around 350 feet above a rough sea. As we approached the line of breakers at the cape, the engine stopped suddenly. Turn and land in the heavy surf with resulting smash-up? Or chance a glide with a dead stick, with a helping wind behind us, across the three-eighths of a mile of sand dunes to the smooth water of Pamlico Sound? There wasn't time for ponderous weigh-ing of all possibilities: instant decision had to be made. We glided across the sand dunes; the last fifty yards the hull was inches above the sand. We touched down in the shallow water — safe. I sent a sample of the wax-like substance from the carburetor, which clogged the jets, to the Uni-versity of North Carolina: their analysts found it to be 'Alumina', a substance formed by reaction of gasoline with aluminium. This information was sent to US Navy Department, Washington. Result: Venus carburetors were changed from aluminium to another metal. There were no more engine stoppages from clogged carburetor jets.

One day, von Paulsen in one plane, and I in another returned from a search off Cape Hatteras, to Kinnikeet, and refuelled. There were about 35 minutes of daylight remaining. So we planned to land and stay overnight at one of the Life Saving Stations. Just as we started to take off, I told von Paulsen I had changed my mind, and I would try a night flight and landing, and von Paulsen could stop overnight at the Life Saving Station, which he did. I continued and picked up the lights of Morehead City easily, flew over it at low altitude and came down in a glide to land in Bogue Sound off the Air Station a mile west of Morehead City. There were absolutely no lights. There were many channel day-markers on pilings, but on an absolutely pitch-black night, they were a serious hazard, not a help. There was nothing to give me an idea of my height above the water. I put her in as slow a glide as I felt would let me have control and *prayed*. I hit the water at a goodly speed and bounced back into the air. After another bounce, I was down safely, not having hit anything. By the time I approached the ramp, the Air Station had turned on all lights. I vowed never again to make a night flight unless on a bit of water with sufficient lights to let me see how far the water was from the hull.

Coast Guard Air Station at Morehead City, North Carolina, remained in commission until July 1922. I received orders to place the Station out of commission and transfer planes and equipment elsewhere for storage. Personnel were transferred to other assignments. A few enlisted personnel under Carpenter Tobiason were left to complete shipments and clean up. I was transferred to Charleston, South Carolina, as Captain of the Port, later to a cruising cutter. Thus ended the first stage of Coast Guard Aviation.

The Chance-Vought UO-4 two-seat tandem observation biplane on floats was included in the first purchase of aircraft for Coast Guard aviation. Two were acquired and were in use between 1926 and 1934. UO-4 CG-5 was based at Section Base #7 at Gloucester, Massachusetts; UO-4 CG-4 was at Section Base #9 at Cape May, New Jersey. (William T. Larkins)

In May 1919, four US Navy Curtiss seaplanes attempted to fly the Atlantic. One seaplane, the NC-4, ultimately succeeded piloted by Lieutenant Elmer F Stone, USCG. This rare photo depicts the NC-4 crew: Lieutenant (jg) W Hinton, US Navy, Lieutenant Commander A C Read, US Navy — aircraft captain — and Lieutenant Elmer F Stone USCG. (USCG)

The second and permanent stage commenced in 1925. Lieutenant Commander Carl C von Paulsen, commanding Coast Guard Section Base #7 at Gloucester, Massachusetts, knowing the value of aviation for sea searching, initiated action to get an airplane to aid in his patrol boat searches. These were the days of prohibition and rum runners. The Coast Guard had established many Section Bases along all its coasts to stop the illegal importing of liquor by sea. From these bases, patrol boats searched at sea for rum runners, carrying contraband liquors. On the Atlantic coast, these vessels loaded up with liquor in various ports, (on east coast of US the French islands of St Pierre and Miquelon, and the British islands of the Bahamas opposite Florida were the two main supply sources).

'Rummies' remained outside the 'twelve mile limit' from the US, waiting for high speed motor boats which would dash out, load up and dash back to shore. When a Coast Guard cutter located a rum runner at sea, it would remain with it, thus preventing transfers to a shore vessel. But there were so many rum runners, and the ocean is so big, and the patrol boats had to replenish fuel and supplies, that it was often a heart breaking task. Von Paulsen as a flier knew the value of planes for searching at sea. He interested Lieutenant Commander Stephen S Yeandle, aide to Rear Admiral Frederick Billard, Commandant of the Coast Guard, in the idea of getting planes for searching the ocean for rum runners. Yeandle in turn discussed the idea with Admiral Billard who favored it. But there was no money, no appropriation. In spite of this, they planned and 'scummed schemes', all on a shoestring. An old UO-1 single float biplane with a 200 horse-power motor had been stored in a hangar at Cape May Section Base. It was surplus. Some enlisted personnel from the first CG Air Station at Morehead City were at Section Base #7. A small unused island belonging to US Fisheries near Section Base #7 was acquired for temporary use. It was called 'Ten Pound Island'. A large surplus tent was acquired from the Army for $1.00. It became the 'hangar'. Coast Guard Aviation was starting again. Von Paulsen and Melka flew the old crate searching at sea for rum runners and keeping an eye on patrol boats. A year later Admiral Billard was successful in obtaining from Congress an appropriation for five planes for the Coast Guard with some equipment. Three were sent to Ten Pound Island and two to Cape May. Thus the pulling infant was given sustenance, was carefully nurtured, and grew to its present efficient stature.

But the story of the 'Rebirth of Coast Guard Aviation' should be told by Captain von Paulsen. He had very extensive flying experience; he retired in 1945.

Close-up of the ungainly Loening OL-5 amphibian CG-3 warming up at Gloucester, Massachusetts, and showing the cockpit area and the flimsy undercarriage. Three OL-5s were commissioned in 1926. This photo clearly shows the USCG markings introduced to these first aircraft purchased for Coast Guard aviation. (USCG)

At this time, and as late as 1931, the Coast Guard numbered its aircraft in the sequence that they were acquired, starting with number 1. Thus, the three Loening OL-5s were given the aircraft serial numbers CG-1, CG-2, and CG-3 respectively. CG-1 was delivered on 14 October 1926, CG-2 sometime that same month, and CG-3 on 3 November 1926. All were commissioned in December of that year. CG-1 and CG-3 went to Ten Pound Island in Gloucester harbor and the other Loening CG-2 was stationed at Cape May in New Jersey. The three amphibians immediately went into service and saw extensive use. By 1 September 1928, CG-1 had flown 136 hours 50 minutes, CG-2 453 hours 55 minutes and CG-3 526 hours 30 minutes.

The acquisition of the OL-5s created a specific need for standard aircraft radio equipment but, because of the nature of their duties, such as scouting and rescue operations over water, neither US Navy nor available commercial types seemed suitable. As a result, the first standard Coast Guard radio equipment was designed and assembled by a Coast Guardsman, Radio Electrician A C Descoteaux.

This radio, battery operated to make it entirely independent of the aircraft electrical system and to insure its usefulness in the event of a forced landing at sea, provided two-way continuous wave telegraph and high quality voice communication. The spoken word could be transmitted 150 miles, whilst signals from the morse key could reach as far as 1,200 miles. The set consisted of a transmitter and receiver that weighed a total of ninety pounds.

The Descoteaux radio underwent its most demanding test on 13 June 1929, when its inventor, broadcasting from the observer's seat in one of the Loenings, described the *Yellow Bird* as it took off at Old Orchard Beach, Maine, to begin its successful flight to Santander, Spain. His words were retransmitted by a commercial radio network, so that thousands heard the Coast Guardsman tell how the big aircraft struggled skyward carrying its French crew — Armemo Lotti, Jean Assolaut and Rene Lefevre, plus an American stowaway.

It was the work of Descoteaux and C T Bolt of the communications section at Coast Guard Headquarters which resulted in the use of the first loop type aerial, radio direction finder.

These first aircraft purchased especially for Coast Guard aviation, the three Loening OL-5 amphibian, had been specially constructed for Coast Guard use, being of stronger build and greater fuel capacity than US Navy aircraft of the same make. The OL-5 was a biplane amphibian powered by a 400 hp inverted Liberty engine that gave it a top speed of ninety mph and enabled it to cruise at sixty-five mph for distances approaching 450 miles. This powerplant consumed twenty gallons of gasoline each hour from tanks holding 135 gallons at cruising speed. The amphibian could carry one passenger in addition to the pilot and observer. They were ordered from the Loening Aeronautical Engineering Company of New York, each costing $32,710. The remaining money from the Congress vote was used to purchase two Chance Vought UO-4s, improved versions of the UO-1 used so successfully flown by Commander Carl C von Paulsen and Ensign L M Melka from Gloucester, Massachusetts, in 1925.

The good work accomplished by the three OL-5s persuaded the Commandant of the Coast Guard, Rear Admiral F C Billard, that the air arm ought to be enlarged because of the manifold uses of aircraft. The duties listed by the Commandant were possibly the very first SOPs (Standing Operating Procedures) issued by Coast Guard Headquarters. So OL-5 crews spent time hunting schools of fish for local fishing fleets, and on one occasion during their law enforcement activity, machine gunned and sunk 250 cases of liquor thrown overboard from a rum runner. They took aerial photographs and patrolled beaches along the coast line.

Resting on its beaching trolley is one of the two Coast Guard UO-4 seaplanes. They were powered by a 200 hp aircooled Wright J-5 engine, and had a gasoline capacity of sixty gallons giving a cruising radius of 350 miles. They carried a Browning machine gun and were fitted with radio equipment.
(via Peter M. Bowers)

Flying an OL-5 out of Cape May in the spring of 1929, Ensign W E Anderson spotted the yacht *Nomad* wallowing in the trough of a heavy sea. He radioed a patrol boat which came alongside the sinking vessel. A boarding party found all hands inebriated, one dead and the helm awash. *Nomad* would certainly have foundered except for Coast Guard aviation.

A short time later, a Loening OL-5 demonstrated how Coast Guard amphibians could capture criminals. On 3 September 1929, Chief Gunner C T Thrun and his two crewmen were testing the radio in OL-5 CG-2. While flying over Murder Kill Inlet, Delaware, he received a message that a sloop had been stolen from the Riverton Yacht Club, some way up the Delaware River, above Philadelphia. As soon as he had obtained an accurate description of the stolen vessel, Gunner Thrun set out in pursuit. Within twenty-five minutes he had found the fleeing sloop off New Castle, Delaware, a full half day's sail from any Coast Guard surface vessel. His after action report tells how the chase ended:

1.20 pm — Landed alongside stolen *Bronco* and ordered her to proceed to shallow water and anchor, as I intended to board her.

1.30 pm — Anchored *Bronco* and sent Chief Machinist's Mate C H Harris, armed only with a Very pistol, in seaplane's rubber life boat with instructions to board the *Bronco* and place the crew under arrest.

2.00 pm — Took off with seaplane No 2 in order to get in communication with Section Base Nine by radio from the air, as Base Nine or patrol boats could not be raised while resting in the water.

2.05 pm — Got into radio communication with Section Base Nine and received instructions to await arrival of CG-182.

4.30 pm — Turned over sloop *Bronco* with two prisoners to CG-182.

Commander C. G. von Paulsen, USCG, Commanding Officer of Coast Guard Section Base #7, Gloucester, Massachusetts, was the inventor of the device by which a seaplane carries a line to a vessel in distress off the coast — too far for the shot-line to reach. The line is dropped over the vessel, and the Coast Guardsmen on shore rig up the breeches buoy and the survivors are safely brought ashore by this means. This photo taken on 4 May 1927 shows the line attachment under the fuselage of a Chance Vought UO-4 aircraft. (USCG)

The first OL-5 to perish was CG-3, which crashed on 10 November 1929. A message from the Commander, Coast Guard Section Base Seven, Gloucester, Massachusetts, advised Coast Guard Headquarters that:

SEA PLANE NUMBER THREE TOTALLY WRECKED AT 0955 BY STRIKING MAST OF FISHING VESSEL JACKIE B IN GLOUCESTER HARBOR STOP LIEUTENANT MELKA MACHINIST KENLY AND RADIO ELECTRICIAN DESCOTEAUX IN HOSPITAL SUFFERING FROM SHOCK BUT NOT IN DANGER LIST STOP NO CIVILIANS INJURED.

Eight months later, on 28 July 1930, the Assistant Secretary of the Treasury Department authorized the payment of the $545.33 claim of the owner of the *Jackie B,* John F Barrett, whose forestay had been struck by the right wing of CG-3, flown by Lieutenant (jg) Leonard M Melka. The Treasury official explained that the damage had been 'caused by the negligence of one of the employees of the Coast Guard Seaplane OL-5 No 3, while acting in the scope of his employment'.

As the claims for damages caused by CG-3 were being settled, CG-1 went to its doom. The amphibian flew to New London, Connecticut, to patrol a yacht race, only to crash as it tried to take off among the crowd of vessels that were preparing for the event. On 21 June 1930, OL-5 CG-1 hit the superstructure of the yacht *Whiz,* destroying the pilot house and showering those on board with broken glass, and other debris. Two sailors sustained bruises, but these were the only injuries suffered by crewmen or passengers. The amphibian sank almost immediately, but the pilot, Lieutenant Norman N Nelson, and his passenger, Commander Eugene A Coffin, got clear of their safety belts and surfaced without receiving serious harm. A board of investigation studied the incident and concluded that 'the basic cause of the collision . . . was the visit of the OL-5 No 1 to New London, Connecticut, on race day', when congested waters made a large seaplane of this type 'utterly unsuited for the mission alleged'.

The three Loenings deserve credit for more than just being the Coast Guard's first aircraft. These amphibians, along with the two Chance Vought UO-4 seaplanes authorized at the same time, were the foundation upon which Coast Guard Aviation rests. Had the aircraft been less dependable and the aviators less skilled and imaginative, the Coast Guard might well have abandoned the experiment.

CHAPTER TWO
The Blue & Silver Period

The years 1927 to 1936 have been described as the Coast Guard's 'blue and silver period'. From the first Loening OL-5 until the introduction of the 'V' serial system in 1936, every Coast Guard had a distinct colour scheme. Until 1927, US Navy colours were used, with the vertical red, white and blue stripes on the rudder. After 1927 all Coast Guard aircraft had contemporary dark blue fuselages, the top of the wing and horizontal tail surfaces were chrome yellow and the underside silver. The underside of the hull, on flying boats, was painted silver, with the FLB-type wing floats being all silver, and the Douglas Dolpin's half silver and half blue. The entire vertical tail surface of each aircraft was divided into three sections: red, white and blue as before 1927. On flying boats the engine nacelles were silver and the cowls blue. The name US COAST GUARD was painted in large letters on the side of the fuselage with the letters USCG on the underside of each wing. The letters US were on the top of the port wing, and CG on the top of the starboard wing.

From 1936 to 1941, to provide a more distinctive colour scheme, all aircraft were an overall aluminium colour with the top of the wing chrome yellow along with upper part of the tail surfaces. Commencing in late 1935 the top one-third of the rudder was painted insignia blue, the bottom two-thirds being divided into five equal vertical stripes, three red and two white. The aircraft's model designation was placed in white on the blue section of the rudder, and the serial number was in black under the words US COAST GUARD on the side of the fuselage. The letters USCG were used on the underside of both wings, and the serial number was painted on the bottom of the hull or fuselage. The USCG emblem was placed on the forward part of the hull or fuselage near the pilot's compartment.

These early days primarily rested upon amphibian models, since the necessity of water landings was always uppermost in the mind. The first five aircraft included a trio of Loening OL-5 amphibians, essentially modifications of a US Navy design, but tailored to a derivative with a stronger fuselage and extended fuel capacity. During this period of aviation's romance with flying boat/amphibian craft it was always a moot point whether it was a boat with wings added as an afterthought. The ultimate aim from the beginning of Coast Guard aviation had been a 'flying life boat' and the theory and even deep research continued until well after World War II.

Commander Norman B Hall, later Rear Admiral, USCG, one of the pioneers of Coast Guard Aviation, pauses on the ramp of the US Naval Air Station at Norfolk, Virginia. The USCG Engine School & Repair Base was located here. In the background a crew prepare a General Aviation PJ-1 seaplane for flight. (USCG-APY-11-22-32 GEN)

The last of the OL-5's CG-102 was eventually discarded because of old age in April 1935. The two UO-4's proved more successful, lasting a full life until their flying log books were filled up. During 1931 the Coast Guard borrowed a Naval Aircraft Factory PN-12 twin engined flying boat for evaluation in connection with the proposed design for a new aircraft. A few years earlier, in 1928, an aviation section was established at Coast Guard headquarters under the command of Commander Norman B Hall. It drew up specifications for a multi-mission aircraft which, given the technology of the day, could be met only by a large seaplane or amphibian. To aid distressed mariners, the Coast Guard again developed the concept of 'flying life boats'. These aircraft could fly hundreds of miles, land in an open and frequently uninviting sea and carry out a rescue. It will have been noted that the earliest Coast Guard aircraft were generally adaptations of examples designed for other services, mainly the US Navy, since development funds were often not available. By 1930 this matter was remedied, Congress voting enough money to allow the service to write its own specifications for aircraft.

The single Douglas RD *Procyon* CG-27 was photographed on 9 March 1931 at the Douglas factory prior to delivery. It is a flying boat and the wheels etc. belong to the beaching gear. In a similar aircraft Lt Cdr Elmer F Stone assisted in the search for the survivors of the US Navy dirigible *Akron* which crashed off the New Jersey coast in 1933. (Douglas Aircraft via William T. Larkins)

Expanding, testing, experimenting, the 1930s Coast Guard took on board a galaxy of custom built aircraft.

When the Douglas Aircraft Company of Santa Monica, California introduced a twin-engined commercial amphibian in 1930, the US armed forces were quick to express their interest. The new model, named *Dolphin,* featured an all-metal hull with provision for eight people including pilot and co-pilot, a plywood-covered cantilever wing and two tractor

Pratt & Whitney R-1340-96 engines mounted in separate nacelles above the wing. First procurement was by the Coast Guard in 1931. Great confusion has existed over the correct identification of the various *Dolphin* models used by the Coast Guard as no less than four different models were in service during a period when the Coast Guard serial numbering system changed twice. The first production *Dolphin* built was delivered to the Coast Guard in New York on 9 March 1931, direct from the Douglas factory. It was designated plain 'RD' and named *Procyon* but was a flying boat, not an amphibian, and the wheels that show in photos are the beaching gear. The RD-129 *Adhara* was delivered next during July 1932, and the RD-1 *Sirius* was the third to be delivered on 5 August 1932. The strange model designation RD-129, painted on the tail of the amphibian, was a combination of the normal model designation and the individual aircraft number. Apparently RD stood for Multi-engine Transport, Douglas. The first Douglas RD-4 was delivered on 20 February 1935, nearly three years later. All four RD types were externally different in fuselage, engine and tail configuration.

In 1931 the US Army Air Corps ordered one standard O-38B aircraft from the Douglas Aircraft Company for delivery to the Coast Guard. Minor differences in equipment resulted in a designation change to O-38C. It was powered by a Pratt & Whitney R-1690-C engine, had dual controls similar to the O-38A, and other minor changes. It had AA Corps serial 32-394 on Air Corps contract AC-4553. What appears to be a model designation of CG-9 on the tail in some photos is in fact the identification as the ninth aircraft purchased by the Coast Guard. It was commissioned on 11 December 1931 and in 1936 was re-registered V108.

Coast Guard aircraft No 8, listed only as 'seaplane experimental' in the Coast Guard register, was imported from France and placed in commission on 16 December 1931. This flying boat was similar to models used by the French Aeronavale at the time and was built by the Hydravions Schreck-FBA Company of Argenteuil, France. The designer was Louis Schreck and many were in use in Canada where they were known as Schreck Flying Boats. The one the Coast Guard purchased was designated Schreck FBA 17HT-4, a wooden-hulled pusher derived from the FBA designs of World War I. Late in 1930 the Viking Flying Boat Company of New Haven, Connecticut was formed to replace the previous Bourdan Aircraft Company, and they acquired the rights to build the Schreck in the USA. As a result of Coast Guard experience with CG-8 five of these flying boats were ordered from the Viking Company, being built and delivered in 1936. The latter five were powered by a 1240 hp Wright J-6-7 radial engine, and designated OO-1.

Six Vought O2U-2 *Corsair* landplanes were purchased from a US Navy production batch of thirty-seven during 1934. Several were based at San Antonio, Texas, with the Air Patrol Detachment assisting the US Border Patrol in the prevention of illegal immigrants. All but one were disposed of in 1937. Depicted is the first one for the Coast Guard with serial 301. (Gordon S. Williams)

Resplendent in the Coast Guard's blue and silver livery with the top of the wings in chrome yellow, this single Douglas O-38C observation aircraft was commissioned by the Coast Guard on 11 December 1931. The CG9 on the tail indicates it was the ninth aircraft in the Coast Guard inventory, later becoming V108. It was decommissioned in April 1934 after a crash. (Museum of Flight)

The five flying life boats for the US Coast Guard marked the swan song of the American Fokker organization. The sleek twin-pusher flying-boats were designed by the Fokker Aircraft Corporation of America as Model AF-15 in a Coast Guard design competition involving eight companies for a patrol and open-sea rescue boat. By the time that Fokker was declared the winner, the company had become a division of the General Aviation Corporation with manufacturing facilities transferred to Dundalk, Maryland. These aircraft were delivered in 1932, and for many years were known simply as the 'Flying Life Boats' and this appeared along with the serial number on the tail of each, serving as a model designation. The first was erroneously marked FLB-8 when it was commissioned in January 1932, but this was soon changed to the correct FLB-51. Later, when General Aviation became North American, the PJ-1 model designation was adopted, but for many years Coast Guard aviators only knew them as FLBs.

This Stinson R3Q-1 *Reliant* was the only one of its type used by the Coast Guard based at Floyd Bennett Field, Brooklyn, New York. Commissioned in 1934, it was used as an electronic test aircraft. It was a four place cabin monoplane powered by a Lycoming R-680-4 engine giving a range of 350 miles. In 1937 it operated out of Cape May, New Jersey. (Gordon S. Williams)

The first flying boat, FLB 51 *Antares,* was completely modified in 1933, being sent to the Naval Aircraft Factory and converted to a tractor design. The engine nacelles and cowlings were changed, and the engine mounts, pilot's cockpit and other sections were modified. This changed the model designation for this one aircraft to PJ-2. All the Douglas RD's and the General Aviation PJ's were named after stars, the name appearing on each side of the nose and often served as the only accurate means of identification of the individual aircraft. The FLBs had a separate radio and a radio direction finder included in their layout.

In one rescue incident with a PJ-1, Lieutenant Commander Carl von Paulsen set the *Arcturus* down in a heavy sea in January 1933 off Cape Canaveral and rescued a boy adrift in a skiff. The flying boat sustained so much damage during the open water landing that it could not take off. This was the fate on a number of ocean rescues which had to be attempted when no other rescue craft could be directed to the scene by the aircraft. Ultimately, the *Arcturus* washed onto the beach and all, including the boy, were saved.

The first of ten Douglas RD-4 amphibians were delivered in November 1934. The solo models of the RD were powered by Wright Whirlwind engines, whilst the RD-4 was fitted with Pratt & Whitney R-1340-96 Twin Wasps. These Douglas aircraft had a range of almost 800 miles, cruised at 105 mph with a maximum speed of 162 mph and had a service ceiling of nearly 16,000 feet. These new Coast Guard amphibians were used extensively in search and rescue missions and as flying life boats, often flying far out to sea from the several Coast Guard air stations now being established to rescue stricken mariners or to rush seamen in need of urgent medical attention to hospitals ashore.

During 1926, the Chance Vought Corporation designed a new observation biplane for the US Navy, combining experience gained from early types such as the UO-1 and UO-4 used by the Coast Guard, and powered by the new Pratt & Whitney Wasp engine. As well as being the first US Navy aircraft designed round this famous engine, it was one of the first to have an all-steel-tube fuselage. This was designated O2U-1 *Corsair.* Production continued in 1928 with the O2U-2 model. Thirty-seven were built, of which six were allocated to the Coast Guard. This model was distinguished by minor alterations which included dihedral on the lower wing, a different cut-out shape in the upper center section and a large rudder. All were disposed of during 1937, except the second in the batch — V118 — which was disposed of in 1940.

In 1934 Henry Morenthau became the Secretary of the US Treasury. He was an aviation enthusiast and supported its expansion within the Coast Guard. On 9 March 1934 he transferred the aviation detachment of the US Customs

Built by the Hall Aluminium Company, seven of these PH-2 flying boats saw service with the Coast Guard between 1934 and 1944. Photo shows V169 whilst based at Port Angeles in Washington State. It appears to have spent the early World War II years at Miami, Florida. (Gordon S. Williams)

Service to the Coast Guard. In fact the material benefits of this transfer were small because they introduced into the Coast Guard a conglomeration of aircraft that were mostly poor in condition and impossible to maintain. A total of no less than fifteen aircraft were turned over to the Coast Guard.

Grumman JF-2 *Duck* V148 was delivered from the factory to Port Angeles air station on 21 November 1935 by Lieutenant C F Edge. This type was very popular with Coast Guard aviators and they even broke speed and load carrying records with it. This photo shows V148 in the snow covered mountain terrain which surrounds Port Angeles in Washington State. (Gordon S. Williams)

A Waco J2W-1, one of three purchased by the Coast Guard, is seen secured for sea, on board the Coast Guard cutter *Spencer* at Cordova, Alaska, in February 1938. These aircraft were versatile, being used with floats or wheels or fitted with skis for take-offs and landings on ice. All three eventually became attached to the Air Patrol Detachment based at El Paso, Texas, and were later destroyed in crashes during 1939. (USCG)

They consisted of types confiscated by the Customs Service for smuggling, violation of flying regulations, or similar misconduct. The Customs Service had pressed them into their service, using them mainly on border patrols. The list, which is reconstructed from the memory of Coast Guard aviation old-timers, included two Curtiss *Falcons*; two Curtiss *Robins*; a Travel-Aire 3000; a Ryan; two Waco 10s; a Fairchild 71; a Douglas *Mailwing*; a Pilgrim; a Sikorsky S-39; a Flamingo, and two New Standards. Some were flown after accession, but after a few crashes the rest were destroyed in the interests of standardization as all were obsolescent. Only the two New Standards were retained, re-engined and refurbished to become NT-2s. However, of the two Curtiss *Falcons* listed, NC-112E apparently went to the Coast Guard as early as August 1932, whilst the other, NC-301E, had been seized by the Customs Service about June 1932 and transferred to the Coast Guard in May 1934.

The Secretary's enthusiasm for Coast Guard aviation was important to its development. He obtained Public Works Administration funds for the purchase of new aircraft and additional air stations. By 1936 the Coast Guard had six air stations, two air detachments and forty-two aircraft. Also during the 1930s, the marriage between the Coast Guard cutter and aircraft took place. The 327-foot cutters each embarked a Grumman JF-2 *Duck* utility amphibian. These aircraft-equipped cutters were designed to patrol against opium smuggling off the West Coast, fisheries violations in Alaskan waters and to serve on plane guard duty in the Atlantic to protect the embryonic trans-continental air service. The tragic sinking of the *Titanic* in 1912 led to the establishment of the International Ice Patrol because the JF-2, several of which were assigned to the larger cutters on a regular basis, was particularly useful for this purpose. The rugged Grumman amphibian extended greatly the ability of the Coast Guard to forewarn merchant ships of impending disaster. Used in this manner the JF-2 ranged far and wide in northern latitudes, reaching far beyond the normal operating limits of coastal air stations. Flying along the northern ice pack the Grumman biplane navigated into many a frigid bay to rescue drowning aviators or to pick up medical cases from ships, often under the most hazardous conditions.

Hardly fitting the category of miscellaneous were several classic examples of sea and float planes, taken from proven US Navy designs, and modified for Coast Guard use between 1934 and 1941. These included the fourteen Grumman JF-2 *Duck* utility amphibians ordered with special equipment and engine change to a 750 hp Wright Cyclone R-1820-50. Four of these aircraft were returned to the US Navy during 1941 whilst V144 crashed at St Petersburg, Florida on 29 September 1940 on a night training flight. All were acquired on a US Navy contract and delivered during 1934.

The only Northrop RT-1 was nicknamed the *Golden Goose* and was occasionally used to transport Secretary of the Treasury, Henry Morgenthau Jr. It was commissioned during February 1935 and, although replaced in April 1936, it remained in Coast Guard service until December 1940 when it was sold. In this photo it carries the VIP insignia of a two-star Admiral on the engine cowl. (Gordon S. Williams)

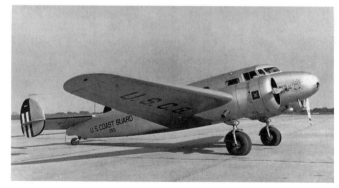

This single Coast Guard Lockheed R30-1 *Electra* was used as an Admiral's Flagship. It was acquired from the US Navy, more specifically the US Marine Corps, in March 1936 before being traded for a Grumman JF-2 *Duck*. (Gordon S. Williams)

With the expansion of its air station network during the 1930s, administrators of the Coast Guard service sited each facility to complement the surface fleet as well as establishing aircraft where the action was. While the Coast Guard is usually shown in drama performing its brilliant sea rescue work, the normal workaday activity takes place close to the coastline. Here is the province of the weekend sailor, crowds of small boats whose misfortunes liberally sprinkle the log book entries of most stations. When the 1930s closed, the end of another stage of Coast Guard aviation expansion found some fifty aircraft scattered around the USA, a diminutive but important force. Obviously the maintenance had to be outstanding since so little time on the ground could be tolerated. Aircraft were based at air stations located at Brooklyn, New York; San Diego and San Francisco, California; Salem, Massachusetts; Elizabeth City, North Carolina; Miami and St Petersburg, Florida; Biloxi, Mississippi; New Orleans, Louisiana; Corpus Christi, Texas and Port Angeles, Washington State. Considering the great distances involved and the dispersal, the aviation units had a great deal of responsibility just providing routine patrols.

The Consolidated Model 21-A was a commercial development of the very popular US Army PT-11 trainer, which was also used by the US Navy. The Coast Guard purchased one in 1932, designated N4Y-1 and used as a training aircraft at Cape May. Power was by a Lycoming R-680-6 radial engine and it was possibly used for administrative and courier duties. (Gordon S. Williams)

Serial Number Assignment

Because so little has been published about the US Coast Guard there can be little wonder that the correct overall picture of Coast Guard Aviation has never been fully understood, especially when one realizes that the aircraft serial numbering system or identification numbers have undergone no less than five complete changes over the years. This has resulted in some aircraft carrying as many as three different serials, at different times of course, others two and some only one. For example, the Douglas RD-1, named *Sirius* was at first numbered 28, later becoming 128 and still later V109. The General Aviation PJ-1 named *Altair* was first numbered 52, then 252, and later V112 and in addition was known as FLB-52 (Flying Life Boat 52). Photos of Coast Guard PJ-1s can show fifteen different serial numbers, although there were only five aircraft ever in use at one time!

A system was adopted during 1927 involving both a one and two digit serial on only sixteen aircraft which were broken up into selective groups so that the Douglas *Dolphins* fell into the 20 serial division and the General Aviation FLBs into the 50 series.

In 1934 the Coast Guard adopted a new three-digit grouping series: 100 for amphibians, 200 for flying-boats, 300 for landplanes, and 400 for convertible designs that could operate from the air stations' land facility. On 13 October 1936, at 00.01 hours, all Coast Guard aircraft serial numbers were changed completely. This was a sweeping revision which included not only all aircraft in service at the time, but for administration purposes every aircraft that the Coast Guard had ever flown, regardless of whether it had already been destroyed or disposed of. Thus, the first ever Coast Guard registered aircraft, a Loening OL-5 (CG-1) became 'V101' under the new system. The purpose of the V prefix was to differentiate the radio call letter or call sign from the W used by Coast Guard surface vessels. The V system was consecutive and complete, with no numbers being omitted, as had been the case with the previous two systems. This system was not only unique, but it stayed in effect for nearly ten years.

In June 1936 the Hall Aluminium Aircraft Corporation of Bristol, Pennsylvania, received a contract from the Coast Guard for seven of its PH-2 patrol and air sea rescue flying boats. These were powered by two 750 hp Wright R-1820F-51 engines and had special equipment fitted for the Coast Guard role. One of these PH-2 flying boats made headlines shortly after the opening of the San Diego Coast Guard Air Station in California.

The episode occurred when a message came over the radio, advising that a sick seaman was in need of medical attention. At a first glimpse it appeared impossible to despatch an aircraft since the vessel on which the seaman worked was over 800 miles south whilst the Hall PH-2s range was but 600 miles. Improvising as always, the Coast Guard personnel at San Diego loaded several barrels of aviation fuel on board a cutter, setting sail for the lower Californian peninsular.

Two Fairchild J2K-1 aircraft were used by the Coast Guard and based at St Petersburg, Florida. Two J2K-2s were also purchased, these operating out of Charleston, South Carolina. Depicted is J2K-1 V160 commissioned in 1937. It crashed during August 1940. (Fairchild)

Excellent night refuelling shot depicting one of the three Curtiss SOC-4 *Seagull* two-seat observation aircraft delivered to the Coast Guard early in 1938. One — V171 — was converted to landplane configuration and it was also attached to the cutter *Bibb*. Photo depicts V173 at Port Angeles, Washington. All three went to the US Navy in 1942. (Gordon S. Williams)

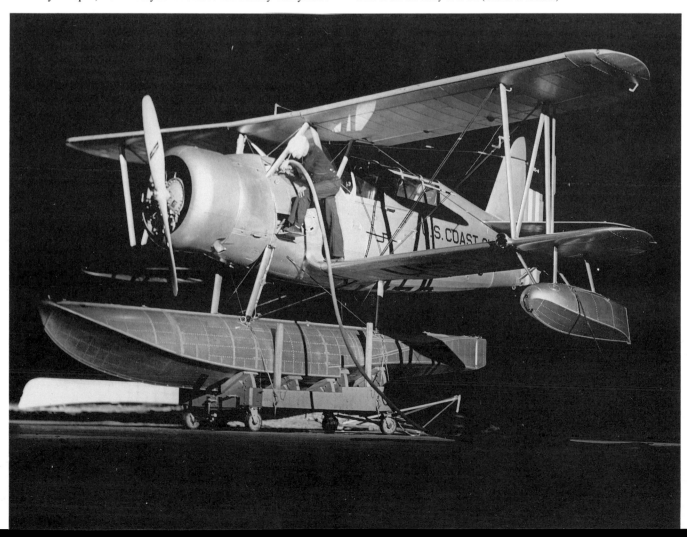

The Sikorsky S-39 also used in the making of the 1939 film *Coast Guard* was not exactly a stranger to the Coast Guard as they had borrowed one in 1930 to patrol yacht races, and one was included in the fifteen miscellaneous aircraft imported from the Customs Service in 1934. (Dustin Carter Collection)

Taking off some hours later the Hall flying boat made a rendezvous in a Mexican bay, refuelled and then flew on to pick up the stricken sailor. Reversing this procedure the aircraft flew black into San Diego fifteen hours after take-off.

It was perhaps logical that the early period of Coast Guard Aviation involved float planes and amphibians. The second decade provided a home for several interesting land base types. During 1935 two four-seat Stinson SR-5 *Reliant* cabin monoplanes were acquired by the US Navy. One went to the Coast Guard as RQ-1 381 later redesignated XR3Q-1 and finally R3Q-1. It was powered by a 225 hp Lycoming R-680-6 engine and had a maximum speed of 133 mph. It was a one-off aircraft, purchased specifically to conduct research and development into radio communications, a matter which was always of great significance to an organization like the Coast Guard when flying the trackless oceans. Of all the US services none was more determined to upgrade its ability to be heard.

The Hall PH-3 was an improved version of the earlier PH-2, with a refined cockpit area, and the two Wright 750 hp R-1820F-51 engines were fitted with long-chord NACA cowlings. Seven were ordered in 1939 which saw extensive service during World War II on anti-submarine patrols and were used in the development of a co-ordinated search and rescue organisation. Depicted is a Hall PH-3 with engines running on the ramp of an unknown Coast Guard air station. (USCG)

The one and only Douglas RD-2 procured for the Coast Guard was used as an administrative transport for the US Secretary of the Treasury. It was given the serial 111 and the name *Adhara*. It was purchased in 1932 and its claim to fame was that it could take off in 594 feet with nil wind. It crashed during March 1937. (Peter M. Bowers Collection)

The Coast Guard has long been responsible for providing official air transportation for the cabinet-level Secretary of the US Treasury, an activity it performs to this day. Amongst the wide variety of aircraft purchased by the Coast Guard between two World Wars, was a single example of the Northrop *Delta,* a commercial transport. The official designation was RT-1 whilst *Golden Goose* was the nickname for the eight-passenger version of the Northrop. This unique transport was a 1935 acquisition which served until December 1940, when it was taken off active status. Cruising at 210 mph, only a dozen miles under its top speed, the graceful single-engined aircraft could fly 1,700 miles with a 20,000 ft ceiling produced by its 575 hp Wright R-1820 Cyclone engine. A year after the RT-1 went into service the Secretary of the Treasury acquired a twelve-seat Lockheed Electra, designated XR30-1, again the only example of its type purchased during this era. It was delivered to the Coast Guard on 9 April 1936, and was a commercial Model 10-B powered by two Wright R-975E-3 engines which gave a maximum speed of 205 mph.

When Columbia decided to make the film *Coast Guard* in 1939 it is unfortunate that the aircraft used were not the type used by the Coast Guard proper. Depicted is an American *Eagle* carrying fictitious Coast Guard livery and also a heavily disguised engine. The engine cowl is false as the aircraft was powered by an in-line and not a radial. (Peter M. Bowers Collection)

The Waco Aircraft Company of Troy, Ohio, was one of the leading American manufacturers of training and sports biplanes since 1926. In 1936 three cabin model EQC-6 Waco biplanes were procured for the Coast Guard and redesignated as J2W-1s. Unfortunately it was an ill-fated purchase, as all three crashed during 1939, just two years after they were commissioned. They were powered by a 320 hp Wright R-760-E2 engine which gave a maximum speed of 176 mph. Two New Standard NT-2s were not a derivative of the US Navy NT-1 trainer, but were much earlier New Standard D-25A models, powered with the 245 hp Wright J-6-7 engine, which had been captured from smugglers and handed over to the Coast Guard by the US Customs Service in 1934. They were designated NT-2 for convenience.

The one and only Consolidated Model 21-A used by the Coast Guard, was a commercial development of the US Army PT-3 and the US Navy NY trainer series. It was designated N4Y-1 by the Coast Guard and powered by a 165 hp Wright J-6-5 engine giving a maximum speed of 118 mph. Of this galaxy of unique landplanes operated by the Coast Guard, the Wacos were of particular interest as they were periodically fitted with skis for service in Arctic areas.

The lone Martin T4M-1 torpedo scout bomber which appears on the Coast Guard inventory went to the USCG Engine School and Repair Base located at Norfolk, Virginia, on 2 June 1937. It was ex US Navy A-7607 and was obtained from the nearby US Navy station. It was marked 'for ground school instruction only' and was used for the detection of engine trouble and for ground instruction. Its engine was a 525 hp Pratt & Whitney R-1690-24. The aircraft did not carry a Coast Guard serial number and was not classed as operational equipment.

A total of four Fairchild three-seat parasol monoplanes powered by a 145 hp inverted air-cooled Ranger engine were contracted by the Coast Guard during 1936, commissioned the following year and all but one were unfortunately lost in crashes. Two were designated Fairchild J2K-1 V160 and V161, both assigned to the Coast Guard air station at St Petersburg, Florida. V160 crashed in August 1940. Two were designated Fairchild J2K-2 V162 and V163 and assigned to Coast Guard air detachment at Charleston, South Carolina with V162 crashing in May 1941, and V163 in August 1939. Cruising speed was 110 knots with a stalling speed of forty-one knots.

Another proven US Navy type which Coast Guard aviators flew was a trio of Curtiss SOC-4 *Seagulls*. These beautiful, two-place float biplanes were purchased during the first quarter of 1938 and exemplified the final phase of twin-wing days in the service, and along with the JF-2 brought an epoch to its conclusion. A truly handsome design, the SOC-4 was powered by a 600 hp Pratt & Whitney R-1340-18 engine giving a maximum speed of 165 mph whilst its range was nearly 900 miles on a single tank of fuel. These three SOC-4 scouting and observation seaplanes — or landplanes — were the fine *Seagulls* built by the Curtiss-Wright Corporation, Curtiss Wright Aeroplane Division of Buffalo, New York, later models being built by the Naval Aircraft Factory. Purchased at a cost of $48,603 each, this trio survived and were transferred to the US Navy in 1941.

During 1939, in their wisdom, Columbia Pictures made a film called *Coast Guard* starring the well-known film stars Randolph Scott, Ralph Bellamy and the pretty Frances Dee. So the Coast Guard became famous and went to Hollywood. Coast Guard aviation was not forgotten, but unfortunately no aircraft from the Coast Guard inventory were used, the types involved carrying fictitious serial numbers but full USCG livery and markings. These aircraft were based at Burbank Airport in California, the air terminal for Hollywood and its stars. Known types used in the film included an American *Eagle* single-engined biplane carrying the serial 504; a Stearman C3 biplane with the serial 600 and a Sikorsky S-39 flying-boat amphibian ex NC-52V apparently carrying no serial number at all.

By January 1935 Coast Guard aviation had a fleet of thirty mixed aircraft types. This rare photo taken on Christmas Day 1934 depicts half the Miami based aircraft, consisting of the Douglas RD-1 128 *Sirius* in the lead, flanked by two General Aviation PJ-1s, 255 *Arcturus* and 254 *Acamar*, both carrying the FLB — Flying Life Boat — designation on the tail. The vessel is the USCG cutter *Pandora*. (USCG)

The Curtiss SOC-4 *Seagull* was a conventional biplane capable of operating on floats or wheels. Seen here is a US Coast Guard landplane version V171 seen during 1941, the palm tree indicating a tropical USCG air station. The three final *Seagulls* built, designated SOC-4, served with the USCG as V171/2/3, going to the US Navy in 1942 as BuNo 48243/4/5. (William T. Larkins)

During 1934, the US Customs Service turned fifteen miscellaneous aircraft over to the Coast Guard. They had been confiscated for offences such as smuggling, violation of flying regulations or similar misconduct, and were pressed into use by the US Customs Service for border patrols. The list included two Curtiss Falcons, two Curtiss Robins, a Travel-Aire 3000, a Ryan, two Waco 10s, a Fairchild 71, a Douglas Mailwing, a Pilgrim, a Sikorsky S-39, a Flamingo and two New Standards. The photo shows a Curtiss O-11A Falcon with the US Customs Service emblem on the fin. (Peter M. Bowers Collection)

On 8 July 1940 two Great Lakes BG-1 carrier based dive bombers went to the Coast Guard Engine School and Repair Base at Norfolk, Virginia. They were ex-US Navy both having previously served with the US Navy since 1935. They were transferred from the nearby US Navy establishment with paper-work reference 'NAS, Norfolk letr. NA8/L11-6/P21 (40-Ly) of 7-8-40'. BG-1 with US Navy BuNo 9506 had completed 1,433 hours of flight, and BuNo 9519 1,161 hours. Both had a 750 hp Pratt & Whitney R-1535-66 engine. No Coast Guard serial number was issued.

Entering the 1930s with but five aircraft, the Coast Guard was to end that decade with ten times more, though it hardly represented a moderate force when one contemplated the far-reaching responsibilities involved. The service was standing on the threshold of a great expansion necessitated by its role in World War II. Early pioneers of aviation history would have been more than amazed at the forecast changes. Unlike

Below: A single *Flamingo* was amongst the aircraft transferred to the USCG from the US Customs Service on 9 March 1934, and had been confiscated. After a few crashes they were mostly destroyed as all were obsolescent. Only two New Standards were retained. Seen here is a Flamingo G2W. (via Peter M. Bowers)

Above: Two Curtiss Robins were included in the fifteen aircraft transferred to the USCG from the US Customs Service. They had the civil registrations NC-112E and NC-301E and had been pressed into service and used on border patrols. The first one went to the USCG in 1932, the second in May 1934. (via Peter M. Bowers)

Another film aircraft depicting a type — Stearman C3 — never used by the Coast Guard. It was numbered 600 and is seen parked at the Union Air Terminal at Burbank Airport, California, during filming of *Coast Guard* in 1939. (Dustin Carter Collection)

its previous wartime affiliation under the US Navy, this smallest service was ready to flex its own muscles. The US Navy would be in control but this time the Coast Guard warriors would have their own identity for the forthcoming conflict. Restricted to no more than a couple of dozen aircraft during any previous year in its existence, suddenly the Coast Guard was to experience an abundance of types. Compared to US Army and US Navy activities it was not much, but to the Coast Guard aviators it seemed like a veritable fleet — as well as a challenge.

Below: This Waco 10 biplane was one of two transferred from the US Customs Service to the USCG in March 1934. Fifteen aircraft, mainly civil models, were transferred, and after a series of crashes the miniature air force was abandoned in a move towards standardization. (via Peter M. Bowers)

Above: A single Fairchild 71 such as the one illustrated, was included in the fifteen aircraft transferred from the US Customs Service. They were in poor condition, and almost impossible to maintain. They had been involved in smuggling, violation of flying regulations, or similar misconduct. (via Peter M. Bowers)

As though reaching back into the past, the Coast Guard made one final purchase of Hall seaplanes, with an order for seven of these somewhat anachronistic twin-engined biplanes during 1940 and 1941. In June 1936 the service had contracted for seven PH-2s to be used on air sea rescue duties, these remaining in service until 1941. The range of the new Hall PH-3 flying-boat was over 2,000 miles. They were powered by two 750 hp Wright R-1820F-51 engines giving a maximum speed of 160 mph and a service ceiling of over 21,000 feet. Although they had modern design features around the cabin area, the tail surfaces were out of the 1920s. Ordered in 1939 the PH-3 had a more refined enclosure for the cockpit, and the engines were fitted with long chord NACA cowlings. After Pearl Harbor they were given standard US Navy finish in place of the natural metal, and some were adapted for anti-submarine patrols. One PH-3 crashed during November 1941, ten months after delivery, whilst another was officially taken off the commissioned list in March 1944. The precise fate of the others has gone unnoticed in the passage of time. By this time the Coast Guard was involved with others in World War II and a few examples of somewhat old fashioned aircraft types could be written off the inventory with very little concern.

The old was quickly fading into memory. World War II accelerated the growth of aviation within all of the US armed services including the Coast Guard. Now the great drama of human conflict would unfold with an impact upon Coast Guard Aviation unlike anything it had ever experienced. Its personnel were fully aware of the dark war clouds that had built up over Europe.

CHAPTER THREE
Into Battle – World War II

On 28 January 1915 the US Revenue Cutter Service and the US Life-Saving Service were combined to form the United States Coast Guard. The law combining the two Services stated that the Coast Guard was to be an armed service at all times and made provisions for its transfer to the US Navy when needed. In fact, this had been the practice since 1798, when the US Navy was created, but for the first time this relation was defined in law. On the morning of 6 April 1917 a coded despatch was sent from Washington by radio and by land wire to every cutter and shore station of the Coast Guard. Officers and enlisted men, vessels and units of all sorts began operating as part of the US Navy.

Following the outbreak of hostilities in Europe in 1939, the Coast Guard carried out extensive patrols to enforce the neutrality proclaimed by the President on 5 September 1939. Port security began on 20 June 1940 when President Roosevelt invoked the Espionage Act of 1917, which governed the anchorage and movement of all ships in US waters and protected American ships, harbors and waters. Shortly afterwards, the Dangerous Cargo Act gave the Coast Guard jurisdiction over ships carrying high explosives and dangerous cargoes. In March 1941, the Coast Guard seized twenty-eight Italian, two German and thirty-five Danish merchant ships.

On 9 April 1941 Greenland was incorporated into a hemispheric defense system. The Coast Guard was the primary military service responsible for these cold-water operations, which continued throughout the war. During the summer of 1941, prior to the USA's entry into World War II, the cutter *Duane* with a Curtiss SOC-4 on board surveyed the coast of Greenland for potential airfield sites. Individual Coast Guard cutters and units were assigned to the US Navy during the spring of 1941. On 1 November 1941, the remainder of the Coast Guard, which included all aviation units, aircraft and personnel, was ordered to operate as part of the US Navy. Among the most important Coast Guard undertakings, in addition to the operations in Greenland, were anti-submarine warfare escort, amphibious landings, search and rescue, beach patrol, port security, and LORAN (long range navigation) duty.

Combat ready — Coast Guard aviators rush to their aircraft at an Atlantic seaboard air station, in order to make a rendezvous with another convoy of merchant ships. Anti-submarine (ASW) patrols were maintained throughout the first few years of World War II by the Coast Guard, protecting Allied shipping. (USCG)

After Pearl Harbor, aircraft flying from Coast Guard cutters searched for and helped locate German weather stations in the frozen northern areas of Greenland which were providing critical data to U-boats operating in the North Atlantic. The stations were captured by the Coast Guard. Also, Coast Guard aircraft performed harrowing rescues by flying through snow storms and landing on the ice pack to aid distressed Allied air crews who had crashed while attempting to ferry aircraft across the Atlantic. Coast Guard cutters, boats and aircraft rescued more than 1,500 survivors of torpedo attacks in areas adjacent to the US. Coast Guard manned ships sank eleven enemy submarines and Coast Guard aircraft sank one. Often Coast Guard aircraft rescued survivors by landing in the open sea and on occasion the aircraft had to taxi ashore because weight of those rescued prevented the aircraft from taking off.

Before the USA entered World War II, neutrality patrols were carried out on all Atlantic seaboards and harbors. Depicted is a Grumman JRF-3 *Goose* V190 based at Brooklyn air station seen on patrol over shipping in New York harbor on 11 April 1941. (Fred Kissner Collection via Grumman)

The early years of Coast Guard aviation had been hard ones. The early aviators were dashing and courageous young men, or foolhardy gamblers, but all were pioneers. Elmer Stone, listed as Coast Guard Aviator 1, was a good example. The early Coast Guard aircraft were rugged but carried out the tasks those very first SOPs (Standing Operating Procedures) laid down. As Congress appropriated more money, more Coast Guard pilots were selected and eventually sent for training with the US Navy at Pensacola, Florida. Coast Guard Aviator #91, Richard Baxter, recalls that a pre-flight training course for several officers and some fifteen enlisted men was given at Charleston Air Station, South Carolina. This was to select the ten men and four officers who would go to Pensacola. For training purposes an aviation school for enlisted personnel was founded at Cape May. The Coast Guard Engine School and Repair Base had been established alongside the US Navy at Norfolk, Virginia.

This Lockheed R50-1 *Lodestar* was delivered to the Coast Guard on 14 May 1940 and used as an executive transport for the US Treasury Department and for Coast Guard VIPs. It was a Lockheed Model 18 which survived World War II and was later sold. (Lockheed via William T. Larkins)

To design a flying machine is nothing; to build it is not much; to test it is everything, Otto Lilienthal (1848-1896). When Lieutenant Robert Donohue test flew that HS-2L flying boat at Morehead City, in the early days, to prove that it could be brought out of a spin, he was expressing the individual enthusiasm of those early aviators. He must have spent many hours working out the intricate plan involved in that successful test flight. Donohue retired as a Rear Admiral. There were losses of course. On 29 September 1940 the Coast Guard lost Lieutenant T G Miller and Seaman 2nd Class T B Redman when their Grumman JF-2 V145 crashed in the water near St Petersburg air station whilst on a local night training flight.

The tasks men and machine were allotted were many and various. Commencing in 1935 the Coast Guard had conducted an annual survey of migratory waterfowl along the east coast for the Biological Survey. Aircraft, invaluable in the enforcement of the US neutrality laws, were also utilized in detecting illicit distilleries. In 1939 more than a thousand such stills were located by Coast Guard aircraft cooperating with the Alcohol Tax Unit of the Treasury Department.

In January 1940 the El Paso Coast Guard air station was officially closed and custody of the hangar released to the US Army. Officers, men and equipment from this Texan base were reassigned to other stations on the east and west coast. Elizabeth City Air Station, the newest and most completely equipped air station maintained by the Coast Guard, was put into commission on 15 August 1940. Assigned were three PH-3 seaplanes, three Grumman JRF-2 amphibians, and four Fairchild J2K- landplanes. During December 1940 a contract was drawn up for the purchase of three additional Grumman JRF-2 amphibians, all to be equipped with automatic pilot and provision for single lens aerial mapping camera. Two were to be fitted with de-icing equipment, the one without to be assigned to the Honolulu Coast Guard District. Delivery of these new Grummans was expected within three months. Proposals had been solicited for approximately eight light utility amphibian aircraft for delivery during that fiscal year. It was expected that the new Consolidated PBY-5 would be accepted into Coast Guard service. Plans were put into force to modify this new acquisition to carry the Coast & Geodetic Survey's nine-lens aerial mapping camera, the installation to be carried out at the San Diego Air Station which was also fitted out as a repair and modification base. According to the Coast Guard register of aircraft the craft was first listed in 1941, being allocated V189 and based at San Francisco after modification. It was ex US Navy BuNo 2290.

It is not generally known that Coast Guard aviators, in addition to their normal duties, were setting up various records with their aircraft. On 20 December 1934 Commander Elmer F Stone set up a speed record of 191.734 miles per hour in a Grumman JF-2 V167 at Buckroe Beach, Virginia when he flew a set three kilometer course. On 25 June 1935 Lieutenant Burke, in another JF-2, set a further record on 173.945 miles per hour over a 100 kilometer course carrying a 500 kilogram load. Two days later a Coast Guard aviator established an altitude record of 17,877 feet whilst carrying a 500 kilogram load. The huge Hall PH-2, built in 1938, had a take-off time of less than twenty seconds in calm weather, and it was reported that Lieutenant Carl B Olsen lifted PH-2 V164 off the water in five seconds during take-off performance tests.

Rescue exploits by the early aviators and aircraft were becoming legendary. In 1933 when two seamen were severely injured in a boiler explosion on a ship off the Jersey coast, a Cape May-based PJ-1 FLB-52 saved their lives by picking them up at sea and transferring them to a hospital in Philadelphia in under two hours. A passenger on board the US Army transport *Republic* en route from Panama to New York became critically ill. An emergency operation, beyond the capabilities of the transport, was necessary. Help was sought. General Aviation PJ-1 *Arcturus* was lowered down the ramp at Miami Air Station, taxied into Biscayne Bay and flew three hours in darkness and a storm. Using radio bearings, the ship's searchlight beams were located. *Arcturus* circled and landed off the ship's bow. The patient and his wife were transferred by ship's lifeboat. *Republic* indicated wind direction by searchlight and *Arcturus* rose out of the rough sea. This difficult mission took seven hours — and a life was saved.

In 1926 the Coast Guard procured its first five aircraft. After this the aviation branch grew steadily and rapidly – and so did the statistics. By 1933 the service had thirteen aircraft and fourteen aviators: three years later, in 1936, there were forty-five aircraft and twenty-seven aviators on active assignment. In the period between 1927 and 1934, the number of flights for all Coast Guard air stations combined increased from 258 to 1,200. Miles flown in 1927 were 28,235; in 1934 they totalled 219,572. Cases of assistance rendered went from twelve to forty-four, and hours flown increased from 366 to 2,752. Nine air stations were in commission. Traverse City, Michigan, was selected by the Coast Guard as the point from which to pursue a further study of Great Lakes flying conditions, preparatory to the establishment of a permanent air station on those waters. During June 1940 a Grumman JRF-2 with supporting personnel were sent to Traverse City for temporary duty (TDY) until 1 October 1940. They investigated and made a report to the appropriate board. Preliminary flight training and indoctrination was given to officers and enlisted men at the air station located at Charleston, South Carolina during early 1941 prior to their selection for flight training at Pensacola with the US Navy, which had allocated the Coast Guard a quota of ten men to be trained between January and June 1941. In order to speed up this flight training programme two Grumman JF-2s V135 and V141 were transferred to the US Navy in exchange for three Naval Aircraft Factory N3N-3 primary trainers.

The air patrol detachment set up at Traverse City was not idle. It was playing an important part in ice-breaking

A Grumman J2F-2 *Duck* BuNo 0794 seaplane, attached to the Coast Guard cutter *North Star* on the Greenland patrol during World War II, is lowered over the side prior to another patrol. The aircraft is carrying early wartime US Navy type markings, and is an ex US Navy aircraft. (USCG)

operations in the Great Lakes area. Grumman JRF-3 V192 had made eighteen reconnaissance flights between 1 April and 16 April 1941, logging sixty-nine hours flying time. The new Coast Guard air station at San Francisco, adjacent to the airport and the water, was officially dedicated on 15 February 1941 at a cost of $600,000. Earlier in the month, on 2 February, the new Consolidated PBY-5 V189 operating out of San Diego, performed a double rescue in one day. Inspection of Coast Guard stations and units by aircraft was made the subject of a special evaluation by the Cleveland Coast Guard District, with results which led to the recommendation that this practice be regularly instituted. Grumman JRF-3 amphibian V192 was used for this experiment. During June 1941, Grumman JRF-3 V191 from the air station at Brooklyn, New York, transported a sick child. During September 1941, Douglas RD-4 V126, attached to San Francisco air station, crashed into the Pacific whilst making a routine patrol flight west of the Farallon Islands. The crew of three were killed.

Coast Guard air stations were strategically located in coastal areas where opportunities for liaison with ships and the lifeboat rescue activities were greatest. Inasmuch as the Coast Guard is part of the US Navy during war, the location of these stations was planned so as to enable them to be a part of the national defense pattern. A milestone occurred in 1939 when the volunteer organization known today as the Coast Guard Auxiliary, with a total membership of some 40,000 personnel, was created. The Auxiliary, working side by side with the regular Coast Guard has significantly contributed to solving the enforcement problem. The 1940 Motorboat Act improved safety standards.

Intended to be non-combatant, Coast Guard aviation plunged with a fervor into World War II, proud of its accomplishments so far, now ready to match in some roles the duties of its much larger cousin, the US Navy. Coast Guard aviation in World War II was chiefly concerned with patrol and rescue. These two functions were almost inseparable, for whichever purpose a mission served, the other was almost sure to be involved, directly or indirectly. Patrols were, in the final analysis, to protect the shores and coastal shipping, but no opportunity to save life or property at sea was ever overlooked and many opportunities arose.

The Coast Guard began its wartime operations under the Secretary of the Navy, in accordance with the law and an executive directive dated 1 November 1941. Coast Guard aviation stations or bases were included in the US Naval District aeronautic organization for military purposes and over-all general direction but were maintained logistically by the Coast Guard officer in command of the base or station, heading for this purpose through the Senior Coast Guard Officer of the Naval District. San Francisco air station was in the 12th Naval District. On 1 November 1941 a total of nine air stations and fifty-six aircraft from the Coast Guard were transferred to US Navy jurisdiction. These were as follows:

Salem, Mass. 3
Elizabeth City 10
St Petersburg 5
San Diego, Calif. 4
Port Angeles, Wash. 3
Brooklyn, NY 8
Miami, Florida 6
Biloxi, Miss. 6
San Francisco

The remaining four aircraft were on special assignments; one JRF-3 V192 at Traverse City, Michigan; one JRF-2 V187 with the Honolulu District; one JF-2 V135 based on the cutter *Taney*; and one JF-2 V141 on detachment at Charleston, South Carolina.

This Stearman N2S-3 BuNo 4342 of the US Navy was photographed at Concord, California, during October 1946 and was similar to the eleven N2S-3 *Kaydet* trainers which served the USCG between 1943 and 1947. This famous trainer was initiated as a private venture in 1934 and trained thousands of Allied pilots during World War II. (William T. Larkins)

On 26 December 1941, before an audience which included the Coast Guard Commandant and the Assistant Commandant, the Secretary of the US Treasury, Henry Moregenthau, awarded Distinguished Flying Crosses to an officer and three enlisted men of the Coast Guard at his office in Washington DC. The secretary stated:

> On the late afternoon of 3 October 1941, Lieutenant Sinton was pilot of Coast Guard Lockheed R50-1 V188 with the Secretary of the Treasury on board, and while executing an instrument let-down to break through the overcast preparatory to landing at New Hackensack, New Jersey, the aircraft crashed through tree tops and was severely damaged. An imminent crash landing seemed certain, but the pilot and crew kept the damaged plane in the air, and after a flight of almost two hours in low visibility and darkness arrived over Philadelphia where clear weather prevailed. Because of the condition of the airplane a dangerous landing at high speed was necessary and it was successfully accomplished without injury to the persons on board or further damage to the airplane. The courage . . .

This was just one of the many citations for the Coast Guard and its aviators.

After Coast Guard aviation went to war alongside the US Navy in November 1941 they retained the 'V' serial system on their own aircraft, but new US aircraft acquired by the Coast Guard kept their US Navy Bureau Numbers. During 1941 two-tone camouflage was adopted, at first with the national markings having red center stars and after Pearl Harbor with very large centerless stars. The rudders of some amphibians were painted with horizontal bars, seven red and six white, but this US Navy variation of prewar Army rudder stripes was only in use up to 15 May 1942.

Long before Pearl Harbor, Coast Guard aviation operated in Greenland from cutter-based aircraft. Without *Northland*'s Curtiss SOC-4, the South Greenland Survey Expedition could not satisfactorily have made its survey. After war was declared, Coast Guard aircraft, flying from cutters, maintained anti-submarine patrols over wide areas of the ocean. In their flights on coastal patrol and over convoy lanes, the Greenland aviators toughest battles were against the elements: gales, icy rains, heavy fogs, and unexpected storms. Attempting a landing on the ice cap presented new dangers in the form of treacherous crevasses and the sudden cracking of ice which earlier had appeared solid enough for a safe landing.

The Grumman JF-2 *Duck* V140 appeared on the Coast Guard aircraft register during 1937, when it was assigned to Miami air station. It moved to Charleston, South Carolina, in 1940, returning to Miami the following year. In 1942 it was based at San Francisco air station, where it received its World War II camouflage. It is depicted with the tail stripes of the 1942 period flying over the lovely Bay area. (USCG)

On 12 September 1941 the ice-going cutter *Northland*, which had been built for service in Alaskan waters took into 'protective *custody*' the Norwegian trawler *Boskoe* and captured three German radiomen ashore. During the spring of 1941, the cutter, along with its aircraft, had been brought around to the east coast for duty in Greenland waters. The *Boskoe* was the US' first naval capture of World War II.

During the summer of 1941 the cutter *Duane*, with a Curtiss SOC-4 on board, surveyed the coast of Greenland for potential airfield sites. After hostilities commenced, aircraft flying from cutters searched for and helped locate German weather stations in the frozen northern wastes of Greenland. These stations were providing critical data to U-boats operating in the North Atlantic. The personnel and the stations were captured by the Coast Guard.

Lieutenant John A Pritchard Jr, a Coast Guard aviator, operating from his mother ship, *Northland*, successfully flew the hazardous air lanes of the North Atlantic for nine months in his amphibian. In November 1942 three Canadian airmen came down on the Greenland ice cap, not far inland from the coast. The Coast Guard was assigned to rescue them, and Lieutenant Pritchard led a rescue party ashore to hunt in the icy wasteland. *Northland*, anchored in a fjord at the edge of the ice cap, fired flares and star shells and broadcast a Morse code message, 'Move back from the edge of the glacier and bear south to meet landing party'. The Canadians went wild with joy. It was their fourteenth day of torture and suspense, and they had almost given up hope.

The US Coast Guard operated eighteen Boeing B-17 *Flying Fortress* aircraft acquired as surplus from the US Air Force in 1945 and modified for new roles. Designated PB-1G, the USCG used them as a long-range air-sea rescue aircraft capable of being fitted with an external lifeboat. Others were used on the International Ice Patrol and one was modified for aerial survey work. (USCG)

Below: Grumman JRF-5G *Goose* BuNo 84792, another ex US Navy aircraft, seen parked at San Francisco US Coast Guard air station, California, during September 1951. At this time the markings were standard for flying boats and amphibians, their prime role being air-sea rescue. (William T. Larkins)

Air to air photo taken on 20 January 1964 of the US Coast Guard Grumman VC-4A *Gulfstream I* transport 1380 marked Arlington on the fin and based at the air detachment at National Airport, Washington DC. It was built in 1963 and is still in service today but based at Elizabeth City, North Carolina. (USCG)

The Douglas C-54 *Skymaster* served the USCG between 1945 and 1962, and some six ex US Air Force and US Navy R5D- models were utilized on a wide variety of duties, including the International Iceberg Patrol, calibration of LORAN stations etc. The type served in Argentia, Newfoundland and at Elizabeth City, North Carolina. (USCG)

Right: A Fairchild C-123B *Provider* transport aircraft of the US Coast Guard based at Honolulu, Hawaii, seen in flight over the Pacific Ocean on 28 April 1961. Six of these transports were used by the USCG when based at far-flung air detachments like Guam in the Pacific, Naples in Italy and Kodiak in Alaska. (USCG)

Martin P5M-1G *Marlin* 1285 seen in take-off sequence. Seven of these were delivered to the US Coast Guard, with four of the later P5M-2G model being delivered in 1961 with the anti-submarine gear removed and air-sea rescue equipment added. (USCG)

Historic photo depicting three US Coast Guard types which include a Boeing PB-1G *Flying Fortress*, an early Lockheed HC-130B *Hercules* and a Douglas C-54 *Skymaster*. (USCG)

The first Lockheed HC-130 *Hercules* was delivered to the US Coast Guard during December 1959. It had c/n 3529, was a Lockheed model 282-2B and was allocated the US Air Force serial 58-5396. As can be seen in this early photo the transport had high visibility markings. Its first assignment was to Elizabeth City, North Carolina. (USCG)

Using skis and snow shoes, the Coast Guard shore party, after many hardships in sub-zero weather, finally found the Canadians and carried them to the cutter. The stranded men were on the verge of collapse and almost frozen. They had made a bonfire of their parkas in a desperate attempt to attract attention. Taken on board *Northland*, they were rushed to the sick bay and treated for shock and exposure. The Canadian Government presented a plaque to the Coast Guard to commemorate the rescue.

Five days later, *Northland* received word that the crew of a Boeing B-17 *Flying Fortress* of the US Army Air Corps, lost two weeks previously on the ice cap, had made contact with other US Army aircraft and were about forty miles from Comanche Bay. The Coast Guard was requested to attempt a rescue. *Northland* ploughed her way through the ice as far as possible toward the scene of the disaster. Lieutenant Pritchard requested permission to fly the rescue operation, proposing to land his Grumman J2F *Duck* on the snow and ice with pontoons, which would work like runners. His amphibian soon climbed out of the fog to 2,000 feet to the ice cap, and Radioman Benjamin A Bottoms transmitted a message to the grounded bomber indicating they were landing. The stranded US Army crew signalled that it was very dangerous, but Pritchard ignored their warning and landed safely. He then set out on foot to pick up the survivors four miles away.

He found the men almost starved and half frozen, but they received Lieutenant Pritchard with joyous shouts. One man had a broken arm and two others were also suffering from injuries, but these were fortunately all walking casualties. The remainder of the crew were more seriously injured. These soon received attention, then assisted by the sturdiest, Pritchard led the three back to his aircraft, but could only fly with two. The third man, Corporal L A Hayworth, had to wait for a return trip the following day. The J2F reached *Northland* after dark, but a landing was made with the aid of the cutter's searchlight.

Next morning Pritchard and Bottoms took off in a blinding snowstorm for the third man on the ice cap. Despite warnings from the *Northland* just prior to landing that bad weather was setting in, and despite orders to return, Pritchard repeated his splendid performance of the day before and took the remaining airman on his amphibian. Bottoms transmitted a message to the cutter that they had recovered the survivor and were airborne again. On board the cutter, anxious personnel awaited the hum of the returning plane. Messages from the J2F suddenly stopped. The storm had increased in intensity, and somewhere on the return flight the pilot had lost his bearings. Search parties were driven back by the howling gale.

On 4 December 1942 five volunteers from *Northland* went ashore under the leadership of Ensign Richard L Fuller USCG to locate Pritchard's amphibian. These men waged a stirring battle for several days on snow shoes. On the night of the second day they and *Northland* saw a light to the northeast of Atterbury Dome, on the ice cap, and two days later were able to investigate. An assumed position of the aircraft had been given them, but a painstaking, heroic search for several days failed to locate it. The party broke camp on 11 December, and after a long, arduous journey, they returned to the beach and *Northland*. Since the cutter now had no J2F, ultimate rescue of the rest of the *Flying Fortress* crew was accomplished by a US Navy and Army aircraft under Lieutenant Bernard Dunlop US Navy (Reserve) and Colonel Bernt Balchen, US Army.

Some four months later, Colonel Balchen flew over Pritchard's lost J2F and reported it six to eight miles from its originally reported position. Lieutenant Pritchard and Radioman Bottoms were listed as missing in action, and in 1943 each received a posthumous award of the Distinguished Flying Cross.

An example of cooperation during attack was that of Coast Guard J2F-5 *Duck* BuNo 00796 from Elizabeth City air station. This amphibian was escorting the US tanker *William A Rockefeller*, 14,054 tons, at 1217 hours on 28 June 1942. It was on the port beam of the tanker, in position 35° 07′, 75° 07′W, about forty miles off Cape Hatteras, when the pilot saw a tremendous explosion and the tanker burst into flames. At the same moment a submerged submarine cruising at about thirty feet was sighted 3,000 yards on the tanker's port beam. The J2F, which was 1,200 feet above the burning tanker, made a full throttle dive on the submarine, but by the time it had arrived at the bomb release point, the enemy had disappeared. The pilot dropped two depth charges at one second intervals, set for fifty-foot depth, in the best ascertainable position, but with no visible results. Then the pilot flew at top speed to CGC-470, a cutter which was five miles distant. This vessel turned towards the scene and the pilot dropped two smoke flares on the spot where the depth charges had detonated, CGC-470 then patterned seven depth charges around the smoke flares with no visible results, after which she began picking up tanker survivors from lifeboats. The J2F directed her to one man stranded on top of an overturned lifeboat and to another clinging to a piece of wreckage. There were no casualties, and the entire tanker crew of fifty was saved.

Rare photo of a Coast Guard Douglas RD-4 in wartime camouflage preparing for take-off from San Francisco air station. During August 1943 RD-4 V128 was based at Miami, V127 at San Diego and V133 at San Francisco. The *Dolphin* was used on anti-submarine patrols over the Pacific. (USCG)

Earlier in the year, on 27 January 1942, a dual role of bombing the enemy from the air and bringing aid to survivors was once more played by Coast Guard Grumman JRF-2 *Goose* V175, piloted by Lieutenant Commander R L Burke from the Elizabeth City air station. The JRF received a distress call from the 7,096-ton US tanker *Frances E Powell* indicating that she was being overtaken by a submarine eight miles off Currituck Light, south of Virginia Beach. The tanker was sunk soon afterward. A Coast Guard Grumman J2F-5 *Duck* first sighted the submarine and dropped two depth charges within a hundred feet of the now submerged marauder. Then Commander Burke in V175 dropped a grapnel with a hundred feet of line and two life jackets to buoy the spot so that destroyers could later depth charge the area. It seemed likely that the enemy had been damaged because Burke later saw and photographed what appeared to be a distress buoy from a submarine. All but four of the tanker's crew of thirty-two were eventually saved by surface craft summoned to the scene by the two Coast Guard aircraft.

From the commencement of hostilities in 1941 to June 1943, Coast Guard aircraft delivered sixty-one bombing attacks on enemy submarines, located over 1,000 survivors and actually rescued ninety-five persons without assistance. During fiscal year 1943, over 11,000 flights were made, including administrative, test flights, training, assistance, ambulance, law enforcement, and patrol flights. These involved sorties against enemy submarines, aerial coverage of merchant and naval vessels, and numerous reconnaissance patrols over the offshore waters of the continental US, Greenland, Labrador, Alaska, Canada, Mexico, the West Indies and Cuba.

Waterfront scene at San Francisco air station during 1942 with a Consolidated PBY-5 *Catalina* V189 being manhandled after a flight, whilst two Douglas RD-4 *Dolphins* V126 and V128 are parked behind. All carry the wartime drab camouflage finish. (USCG via William T. Larkins)

From the spring of 1942 until the threat of enemy raids along the US coastline diminished, the Coast Guard air stations were primarily engaged in anti-submarine patrols and auxiliary missions. In general the duty consisted of patrol and scouting activity off the principal ports and coastal waters and from 100 to 200 miles out to sea. The port approaches were especially important. Convoy escort duty was performed to the extent the cruising radius of the aircraft permitted. Uppermost in the purpose of these patrols carried out by both Coast Guard and US Navy planes was protection of shipping from hostile submarines. Special scouting was done in connection with the arrival and departure of US and Allied naval and merchant vessels. Suspicious craft were investigated in an effort to discover ships refuelling enemy submarines, especially in the waters off the First Naval District covering the north Atlantic where numerous fishermen worked far offshore.

During World War II, Coast Guard manned ships sank eleven enemy submarines and Coast Guard aircraft sank one.

Coast Guardsmen are seen loading a potent depth bomb into position on a Coast Guard Vought OS2U-3 *Kingfisher* at an air station somewhere on the Atlantic seaboard. During World War II these airborne mariners kept a constant vigil, protecting convoys from lurking enemy submarines. (USCG)

On 1 August 1942 a Coast Guard utility amphibian, a Grumman J4F-1 *Widgeon* V212, piloted by Chief Aviation Pilot Henry Clark White, bombed a German submarine in the Gulf of Mexico about a hundred miles south of Houma, Louisiana. Chief White with Radioman First Class George Henderson Boggs Jr as his only crewman, was patrolling an assigned area near a buoy marking a sunken United Fruit ship. At 13.37 hours, White sighted on his starboard bow a surfaced and stopped submarine. Boggs immediately sent an SOS message, indicating position.

Chief White thought that circling and making the attack from the stern would be most effective; but while he was circling the submarine began to submerge. Therefore, he started his attack immediately from abeam at an altitude of 1,500 feet and one-half mile distant. As the submarine was going under fast, White went into a fifty degree dive and released his bomb from an altitude of 250 feet. The submarine had been visible during the entire approach, and though under the surface when the bomb was released, it was clearly seen.

Submarine U-166 had been launched on 3 November 1941, had a 1,120 tons displacement, was 252 feet long and was a Type IXC model. It must have seemed a far cry from the climate of Northern Europe as it languished in the hot humidity of the Gulf of Mexico. One can only imagine how the crew felt when the raucous klaxon announced a crash dive, as they were about to be attacked by Coast Guard J4F-1 *Widgeon*.

Boggs, with his head out of the J4F window, saw the bomb strike the water and explode in what appeared to be a direct hit. White pulled out of the dive and came round to observe results; no debris was seen, but various patches of oil coming to the surface bore witness to heavy damage at least.

After the attack, two US Army Air Corps observation aircraft came on the scene just off the Mississippi Delta in the Gulf of Mexico, and White's relief aircraft arrived. White remained in the vicinity for about an hour, and then departed for his base at Houma air station, Louisiana, where he was attached to Squadron 212 USCG. It later transpired that he had made a direct hit and the submarine U-166 had been completely destroyed. It was the only submarine sunk by Coast Guard aviation during World War II. White, then a Lieutenant, was awarded the Distinguished Flying Cross and Boggs received the Air Medal for his participation in the sinking.

The G-44 Grumman *Widgeon* utility amphibian flying boat was flown for the first time in July 1940 and was designed for the commercial market. The twenty-second production model was, however, a three-seat anti-submarine patrol and utility model for the Coast Guard, some twenty-five being delivered in 1941. However, the J4F-1 could carry only one depth charge or bomb attached to a rack under the starboard wing root, and with the crew reduced to two had a 'negative rate of climb' on one engine, thus being unsuitable for use at any great range from the shore. The famed Grumman J4F-1 V212 survived World War II and was sold as war surplus to the US Department of the Interior and over the years carried the US Civil Registrations N743, N2770A and N324BC. The aircraft has now been restored to Coast Guard livery and is on display at the US Naval Aviation Museum located at Pensacola, Florida.

Most air patrol work was hard, very routine and without any special excitement. Regular harbor, inshore and offshore patrols, often as far as 500 or 600 miles out to sea, were not very spectacular and most of the pleasure of flying was lost in the constant vigil required. Pilots were continually on the lookout for obstructions, derelicts or surface craft that had to be identified. Nevertheless, every Coast Guard pilot had his thrilling moments. At any time a routine patrol might be interrupted by a radio message sending the aircraft out on an emergency mission, a ship might be lost, a boat wrecked or a vessel sinking and its crew in dire need of assistance. 'Mercy flights' gained an enviable reputation.

The early days of World War II were neither easy nor satisfying for Coast Guard aviation. For example, the first station order received by the Elizabeth City air station, North Carolina, from the US Navy after the declaration of war was for an air patrol of 'steamer lanes and offshore approaches to Chesapeake Capes; an alert for enemy submarines'. This patrol, extending fifty miles to sea and south to Cape Lookout, was maintained every day that weather conditions permitted. Thirteen pilots and only ten aircraft were available for anti-submarine patrols, but positive achievements in repelling enemy operations off the coast were largely negated because the aircraft were unarmed. Merchant vessels were being sunk daily, while pilots stood by helpless, unable to do more than turn in an outraged report. Despite requests for modern planes, adequately armed for combatting submarines, it was not until 22 January 1942 that armed aircraft were assigned to the station. Two were then received, equipped with machine guns and bomb racks, but they were poorly adapted for submarine warfare. It was December 1943 before adequate fighting planes were procured and by then the danger from submarines was largely over.

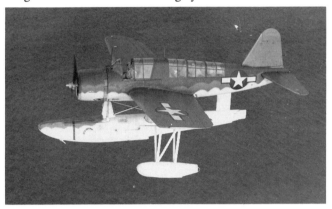

Airborne over an Atlantic Allied convoy of mixed vessels, a Coast Guard Vought OS2U-3 *Kingfisher* is seen on patrol, keeping a sharp lookout for undersea marauders. Depth charges carried beneath the wing can be dropped in an instant. The ceaseless guarding of such convoys by USCG planes and cutters contributed greatly to the reduction in ship tonnage losses. (USCG)

The outstanding work of Coast Guard aviation remained little known to the general public during World War II — only when some dramatic incident was publicized was it given any general acclaim. Yet numerous operations were undertaken during the war years. While many statistics are available, there are many interesting and informative figures taken from Aircraft Operations Reports which can be cited to show the scope of operations by the nine Coast Guard air stations. In the fiscal years 1943 and 1944, Coast Guard aircraft spent a total of 131,277 hours in flight. There were 42,282 training, test, patrol and administrative flights and 1,295 assistance flights. A total of 12,365,072 miles was cruised and an area of 85,957,671 square miles searched. In all, 207,522 vessels and aircraft were identified, 194 vessels and aircraft, and 207 disabled or overdue airplanes were assisted, 659 persons received help and 175 medical cases were transported. Other persons transported totalled 4,422, and cases of assistance to other US Government departments numbered 305.

In January 1942 a Coast Guard aircraft from the Salem air station in Massachusetts was ordered to get airborne when the US Navy Information Centre requested information about the sinking of an unidentified tanker. The plane sighted the partly sunk vessel in a vertical position, with its bow extending about twenty feet above the water. The area was searched for survivors and enemy craft. A life raft and lifeboats with survivors were located within a five mile radius of the derelict tanker and the Coast Guard airplane informed five commercial fishing vessels who were nearby of the situation and they picked up the survivors.

From time to time Coast Guard pilots would chance the dangers of crashing and effect successful landings in order to give succour to the dying or helpless. The first such landing by an aircraft based at Elizabeth City air base was made by the unarmed Hall PH-3 V183 on 1 May 1942, when thirteen survivors were saved after drifting at sea for six days. Two men, one seriously injured, were flown to Norfolk, Virginia, whilst the remaining eleven were picked up by a Coast Guard cutter. The following day another offshore landing saved the lives of two men adrift on a raft. Perhaps the most spectacular rescue from Elizabeth City was made in July 1942 when Lieutenant Richard L Burke and his co-pilot Lieutenant R W Blouin picked up seven German survivors from the submarine *Dergin,* which had been sunk by a US Army aircraft. Burke was awarded his second Distinguished Flying Cross for this exploit.

A pair of Coast Guard Grumman J4F-1 *Widgeons* in an early camouflage scheme are seen on patrol over an Allied merchant ship during the early part of World War II. The rugged Grumman amphibian was capable of carrying depth charges and bombs. Twenty-five of this type served between 1941 and 1948. (USCG)

On 3 April 1943 Lieutenant J N Schrader, whilst patrolling out of the Miami Coast Guard air station in a Vought OS2U-3 *Kingfisher* observation and scout aircraft, received a radio message to search for survivors of the torpedoed tanker *Gulfstate*. Upon sighting the remains of the tanker, he was able to spot three groups of survivors. Dropping his depth charges, he landed in the ocean and picked up the three men in the first group. He taxied to the second group, gave them a rubber raft for support, and carried on to the assistance of the third group, one of whom was badly injured with burns. Taking this man on board his already overloaded OS2U aircraft, Schrader stood by to protect the drifting survivors from sharks until other Coast Guard aircraft arrived to assist him.

The Vought OS2U-3 was a workhorse for the Coast Guard and they carried the burden of early anti-submarine warfare along US coastal waters. Beginning in March 1942, the Coast Guard eventually acquired fifty-three of these aircraft and they served until retirement in October 1944. Equipped with one depth charge or bomb plus a full load of fuel they could manage a patrol of six hours duration. By August 1943 the *Kingfisher* was part of the aviation inventory at six major Coast Guard air stations. Salem had eight, Elizabeth City had eight, Miami had nine, Biloxi had six and San Francisco five. During 1943 three of these aircraft were airborne from Elizabeth City on a routine patrol when they spotted sailors in the water about thirty miles east of Cape Hatteras. All three aircraft made off-shore landings, and picked up all the survivors who rested on the wings until a boat arrived from Elizabeth City to take the rescued. They were all survivors from a tanker torpedoed off Cape Hatteras.

It will now be realized that most Coast Guard aviation units performed a far greater service in rescuing or aiding survivors as a by-product of anti-submarine patrols, than in scaring off enemy submarines. The patrols were, for the most part, little less than harassing agents. Day after day, pilots gave what assistance they could to the victims of torpedoed vessels. Seaplanes could land in the water and pick up survivors, but others could only pause in their patrol to stand by until other surface rescue craft arrived. But many enemy submarines were contacted. Several were attacked and damaged or disabled. Coast Guard action reports record numerous attacks which helped to drive enemy submarines from the US coastal areas.

A noteworthy service developed by Coast Guard aviation, especially in the lower Atlantic coast and the Gulf areas, was the hurricane warning system for small craft. When hurricanes threatened, Coast Guard planes dropped warning blocks to off-shore vessels not equipped with radio. These warnings were particularly valuable to local fishermen, yacht owners and vessels engaged in the sponge fishing industry and many vessels reached shelter which might otherwise have been caught in dangerous storms.

Patrol Squadron Six

The history of Coast Guard aviation in World War II is replete with accounts of heroic service and devotion to duty under the most difficult conditions. One such chapter recounts the story of how Coast Guard aviators, in one inhospitable corner of the earth, assumed and carried out with great skill and courage the mission of maritime patrol traditionally assigned to the US Navy.

During the early years of World War II in the North Atlantic, German submarines harassed and sank Allied ships with virtual impunity. On 9 April 1941, by agreement with the Danish government, the US undertook the defense of Greenland. The Act of Havana of 30 July 1940 had already conferred upon the USA the responsibility for the defense of the western hemisphere.

The Coast Guard's long association with the International Ice Patrol and the Bering Sea Patrol made that service uniquely qualified for Arctic operations. Consequently, during October 1941, Commander Edward H Smith, USCG was appointed overall commander for Greenland defense reporting to the Commander in Chief, Atlantic Fleet.

With the entry of the United States into the war, the air patrol requirement in the Greenland area was greatly expanded. From this requirement was born a special patrol squadron manned entirely by Coast Guard personnel and considered by many to be the most colourful of all the Coast Guard aviation units of World War II.

On 5 October 1943 Patrol Squadron Six (VP-6 CG) was officially established by the US Navy at Argentia, Newfoundland, relieving the US Navy's Bombing Squadron 126. The new squadron's home base was at Narsarssuak, Greenland, code name *Bluie West-One* (BW-1). Designated as a unit of the huge Atlantic Fleet, it was under the direct operational control of Commander Task Force Twenty-Four (CTF-24) with administrative control vested in Commander Fleet Air Wing Nine (CFAW-9). All personnel matters, however, remained the responsibility of Coast Guard Headquarters.

Commander Donald B MacDiarmid, Coast Guard Aviator #59, a seasoned professional and flying boat expert, was selected to command VP-6. Thirty officers and 145 enlisted men were assigned; twenty-two of the officers were aviators and eight of the enlisted men were also aviation pilots, most with considerable flying experience. All of the aircraft and ground crewmen had years of aviation service, every bit of which would be taxed to the limits during the more than two years of flying they would accomplish in the hostile environment of the North Atlantic.

The aircraft assignment called for ten Consolidated PBY-5A *Catalina* patrol bombers, nine to be operational with one spare. However, because of delivery problems, flying operations commenced with only six aircraft. The PBY was a remarkable aircraft and quickly gained the respect and affection of pilots and crewmen for its rugged dependability.

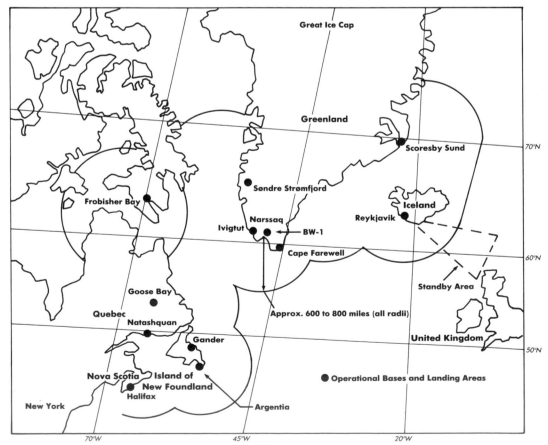

A map showing the VPB-6 operational areas.

It could carry 4,000 pounds of bombs, two torpedoes or four 325lb depth charges. Cruising range at 105 knots was over 2,000 miles. It did magnificent work and was employed for every conceivable mission. Some units nicknamed it *Dumbo*. It could carry a crew of between seven and nine, and by 1945 the Coast Guard had no less than 114 on its inventory.

The mission of VP-6 was five-fold: anti-submarine patrol, known as ASW (anti-submarine warfare); air support for North Atlantic convoys; search and rescue; surveying and reporting ice conditions; delivering essential mail and medical supplies to military bases and civilian villages and outposts. German U-boats were operating almost at will in the North Atlantic and the number of convoy sinkings was staggering, giving VP-6's rescue duties high priority.

On 28 November 1943, not long after VP-6 had been commissioned, a US Army Air Force Beechcraft AT-7 twin-engined trainer was reported lost, and several *Catalinas* from Narsarssuak conducted a search over a wide area. Lieutenant A W Weuker finally located the wrecked advanced training aircraft on the edge of the Sukkertoppen Ice Cap on 1 December. On the second flight six days later, Weuker marked the spot with flag stakes; on 21 December photographs were finally taken successfully to guide a rescue party. A Coast Guard PBY-5A from VP-6 directed the actual rescue party, on 5 January 1944, over the last ten miles to the wreckage, dropped provisions to the rescuers, and two days later contacted the rescue group on the return trek and again dropped provisions.

As additional PBYs became available, the units area of operations broadened in scope and detachments were established at several locations. Two PBYs and crews were based at Reykjavik, Iceland, furnishing air cover for US Navy and Coast Guard vessels operating against the enemy and providing ASW services for North Atlantic convoys and search and rescue operations in conjunction with the Royal Air Force Coastal Command. Whilst carrying out their missions, these units provided their own ground support.

An additional detachment of two aircraft and crews was assigned to the Canadian Arctic in support of vessels entering the Hudson Bay area during the navigation season. Anti-submarine patrols were required in the Hudson Strait, Ungava Bay and Frobisher Bay area regions. Two more aircraft were assigned on a rotational basis to the US Naval Air Facility at Argentia, Newfoundland, where all major repairs to the *Catalinas* were carried out. The widespread dispersal of aircraft and crews posed many administrative and

logistical problems which made an already difficult situation even more unwieldy. But that was the hand VP-6 of the Coast Guard was dealt, and play it they did.

The operation was focused on Greenland, the largest island in the world, which lies almost entirely within the Arctic Circle. It is 1,600 miles north to south and nearly 800 miles wide. Eighty-five per cent of the island is covered with a great ice cap of unbelievable thickness. It was not uncommon for VP-6 aircraft to fly thousands of miles over the ice cap under the most trying weather conditions in a single search. Strong wings of 120 to 150 knots were a constant threat. Flying in those weather conditions, far from bases and with few navigation aids, required a high degree of pilot skill and courage. Only well trained, savvy pilots and crews could have survived.

The Consolidated PBYs of VP-6 often sighted stranded vessels and crews that had sometimes been adrift for weeks in stormy seas. Two officers and twenty enlisted men on board the 110-foot British trawler HMS *Strathella*, disabled in a heavy storm, faced death after being adrift in the North Atlantic for over a month. They were dramatically rescued on 13 February 1944 by the combined efforts of a Coast Guard PBY-5A, piloted by Lieutenant Commander John D McCubbin, on a routine air patrol to check ice conditions and deliver mail, and the Coast Guard cutter *Madoc*. Sighting a red flare in position 60° 03′ N, 45° 24′ W, west of Cape Farewell, McCubbin requested the ship's identity by blinker light, received her name in like manner, and was told of these victims being adrift for five weeks, their food and water exhausted and their radio unserviceable. McCubbin radioed to shore and within the hour *Madoc* was on its way to the rescue. It towed *Strathella* 100 miles safely to the Greenland base. A second VP-6 PBY-5A was also involved in the rescue.

That rescue and hundreds of others were carried out by VP-6 during its twenty-seven months of operations, frequently during high winds and near-zero visibility. During a three-month period in early 1944, for example, Lieutenant Carl H Allen, USCG, flew more than a hundred hours each month over difficult Arctic terrain to and from convoy support duty and ice patrol. One flight took him over the magnetic North Pole.

Only seven of the improved Hall PH-3 flying boats were delivered to the Coast Guard in 1940 and continued in service until 1944. This photo shows a PH-3 in unusual finish during World War II. The national insignia is positioned on the rear of the fuselage, and the blue tail marking is retained. In August 1943 six of the seven were still in service. (USCG)

By early 1944, rapid expansion of Coast Guard aviation had produced a shortage of seasoned pilots and crews. The squadron was forced to maintain a comprehensive training schedule to ensure its crews were at peak readiness. To provide some relief for the squadron, a pre-training syllabus was set up at Coast Guard air station, Elizabeth City, North Carolina. Coast Guard Headquarters meanwhile decreed that a one-year tour of duty in Arctic regions was sufficient, and ordered that pilots and crews not requesting an extension of their tour be relieved as soon as possible. Reliefs therefore were staggered over a four-month period to permit absorption and orientation for replacements without disruption of operations.

On 15 May 1944 Commander William I Swanston, USCG relieved Commander MacDiarmid as commanding officer of VP-6, and Lieutenant Commander G Russell 'Bobo' Evans, USCG became executive officer. By then the squadron had twelve PBY-5A aircraft, with two in Iceland, two assigned to Canadian Arctic, three at Argentia and five at BW-1 Narsarssuak.

Throughout the summer of 1944, the squadron was extremely busy. An expanded part of VP-6's operations involved ASW operations in the Baffin Bay, Davis Strait and Labrador Sea areas to protect US ships transporting cryolite, urgently needed in the production of aluminium for the US aircraft production programme.

To comply with a US Navy directive dated 1 October 1944, patrol squadrons (VP) and multi-engine bombing squadrons (VB) were renamed and redesignated patrol bombing squadrons. Thus VP-6 (CG) became VPB-6 (CG).

From September through to 16 November 1944 two PBYs and their crews commanded by Lieutenant Commander Evans, operated from Reykjavik and provided ASW sweeps, ice reconnaissance and logistic support for a task group of four Coast Guard cutters engaged in smashing a Nazi effort to establish weather stations in north-east Greenland. In the autumn, winds of gale force sometimes produced turbulence so severe that bombs had to be jettisoned.

Telling of his experiences flying from Reykjavik, Iceland, former VPB-6 executive officer Captain G R Evans, USCG (Ret) said:

> The airport was under repair most of the time and only half of the 150-foot wide runway was available to us. At night, we actually navigated our *Catalina* around obstacles during take-off and landing. We were motivated to achieve accuracy by the line of 50-gallon drums separating the two halves of the runway. The oil drums were virtually under one wing each time we had made a take-off or landing. The wing-span of the PBY-5A was 140 feet.

Another time we became completely weathered out of Iceland with none of the alternates open. So, we flew all the way to Stornoway, Scotland. We arrived in a blinding rain storm without an assigned IFF — Identification Friend or Foe — code and made our landing approach by a ground-controlled system we had never used before. Sometime later, I learned that my two crews and others in the squadron had affectionately dubbed our extensive flying programme in Iceland *Bobo's Flying Circus*.

At BW-1 Narsarssuak, surface winds were rarely less than twenty-five knots. The single concrete runway had a considerable slope down from the edge of a mountain towards Narsarssuak Fjord. Thus, all take-offs were downhill and landings were uphill regardless of the wind direction. Under inclement weather conditions, it was necessary to fly up or down the fjord at low altitudes to get in or out of BW-1. With 4,000-foot mountains on each side, it was like flying down a giant tunnel. Its elevation was 112 feet above sea level and was positioned 61° 10′ N, 45° 26′ W.

Recalling those days, Commander John C Redfield, USCG (Ret) said:

> Most of the time, our return to BW-1 during bad weather conditions was an exercise in nail chewing, turning to stark terror. We had very few instrument landing aids. Sometimes when we were inbound up the fjord with one-quarter to one-half mile visibility, we would receive a report that another plane had just departed BW-1 on a priority flight and was outbound down the fjord. Sure was good for growing gray hair. After radar was finally installed, we were better off. We could fly up the fjord at 400 to 600 foot altitudes and negotiate the twists and turns as directed by the radar operator. At the last turn to the west, if we couldn't see BW-1, less than a mile away, we would pull up and climb out.

Curtiss SO3C-1 *Seagull* landplane is readied for take-off at Port Angeles Coast Guard air station during 1943. A total of forty-eight of these scout aircraft were delivered between 1943 and 1944 for use by the Coast Guard. Some retained their floats, others were used as landplanes. In August 1943 six were based at Brooklyn, and six at Biloxi. (Gordon S. Williams)

Lieutenant Commander William C Wallace, USCG (Ret) said of his VPB-6 days:

> Even though there were many problems and difficult things about flying the Arctic in those days, there was beauty unsurpassed at times, such as the aurora borealis — the Northern Lights — which were beautiful and awesome with streamers of red, green and yellow across the heavens. The stark isolation of the ragged peaks and rocks along the shorelines, the tremendous icebergs and solid ice fields stretching to the horizon, days without nights and eternal nights in winter, the nearness and remoteness of the great ice cap where depth perception was non existent, made lasting impressions.

An armed Vought OS2U-3 *Kingfisher* takes off from an unidentified Atlantic seaboard Coast Guard air station on anti-submarine patrol. Under each wing is carried a bomb — bad news for any enemy U-boat that may be spotted by the ensign pilot. The type served the Coast Guard between 1941 and 1944. (USCG)

Like any other squadron, VPB-6 had its characters. There were Lieutenants Harry H 'Shakey' Eckels, whom everybody teased about his red nose; E P 'Barefoot' Ward who could never find his shoes; Frank 'Wallbuster' Hodge, former football player, who lived up to his nickname; and Carl H 'Deacon' Allen and William H 'Bull' Durham who were full of humour, jokes and sea stories. They were experienced pilots and were a real inspiration to new and less experienced pilots coming into the squadron. Said one former squadon member, 'Those men were the real heroes. They kept us laughing and helped to make Arctic duty bearable for everyone in the squadron.'

Recreation was available at BW-1, such as movies, bowling, skiing, skeet shooting and, occasionally, a USO show. At Argentia, known as the Utopia of the North, all the comforts of the USA could be had — almost. Because of crew rotation, everyone usually had two tours there.

The surrender of Germany in May 1945 brought U-boat activity to a standstill. However, VPB-6's operations in search and rescue, ice patrol, logistic support of military bases, LORAN stations and civilian facilities continued unabated. An entry on 22 May 1945 reported a typical day's operation from BW-1 after hostilities ceased in Europe: BPY-5A BuNo 46575 departed BW-1 in the early morning to survey ice conditions along the west coast of Greenland. En route, passengers were landed at Ivigtut. PBY-5A BuNo 46458 returned to BW-1 with passengers and mail from BW-8. By 08.00 hours, the US Army Air Force advised VPB-6 that a Consolidated B-24 *Liberator* heading for Iceland from Goose Bay, Labrador, was in distress with two engines out. The PBY-5A BuNo 46572 responded immediately and, within one hour, the B-24 was contacted and escorted safely to BW-1. After refuelling, BuNo 46572 departed BW-1 again on ice patrol, plotted an ice navigation chart and dropped it at Ivigtut to assist a ship convoy moving down the Davis Strait.

One Howard GH-2 and two GH-3 high-wing monoplanes were delivered to the Coast Guard in 1944. They were used for proficiency and instrument training. One GH-3 was based at San Francisco air station in November 1944. They were known as the *Nightingale*. (Bureau of Aeronautics 72-AC-30H-4 National Archives)

While returning from this mission, the crew received a report that a US Army Air Force Boeing B-17E *Flying Fortress* en route to Goose Bay from Iceland was in distress, with two engines out and a third engine smoking badly. Interception was made and the disabled bomber was escorted up the fifty-mile fjord to BW-1, where the third engine quit while landing. Lieutenant Allen in PBY-5A BuNo 46510 departed with twenty passengers en route to Stephenville, Newfoundland. On his return flight he was ordered to search for another US Army Air Force B-24 *Liberator* reported down near Port-au-Choix. Allen located the plane on a beach, landed his PBY in the water nearby, picked up the downed crew and flew them safely to Stephenville.

On 30 May 1945 Commander Loren H Seeger, USCG relieved Commander Swanston as commanding officer of VPB-6. On 12 July administrative control of the squadron was transferred from Commander Fleet Air Wing Nine to Commandant US Coast Guard and it was redesignated a non-combat squadron. Operational control, however, was retained by Commander Task Force Twenty-Four. In August 1945 VPB-6 received a directive to transfer its base headquarters from BW-1 Narsarssuak to the US Navy facility at Argentia, Newfoundland, where it was disestablished as a US Navy squadron in January 1946.

The accomplishments of this outstanding World War II Coast guard squadron have remained relatively unknown. However, the men who served on Arctic duty and the Greenland Patrol and their dedication to the job assigned added a heroic chapter to the story of Coast Guard Aviation.

Consolidated PBY-5A *Catalina* of the Coast Guard prepares for another patrol over the Pacific from San Francisco air station. Over a hundred of the PBY, nicknamed 'Dumbo', served with the Coast Guard between 1942 and 1954. It did magnificent work, being employed on every conceivable mission. In the background is parked an SNJ-5 *Texan*. (Gordon S. Williams)

Air Sea Rescue

By October 1944, the submarine menace along the Atlantic Sea Frontier had largely disappeared, though occasional sinkings continued. Coast Guard aviation had generally ceased anti-submarine patrols at that time, and the organization underwent transition to an integral part of the newly-organized Air Sea Rescue Forces. As naval, air force and merchant marine operations daily increased, the number of aircraft and vessels requiring assistance grew constantly. It was to facilitate saving the lives of countless aviators and seamen that Air Sea Rescue was born. Thereafter, wartime air activity was almost entirely confined to rescue operations, the normal peacetime function of this fifth branch of the US Services.

The first Air Sea Rescue unit was established at San Diego, California, during December 1943. The regular National Air Sea Rescue Agency was established in Washington DC on 22 February 1944, and its administration was placed under the Coast Guard. Maximum co-ordination of all rescue efforts of the Army, Navy and Coast Guard was the major responsibility of each regional Air Sea Rescue Task Unit, headed by the commanding officer of the Coast Guard air station. Except where this Agency was concerned with rescues before the end of World War II, it was primarily a postwar organization. Upon receipt of information from any source that an accident had occurred, the sector headquarters sent out an appropriate search from the nearest task unit or, if the situation warranted, indicated a general 'alert' for the entire section area. Thus, all services, operating under a unified command, co-ordinated their activities in a general search.

A very rare photo depicting an airborne lifeboat being hoisted into position under the wing of a Coast Guard Consolidated PBY-5A *Catalina*. This amphibian was one of the most versatile craft utilized by many Allied forces during World War II. It had a range of nearly 2,500 miles and could carry four 1,000 lb bombs under its wings. It was 1954 before the last one was graciously retired from Coast Guard service. (Peter M. Bowers)

In May 1943 a Salem air station aircraft on patrol intercepted a message regarding an airplane down in the sea north of Peaked Hill Bar at the tip of Cape Cod. Proceeding to the scene, the pilot located an overturned lifeboat and a man on a raft nearby. Three other aircraft were circling overhead. The only vessel in sight was a disabled trawler, from which two dories were rowing toward the life raft. The Coast Guard airplane dropped its depth charges clear of the scene, and landed on the water a mile off the beach. It taxied to the dory, which had picked up the survivor of the crashed aircraft who was suffering from head injuries and exposure. He was taken on board the Salem Coast Guard airplane and flown to the US Naval Air Station located at Squantum.

After the hurricane of 14 September 1944, an amphibian from the Salem air station was the first aircraft under Commander Northern Air Patrol to go out. A photographic survey was made of the damage along the coast, and an unsuccessful search was conducted for the Vineyard South Lightship which was later discovered to have foundered at her mooring.

Just one year earlier, during September 1943, Ensign W M Braswell, flying from the Miami Coast Guard air station, and still in a weakened condition from recent hospitalization, landed near a Pan American Airways aircraft that had crashed in Biscayne Bay. Risking his own life, he swam to the submerged aircraft, unstrapped the pilot and, with the aid of his radioman, rescued the pilot and two other survivors. Artificial respiration brought all three unconscious men to life before they were turned over to the Coast Guard crash boat for medical treatment. Rescues of this character indicated more than a mere strict adherence to duty.

By 1942 most of the US Coast Guard Aviation fleet of unique types began to appear in warpaint. This rare photo, taken at air station San Francisco on 3 June 1942, shows two Douglas RD-4 *Dolphins*, V128 and V133, plus one Hall PH-3 which is either V180 or V181. (William T. Larkins)

One rescue during patrol by a Coast Guard aircraft from the St Petersburg air station is another example of how patrol and air sea rescue duties were combined. In December 1944 Ensign F T Merritt accomplished a dramatic rescue of a US Navy pilot who had apparently collided with a tow aircraft during practice gunnery exercise and had been forced to bail out. Returning from a routine administrative flight to Cuba, Merritt and his crew were instructed to search for survivors of a US Army Air Force B-24 *Liberator*. While thus engaged they spotted and investigated an SOS dye marker about twenty miles off Daytona Beach. An injured fighter pilot was discovered on a life raft. Merritt effected a safe landing, picked up the injured pilot and delivered him safely to the hospital at his Daytona base.

Sometimes Coast Guard aircraft had to work well inland from the coast. Typical of the harmonious coordination of all types of Air Sea rescue units was the rescue of six members of the crew of a US Navy patrol airplane which crashed in thick fog about 130 miles northeast of Seattle in Washington State. The rescue necessitated a six day search from 14 to 20 January 1945 over the rugged Cascade Mountains, under the most trying weather conditions. Amid snow and rain, without shelter or rest, Army, Navy, Coast Guard and Forest Service crews searched. By 17 January four men had been found. The Army and Navy secured search operations after that but the Coast Guard and Forest Service continued the attempt until the other two crew members were rescued. The lives of five of the six men were saved. Coast Guard aircraft from Port Angeles air station were heavily involved.

After VE-Day in Europe during May 1945, plans were made for a huge redeployment of aircraft and personnel from the ETO (European Theatre of Operations) and the MTO (Mediterranean Theatre of Operations). This was the task of US Air Transport Command, designated 'White Project', and involving the return to the USA of some 2,825 heavy bombers from Europe and 1,240 from the Mediterranean. These, with varying numbers of passengers, were to be flown to the US by full combat crews. All three major Atlantic routes were utilized. On the North Atlantic route there was a small epidemic of ditchings, inspired by faulty fuel gauges, but the total accident rate was extremely low. During the course of the project 5,965 aircraft made the westward crossing of the Atlantic, all but 521 by the end of August 1945. The last large contingent consisted of 433 Boeing B-17 *Flying Fortresses*, which came home in September and October via the South Atlantic airway. In addition to 50,764 crew members, an average of eight to each aircraft, the airplanes brought home an additional 33,850 passengers, many of them aircrew. In all, the returnees numbered over 84,000, a substantial figure by any standard. Air Sea Rescue and the Coast Guard were on stand-by.

As an example of Air Sea Rescue experience in the later days of World War II, after most anti-submarine patrols had been secured, the records of the Northern California sector of the Western Sea Frontier may be mentioned. Of the total of thirty-eight crashes involving thirty-seven aircraft and ninety-eight personnel, from March 1944 to January 1945, forty-two persons were saved, fifty-one were beyond assistance, and only five were lost who might have been saved.

Coast Guard aviation proved itself time and time again during the crucial war years. While air patrols were largely preventive and few tangible results can be cited, the number of lives and the value of property saved was, in total, highly impressive. The airmen, in their devotion to duty and in their efficient execution of assignments, fully lived up to the fine traditions of the Service.

The age of the helicopter for Coast Guard rescue work was only just beginning in these war years and has not been forgotten. It is featured in Chapters 4 and 5.

CHAPTER FOUR
The Early Post-War Years

Total Coast Guard personnel during World War II numbered 231,000 men and 10,000 women. Of these, 1,918 died, a third losing their life in action. Almost 2,000 Coast Guardsmen, including aviators, were decorated. After demobilization, personnel figures reached a low of 18,687 officers and men in 1947. On 1 January 1946 the US Coast Guard had been returned to the US Treasury Department.

Following the end of World War II — 8 May 1945 in Europe and 14 August 1945 in Japan — US forces remained to assist in both theatres of operations, resulting in still heavy Atlantic and Pacific sea and air traffic to and from the US. By this time, the Air Sea Rescue service had been abandoned, but in view of the ever-increasing over-water aviation activity, both commercial and military, the need for such an organization continued. Consequently, the Secretaries of Commerce, Treasury and Defense, plus the Chairman of the Civil Aeronautics Board and the Federal Communications Commission signed an agreement organizing a Search & Rescue Agency. To avoid confusion and duplication of effort, the Coast Guard was assigned SAR responsibility over water, whilst the US Air Force — formed on 18 September 1947 — was assigned responsibility over the land area of the USA.

Although constructed during World War II, the USCG cutter *Storis* was never intended to carry an aircraft. During her long career in Coast Guard service, 1942 to date, this cutter has been classified as a miscellaneous auxilary (WAG); an icebreaker (WAGB); a buoy tender (WAGL); and a medium endurance cutter. A Grumman J2F-6 *Duck* is seen stowed on board *Storis* in Greenland during the early post-war years. (USCG)

After the Coast Guard combined with the US Navy on 1 November 1941 their aircraft retained the 'V' serial system introduced on 13 October 1936. When drab camouflage was introduced, plus the national insignia, naturally the 'V' serial disappeared from the side of the aircraft, appearing in some cases with the aircraft designation on the tail. However, all Coast Guard documents still referred to the 'V' serial throughout World War II. When all Coast Guard personnel and equipment was returned to the Treasury Department after the war it had a very varied mixture of both 'V' serials and US Navy Bureau Numbers. In some cases the Navy serials were referred to as Coast Guard numbers. With effect from 28 December 1945 the letter 'V' was dropped from the few remaining original Coast Guard aircraft and on 1 January 1951 the numeral '1' was added as a prefix to make up a four-digit number for use as a radio call-sign. At the same time five-digit US Navy serials on Coast Guard aircraft were reduced to their last four digits. The standard location of the serial number remained near the top of the vertical fin until 1947 when, along with the model and service designations, it was moved to a point on the fuselage below the leading edge of the horizontal tail. The serial number, later to become a mixture of USAF and US Navy, was usually in figures a little larger than those used for the model designation and name of the service. Today the last four digits of the serial appear on the nose of the aircraft in figures twelve or more inches high.

The wartime two-tone camouflage disappeared, all aircraft reverting to a general pre-war scheme, being either natural metal finish or painted aluminium. Helicopters were given an overall yellow/orange finish. The name US COAST GUARD was painted on the side of both fixed wing and rotary wing aircraft. The national star and bar insignia was placed on the top of the left wing and the bottom of the right, and on both sides of the fuselage. The letters USCG were on the top right and lower left side of the wings. In addition, all aircraft types considered to have the primary task or mission of Search & Rescue had additional high visibility markings. The upper and lower portion of the wing tips — approximately seven per cent of the wing span — were painted chrome yellow with an additional six inch black band inboard. An orange/yellow band encircled the fuselage, eighteen inches wide on the Grumman JRF Goose, and thirty-six inches wide on all other aircraft. This band was enclosed by a three- or six-inch black band accordingly. The new colour scheme was introduced during December 1952. On helicopters the main rotor blades had varicoloured tips to enhance visibility for Coast Guard personnel working on or near them on the ground. The yellow tail band was actually applied during the latter part of World War II to US Navy and Coast Guard aircraft assigned to Air Sea Rescue, some aircraft even carrying the word RESCUE in black on a yellow background on a panel on the top mainplane.

The baptism with multi-engined aircraft came during this period. The service had flown many twin-engined types until this point of time, but had never flown anything larger until the four-motor sea and landplanes arrived.

Four large Convair PB2Y-3/5 Coronado patrol bomber flying boats were operated by the Coast Guard between 1944 and 1946. They were used for ASW patrols and long-range search and rescue. Powered by four 1200 hp Pratt & Whitney R-1830-88 Wasp engines, this monster seaplane was ideal for extended flights over the ocean with a range of nearly 1,500 statute miles. During the same period five Consolidated PB4Y-1 Liberator land-based patrol bombers were operated. Their low range of nearly 3,000 statute miles made them outstanding platforms for extended searches far offshore. They were delivered in 1944 and 1945 and served until 1951.

Earlier, during the latter part of 1943, some twenty-seven Martin PBM-3 Mariner twin-engine patrol flying boats were delivered to the Coast Guard, these having a useful range of well over 2,000 statute miles, and carrying a load of up to 2,000 lb of bombs or depth charges. Later, in 1945, the first of a batch of forty-one PBM-5s were delivered to serve primarily in the air sea rescue role. At Salem air station, Massachusetts, after a successful experiment with jet assisted take-off, heavier take-off loads were permitted.

Lockheed R50-4 Lodestar BuNo 12453 seen parked at the USCG air detachment located at Washington National Airport on 10 November 1946. The Coast Guard operated three R50-4s, four R50-5s and a single R50-1, all used on VIP and administrative duties as required. Known as the Lodestar, BuNo 12453 carries a four-star VIP symbol on the engine cowl indicating it was used by the Commandant, Coast Guard. (Peter M. Bowers)

Spectacular photo depicting a huge Convair PB2Y-5 Coronado patrol bomber taking off assisted by JATO. Only four PB2Y-3s and -5s were operated by the Coast Guard serving at San Francisco air station. With the Coast Guard they were designated P4Y-2G. (USCG)

Within the Coast Guard aviators there remained the great tradition of the sea. This harked back to the era of World War I when Coast Guard officers and aviators were attached to the US Navy air stations in France; all USCG aviators were trained by the US Navy at Pensacola, Florida, and were well versed in the ways of the sea from a three-year duty on Coast Guard vessels prior to reaching wings standard. Unique as VP-6 (CG) Squadron was in being the only Coast Guard staffed Naval unit in World War II, the organization was only following the tradition established in the 1930s when the cutter-aircraft marriages roamed the desolate bays and ice strewn waters of high latitudes. Once on the ocean, the flying boat or amphibian pilot became a mariner and obeyed the rules of the sea accordingly. World War II introduced strange aircraft types, but the Coast Guard aviators flew side by side with their naval cousins during the period of global hostility which followed.

Having been second in priority to other requirements throughout the early combat period, the Coast Guard by late 1943 was beginning to acquire more modern aircraft. Seven improved versions of the Lockheed Lodestar — four R50-4 and three R50-5 — were assigned by the US Navy for use as executive transports, based at Floyd Bennett Field, New York, Elizabeth City, North Carolina and the Headquarters Detachment established at Washington National Airport.

In the land transport role, ten Curtiss R5C-1 Commando aircraft were operated from Elizabeth City air station, and at the local Aircraft Repair & Supply Center. They were used on a logistic service set up to deliver spare parts and personnel to Coast Guard units worldwide. Long-range fuel tanks were fitted and used between 1943 and 1950. Only the identity of one R5C-1 is known, this being BuNo 39537 which had previously served with the US Marine Corps and been made surplus on 31 May 1947, only to be reinstated with the Coast Guard at Norfolk, Virginia, on 31 July 1948.

Another workhorse used by the Coast Guard in a number of roles, was the Douglas R4D-5, the US Navy version of the ubiquitous DC-3 transport. The first of eight was delivered in late 1943, with the remainder the following year. At least one was based at Port Angeles air station, Washington, to provide support for the Alaskan LORAN chain plus the air detachments at Annette Island and Kodiak Island, Alaska. R4D-5 BuNo 17243 was one of those transports on the Port Angeles inventory.

Deliveries of a smaller twin-engined transport began in 1943. This was the Beechcraft SNB-1 plus JRB-4 and -5, a total of seven being used by various Coast Guard units. One carried specialized equipment and was used by the US Coast & Geodetic Survey in harbor mapping and photography. JRB-4 BuNo 90564 was based at Elizabeth City and used primarily for administrative and proficiency flying. The type was retired in 1958.

In an effort to improve and provide an efficient air sea rescue service at sea, now the Coast Guard's full responsibility, two Curtiss SB2C-4 *Helldiver* aircraft, surplus to the US Navy, were evaluated in 1945. Carrying life rafts and ration packs it was felt time could be eliminated by these 'fast types' on station at the rescue scene. Powered by a Wright R2600-8 engine they had a top speed of about 250 knots. With so many war surplus types to select from, the Coast Guard took advantage in order to improve its long-range air sea rescue capabilities. The USAF had already proved that the four-engined Boeing B-17 *Flying Fortress* could be fitted with a large airborne lifeboat which fitted in under the bomb bay. In 1945 the Coast Guard took delivery of the first of eighteen Boeing PG-1Gs as they were designated, all capable of carrying the airborne lifeboat. The type was useful on the International Ice Patrol, and for both coastal and geodetic survey photo mapping tasks. It was the most successful of the adapted long-range search aircraft used by the Coast Guard.

Held in storage by the USAF, the first was transferred to the Coast Guard during September 1946. One of these eighteen *Flying Fortresses* to be configured for SAR was CG-77254. It was a unique aircraft having only 52½ hours of flight time on the airframe. It was converted for photo survey work, her armament was removed, the bomb bay sealed and loaded with oxygen tanks. A massive hole was cut under the fuselage in order that a special US Coast & Geodetic Survey one and a half million dollar nine-lens aerial mapping camera could be installed. Only the World War II Norden bombsight remained to be used for pinpointing targets for the camera.

With the nine-lens camera the PB-1G could photograph 313 square miles of terrain with one click of the shutter whilst operating at 21,780 feet. Most of the task was conducted at altitudes between 20,000 and 30,000 feet. For twelve years CG-77254 ranged from Puerto Rico to Alaska recording the face of the United States for the Hydrographic Office. During these years it flew almost an even 6,000 hours and more than a million and a half miles. Her career was marred by two accidents, both occurring by coincidence at Hill Air Force Base, Ogden, Utah: one was a taxiing accident with a mobile tower being moved across the field which slightly damaged one wing, the other when she was struck by an unknown aircraft whilst parked. This damaged her nose.

As the years passed, the once familiar silhouette was greeted more and more with awe. She was the last of her type operated by the United States military services. Finally at 1.46 p.m. on Wednesday 14 October 1959, CG-77254 made her final landing at Elizabeth City air station, North Carolina, bringing to an end yet another great era in Coast Guard aviation history. For twelve of her fourteen years of service with USCG aviation she had operated as a special photo mapping mount. She was finally broken up at Elizabeth City on 17 February 1960.

During 1945 nine single fin Convair PB4Y-2G *Privateer* land-based patrol aircraft went on the Coast Guard inventory. With a range of nearly 3,000 miles their long-range capability and reliability made them particularly suitable for use over the Pacific Ocean. They were used for air sea rescue and for weather reconnaissance duties at the San Francisco air station, and at Barbers Point in Hawaii, and spent many thousands of hours over the blue of the Pacific.

Another four-engined type delivered during 1945 was the Douglas R5D *Skymaster*. A total of fourteen were delivered and used in a wide variety of missions including search and rescue, International Ice Patrol, photo-mapping and research and development with electronics. They were based at Elizabeth City, North Carolina, Argentia, Newfoundland, San Francisco, California and Barbers Point, Hawaii. They were a mixture of ex-USAF C-54 transports, including two EC-54U for electronic test, and US Navy R5D-3 and R5D-4s which served the Coast Guard until 1962 on world wide tasks.

Martin PBM-5G BuNo 84732 based at Salem air station, Massachusetts, seen using JATO for a maximum performance departure. The Coast Guard operated no less than twenty-seven PBM-3 models and forty-one PBM-5Gs between 1943 and 1956. They were powered by two 1700 hp Wright R-2600-12 engines. (USCG)

Early Helicopter Development

By 1941 the Coast Guard was seriously interested in developing the helicopter for search and rescue. Lieutenant Commander William Kossler had represented the Coast Guard on an inter-agency board formed in 1938 for the evaluation of experimental aircraft, including the helicopter. World War II interrupted these plans and stalled further development of the concept of the marriage of fixed wing aircraft to the cutter. Between 1937 and 1941 a variety of aircraft operated from the 327-foot class vessel. Usually, an aircraft would be assigned to a cutter for a number of months, whilst the ship was employed on a particular mission. Typical of such duty was the Bering Sea Patrol. For example, *Spencer* received a Waco J2W-1 in 1937 which was one of three the Coast Guard acquired that year. Grumman J2F *Ducks* were assigned to *Taney* in 1937 and to *Alexander Hamilton* and *Spencer* in 1938, fourteen of these Grummans being obtained in the mid-1930s. Curtiss SOC-4 *Seagulls* were assigned to *Bibb* in 1938 and *Duane* in 1941. They were the last aircraft to operate from a 327-footer (*Spencer,* which surveyed parts of Greenland). The 327s lost their aircraft at the beginning of World War II because they were required for convoy escort duty, whilst others were armed for ASW. The large quarterdecks, once used to stow aircraft, were fitted with five-inch, fifty-one-caliber guns, long depth charge racks and K-guns.

Curtiss SB2C-4 *Helldiver* similar to the two evaluated by the Coast Guard between 1945 and 1947 in an effort to expedite rescue operations. A high speed dash to the disaster scene, providing life rafts and rations pending the arrival of rescue by floating boat or surface vessel was the idea, but never implemented. (Navy Department — National Archives 80-G-243646)

Beechcraft JRB-4 BuNo 90580 light transport, one of seven used by the Coast Guard between 1943 and 1958. This particular aircraft was from a batch of fifty USAAF C-45F-BH *Expeditors.* The Coast Guard transports were a mixture of SNB-1 and JRB-4 and -5 models as used by the US Navy. (Howard Levy)

In 1941 *Northland,* an ice-going gunboat, was fitted to carry an aircraft on her quarterdeck. Another cutter adapted to carry an aircraft was the wooden-hulled *North Star,* acquired by the Coast Guard in May 1941 from the US Department of the Interior. A third cutter modified to carry an aircraft was the 230-foot *Storis,* built during the opening days of the war to serve as a supply ship for remote Greenland stations. All three cutters were modified to carry a Grumman J2F-5 *Duck* on their quarterdecks. In all cases, the aircraft had to be lifted on and off the cutters by booms. These were very much a part of the Greenland Patrol until the *Wind* class was commissioned.

The new *Wind* class cutters were designed specifically as aircraft-carrying, ice-breaking gunboats for Greenland duty and were destined to replace the collection of makeshift aviation cutters. The *Winds* were the first cutters to be equipped with catapults and each carried a Grumman J2F *Duck.* Initially, four *Wind* units were built for the Coast Guard, three of which were transferred to the Soviet Union under lend-lease before the close of the war. One replacement was built for the Coast Guard and two for the US Navy.

The Coast Guard's ultimate aircraft-carrying cutter was to have been the 255-foot class. As the follow-on to the 327, she was to have carried a catapult-launched aircraft. However, due to wartime construction demands and technological changes, the new cutters resembled the *Wind* class more closely than they did the 327s. During the final design stages, the capability to carry an aircraft was dropped, because the need to carry a ship-borne aircraft became less critical as the war progressed.

Curtiss R5C-1 *Commando,* one of ten operated as a logistic transport by the Coast Guard between 1943 and 1950. They were ex US Marine Corps transports, used world-wide and based at Elizabeth City, North Carolina. Long-range tanks were fitted giving it a long-range capability. (Navy Department — National Archives 80-G-79995)

It was back in 1936 when aircraft and cutter were teamed for the first time when the first 327-foot Coast Guard cutter was commissioned. At that time, opium smuggling was increasing on the west coast of the US. Freighters coming from the Orient dropped drugs far offshore in watertight containers which were picked up by small coastal utility, fishing or pleasure craft or perhaps seaplanes. By the mid-1930s, the best solution to the problem of intercepting drug traffic was a large cutter carrying its own reconnaissance aircraft. The Coast Guard also needed the cutter-aircraft team in Alaska. Throughout the late nineteenth century, cutters patrolled the Bering Sea, particularly looking for illegal sealers. The Japanese had terminated a number of fishing treaties and, as tensions grew between Japan and the US during the 1930s, these northern waters took on an added importance. Intercontinental air traffic was coming of age. Airliners would soon be flying across the oceans, each carrying forty passengers. Unlike the passenger carrying flying boat, the airplane had few emergency options over water. If it went down, the Coast Guard rescuers would have to find the distressed aircraft quickly and arrive at the scene without delay. Since an aircraft operating from a large, seaworthy cutter offered the best rescue platform the 327-foot class was built to meet these needs.

The marriage of fixed wing aircraft and the cutter lasted slightly more than a decade. Fixed wing aircraft on small vessels were destined to be replaced by helicopters. Today, all medium and high-endurance Coast Guard cutters are equipped with helicopter pads, often operating and housing two, which is testimony to the great value of small-deck naval aviation which the Coast Guard has adopted.

A legacy from the early years, when money for equipment was hard to come by, is that Coast Guard aviation has the tremendous ability to improvise. In the immediate post-World War II period this heritage was frequently in demand. The war surplus market in used aircraft was large and so the Coast Guard plodded on with a variety of aircraft, resulting in a fleet of types that was as unique as ever. The following status of aircraft for May 1947 and January 1950 is in itself unique, as it shows not only the types which were retained in service but also their numbers, plus new types incorporated in the Coast Guard inventory.

One trip to go before retirement. Final briefing for the crew of Coast Guard Boeing PB-1G 7254 at Seattle, Washington DC, on 4 September 1959 prior to the final aerial photo mapping mission for the US Coast & Geodectic Survey. Left to right: Terrance K O'Driscoll, photographer; Lieutenant R C Branham, USCG co-pilot; Carl T Johnson, USCG Aviation Electronicsman Second Class; Lieutenant Commander Arthur R Benton, USCG Navigator; Willard E Brown, USCG Aviation Machinist Mate First Class; Lieutenant Commander Fred T Merritt USCG, aircraft captain; J T Smith, survey photographer; Richard G Schmidt, USCG Aviation Machinist Mate First Class and John A Worsham USCG, Aviation Machinist Mate Second Class. (USCG)

May 1947	January 1950
56 Consolidated PBY-5A *Catalina*	32 Consolidated PBY-5A *Catalina*
24 Martin PBM-5 *Mariner*	19 Grumman JRF-5 *Goose*
19 Grumman JRF- *Goose*	15 Martin PBM-5G *Mariner*
19 Sikorsky HOS-1 helicopter	12 Boeing PB-1G *Flying Fortress*
15 Boeing PB-1G *Flying Fortress*	5 Sikorsky HO3S-1G helicopter
15 Grumman J4F- *Widgeon*	5 Beech JRB-4 *Expeditor*
10 North American SNJ- *Texan*	4 Douglas R4D-5 *Skytrain*
8 Douglas R4D- *Skytrain*	4 Grumman J4F-2 *Widgeon*
6 Sikorsky HNS-1 helicopter	3 Piasecki HRP-1 helicopter
5 Beech JRB-4 *Expeditor*	2 Lockheed R50-4 *Lodestar*
4 Grumman J2F- *Duck*	2 Lockheed R50-5 *Lodestar*
2 Lockheed R50- *Lodestar*	2 Bell HTL-1 helicopter
2 Consolidated PB4Y-2 *Privateer*	2 Curtiss R5C-1 *Commando*
1 Beech SNB- *Expeditor*	1 Sikorsky HO2S-1 helicopter
1 Sikorsky HO2S-1 helicopter	1 Douglas R5D-5 *Skymaster*
187 Total	109 Total

Despite the fact that as from 28 December 1945 the prefix letter V was dropped from Coast Guard aircraft, odd V prefixed US Navy aircraft in Coast Guard service were recorded. On 3 April 1947 two were recorded at San Francisco air station: Boeing PB-1G V77256 and Martin PBM-5G V84728. With effect from 1 January 1951 a new listing of Coast Guard aircraft serial numbers commenced. It continued numerically with the prefix 1 replacing the V, so the nine Sikorsky HO3S-1G helicopters which were painted 230 to 238 prior to 1 January 1951 would have been V230 to V238, had the V system still been in effect. Instead they were the first aircraft numbered under the system which is still in effect today, and became 1230 to 1238. Model designations for new Coast Guard aircraft were similar to US Navy models using Navy suffix letters to denote task etc. Sikorsky helicopters 1253 and 1254 were delivered in December 1951 as HO4S-2s, becoming HO4S-2Gs (the G denoting Search & Rescue, later Coast Guard) under USCG Painting & Instructions Memo 7-51, which specified that all helicopters were considered to have the primary mission of Search and Rescue.

Largely equipped with World War II designs from 1945 onwards, the Coast Guard contracting office responsible for aviation procurements saw little action until the early 1950s, especially with regard to fixed wing models. The exception was in helicopter development, where some action gave spirit to an organization that had reverted to its peacetime role of Search & Rescue. The years when the perilous drama of the U-boat war had kept the aviators' adrenalin flowing were now over.

Coast Guard flying boat operations had their heyday immediately after World War II. As already indicated, the service had no less than fifty-six PBY-5A *Catalinas* on inventory on 1 May 1947, plus twenty-four Martin PBM-5 *Mariners,* these stemming from an original wartime order. By 1954 the *Catalina* had been struck off the active duty list, whilst the variants of the *Mariner* were sustained much longer. The service acquired seven Martin P5M-1G *Marlin* twin engined flying boats powered by 3,450 hp Wright R-3350-32WA engines. Four of the T tail versions of the *Marlin,* designated P5M-2G were purchased in 1956, because this version was more effective than the earlier P5M-1G. Plagued by the high cost of both maintenance and operation, all the Marlins were struck off charge during 1961, when the P5M-2Gs were traded to the US Department of Defense for Grumman HU-16E *Albatross* amphibians. This brought to a close the era of the large flying boat.

There was no recorded delivery of new aircraft, either fixed or rotary wing, during 1957 but plans for the reorganization of the Coast Guard air fleet were presented to the US Congress during that year. The following year saw new types of aircraft introduced to the Coast Guard inventory. These included the first of a batch of six Fairfield C-123 *Provider* twin-engined transports ex-USAF, the first of a quota of Grumman UF-2G *Albatross* twin-engined amphibians, an updated version of the early UF-1G and the first of a quota of Bell HUL-1G helicopters, an improved Bell HTL with two-bladed rotor, skids and hoist. The Coast Guard also took delivery of the first of a quota of Sikorsky HUS-1G helicopters with four-blade rotor, hoist and automatic stabilization equipment, plus Doppler navigation equipment fitted. The order book looked good, as no less than fifty-six helicopters of various lineage were destined for Coast Guard use. Two new VIP executive transports were ordered and delivered to the USCG air detachment located at Washington National Airport. Commercially known as the Martin 404, these were known as VC-3A at a unit cost of $647,140 on Contract Tcg-38422 and were completely new. The aircraft were used for administrative support of Coast Guard HQ and the Treasury Department until 1967, and the Department of Transportation from 1967 until 1969. A Grumman VC-4A *Gulfstream I* executive prop-jet was delivered to the air detachment at Washington National during 1963, providing a fast comfortable executive transport for the USCG Commandant and the Secretary of Transportation. This was joined later by a Grumman VC-11A *Gulfstream II* executive jet. Both aircraft were powered by Rolls-Royce engines, the *Gulfstream I* by two Darts, and the *II* by two Speys — both are still in service. (Reference the Coast Guard serial system, these two are the oddballs carrying a two-digit serial '01' and '02'.)

Only nine of these impressive Convair P4Y-2C *Privateer* long-range patrol aircraft were used by the Coast Guard, serving between 1945 and 1949. This unique photo depicts four *Privateers* from the San Francisco air station on a morning patrol heading north past the Golden Gate Bridge towards the hills of Marin County. (USCG)

Several versions of the USAF-developed C-130 *Hercules* were ordered by the US Navy, Marine and Coast Guard and deliveries commenced in 1958. The Coast Guard acquired twelve Hercules for air sea rescue duties, which were designated R8V-1G when ordered, delivered as SC-130B and redesignated HC-130B in 1962. The US Navy mission — manufacturer — numbering system, also used by the Coast Guard, survived until 18 September 1962, when the US Department of Defense combined all USAF and US Navy/Coast Guard aircraft designations into the existing USAF system. The transition to the new system was eased for US Navy and Coast Guard personnel and others well-versed in the old system by using dual designations on the aircraft for a year or so.

This Martin P5M-2G *Marlin* 1312 was one of four operated by the Coast Guard. Accepted from Glenn L Martin at the Baltimore factory on 7 February 1956, it was assigned to Elizabeth City air station for long range air-sea rescue work. It had an increase in power of 200 hp over the earlier P5M-1G and was five feet longer. The interior electronics were updated and crew comfort for long patrols was improved. (USCG)

It is not generally known that two Convair R4Y-2 transports similar to the commercial Convair CV-440 airliner were delivered to the Coast Guard in 1957. Originally ordered as USAF C-131A 57-2551/2 c/n 481/2 they were allocated US Navy BuNo's 145962/3 and were designated C-131G in 1962 under the new designation system. However it is felt that these two transports were evaluated only by the Coast Guard whilst looking for VIP aircraft to replace the Martin RM-1Z, later VC-3A aircraft.

A total of seven Stinson OY-1 *Sentinel* light aircraft were acquired in 1948. Four were used operationally whilst the remaining three were cannibalized for spares. The type had been used in large numbers during World War II as artillery spotters. Among Coast Guard duties, the OY-1s were used to spot illicit stills for the Alcoholic Tax Unit of the Internal Revenue Service. For these operations they were based at Elizabeth City air station, North Carolina, but at least one OY-1 14870 ex-USAF L-5-VW 42-14870 was based at San Diego air station and was photographed on 25 October 1948.

After World War II many of the original V registered Coast Guard aircraft were included in the huge stocks for sale by the WAA — War Assets Administration. Depicted is Grumman JRF-2 V174, the first ever *Goose* in Coast Guard service, still showing signs of wartime drab finish, but sporting a yellow fuselage band and yellow wing floats. Photo taken on 31 January 1947 at Buchanan Field, Concord, California. (William T. Larkins)

The responsibilities of Coast Guard fixed wing aviation had increased tremendously following World War II. In 1946, Coast Guard aircraft were used for the first time on the International Ice Patrol, a practice that continues to this day. The primary objective of these Ice Patrol flights is to observe ice floating in the vicinity of the Grand Banks, so that shipping in that area can be advised of conditions throughout the iceberg season. Ice Patrol flight tracks are normally between 1,000 and 1,500 nautical miles long — from six to eight hours flight time.

After the end of World War II, Coast Guard aircraft were also used increasingly to intercept the escort aircraft that were experiencing mechanical problems. The presence of the Coast Guard aircraft was always reassuring to both passengers and flight crews. During the 1950s the Coast Guard developed open-ocean ditching techniques that are still in use by commercial airliners today following the experiments conducted and evaluated by Captain Donald B MacDiarmid USCG.

Whilst Commanding Officer of the San Diego air station in California, Commander MacDiarmid USCG used a PBM-5G *Mariner* for research tests in both the Atlantic and Pacific Oceans and the Gulf of Mexico — in fact wherever the seas were roughest. Landings were frequently made in seas as high as eighteen feet and in winds up to twenty-three knots, far too rough for small surface craft rescue work. The results of this research work resulted in the preparation of an internationally accepted manual on air sea rescue techniques. The Octave Chanute Award for 1950 was awarded to Commander MacDiarmid. The citation is presented in the name of the pioneer aeronautical investigator who died in 1910 to the pilot who annually makes the most notable contribution to flying. Commander MacDiarmid was cited for 'outstanding contributions to air sea rescue techniques by the scientific analysis and correlation of the effect of wind and waves on sea planes during landings, manoeuvering and take-off'. In 1986 Donald MacDiarmid was enshrined in the Naval Aviation Museum at Pensacola, Florida.

During the Korean War 1950-53, the Coast Guard performed a variety of tasks and established air detachments throughout the Pacific. Additional weather station sites were established to help guard the flow of troops and supplies to Korea. The air detachments were constantly on search and rescue alert to safeguard the tens of thousands of United Nations troops that were being airlifted across the ocean.

Grumman Albatross

Work commenced in 1944 on a general purpose amphibian for the US Navy to succeed the JRF *Goose* which served both the US Navy and the Coast Guard during the war years. The Grumman company had the benefit of more than ten years' experience in the design and production of amphibians for the US Navy, and the new type, the Grumman model G-64, was a continuation of the JRF design philosophy. It featured a conventional two-step hull into the sides of which the main wheels retracted, a high wing with fixed stabilizing floats, and a single tail unit.

When the US Navy selected the G-64 for construction it assigned the designation XJR2F-1 to the prototype. The JR indicated utility transport, and JR2F-1 was the first of five successive designations applied to these US Navy amphibians after the first order was placed. The prototype flew on 24 October 1947 and evaluation flying not only led the US Navy to confirm its proposed order but also aroused US Air Force interest in the type because its Air Sea Rescue Service was being consolidated at the time. This eventually resulted in US Air Force orders under the designation SA-16A-GR. After the JR category had been abandoned by the US Navy, the *Albatross* was tentatively redesignated PF-1 in the patrol category, and then became the UF-1 in the US Navy's new utility series.

The new amphibian entered military service in July 1949, with an eventual total of 465 airplanes being built and delivered to the US Navy, the US Air Force and the Coast Guard. The USCG quickly recognized the capability of the SA-16 as a search and rescue vehicle and entered into the joint-service agreement to procure aircraft at a cost of approximately $59,000 each. Under Contract No 10988 four UF-1CG aircraft were procured for the Coast Guard with USCG numbers 1240 to 1243. The first *Albatross* to enter operational service with the USCG was 1240 which was picked up at the Bethpage plant near New York on 7 May 1951 by Lieutenant (jg) C R Leisy, Lieutenant (jg) A E Flannegan, AD1 E J Slanzik, AD1 C W Hughes, AT1 D S Bishop and AL1 M W Salovitch. Captain C B Olsen, Chief of the Aviation Division at Headquarters, accompanied the crew on the flight and delivered the aircraft to USCG air station Brooklyn, New York. This was the first of some eighty *Albatross* amphibians to be commissioned in the Coast Guard. Not every aircraft flew missions with the Coast Guard, as some were re-purchased by the US Navy for use in the Korean conflict. A second order for the Coast Guard involved nine aircraft under Contract No 51-118 priced at $52,000 each with numbers 1259 to 1267, the first from this batch being delivered in March 1952. A second batch of nine followed under Contract No 51-656 with numbers 1271 to 1279, the first being delivered in March 1953.

The new aircraft were immediately pressed into service as replacements for the myriad of aircraft the Coast Guard had been operating since World War II. The Boeing SB-17s, Douglas R4D- (DC-3), Consolidated PBY- and Martin P5M- aircraft were flown to their final resting place as soon as Coast Guard pilots could be trained and qualified in the new aircraft. Those aircraft originally purchased were soon augmented by additional amphibians received from the US Navy and Air Force. This followed a fourth USCG contract No 53-394 for eight UF-1CGs numbered 1280 to 1294, the first of which was delivered in January 1954. By this time the Coast Guard was placed totally in charge of Search & Rescue over the waters of the US and its territories. A total of fifty ex-US Air Force SA-16 *Albatross* amphibians were transferred to Coast Guard Aviation. The first fifteen were numbered 52-121 to 52-135 with the first three being delivered in December 1953, the next five in January 1954 and the final eight in this batch in February 1954.

The Achilles' heel of the early UF-1CG *Albatross,* which led to a number of accidents, was traced to the wing design.

The original production aircraft had one extremely undesirable characteristic. Single-engine operation consisted of a controlled descent — and some were more controlled than others! The Grumman engineers got to the bottom of the problem by extending the wing from eighty feet to ninety-six feet eight inches. This modification resulted in a vast improvement in performance, since single-engine flight at altitude was made possible. Maximum gross weight was increased by 5,000 lbs. Cruise airspeed was increased by more than twenty-five knots with no increase in fuel consumption. Stall speed was lowered from seventy to sixty-four knots and the maximum range was extended some 500 miles. The Coast Guard converted all of their early A models to the new stretched wing version, designated UF-2G during the latter part of the fifties.

The *Albatross* has flown well over 500,000 hours on a variety of missions during its twenty-six years of operation with the Coast Guard. Many of these missions have brought glory and honor to the Coast Guard, to the aviators involved and to the aircraft itself.

During the early 'sixties, seventy-one HU-16E aircraft were operational. The aircraft were scattered among nineteen air stations in the continental US, Alaska and overseas, with the major concentration at USCG air station Miami, Florida. Ten aircraft were flown on a myriad of Search & Rescue missions and Cuban Patrols from the Biscayne Bay water base. Thousands of Cuban refugees owe their lives to the men who patrolled the water between Cuba and Florida since daily flights were conducted by Coast Guard airmen armed only with Thompson sub-machine guns to locate the refugees who fled Castro's Cuba in ever-increasing numbers, on board anything that would float. It was not unusual to find ten or twelve people clinging to makeshift rafts, tyre tubes, floating bathtubs and wooden crates.

The *Albatross* was not alone on its vigil. Heavily armed Cuban gunboats and aircraft also patrolled these waters searching for the refugees and the fate of those who were found by these forces and returned to Cuba is not known, but during one five-week period over 8,000 refugees arrived safely in Key West. The Coast Guard Patrol Forces in the Florida Straits consisted of ships, helicopters and, overseeing and directing the operation, the ever present *Albatross.*

Grumman UF-1G *Albatross* amphibian 1262 is an excellent example of original USCG post-war livery. All of the initial thirty aircraft were later modified and re-designated HU-16E. Records reveal that this amphibian was amongst other Coast Guard aircraft in- storage at the huge Military Aircraft Storage & Disposition Centre located at Davis-Monthan AFB in Arizona. (Gordon S. Williams)

A glance at the HU-16E does not inspire thoughts of speed and power; however, the *Albatross* is the holder of nine world class amphibian records, certified by the Federation Aeronautique International (FAI), the world's governing body for aviation records. The records were established as a result of a tri-service venture by the Coast Guard, US Navy and US Air Force and are still in effect. Moreover unless interest in amphibian aircraft development is renewed, these records may stand forever. Records established by Grumman HU-16E *Albatross* 7255 are as follows:

1, 2 *Speed over a 1,000 km closed course with a 1,000 kg and 2,000 kg load* — Established by Commander Wallace C Dahlgreen and Commander William G Fenlon USCG on 13 August 1962 at a speed of 201.5 knots.

3 *Speed over a 5,000 km closed course with a 1,000 kg load* — Established on 15 and 16 September 1962 by two US Navy pilots flying the Coast Guard aircraft at a speed of 131.5 knots.

4, 5 *Altitude with a 1,000 kg load and altitude with a 2,000 kg load* — Established on 12 September 1962 by two US Navy pilots flying the Coast Guard aircraft at altitudes of 29,475 ft and 27,405 ft respectively.

6 *Distance – non-stop* — Established on 24 October 1962 on a flight from USCG air station Kodiak, Alaska to the US Naval Air Station at Pensacola, Florida, a distance of 3,104 nautical miles, by Commander William G Fenlon, Commander Wallace G Dahlgreen, Lieutenant W Senn and Chief W Taggart USCG.

During its twenty-six years of service with the Coast Guard, the *Albatross,* known affectionately as *Goats, Whispergoats* and *Dumbo* to name a few, has seen its share of tragedies as well as spectacular accomplishments. The US Air Force Rescue Service's motto 'That Others May Live' seems an appropriate way of eulogizing those thirty-three Coast Guard airmen who gave their lives for their fellow men:

UF-1G 2121 was flown from Annette, Alaska to Haines, Alaska on 14 December 1954 to perform a medical evacuation. The aircraft crashed during a water take-off, possibly due to a layer of ice which had built up on its wing during the wait for the patient to be delivered. The following airmen were killed: AL1 C E Habecker, AD1 A P Turnier and AL3 D E John.

UF-1G 1278 was performing a water jet assisted take-off (JATO) demonstration from the air station Salem, Massachusetts on 18 May 1957. Lift-off occurred with insufficient airspeed and the aircraft stalled and crashed. Crew members killed were: Lieutenant Commander A P. Hartt Jr. and AO2 W J Tarker Jr.

Two Martin RM-1Z aircraft were purchased during 1952 for use as VIP transports, being the equivalent of the commercial Martin 404 airliner. Powered by two Pratt & Whitney R-2800-34 engines, they were ordered as RM-1G but went into service designated RM-1Z with executive interiors. Still serving in 1962, they were then re-designated VC-3A in the new US unified system. Photo depicts both transports 1282 and 1283 c/n 14290-1 outside the Martin factory prior to delivery. (AP Photo Library)

UF-1G 1259 crashed on its take-off run from the Brooklyn, New York air station on 22 August 1957. The flight was scheduled as a test flight following maintenance. The crash was caused by either reversed or jammed aileron controls. The following Coast Guard aviators were killed: Lieutenant Commander C S Lebaw, Lieutenant R A Faucher, AD3 M R Ross and AL3 G R Fox.

HU-16E 7233 crashed into a mountain ridge on 3 July 1964 whilst attempting an instrument approach to the air station at Annette, Alaska after a long search mission. The following airmen were killed: Lieutenant Commander J N Andrassy, Lieutenant R A Perchard, AO1 H W Olson, AM2 D G Malena and AT3 E D Krajniak.

HU-16E 1271 crashed on 8 February 1967 at St Paul Island, Alaska while attemping to make a landing during severely deteriorating weather conditions. Miraculously, the only crew member killed was AT2 F R Edmunds.

HU-16E 1240 was conducting a night search out of air station St Petersburg, Florida during low visibility conditions on 5 March 1967. The aircraft located the vessel in distress and was attempting to drop de-watering equipment when it crashed into the Gulf of Mexico. The entire crew was lost and included: Lieutenant C E Hanna, Lieutenant (jg) C F Shaw, AD1 R H Studstill, AT1 C M Powlus, AT2 J B Thompson and AE3 A L Wilson.

HU-16E 7237 departed Annette air station in Alaska engaged in a search over mountainous terrain for a crashed aircraft on 15 June 1967. The aircraft apparently flew into a box canyon and crashed. Crew members killed were: Lieutenant R D Brown, Lieutenant D J Bain and AT1 R W Striff.

HU-16E 2128 departed air station San Francisco, California on 7 August 1967 to search for an overdue boat along the Californian coastline during low visibility conditions. The boat was located. While attempting to accurately fix the position of the vessel for surface assistance the aircraft crashed into mountainous terrain. Coast Guard aviators killed included: Lieutenant (jg) F T Charles, AD3 W G Prowitt and AD3 J G Medek.

HU-16E 2123 departed the air station located at Corpus Christi, Texas on 21 September 1973 to conduct an over watch search in company with a HH-52A *Seaguard* helicopter. The aircraft was providing night illumination by dropping Mk.45 flares. One flare apparently ignited accidentally, filling the aircraft with intense smoke. The aircraft crashed into the Gulf of Mexico. The following Coast Guard aviators were killed: Lieutenant Commander F W Miller, Lieutenant (jg) J M Mack, AD1 H G Brown, AM2 B R Gaskins, AT2 J F Harrison and AT2 J P Pledger.

The Grumman *Albatross* proved to be an adaptable aircraft that fitted well into the Coast Guard multi-mission roles. Its traditional Search & Rescue role was expanded to include law enforcement protection duties with the necessary addition of new equipment for these missions. The life of the HU-16E was fixed at 11,000 flight hours. Laboratory fatigue tests were conducted at the US Naval Air Development Center (NADC) at Warminster, Pennsylvania which clearly determined that catastrophic failure of the wing was a definite possibility if flight operations were continued beyond this limit.

A daily scene at San Francisco air station, California, showing the three main types of the day operated by the USCG twenty years ago. Parked on the apron can be seen a Grumman HU-16E *Albatross* amphibian, a Lockheed HC-130 *Hercules* long-range patrol transport, and a Sikorsky HH-52A *Seaguard* helio. (AP Photo Library)

Apron scene at New Orleans air station, Louisiana, on 19 March 1964 showing a Sikorsky HH-52A *Seaguard* helio 1373 parked alongside a veteran Grumman HU-16E *Albatross* 2123 amphibian, the two types in use at this US Coast Guard unit. Note the high visibility markings. (USCG)

Seen in the vicinity of the coastline near Cape Cod air station, Massachusetts, is a formation trio; a Grumman HU-16E *Albatross* 7249 following a Sikorsky HH-3F *Pelican* 1470 and a Sikorsky HH-52A *Seaguard* helio on 13 July 1971. These are the major rescue types of aircraft in service that can land on water and pick up survivors. (USCG)

Between 1951 and 1977 the Grumman *Albatross* served the USCG as a venerable workhorse. After receiving an initial batch of thirty-four from the manufacturer, a further seventy-seven were received from US Air Force stocks. First models were designated UF-1G, modified later to UF-2G, and in 1962 standardized along with USAF and US Navy models to HU-16E. Shown here is 1271. (USCG)

Right: An iceberg located off Gull Island, Newfoundland, is used as a target for thermite and petroleum bombs dropped from a US Coast Guard Grumman UF-2G *Albatross* on 17 July 1958. The empty bomb cradle can be seen under the wing. The International Ice Patrol for 1959 was involved in iceberg destruction tests. (USCG)

Grumman HU-16E *Albatross* 7245 from Brooklyn air station, New York, seen on a routine patrol over the Atlantic Ocean. In addition to a batch purchased direct from Grumman, a further batch was transferred from US Air Force surplus stocks. (USCG)

Above: An aerial view of Elizabeth City air station, North Carolina, taken on 6 March 1966, with a number of fixed wing aircraft, including HC-130 *Hercules* and helicopters parked on the apron. The control tower is manned by USCG personnel. (USCG)

Below: The Grumman *Albatross* amphibian proved to be more than a workhorse for the US Coast Guard, commencing with thirty-four UF-1G aircraft converted to UF-2G standard. Later some thirty-seven were obtained from US Air Force stocks and the type was re-designated HU-16E in 1962. Seen here is HU-16E 7209 based at Port Angeles air station in Washington State. (USCG)

US Coast Guard crewmen prepare to winch a 1,000 lb thermate bomb to the underwing of a Grumman UF-2G 7240 at Argentia, Newfoundland, on 17 July 1959 during the International Ice Patrol period. It was part of a research project to determine deterioration effects on icebergs through intense heat from bombs. (USCG)

By the mid 1970s the active fleet of USCG *Albatross* amphibians had dwindled to twenty, located at five air stations. These aircraft were retired as they approached the 11,000 flight hour limit. During October 1977, HU-16E 7236 departed air station Traverse City, Michigan on its last flight, to the US Naval Air Museum at Pensacola, Florida. Here she resides with the resplendent Coast Guard colours adding a touch of class to the silver and grey naval aircraft. Built in 1953 and originally destined for the US Air Force she commenced her career with the Coast Guard in 1958 and participated in numerous Search & Rescue missions throughout the world. Her final resting place should be much more comfortable than the harsh environment of the Arizona desert at the home of the 2704th Air Force Storage & Disposition Group, Military Aircraft Storage & Disposition Center (MASDC) (now re-designated the Aerospace Maintenance & Regeneration Center (AMARC)) located at Davis-Monthan Air Force base, where many of her sister *Albatross* aircraft were initially placed in storage and then broken up. Nearly forty HU-16E amphibians were in storage during the mid-1970s.

This North American B-25J-30-NC 44-31357, unofficially borrowed from the US Army Air Force in 1945, was apparently never on the Coast Guard inventory. It is seen parked at Kiangwan Field, Shanghai, China.
(D. W. Lucabaugh via Fred C. Dicky Jr Collection)

Parked on the ramp at the US Coast Guard air station at San Francisco is Martin PBM-5G *Mariner* BuNo 84686 with the US national insignia known as the 'star and bar' on the nose. The search radar housing is just aft of the cockpit. (William T. Larkins)

The many missions of the *Albatross* were taken over on an interim basis by seventeen Convair HC-131A *Samaritan* aircraft which were reactivated from US Air Force stocks held in storage at Davis-Monthan AFB. These aircraft were overhauled by a commercial contractor, modified to a USCG Search & Rescue configuration at the Aircraft Repair & Supply Center at Elizabeth City, North Carolina and then placed into operational service at four air stations. These aircraft covered the Coast Guard medium range surveillance (MRS) missions until the ultimate replacement arrived, the twin-engined HU-25A *Guardian,* which commenced its operational service in the early 1980s.

Sikorsky HH-52A Seaguard

During July 1962 Sikorsky Aircraft, a division of the United Aircraft Corporation of Stratford, Connecticut, announced that the single turbine Sikorsky S-62, the first amphibious helicopter built with a flying boat hull, had been selected by the Coast Guard as its medium range Search & Rescue helicopter. Some years earlier the USCG had been looking for a replacement for its Sikorsky HUS-1G later HH-34F helicopters for that purpose. A contract was signed and settled on 21 June 1962. The craft was originally designated HU2S-1G, later HH-52A. Powered by a 1,250 shp General Electric T58-GE-8 turboshaft engine, it had a single rotor with a cruising speed of ninety to ninety-five knots and a carrying capacity of 2,900 lbs. Equipped with automatic stabilization equipment it introduced substantial improvement to helicopter instrument flight operation.

The boat-shaped hull of this new Coast Guard helicopter, coupled with a unique rescue platform designed according to a USCG specification, revolutionized helicopter rescue techniques and provided a marked increase in the flexibility of all helicopter operations over water. It was capable of flying out approximately 150 miles, picking up an injured person with the rescue hoist or by landing in the water and returning to its home base with a ten per cent margin of fuel remaining. In addition to shore-based operations the HH-52A has been deployed on Coast Guard icebreakers and cutters for extended periods. The purchase price for the airframe apparently ranged from quarter of a million to over half a million $US.

On 9 January 1963 the Coast Guard Commandant, Admiral E J Roland and his acceptance committee attended ceremonies at the Sikorsky plant for the first of nearly one hundred of the new HH-52A *Seaguard* helicopters, these being numbered 1352-1355. On 25 January 1963 Commander John M Waters, commanding officer of the USCG air station at Salem, Massachusetts, took delivery of the first, 1352, this being followed by two more. The initial USCG order was for twenty-eight HH-52A helicopters. Development trials had been completed both by Sikorsky and the Coast Guard using an S-62 registered N880 as early as February 1962.

In addition to Search & Rescue assignments, the HH-52A missions included aids to navigation, port security and law enforcement, inter-agency cooperation in natural disasters, military readiness and general logistics. As of 30 September 1977 the Coast Guard had sixty-nine HH-52A *Seaguards* in the operational fleet, supported by approximately twenty per cent of each type in overhaul at all times. Five spare HH-52A airframes were activated at this time for deployment aboard USCG 378-foot and 210-foot cutters. Four of the HH-52As were assigned to air station Kodiak, Alaska, the fifth assigned to air station Corpus Christi.

Here in 1988 the Coast Guard's Short Range Recovery mission is being taken over from the HH-52A by ninety Aerospatiale SA-365N helicopters known as the HH-65A *Dolphin*.

International Ice Patrol

It was the collision between the unsinkable *Titanic* and an iceberg in April 1912, with a loss of more than 1,500 lives, that shocked the maritime nations into action to prevent such a tragedy from happening again. In 1912 and 1913 the US Navy carried out the International Ice Patrol. In 1914 it was assigned to the Revenue Cutter Service and became a Coast Guard responsibility in 1915 when the Revenue Cutter Service and the Life-Saving Service were merged. The cost is now apportioned among twenty maritime nations based on their tonnage moving through the North Atlantic.

Since 1914 the US Coast Guard has been tasked with operating the International Ice Patrol in the North Atlantic and has proved to be an outstanding example of international collaboration. Each year, from March to September, Coast Guard HC-130H aircraft flying out of the Canadian Armed Forces base at Gander, Newfoundland patrol a 33,000 square mile area off the Grand Banks, a rugged section of the North Atlantic, crossed by the busiest shipping lanes in the world, which is also the natural route for thousands of icebergs that break off the western coast of Greenland in spring and are carried south on the Labrador Current. Drifting at a speed of ten miles a day, it can take three years for icebergs from the time they 'calve' or split off Greenland's ice cap until they melt in the warmer waters off Newfoundland and during the long journey they pose a tremendous threat to ships. Even a relatively small iceberg can rip a ship's hull to shreds in seconds.

The Coast Guard mission is to locate the icebergs, plot their paths and send out radio warnings to ships at sea. But behind those twice-a-day bulletins are hours of hazardous and tedious flying, often in thick fog and over stormy seas. The Coast Guard, a small service with a high morale and a great professionalism, is justly proud of the fact that not a single life has been lost by a commercial ship in the North Atlantic due to an iceberg collision since the International Ice Patrol mission began.

Initially the task was done by patrol ships but soon the job became a joint aircraft and ship mission. Today the big job is handled almost entirely by the Coast Guard's long range Lockheed HC-130H *Hercules* patrol planes based at Elizabeth City, North Carolina. Between 1945 and their retirement in 1957 the Coast Guard used the Boeing PB-1G *Flying Fortress* for the ice patrol duty, followed by the Douglas R5D-*Skymaster* which served the USCG from 1945 to 1962 when retired.

Four Stinson OY-1 *Sentinel* light aircraft were procured in 1948 and were used primarily as spotters for the Alcohol Tax Unit of the US Treasury Department. Helping the 'Revenooers' in locating illicit stills, they were based at Elizabeth City serving in the Mid-Atlantic Moonshine area. Depicted is OY-1 14870, ex US Air Force 42-14870 taken from the waist turret of a USCG PBY-5A *Catalina* in the vicinity of San Diego on 25 October 1948. (William T. Larkins)

In July 1959 a step in the first known systematic attempt by man at destroying icebergs from aircraft was taken. This was the use of 1,000 lb thermite bombs as part of a research project of the ice patrol force to determine deterioration effects on icebergs from the intense heat of these bombs. They used cluster type bombs enclosing small thermite bomblets, each capable of burning at a temperature of 4,300° Fahrenheit, half the surface temperature of the sun. In June and July 1959, at the height of that year's severe ice season, USCG aviators dropped twenty cluster bombs of thermite and lesser heat-producing petroleum types one at a time on selected icebergs in the foggy Grand Banks of Newfoundland using a standard operational type Coast Guard Grumman UF-2G *Albatross* amphibian ordinarily used for patrol and Search & Rescue.

A US Coast Guard HC-130 hedge-hopping a row of icebergs off the coast of Labrador selected the iceberg in the foreground for dye bomb marking. On low level passes, USCG crewmen dropped a glass jug 'bomb' filled with calcium chloride and rhodamine. The pellets allowed bright vermilion dye to penetrate the ice to the depth of about one inch which ensured the iceberg would remain marked for eight to ten days. (Lockheed)

Seen in drab warpaint is a Grumman JRF-5 *Goose* at the US Coast Guard air station at San Francisco on 3 April 1947, still retaining its wartime 'star and bar' insignia minus the centreline red stripe. (William T. Larkins)

Never had an iceberg been destroyed other than through its normal course of melting in warm currents and warm air. The tests in previous years on this massive menace to North Atlantic shipping traffic had involved men firing guns and torpedoes from ships, and even risking the hazards of boarding drifting icebergs in order to plant high explosives. In 1959 the Ice Patrol proved that a standard aircraft was capable of successfully dropping bombs on icebergs and encouraged this method for future tests. Unfortunately we are unable to discover the results of these unique tests and the findings from the research project.

During the 1983 International Ice Patrol season, one of the veteran Coast Guard aviators employed on the task was Lieutenant Commander William Schleich, who at that time held the USCG record of twenty-three Ice Patrol missions as a Lockheed C-130 *Hercules* pilot. His duty as aircraft commander for the 11 to 16 July 1983 ice patrol mission, his twenty-third, was his last. On return he was assigned to the air station at Mobile, Alabama to commence intensive

The scene in the Sikorsky hangar as the first four HH-52A helicopters are accepted by the US Coast Guard on 9 January 1963. They are 1352/3/4/5, the latter being handed over to the US Naval Aviation Museum in Pensacola, Florida, by Admiral Donald C Thompson on 10 March 1988. Present was Commander Dick Shelley who delivered the helio to Salem air station, its first duty station. (USCG)

training on the new HU-25A *Guardian* aircraft.

Schleich recalled:

> I first went on ice patrol out of Prince Edward Island, a Canadian Armed Forces base. We worked there until '73, when we moved to St John's. In 1982 we moved to Gander . . . In the early days we flew the ice patrol in the C-130 without the extra range available on the current H model. All we had was the Doppler navigation equipment; no side-looking radar, no inertial navigation system (INS). We went out and did the mission on the Doppler and accepted whatever error we had. It was all visual sighting at that time. Sometimes we'd go a week at a time without seeing the surface of the water. We'd go out and try to find a clear area to search. If we didn't find it, we'd go back home. Now, with this side looking airborne radar (SLAR), we can go in any kind of weather.

The endurance of the C-130 is legendary among veteran Coast Guard aviators. Lieutenant Commander Schleich talks of retired USCG pilot Matt Ahearn who made a one-engine landing in Greenland:

> Matt was on Ice Patrol with his outboard engines shut down to conserve fuel. Number 3 engine caught fire. He couldn't start his outboard engines because they were frozen. He shut down Number 3. The plane was still flyable . . . just using Number 2. Sondestrom, Greenland, has only a one-way runway. He was light and made a successful landing.

The year 1983 will go down as the second biggest year for icebergs since the sinking of the *Titanic* in 1912. Almost two thousand icebergs were sighted in the North Atlantic, over 1,400 of which drifted south of the 'magic' line of 48° north latitude, in the Great Circle shipping lanes where the *Titanic* met its fate. At one point some three hundred icebergs were under observation by the Coast Guard Ice Patrol.

CHAPTER FIVE
The Rotary Wing Period

In the hands of US Coast Guard aviators, helicopters have saved thousands of lives in the forty-five years since the first Sikorsky R-4 was delivered to the air station at Floyd Bennett Field, Brooklyn, New York. From the very beginning of helicopter development, the service has shown its awareness of the potential value of rotary-wing aircraft in the performance of Coast Guard functions and by 1941 the Coast Guard was seriously interested in developing the helicopter for search and rescue. Lieutenant Commander William Kossler USCG had represented the Coast Guard on an inter-agency board formed as early as 1938 for the evaluation of experimental aircraft, including the helicopter. World War II interrupted these plans.

Mankind has never seen anything like the helicopter. With helicopters in service around the world, one can still appreciate the reaction of the US Army flier in the early 1940s who, watching a helicopter perform for the very first time, exclaimed: 'I see it, but I don't believe it'. On 14 September 1939, Igor I Sikorsky lifted the wheels of his famous VS-300 just inches off the ground at Stratford, Connecticut. This brief flight, witnessed by a few engineers and mechanics, proved to be an aviation milestone, leading to a series of helicopter advances that made the helicopter for the first time an instrument of practical use to mankind.

If the twentieth century's first global conflict was to forge a role for aircraft in Coast Guard thinking, the second was to bring about maturity and a major change of direction. Committed as were all major aircraft users to fixed-wing aircraft, the service as always was game to entertain and test new concepts. In a visionary way the Coast Guard was somewhat ahead of the other services in one area . . . helicopters, although admittedly during its early years the helicopter had one major handicap — the pilot needed three hands in order to fly it!

In its constant vigil over life and property, the Coast Guard today employs a wide variety of ships, planes and aids to navigation. A Coast Guard Sikorsky HNS-1 helicopter hovers near the Boston lighthouse, which has stood guard at the present site on the New England coast since 1716. (USCG)

After witnessing early flight trials and tests of the Sikorsky VS-300, Commander W A Burton USCG, Commanding Officer of the Brooklyn air station, New York, reported:

> The helicopter in its present stage of development has many advantages of the blimp and few of the disadvantages. It hovers and manoeuvres with more facility in rough air than the blimp. It can land and take off in less space. It does not require a large ground handling crew. It does not need a large hangar. There is a sufficient range — about two hours — in this particular model to make its use entirely practical for harbor patrol and other Coast Guard duties.

Anxious moment on board the US tanker *Bunker Hill* on 7 May 1943, a few miles east of Stratford Point Light, Connecticut. Fifty observers, including Mr Igor Sikorsky and Commander Frank A Erickson USCG, watch closely as Colonel Frank Gregory USAAF lifts and lands a Sikorsky XR-4 helicopter. Conditions varied from flat calm at anchor to fifteen knots with twelve knot winds blowing across the converted landing area. (USCG)

In June 1942 Commander F A Leamy USCG, Chief of Aviation Operations, strongly urged the purchase of a number of Sikorsky helicopters for training and experimental development. Lieutenant Commander Frank A Erickson USCG, an officer destined to play a major role in the adaptation of the helicopter to Coast Guard use, described in a memorandum in June 1942 a flight demonstration he had viewed at the Sikorsky plant in Stratford, Connecticut:

> The life saving and law enforcement possibilities of the helicopter have heretofore been especially stressed. However, this machine can fulfill an even more important role, that is in providing aerial protection for convoys against submarine action, an important function of Coast Guard aviation.

The first US Coast Guard helicopter detachment, headed by Lieutenant Commander Frank A Erickson, the first Coast Guardsman to qualify as a helicopter pilot, who pioneered rotary wing development for military use. The USCG were responsible for training all Allied helicopter pilots at Brooklyn air station, New York. (USCG)

Commander Erickson suggested that five of the Sikorsky XR-4s then being built for the US Army Air Force and which would be in use early in 1943, could give far greater protection for a convoy than a similar number of blimps or aircraft. This type of helicopter was reputed to be able to carry a crew of two, a 325 lb depth charge, radio and other equipment, and fuel for about four hours.

The great successes of Sikorsky with the VS-300 prompted the US Army Air Corps (which became the US Army Air Force on 20 June 1941) to award a contract to Sikorsky Aircraft for an experimental machine, the XR-4, which first flew on 14 January 1942. Following a US Navy decision to procure helicopters made in July 1942, action was taken later the same year to obtain a single YR-4B from the USAAF, with the designation HNS-1. The spotlight of public interest in helicopters for the Coast Guard was first turned on when Brooklyn Air Station, New York, was designated as a helicopter training base on 19 November 1943. The Coast Guard were to procure no less than twenty-one Sikorsky HNS-1 machines at a unit cost of $43,940. Prior to their arrival, three helicopters were loaned by the US Navy. Commander of the new training school was Commander Frank A Erickson USCG. Even in those early days several spectacular rescues were made by the new machines.

Programme delays and first tests

In January 1943 the UK placed an order for 200 Sikorsky helicopters and opened negotiations for 800 more. At this time, the Coast Guard had two Sikorsky R-6 helicopters on order. Shortly after this, Vice Admiral R R Waesche USCG Commandant, had a conference with Admiral E J King, Chief of Naval Operations, concerning the lagging development of helicopters for naval service. On 15 February 1943 Admiral King issued a directive to the Chief of the Bureau of Aeronautics that effectively launched a development programme. He ordered that the testing and evaluation of helicopters be initiated and carried through quickly to determine their practical value for operating from merchant ships in ocean convoys. The tests were to be conducted by the Bureau of Aeronautics, and the Coast Guard, with the Maritime commission providing a merchant ship with suitable platform, the US Army Air Force providing three YR-4A helicopters and the Coast Guard supplying the aviators.

A 'Combined Board for the Evaluation of the Helicopter in Anti-Submarine Warfare' was formed, consisting of representatives of the Bureau of Aeronautics, Great Britain, the Coast Guard and the Commander in Chief US Fleet. Later, representatives of the War Shipping Board (August 1943) and the National Advisory Commission for Aeronautics (September 1943) were added to the board.

The first tests got underway on 7 May 1943. Fifty observers were on hand when Colonel Frank Gregory USAAF, gave a convincing demonstration of the Sikorsky XR-4 aboard the US tanker *Bunker Hill* in Long Island Sound. Observers from various military agencies attended, as did Igor Sikorsky, the builder and designer. The Coast Guard was represented by Lieutenant Commander Frank A Erickson. Colonel Gregory made more than twenty flights from a small strip deck previously used for deck cargo. He landed under conditions varying from flat calm, with no movement of the vessel, to full fifteen-knot cruising speed with an approximate twelve-knot wind varying in direction from ahead to astern. The helicopter successfully completed every landing with precision, proving itself entirely practicable in the opinion of at least one observer, Mr Grover C Loening, Consultant on Aircraft, War Production Board. This gentleman was none other than the Grover G Loening who designed the first aircraft procured by the Coast Guard, the Loening OL-5. The only difficulty experienced was holding the helicopter on a deck slippery with salt spray.

Enthusiasm naturally ran high following these first tests. Action was taken to provide two ships with landing decks for helicopters, the *Governer Cobb,* a merchant vessel to be operated by the Coast Guard, and the SS *Daghestan,* another merchant vessel being operated by the British under Lend Lease. The combined board had concluded that a three-phase shipboard testing programme would determine whether or not the helicopter was ready to go to war in a convoy.

Phase I: Calm water, as in Chesapeake Bay, to familiarize the pilots with shipboard take-off and recovery technique.
Phase II: Open sea tests to establish the effect of ship's motion in a seaway on the problem of taking off and alighting.
Phase III: Operations from a ship in a regular convoy to Europe and return.

On 6 July 1943 merchantman *T James Parken* embarked on a two-day cruise between New York and the Virginia Capes to determine the practicability of operating a helicopter for short-range anti-submarine patrol. Two Sikorsky helicopters were employed, the XR-4 and the first of three YR-4As. The landing platform, mounted forty feet above the waterline, was trapezoidal, fifty feet athwartships forward tapering forty feet aft, with a sixty-foot length. During three days, ninety-eight flights were conducted with winds ranging from five to twenty-five knots and varying visibility. The test for Phase I was a complete success.

Phase II commenced on 26 November 1943, when shipboard helicopter trials were conducted on board *Daghestan* in Long Island Sound. Two YR-4B helicopters were embarked, one each from the British and American navies. *Daghestan* raised anchor and proceeded into the Sound. The wind was variable, the sea smooth, and visibility six miles in hazy weather. *Daghestan* built speed up to ten knots. Lieutenant Commander Frank A Erickson USCG led more than three hundred lift-offs and landings. All twenty-six evaluators and observers took turns as pilots and as observers. The only difficulty encountered was with the main rotor blades. In high winds, the vessels had to be turned down wind in order to permit starting and stopping motors. The helicopter was ready for Phase III — the convoy test.

On 2 January 1944 the British Helicopter Service Trial Unit embarked at Bridgeport, Connecticut, and two fragile YR-4B helicopters were carefully lifted on board. *Daghestan* proceeded to New York where US Coast Guard and US Navy observers boarded. The motor vessel then joined a convoy and sailed for Liverpool, England on 6 January. It can be revealed that the helicopter did go to war. The Sikorsky R-4 was used in the jungles of Burma to rescue Allied airmen with great success. Not so successful was its one attempt to fight in the Battle of the Atlantic. On 16 January 1944, a Sikorsky YR-4B rose from the pitching deck of the British motor vessel *Daghestan* in mid-Atlantic. A more demanding trial could not have been devised. *Daghestan,* heavily loaded, rolled and yawed during the entire sixteen-day Atlantic voyage due to rough weather. Ten degree rolls were routine and as the weather worsened, forty-five degree rolls were experienced. The flight deck, fitted on the stern, rose and fell by thirty feet as the bow slammed into the heavy seas, and forty-knot winds whipped across the landing area. A few days out from the USA a winter gale struck and the wind blew at eighty knots for a short period. The helicopter, and for that matter, all of the ingenuity of the Allies, was needed to fight the U-boat. For ten days *Daghestan* ploughed through the Atlantic, experiencing heavy seas, the helicopters lashed to the deck. Finally, on 16 January the weather abated. A successful thirty-minute flight was completed. On the following day, a second thirty-minute flight took place. On 18 January the weather worsened and no further flight operations could be conducted during the voyage.

Many firsts were accomplished by early Coast Guard HNS-1 helicopters and their pilots. Seen here is a Coast Guard HNS-1 BuNo 39036 fitted with a hoist and demonstrating a survivor pick-up. On 1 May 1944 the USCG accomplished the 'first helicopter hoist of a man'. (USCG)

The helicopter had not been adequately developed by January 1944 to allow it to be employed against submarines. Had the German submarine offensive continued to grow rather than peaking in the summer of 1942, perhaps a reorientation of national priorities would have resulted in a greater commitment from the US Treasury to helicopter development. This did not happen, and besides, technology is most often evolutionary and seldom revolutionary. Additional resources would probably have had only a slight catalytic effect. The helicopter was not yet ready to go to war.

Meanwhile at Brooklyn air station, New York, a special movable platform forty feet by sixty feet had been developed which could simulate the motion of a ship's deck at sea. During December 1943, tests were conducted at Brooklyn carrying a stretcher under the fuselage of a Sikorsky HNS-1 at a level about four feet below the bottom of the floats. No difficulties were encountered under all conditions of hovering and cruising flight, nor was it found hazardous to land astride the stretcher. Further development work on stretchers, slings and related equipment progressed rapidly.

The official debut of this type of aircraft came on 3 January 1944, when Commander Frank A Erickson flew the first helicopter mercy mission. He made an emergency flight, in a lashing snowstorm, to take two cases of blood plasma from The Battery to a hospital at Sandy Hook, New Jersey, where there were several survivors from the explosion of destroyer USS *Turner* off New York Harbor in Ambrose Channel. The limited space for landing at the hospital required the services of a helicopter, and this flight was instrumental in saving several lives of US Navy personnel. Accomplishment of the mission with any other type of vehicle would have required hours instead of minutes. As a result of this flight further studies were made to explore the helicopter's possibilities as a flying ambulance.

On 1 April 1944 the first civilian rescue by helicopter occurred. In a routine patrol training flight from Brooklyn, New York, Lieutenant (jg) W C Bolton USCG sighted and rescued a boy from a sand bar after he had been marooned there by the tide off Jamaica Bay, New York. The records from Brooklyn air station show that in the first quarter of 1945 there were 147 assistance flights by USCG helicopters in which a total of 1,123 miles were cruised.

Shortly after the commissioning of Floyd Bennett Field, Brooklyn, New York, as a helicopter training base, the British Admiralty made a request to the Coast Guard to train a number of helicopter pilots and mechanics and Britain supplied four Sikorsky R-4 helicopters for this purpose. More than a hundred pilots and 150 mechanics were trained under this programme. In addition to purely military use, such as anti-submarine duties, the Coast Guard demonstrated and continued to experiment with and employ helicopters in rescue and relief missions. The versatility and maneuverability of the helicopter made it ideal for many Coast Guard operations.

One of three Bell HTL-1 helicopters acquired in 1952 from the US Navy, and used primarily for rescue work. It could carry three people, had a top speed of 92 mph and a range of 110 miles. Depicted is BuNo 122461.
(USCG via William T. Larkins)

In the years following World War II, the flying boat, which had long been associated with the Coast Guard, was gradually replaced by the helicopter. Prior to the establishment of the first helicopter training establishment at Brooklyn air station, the first Coast Guard helicopter detachment was commissioned at the Sikorsky helicopter airport and factory at Bridgeport, Connecticut, on 7 July 1943. A very close liaison was established between Sikorsky, the manufacturer, and the Coast Guard, the user. On 30 October 1943, Commander Frank A Erickson flew the first Coast Guard helicopter from Sikorsky's plant to Floyd Bennett Field.

Photo taken on 30 January 1951 at Elizabeth City air station, North Carolina, depicting the single Coast Guard Kamen K-225 helicopter CG-239 being put through its paces. The 'Flying Banana' helicopter on the ground is a Piasecki HRP-1 1821. (USCG)

During May 1944 the first Sikorsky HNS-1 Coast Guard helicopter BuNo 39040 to be fitted with a hoist was proved and tested. The pilot was Commander Erickson, the man hoisted was E Sikorsky and the location was Brooklyn air station. This was the first helicopter hoist of a man. Today the HNS-1 is preserved in the Sikorsky museum. The hoist, or winch, was a complete success and was immediately approved and put into large scale production. On 2 October 1944, a huge Air Sea Rescue demonstration was held off Manasquan, New Jersey. New techniques were involved including the helicopter hoist. Lieutenant (jg) Stewart Graham USCG, made a demonstration pick-up of a simulated survivor from a Mark II life-raft using the hoist from his Sikorsky NHS-1 helicopter. The new invention required a great deal of research and development prior to being perfected; operating techniques had to be studied and then written into the SOP (Standing Operating Prodecures). Various hoists and strops were perfected, winching techniques developed, exercises and demonstrations were thoroughly examined as the flying hours were built up.

A close look will reveal three Coast Guard types in this photo taken at Elizabeth City air station. In the foreground is a Piasecki HRP-1 'Flying Banana' BuNo 11821 with a Sikorsky HO3S-1 230 airborne; a Curtiss R5C-1 Commando is parked in the background on the left. (USCG)

Helicopters for coast guard

Lieutenant Commander Frank A Erickson USCG, helicopter pioneer, as head of the Coast Guard Rotary Wing Development Project, had a key role in the creation of emergency flotation gear for helicopters. He developed the rescue hoist and other related life-saving equipment and was instrumental in the use of the helicopter as an effective tool for Search & Rescue.

The following is what Frank Erickson had published in 1943.

> Last May I had the privilege of witnessing the first flights of a helicopter from aboard ship. The aircraft was the Sikorsky R-4 flown by Col H F Gregory, USAAF. The platform from which these flights were conducted was located amidships on the vessel. The clearance fore and aft between the bridge and the mast guys was only 70 feet. These operations were conducted in Long Island Sound with smooth sea conditions and a wind of about 15 knots force. The vessel was cruised at various speeds up to 15 knots, hence a relative wind of 30 knots was obtained when headed into the wind which condition gave the maximum air turbulence obtained on the landing platform. Colonel Gregory was able to continue landings and take-offs throughout the maneuvers despite the severe turbulence.
>
> After the demonstration, a famous aeronautical engineer remarked to the effect that had he seen movies of these flights without having

seen them in real life, he would have sworn they were faked. Such are the reactions of many. The usual comment of spectators witnessing the Sikorsky helicopter in flight for the first time is, 'Well, now I have seen everything'. An idea of the flexibility of the control of this versatile aircraft can be gained from the evolutions expected of students upon completion of 25 hours of flight training. Mr C L Morris, chief test pilot for Sikorsky Aircraft, prepared the final check requirements which follow.

Requirements

1 Check on general coordination and smoothness of controls.
2 Take-off and climb sideways at approximately a 45-degree angle to the ground both sides (left and right).
3 Glide in sideways at approximately 45-degree angle and hover prior to landing.
4 Take-off and climb backward (preferably tail into wind). This maneuver might incorporate allowing the craft to turn and continue with forward flight after the craft has reached about 25 to 50 feet altitude.
5 Power-off glide from approximately 300 feet and flare-out at approximately 20 feet, doing the initial flare-out with azimuth stick and then preventing the ship from settling by applying pitch and power.
6 Turning on a spot while hovering, maintaining same rate of turn throughout 360 degrees (both ways).
7 Land into marked area (approximately 20 feet square) with steep glide angle (approximately 60 degrees to ground) from approximately 200 feet altitude.
8 Fly the boundary of a square. This should be done facing into the wind and following each side of the square, stopping at each corner. The vertical variation in altitude should be approximately one foot and the variation from the line should be not more than one foot. Altitude of this maneuver should be approximately 5 feet.

9 Power-off glide with zero airspeed and recovery therefrom both with and without power.
10 'Jump' take-off and get-away.
11 Take-off and steep down wind turns.

A Novel Experience

It is evident that the prospective helicopter pilot must change some of his notions on flying. On occasion I have taken uninitiated 'frozen wing' pilots for flights. Stopping suddenly and settling vertically from 200 feet altitude onto the Brooklyn air station baseball diamond is enough to make the passenger squirm and wish for the moment that he was anywhere else but. A backward take-off with a 180-degree swing into the wind is even more startling. The non-flyer is not troubled by such maneuvers. A Coast Guard Captain remarked after a flight during which similar maneuvers were made that he felt more at ease in the helicopter than in a conventional airplane. It does not follow however that the non-flyer is better suited for helicopter flight training. Helicopter pilots agree that, in its present state, it is probably more difficult to fly than most airplanes. In flight, it is longitudinally unstable, hence must be continuously flown. It is exceedingly sensitive in lateral movements of the stick; the pitch control lever and throttle combination is difficult to master while the stick and pitch lever forces are heavy, requiring considerable physical as well as mental exertion. Sixty hours' flight time per month is a good month's work. No doubt improvements will be made to simplify the controls but they are still in the future. At present there are more controls to be manipulated and greater coordination required than for other types of aircraft. Not all pilots have sufficient coordination for this duty, hence it is a special distinction to qualify as a helicopter pilot.

Many firsts were accomplished by the Coast Guard, and many helicopter firsts by Commander Frank A Erickson USCG. Here is a photo showing the first flotation trials off Elizabeth City with a HO3S-1G. The stabilization aerofoils below rotor head gave a hands-off capability in flight. These were designed by the pilot — Frank Erickson. Date 26 November 1946. (USCG)

Air sense required

As I have indicated above, it is essential that prospective helicopter pilots have a well developed 'air sense'. This can only be acquired by spending time in the air in the actual control of aircraft. The airplane pilot is therefore the logical candidate for helicopter flight training. Just how much time is required before transferring to helicopters is debatable. It appears that the flight student who has completed primary training in airplanes and has acquired at least 100 hours' flight time should have developed 'air sense', yet it should not be too difficult for him to overcome instincts acquired in fixed-wing training which are at variance with helicopter practice.

Frequently I am asked, 'Well, what possible use could a thing like that have?' The helicopter speaks for itself. A few of its many applications for the Coast Guard follow:

Winter scene as a convoy of shipping follows the US Coast Guard icebreaker *Mackinaw* through the Great Lakes on 24 April 1958 as it cuts through the ice to open the 1958 shipping season. The Coast Guard Sikorsky HO3S-1G helicopter on the stern flight deck of the icebreaker is being refuelled. (USCG)

Life saving — For removal of persons from vessels at sea, from the surf, from flooded areas, inaccessible mountain heights, ice caps or swamps. For the transportation of ambulance cases under almost any conditions. For running line from disabled vessels to cutter etc.

Law enforcement — For overhauling and directing of vessels to be boarded into shelter as required. For actual landing of boarding officer aboard vessels; landing or removing pilots and law enforcement officers from incoming or outbound vessels at sea; for directing movements of vessels in enforcement of navigation and anchorage regulations; for making security patrols of harbors and waterfronts, and for scouting jointly Coast Guard patrol craft.

Aid to navigation work — For transportation of men and materials ashore from tenders to isolated aids to navigation or those difficult to reach because of sea conditions; for flight checking of radio aids to navigation.

General utility — For all types of aerial photographic work, for ice operations; for spotting leads for vessels etc; for running of communications lines; for transportation of personnel from ship to shore.

Despite poor weather

It is not necessary that weather conditions be ideal for the operations outlined above. Flights can be carried out in winds in excess of 45 knots. Ceiling and visibility can be far less than that required for the operation of conventional aircraft. In fact, it is possible to equip the helicopter to permit take-off, flight to a distant point and a landing onto 100-foot square area with ceiling and visibility zero. The helicopter is the most nearly perfect amphibious craft in existence. If terrain or sea conditions prevent landing, it can hover while a member of the crew is lowered by rope ladder to perform any function possible under like conditions. There is every reason to believe that as the helicopter is improved it will play an increasingly important role in the Coast Guard.

Commander Frank A Erickson's forecast for the future of the helicopter was correct. Vital also during this time was the zeal with which the Coast Guard and the US Navy developed useful applications for the helicopter. The first actual use of the hydraulic winch hoist in a rescue occurred on 29 November 1945, during a severe storm in the vicinity of Bridgeport, Connecticut. Two crew members of a barge which had broken away from its tow and was in imminent danger of breaking up were successfully rescued by means of a hoist-equipped helicopter sent out from the Sikorsky factory.

Assimilation of post-war equipment into the Coast Guard began in August 1946 with the introduction of the Sikorsky HO3S-1G. Adoption of metal rotor blades for the HO3S- in September 1950 was the result of a development programme between Sikorsky Aircraft and the Coast Guard. Earlier during 1945 the Coast Guard had purchased twenty-seven of the R-6A type helicopter, designated HOS-1G, these being built by Nash Kelvinator under licence from Sikorsky. First acceptance of this type was during September 1944 when the first went to Floyd Bennett Field for evaluation. It was powered by a Franklin 0-405-9 240 hp engine, had a range of 245 miles and could carry three people.

The Sikorsky HO4S- was introduced in November 1951 and later became the standard helicopter provided to Coast Guard air stations for rescue purposes. The HO4S-2G was a proposed version of the HO4S-1 for Coast Guard use in the air sea rescue role, but this was not produced. Instead, twenty-one of the more powerful Wright-engined model were assigned to the Coast Guard. They were designated HH-19G in 1962. Unit cost to the Coast Guard was $177,530. Hundreds of rescues were made with this type, primarily using the hydraulic hoist and the new Coast Guard designed rescue basket, still in use today. All of these helicopters were fitted with *Tugbird*, another ingenious Coast Guard design which provided the capability of towing boats and ships of quite a large size. Eight versions designated HRS-3 were borrowed from the US Navy and were operated for several years. Continued development efforts resulted in provisions for all-weather capabilities, improved night illumination, extended range and payload, plus flexibility and improvement of rescue devices.

By this time other helicopter designers and constructors were busy in this field, and on 18 March 1950 a rather strange machine was delivered to Elizabeth City air station, North Carolina. This was a single Kamen K-225 helicopter originally allocated the USCG serial 239, later 1239. Only nine K-225s were built, of which two went to the US Navy, one to the Coast Guard and one to Turkey. The remainder stayed in the US of which one went to Mississippi on geological survey and two were used for crop dusting. Records show that the Coast Guard Kamen K-225 was manufactured in the former Kamen shop located at Bradley International Airport, Windsor

Locks, Connecticut with a completion date of 9 March 1950. It was one of three K-225s produced under a US Navy Bureau of Aeronautics contract for evaluation of flying qualities, it being felt that the Coast Guard were now experienced enough in the helicopter field to be included. The subject helicopter 1239 was the tenth helicopter produced by Kamen and the seventh K-225.

On 11 May 1950, after evaluation at Elizabeth City by Coast Guard pilots, 1239 went into the workshops for an extended maintenance overhaul and had flown 120 hours. According to an old USCG service report, after its initial evaluation, the helicopter was little used, and then chiefly for pilot refresher training. On 22 March 1954 the aircraft was removed from Coast Guard flight status and apparently returned to the US Navy, who operated it until 30 January 1955, by which time it had a total flight time of 165 hours. It subsequently became surplus to requirements and was sold to the Charlotte Aircraft Corporation, Charlotte, North Carolina. An airworthiness certificate was issued to that company on 24 May 1955, together with Civil Aeronautics registration number N1573M. It appears that the Charlotte Aircraft Corporation flew it an additional sixty hours until 1 October 1955, when it crashed on a tidal flat near Fort Fisher, North Carolina whilst transporting a fishing party to an island nearby. The pilot and two passengers were uninjured. The Kamen K-225 was totally demolished. Total flying hours 237:40.

Apparently the K-225 was remarkable for its stability, with torque forces cancelled out by its contrarotating rotors. It could comfortably be flown and hovered hands off. It was a three-seat open framework rotary wing aircraft with tricycle landing gear and twin contrarotating, intermeshing rotors, full servo-flap control surfaces mounted at seventy-five per cent of rotor radius and control linkage by push-pull rods through a small gimbal ring assembly below the transmission and through the rotor blades to the flaps. Its overall length was thirty-eight feet, its height fourteen feet two inches, rotor diameter thirty-eight feet and maximum gross weight 2,500 pounds. It had a cruising speed of sixty mph at 3,000 engine rpm, with a top speed of seventy-two mph. Other features included: fuel system thirty-eight gallons, gravity feed; electrical system single wire, direct current, twelve-volt system with an engine-driven generator and voltage regulator; powerplant a Lycoming 0-435-A2 six cylinder, horizontally opposed, gasoline pistol air cooled of 225 hp at 3,000 rpm; rotor operating range 200-250 rpm. Its range was 145 miles at cruising speed. The unit cost to the Coast Guard was $37,684 and it was also known as the *Mixmaster*.

Charles H Kamen, later President and Chairman of the huge Aerospace Kamen Corporation, was himself an inventor and during 1945 developed a servo-flap control system for helicopter rotors. Although the Coast Guard only evaluated the single Kamen helicopter, the company produced many for use by the USAF and the US Navy.

Helicopter designer Frank Piasecki favoured the use of the tandem rotor layout which he introduced in the Piasecki HRP-1 *Flying Banana*. The Coast Guard purchased three of these at a unit cost of $256,912 in 1948. They served until 1952 and were powered by a Pratt & Whitney R1840-AN1 engine, had a cruise speed of sixty-four knots and a range of 140 miles. Fitted with a rescue hoist, they carried a crew of two and had the capability of picking up eight survivors. The US Navy BuNos were 111821, 111823 and 111826.

In conjunction with the Coast Guard and the US Navy, Sikorsky was kept active producing advanced models of previous helicopter types. The first US helicopter to have metal rotor blades was the Sikorsky S-52, developed as a two-seater, which made its first flight on 12 February 1947. Later developed into the four-seater S-52-2 and designated HO5S-1G, eight were procured by the Coast Guard under contract Tcg-15513 at a unit cost of $82,928. It had a maximum speed of 110 knots, but its small size, short range and low life capability unfortunately limited its effectiveness.

First flown on 8 December 1945, and granted the first-ever US type approval for a commercial helicopter during March 1946, the Bell Model 47 was still in production twenty years later for both civil and military users. A number of different versions were procured for US Navy use between 1947 and 1958, some of these models going to the Coast Guard. Designated Bell HTL-1, these were part of a service evaluation as training helicopters, powered by a 178 hp Franklin 0-335-1 engine. Only two HTL-1s were purchased by the Coast Guard and were used for a survey of the New York Harbor area under the direction of the Captain of the Port of New York, checking for smuggling, harbor pollution, sabotage and other maritime derelictions. They usually had floats attached, although they were sometimes flown on skids.

A Sikorsky HO4S-3G 1289 from the Coast Guard air station at Port Angeles, Washington, participates in establishing an observation post on Blue Glacier, Mount Olympus, as part of the 1956 International Geophysical activities. The HO4-3G flew in scientists and delicate instruments. Other supplies were dropped by parachute from USAF Douglas C-124 *Globemaster* transports. (USCG)

The major US Navy version of the Bell 47 was the HTL-4, which dispensed with the fabric covering on the rear fuselage framework. The HTL-5 was similar and was powered by a Franklin 0-335-5 engine. Three of this type of Bell helicopter were purchased by the Coast Guard in 1952 and were assigned USCG numbers 1268 to 1270. Unit cost on contract Tcg-19087 was $49,290. They were used on a variety of missions, but their relatively small size and short range limited their effectiveness. They served until 1960. In 1955 a US Navy Bell HTL-4 BuNo 128623 equipped with floats was procured by the Coast Guard. This two-seat single-engined helicopter was used for ice reconnaissance work in Alaska on the USCG cutter *Storis*. It was also used for search and rescue and limited logistics support.

Coast Guard Sikorsky HO4S-1G helicopter 1253 tows the seventy-five-ton USCG tender *Birch* during tests at St Petersburg air station, Florida, on March 24 1958. These tests proved the potential of the type for towing fishing vessels, pleasure and other types of craft in air-sea rescue operations. Tests were made on craft of 794 tons and under. Effective on 1 July 1958, each USCG air station had at least one HO4S-helicopter equipped for towing. (USCG)

During 1959 two Bell model 47G helicopters with the designation HUL-1G were purchased and operated by the Coast Guard until 8 December 1967. These helicopters were fitted with floats and were also used for ice reconnaissance duties from USCG flight deck equipped ships in the Bering Sea and the Gulf of Alaska. The helicopters were based at Coast Guard air station, Kodiak, Alaska. They were re-designated HH-13Q during 1962.

Documentation discovered in USCG HQ archives indicates that two Bell HTL-7 BuNos 145848 and 145853 were loaned by the US Navy to the Coast Guard from 1 August 1962 under Chief of Naval Operations letter OP 502D5/cr, Serial No 2698P50 to the Commandant US Coast Guard. During 1962 they were re-designated TH-13N and even later HH-13N and had a unit value of $163,696. A further letter dated 26 January 1967 from the Department of the Navy, Naval Air Systems Command, gave an extension of loan for these two helicopters until 1 October 1968. On 6 December 1968, a requisition and invoice/shipping document was issued by the Commanding Officer, US Coast Guard air station, Route 1, Box 950, Warrenton, Oregon 97146 and signed on his behalf by Lieutenant (jg) W E Wade, USCG, Supply Officer, indicating that the helicopters BuNo 145848 and 145853 complete with floats and publications were being transferred to the Military Aircraft Storage Disposition Center, Davis Monthan Air Force Base, Tucson, Arizona. The US Navy BuNos for the two earlier HTL-1 helicopters used by the Coast Guard were 122460 and 122461.

The Coast Guard acquired eight of these Sikorsky HO5S-1G helicopters during late 1952 under contract Tcg-15513 at a unit cost of $82,928. They could carry four people and had a top speed of 105 mph giving a range of 190 miles. (AP Photo Library)

During 1959 six Sikorsky HUS-1G helicopters were purchased by the Coast Guard as a replacement for the earlier Sikorsky HO4S-3G. This new helicopter had made its first flight on 8 March 1954 powered by a 1,525 hp Wright R-1820 radial, located obliquely in the nose so that the transmission shaft ran at right angles to the engine straight into the gearbox beneath the rotor hub. Unlike the earlier HO4S- with its nosewheel landing gear, the HUS- had a tailwheel and, to facilitate ship-board stowage, the main rotor blades could be folded aft and the entire rear fuselage and tail rotor folded forward. Some of the Coast Guard models had inflatable flotation gear attached to the wheel undercarriage. It was known as the *Seahorse* and was re-designated HH-34F in 1962. However, Lady Luck was not on the side of the six Coast Guard helicopters. Two were lost in Tampa Bay, Florida, during rescue operations to recover a Boeing B-47 *Stratojet* crew after it had ditched. Both were lost within an hour. Another was lost at sea in the Gulf of Mexico when the helicopter struck the rigging of a fishing boat while hoisting an injured crewman at night. These six Sikorsky helicopters were allocated the USCG serials 1332 to 1336 and 1343.

Bell helicopter operations

A close liaison was maintained between the helicopter manufacturer and the Coast Guard. During February 1952 Coast Guard personnel were ferried to the Bell Helicopter Division Plant located at Fort Worth, Texas, prior to the delivery of the three HTL-5 machines to Floyd Bennett air station, New York. The three delivery pilots were Lieutenant Commander David Oliver, Lieutenant Thomas J Fallon and Lieutenant C W Lockwood.

A year later, whilst on a regular patrol from the Coast Guard Port Security Air Detachment at Floyd Bennett, New York, Lieutenant (jg) Charles W Lockwood and CMM James Boone were flying over Kings Point, Long Island when they spotted flames coming from a large dairy farm. Lockwood landed the maneuverable helicopter and called the local fire department. Airborne again, he quickly located the nearest fire hydrants, then hovered over the highway intersections to direct the fire appliances to the barn. When the firemen arrived on the scene Lieutenant Lockwood and Chief Boone landed again and assisted in laying hoses. Fire Chief Frederick Nineling credited the Coast Guardsmen with preventing a great loss: 'Without their early warning it would have been many thousands more'.

In October 1953, a graphic account of helicopter work aboard an icebreaker was written by Lieutenant (jg) R L Carpenter who piloted one of the two Bell HTL- helicopters in service with the Coast Guard on the cutter *Eastwind*. His co-pilot on many of the flights described was Captain G H Bowerman USCG.

Through the advent of helicopter development, icebreaking operations have become considerably more effective. With the aid of the helicopter, ships have reached out to greater extreme in polar navigation than ever before. The USCG cutter *Eastwind* in the summer of 1952 smashed her way to a scant 440 miles from the North Pole, thus travelling further north than any ship has done before. First, let us take a look at the ship which must push, smash and cajole her way through ice that varies in thickness from that which is found on local lakes and ponds to polar ice that reaches a thickness of ten to twenty feet and has the temper and resilience of mild steel. Six powerful diesel engines propel the ship which is constructed rigidly. A belt of steel close to two inches thick encompasses her about the water line and down to the keel. A sharp structure on the bow enables the ship to cut the ice or, if necessary, ride up on the ice, crushing it with its tremendous weight.

There are comparatively few people who know and understand the art of directing and guiding an icebreaker through the ice. This is not an easy job, and the danger of getting frozen in is ever present. As ice conditions become more difficult the helicopter is used as much as possible. Even in the extreme latitudes, where the ice is a problem all year round, there are passages through the ice known as leads. These vary from a few feet across to as much as several miles. This is where the helicopter comes into the picture.

With the helicopter ranging from a hundred yards to thirty miles out ahead of the ship, it is possible to relay information to the ship about the condition of the ice. Sometimes it is possible to find a clear path for several miles, while at other times it is a matter of yards. Often the ship will travel ten or fifteen miles while making good only three or four in the desired direction. From the time the ship enters the ice until it again breaks clear, the helicopter, pilots and maintenance crew are on immediate call. The pilots assigned to the ship are required to stand watches on the bridge and learn the characteristics of the ships so as to aid them in determining the best path for the ship to follow. Conversely, the ship's officers are encouraged to ride in the helicopter to see things from above. This results in good co-ordination between the ship and the helicopter.

The maintenance crew are on call twenty-four hours a day and must work in all extremes of weather. It is essential that they know their jobs and are equipped to handle all situations, as the ship often operates hundreds of miles from any facilities for repair. The aircraft may fly as many as twelve hours a day during periods of heavy operations. Most are conducted in latitudes that guarantee twenty-four hours of daylight which is a great help to both maintenance and flight. The helicopter is ideal for this type of work due to its versatility. A wind check from the ship is normally obtained for landing and take-off and is maneuvered as necessary. However, at times when the ship is engulfed by ice, it is impossible to maneuvre. This necessitates backing the helicopter into the landing area, a space only a few feet square on the stern. This tricky situation is best dealt with by employing a constant signalman who directs the pilot just where the helicopter should land.

At the sound of the bull horn 'man your flight quarters' the deck is manned by a group of personnel who are trained for any emergency that should occur. A pharmaceutical mate is ready to give first aid in the event of an accident. Likewise a fire fighting party is standing by, and a boat is at the ready to pick the pilot out of the water in the event of a water crash. Direct communications with the bridge by radio, telephone and flags are maintained to forestall any mis-understandings between the bridge and the flight deck. Also, the ship has a team ready to go over the side and traverse the ice to assist the helicopter in the event it crashed on the ice. It is a great comfort to the pilot and observer to know that these people are ready when you are operating hundreds of miles out in the ice pack. All icebreakers employed in the Atlantic Fleet during this period have found it very desirable to have at least one helicopter aboard to help them find their way through the ice.

Sikorsky HO4S-2G helicopter 1254 seen in flight over Manhatten Bridge, New York, during a routine flight from the USCG air station at Brooklyn. This helio, based on the Model S-55, served the Coast Guard from 1951 to 1966 and cost $117,530; the first batch was numbered 1252 to 1258. (USCG)

New Solution to Old Problem

Personnel of the USCG air detachment located at Floyd Bennett Field, New York, came up with a new solution to the problem of handling float-equipped Bell HTL- helicopters on the ground. Commander F W Brown USCG, commanding officer of the detachment, said Coast Guardsmen believed their new dolly to be the 'smallest airport in the world'. The dolly consisted of two support platforms constructed of canvas and steel tubing with connecting bars and tow bar. It could be readily assembled and disassembled and carried aboard the helicopter to use wherever it was needed. It originally weighed sixty pounds but Commander Brown said additional experimentation and re-design would reduce the weight to forty pounds. The platform was equipped with small wheels permitting the helicopter to be moved on a smooth surface easily by two men.

Well marked Coast Guard Bell HTL-5 helicopter 1269 seen parked behind a USCG UF-2G 7246. Serving between 1952 and 1960, the HTL-4/5 were based on the Bell Model 47A and were ex US Navy. They cost $49,290 each. Three were procured under contract No TCG-19087. (William T. Larkins)

Any helicopter pilot and crew involved in rescue operations must know the local landing areas and hospitals for use in an emergency. This photo shows a Sikorsky HO4S-3 helio 1301 landing at Battery Place, New York. It is based at the USCG air station at Brooklyn, New York. (William T. Larkins)

Due to the nature of the tasks they perform Coast Guardsmen make natural subjects for film. During June 1956, star billing was given to the movie *Men Against the Arctic*. Filmed in CinemaScope and Technicolor, the Academy award-winning thirty-minute documentary told the story of the danger-packed, back-breaking assignment of Arctic icebreaking duty. Four Bell HTL- helicopters, normal complement of the patrol's twin icebreakers *Eastwind* and *Westwind,* were shown performing their routine chores acting as an extra set of eyes for the ships' captains by directing navigation in ice-choked waters, surveying conditions ahead and charting the direction, size and number of icebergs.

Through Disney and Coast Guard cameras, borne aloft by the versatile Bell helicopters, audiences were given an intimate introduction to gigantic icebergs, romps across the ice floes with a lumbering polar bear and an entertaining interlude with a playful school of walrus, but in the main the cruise was depicted as it really was, a bitter battle of steel ships and stout-hearted men against the frozen barriers of the Far North. The theme of the movie was the urgency of keeping the sea lanes open to Arctic bases for the cargo ships as long as seasonal weather permitted and of keeping the ice wedge in the area shattered.

Many of the movie's spectacular views of this world of polar glaciers were taken from the Fort Worth built Bell helicopters operated by the Coast Guard and by the inquisitive cameramen. The movie brought to the screen for the first time a panoramic glimpse of the great Thule air and weather base on the northwest shoulder of Greenland from which radar stations and jets maintain a constant vigilance of the north. The last portion of the movie dealt with *Operation Alert* the Coast Guard's annual push north through the polar ice pack. This mission pitted the icebreaker against the almost impenetrable roof of ice on top of the world in an effort to reach and supply an isolated weather station only 400 miles from the North Pole.

A USCG file photo dated 16 April 1958 depicts a model of a new Bell HUL- helicopter, one of the proposed types of aircraft for a modernized US Coast Guard air fleet. This helicopter would have replaced the old Bell HTL- types used by the service.

By the 1960s Coast Guard helicopters were operating in all areas to which their missions carried them. Ice reconnaissance, port security patrols, search and rescue, transportation to isolated points, flood relief, pollution control and law enforcement had all become regular duties for Coast Guard helicopters, and outstanding helicopter rescues of people in peril had now become routine in the Coast Guard.

Sikorsky HOS-1 helicopter 75610 seen parked at its base at Floyd Bennett Field, New York, during 1948. In recognition of its participation in the epic rescue drama in Canada it has been named *Gander Express*. (William T. Larkins)

CHAPTER SIX
Coast Guard Aviation Overseas

On 28 January 1915 the Revenue Cutter Service and the US Life-Saving Service were combined to form the US Coast Guard. The law combining the two Services stated that the Coast Guard was to be an armed service at all times and made provisions for its transfer to the US Navy when needed. In fact, this has been the practice since 1798, when the Navy was created, but for the first time this relation was defined in law. Coast Guardsmen and their forefathers have fought in every conflict since the Constitution became law.

The Coast Guard's constant battle is with the elements. This photo dated 24 August 1946 depicts a Grumman J2F- *Duck* flying over ice and desolate snow capped mountains of the Arctic on a scouting mission. The vast post-war increase of world air traffic added greatly to the role USCG aviation had to play. (USCG)

During August and September 1917, six Coast Guard cutters left the US to join US naval forces in European waters. They constituted Squadron 2 of Division 6 of the patrol forces of the Atlantic Fleet and were based at Gibraltar. A large number of Coast Guard officers held important commands during World War I. Twenty-four commanded naval warships in the war zone, five commanded warships attached to the American Patrol detachment in the Caribbean Sea, twenty-three commanded warships attached to naval districts, five commanded large training camps, and six were assigned to aviation duty — two of them in command of important air stations, one of these in France. Of the 223 commissioned officers of the Coast Guard, seven met their deaths during the war as a result of enemy action.

On 9 April 1941 Greenland was incorporated into a hemispheric defense system. The Coast Guard was the primary military service responsible for these cold-weather operations, which continued throughout World War II. During this conflict Coast Guard personnel manned amphibious ships and craft from the largest troop transports to the smallest attack craft. These landed US Army and Marine Corps forces in every important invasion in North Africa, Italy, France and the Pacific.

During the Korean War 1950-53 the Coast Guard performed a variety of tasks. The service established air detachments throughout the Pacific. These detachments, located at Sangley Point in the Philippines, Guam in the Marianas, Wake Island, Midway in the Hawaiian Islands, Adak in the Aleutian Islands and Barbers Point in the Hawaiian Islands, conducted Search & Rescue to safeguard the tens of thousands of United Nations troops that were being airlifted across the Pacific. In January 1953 a Martin PBM-5 *Mariner* flying from Sangley Point Coast Guard detachment landed in twelve-foot high seas in an attempt to rescue the crew of a US Navy P2V- *Neptune* patrol bomber. After taking the survivors on board it unfortunately crashed on take-off when an engine failed. Five Coast Guard aviators and four US Navy crewmen lost their lives.

The Coast Guard ice-breaker *Northwind* made many visits to both the Arctic and Antarctic, and had the unique capability of carrying a Sikorsky HNS-1 helicopter, a Curtiss SOC- *Seagull,* plus specially designed small boats. The ice-breaker is seen at anchor in the Arctic while crew members explore the surrounding ice. (USCG)

Additional weather station sites were established in the Pacific to help guard and guide the flow of troops and supplies into Korea. A team of about fifty Coast Guardsmen were stationed in Korea to help establish the Korean Coast Guard, which has since evolved into that country's Navy. The Coast Guard also provided communications and meteorological services plus assured port security and numerous other tasks.

Coast Guard HNS-1 piloted by Lieutenant August Kleisch drops gently onto a strip of canvas on Lake Mecatine near a remote weather station. He had on board one of eleven RCAF crash victims rescued from the bleak wilderness of North Labrador. The canvas prevented the floats freezing to the ice. One by one the marooned aircrew were flown from the crash site some thirty-two miles distant. (USCG)

Aviators were among the 7,000 Coast Guard personnel who served in the Vietnam conflict. In April 1968 three Coast Guard helicopter pilots were assigned to the 37th Aerospace Rescue & Recovery Squadron of the USAF based at Da Nang, Vietnam. Pilots were assigned there until November 1972 whilst their USAF counterparts were assigned to stateside Coast Guard air stations. One Coast Guard pilot, Lieutenant Jack Rittichier, died in a rescue attempt. He was attempting to pick up a downed US Marine Corps pilot when his helicopter took heavy enemy ground fire, touched down and burst into flames.

This photo shows the remote island LORAN station 'DUKW', as the Coast Guard flying valet, a PBY- *Catalina,* delivers the vital mail from home, plus cigarettes, fresh fruit, candy, fresh meat and other expendables, including eggs in the form of a crate of chickens. Just one more task for the versatile *Catalina* which served the USCG well over many years. (USCG)

The Coast Guard set up and operated a LORAN system in southeast Asia in order to assist the US Air Force warplanes to achieve precision navigation. It was a difficult task to find transmitting sites, bring in equipment and build the system. The Coast Guard LORAN Construction Detachment began work in January 1966 and on 8 August the navigation network was on the air. LORAN stations were established in Lampang, Sattahip, and Udorn in Thailand and Con Son, Vietnam. Another station was later added in Tan My, Vietnam.

Some 8,000 Coast Guardsmen served in Vietnam. Seven lost their lives and fifty-nine were wounded. There were many awards including thirteen Distinguished Flying Crosses.

The long range aid to navigation chain (LORAN) became a global network installed and maintained by the Coast Guard after a great deal of development. It covered the major shipping areas of both the Pacific and Atlantic Oceans and the Mediterranean Sea. Using the system, trained operators can fix their position to within less than a quarter of a mile. Prior to the present LORAN C world-wide network's being set up, there was a LORAN station located in the Outer Hebrides which was administered on behalf of the Coast Guard by the Naval Air Facility based at RAF Mildenhall, Suffolk, in the United Kingdom, which flew equipment etc. to the station in Douglas C-117D Super DC-3s and later Convair C-131 *Samaritan* transports. Commander Thomas C Bird, USN Commander of the NAF flew many of the logistic missions to the LORAN station, often in atrocious weather conditions, high winds, and with limited navigation facilities. A further hazard was the sheep which grazed on the airfield area, which had to be 'shepherded' to safety by a US Navy crewman prior to take-off. Other early LORAN stations included such exotic locations as French Frigate Shoals in the Pacific.

Canadian rescues

The future of the Coast Guard helicopter in air sea rescue activity was clearly presaged by the dramatic Arctic rescue at Goose Bay in 1945. On 19 April a Royal Canadian Air Force aircraft crashed on the inland snow clad wastes of Labrador. Radio communication having failed, the nine stranded survivors had to patiently await the location of the wreck by scout aircraft before any rescue could be expected. After a day and night search the party was finally located, but a landing could not be affected in that difficult northern wasteland. Supplies and emergency rations were dropped to the men and two ski equipped aircraft were flown to the scene from RCAF Air-Sea Rescue headquarters. One aircraft, commanded by Flight Lieutenant Dave Avent RCAF, was successful in landing, but unfortunately the second aircraft crashed by a nearby lake. Two casualties were flown out by Flight Lieutenant Avent, who returned only to find himself stranded in the thawing snow, unable to take-off.

In addition to the original flyers, two more pilots were now marooned in an almost inaccessible region. In desperation the Eastern Air Command appealed to the Atlantic Division Headquarters at Manchester, New Hampshire. Perhaps a helicopter could reach the stricken airmen. There seemed no other possible chance of rescue. Immediate action was taken by the air sea rescue authorities. At the Coast Guard Floyd Bennett air station in New York a Sikorsky HNS-1 training helicopter was lying dismantled. Working tirelessly during the entire night, the engineering crews worked so that the dismantled helicopter might be ready for loading the following morning. It was transported to Goose Bay in a USAAF Douglas C-54 *Skymaster* transport and hurriedly reassembled. From Goose Bay Lieutenant August Kleisch USCG, flew the helicopter 150 miles to the nearest rescue point in Labrador, and on to the scene of the crash about thirty-five miles beyond.

The first rescue was completed before nightfall of the same day. However, the following morning found the HNS-1 engine frozen and a defroster had to be flown in from Goose Bay before the rescue mission could be resumed. By shuttle trips, all the survivors were flown out during the next two days. Amid very difficult weather conditions, at an altitude of 2,000 feet, Lieutenant Kleisch, in jump take-offs, averaged an hour-and-a-half for each round trip. It was a magnificent performance of skill and efficiency, a perfect example of international cooperation in air sea rescue. The praise of the RCAF was unstinted. Without the use of the Coast Guard helicopter the stranded flyers might have been forced to endure for months the cold and hardships from which they had been rescued in a fortnight. Flight Lieutenant Avent RCAF, expressed the admiration of all his countrymen when he said, 'We certainly owe a lot to the American Coast Guard and the US Air Transport Command'.

On 17 September 1946, Canadian Oceanic Air Traffic Control agencies reported that a Belgian SABENA Douglas DC-4 *Skymaster* airliner with passengers on board had crashed twenty-two miles south-west of Gander, Newfoundland. The aircraft registered 00-CBG c/n 42986/46 had been delivered to the airline just over three months previously on 4 June 1946. It was confirmed that there were survivors but twenty-seven people were dead.

It was 20 September 1946 when orders were received from the Eastern Area Rescue Officer, Captain R L Burke USCG, to prepare an HNS-1 helicopter for immediate shipment to Gander, Newfoundland, to take part in the rescue of survivors of the crashed Belgian airliner. Instructions were given by telephone to Lieutenant A N Fisher USCG, at Elizabeth City air station to begin disassembly of the Sikorsky HNS-1 helicopter for stowage in a Douglas C-54 *Skymaster* transport.

Sikorsky H03S-1 238 seen in the hover at San Francisco US Coast Guard air station in California. An overall yellow finish was used on all USCG helicopters in the early post-war years. The derrick for the rescue winch system is clearly visible. (William T. Larkins)

A Bell HUL-1G, one of two operated by the US Coast Guard, about to alight
on the flight deck of the USCG cutter *Storis* during the 1961 Bering Sea Patrol.
(USCG)

A factory new Sikorsky HUS-1G helicopter 1382, fitted with an auxiliary
droppable fuel tank, visiting the Naval Air Station at Anacostia in the District
of Columbia before proceeding to its assigned air detachment, later air station,
at New Orleans, Louisiana, on 3 May 1960. (USCG)

A Sikorsky HO4S-3G helicopter demonstrating a hoist pick-up of a survivor using a seadrome duoy system at St Petersburg US Coast Guard air station in Florida on 11 January 1963. With the introduction of the helicopter, the USCG entered an inventive field, testing and trying many methods of pick-up, including this one. (USCG)

Right: US Coast Guard Sikorsky HO4S-2G helicopter and the wreck of a Northwest Orient Boeing 720B airliner which crashed forty-three miles west of Miami during February 1963 with thirty-five passengers on board. (USCG)

Right: A Sikorsky HH-3F *Pelican* from San Francisco air station resting on the landing platform at Mile Rocks Light, a facility two miles west of the Golden Gate Bridge. USCG helicopters must land here frequently to service the light. The platform is ninety feet above sea level and landings are hazardous in rough weather. (John Gaffney USCG)

Below: An apron scene at the USCG Aviation Training Centre located at Mobile, Alabama, during November 1987. An HH-65A *Dolphin* prepares for a training flight, whilst a single scarlet finished HH-52A *Seaguard* helicopter is parked. The photo shows an interesting comparison between the two helios and the advance of a generation in design. (John Gaffney USCG)

Right: A Sikorsky HH-52A from the USCG Polar Operations Division (AVTRACEN), Mobile, Alabama. The helio has just returned from temporary duty on an icebreaker and carries rare USCG nose art. It shows a character similar to 'Yosemite Sam' and the words 'Whirleybird Cowboy'. Temporary duty can take helios and crews to either Arctic or Antarctic regions. (John Gaffney USCG)

A US Army Air Force C-54 transport 42-72558 c/n 10663 from Westover Air Force base arrived at Elizabeth City at 9.25 pm. The helicopter was loaded on board and the transport departed at 11.25 pm with the HNS-1 and crew aboard, landing at Gander at 8.55 am the next morning. The HNS-1 was unloaded and assembly began. Whilst this was taking place the pilots were flown to the scene of the crash in a Coast Guard Consolidated PBY-5A from the air detachment based at Argentia, Newfoundland, and plans were discussed for flying the survivors out by helicopter. It was decided to drop lumber at the clearing nearest the crash for the purpose of constructing a small landing platform as the muskeg would not support the weight of the helicopter. A second platform was built on the edge of a lake approximately seven miles from the clearing so that the survivors could be transferred at this point to the PBY-5A *Catalina* and flown to Gander.

While the Elizabeth City HNS-1 helicopter was being prepared for flight, another helicopter, a Sikorsky HOS-1, a more advanced and powerful machine, was also being made ready. This HOS-1 was from the Coast Guard air station at Brooklyn, New York, had arrived in Gander some twenty minutes prior to the Elizabeth City helicopter and was assembled and in the air before the Elizabeth City HNS-1.

However a delay was suffered by the HNS-1 during the initial test flight after assembly and darkness had fallen before the fault could be remedied. The Sikorsky HOS-1 helicopter managed to remove eight of the casualties before dark, all of whom were stretcher cases. The next day both Coast Guard helicopters were used to fly out the remaining survivors plus the fourteen members of the US Army ground rescue team and several others who had arrived to help with the evacuation at the scene of the crash. The following day, after all survivors had been flown out, the investigators and airline officials from SABENA were flown in by helicopter. The Coast Guard officers, all well experienced, were Commander Frank A Erickson, Lieutenant Stewart R Graham and Lieutenant Walter Bolton USCG.

The operation proved that careful coordination of the resources available was vital, and expert flying and caution was required of the pilots in order to avoid accidents. Two near accidents which could have wrecked the helicopters were narrowly averted. On the first flight into the clearing, the landing platform was not ready and Lieutenant Kleisch had to touch down on a tarpaulin spread out on the muskeg. The machine sank into the mire until it was up to the lower fuselage and cut the air intake off. The second near accident happened when a cargo parachute, lying near by, was drawn into the main rotor. The damage suffered was slight, but could have been more serious.

The Consolidated PBY-5A *Catalina* from Coast Guard air detachment at Argentia, Newfoundland, was commanded by Lieutenant Commander Schrader. It was from Wolf Lake that the land rescue party had made their way down a river in rubber boats after being flown in by the PBY-. It took this land team six hours to make the journey from Wolf Lake to the crash scene with rafts in tow. The reverse trip took thirty-six hours because the party was travelling upstream. Chief Aviation Machinist Mate Vannelli USCG, was in charge of the team re-assembling the helicopters and he refused to pause even for chow. Photographer O'Leary USCG was on hand to record the rescue operation, as Aviation Ordnanceman First Class O'Leary USCG also assisted in laying the timber required as a landing platform. In his report, Lieutenant Kleisch praised the Coast Guard mechanics who made early evacuation of the survivors possible. Coordination between the various rescue teams after first transfer was perfect and the Coast Guard employed three PBY-5A *Catalina*s which were kept busy shuttling between Wolf Lake and Gander airport.

Up over and down under

The US Navy's *Operation High Jump* with thirteen ships and 4,000 men was the largest Antarctic expedition ever organized. Led by Admirals Richard E Byrd and Richard H Cruzen, US Navy, it photographed most of the continent's coastline during 1946-47. It included ships, aircraft and personnel from the Coast Guard. A total of twenty-six aircraft accompanied the huge US Navy expedition. This air armada was made up of six Douglas R4D-5 transports, six Martin PBM-5 *Mariner* flying-boats, two Curtiss SOC *Seagulls*, two Grumman J2F-6 *Ducks*, two Convair OY-1 *Sentinels*, a Noorduyn JA-1 *Norseman* on skis and a selection of seven Sikorsky helicopters — one HNS-1, two HOS-1s and four HO3S-1s — which operated from platforms on the forward deck of the icebreakers. Most of the aircraft were painted bright orange for visibility reasons.

A Belgian civil airliner crashed in Newfoundland on 18 September 1946 and the USCG were called to assist. This photo depicts a USCG HNS-1 helicopter airlifting one of the eighteen survivors to a waiting USCG PBY- *Catalina* which will fly the victim to a hospital near Gander Field. (USCG)

No previous expedition into unknown areas of the world ever operated on as vast a scale as Task Force 68 or *Operation High Jump* in its probe of the Antarctic regions. It was the most elaborate expedition sent to the area and included thirteen ships, amongst them two seaplane tenders, an aircraft carrier and a US Coast Guard icebreaker, USS *Northwind*. Full advantage was taken of new techniques developed during World War II, particularly in the fields of electronics and photogrammetry. Helicopters, including a lone USCG Sikorsky HNS-1 043 represented an innovation. They were used largely for ice reconnaissance whilst in the ice pack and for seeking out ice-free areas for the PBM- Mariners to take-off and land.

The Sikorsky HNS-1 BuNo 39045, aptly inscribed '*Labrador Special*', and with nine rescue missions recorded, returns to its home base at Floyd Bennett Field, New York, after the rescue of eleven Canadian aviators who crashed in a remote part of northern Labrador. (USCG)

US Navy, Marine and Coast Guard personnel totalled over 4,700 officers and men and Task Force 68 was absent from the US from December 1946 to April 1947, of which the period from 19 January to 6 February was spent ashore on the continent of Antarctica. These operations provided further proof that polar flying was feasible. Experience once more bore out the fact that the problems of operating aircraft were not basically different from those encountered during the winter months in the northern US, although lack of adequate facilities for service and repair made the problem worse The greatest hazards to flight were low visibility, ice and frost. Ice was generally present in the clouds, particularly at their base, and with de-icing equipment only partially effective the only safe solution was to avoid the clouds. High winds drifted the surface snow and made visibility poor, blending the terrain with the sky and wiping out the horizon so that the general effect was like flying in a bowl of milk. The absence of radio aids and lack of well charted landmarks added to the navigator's problem, a problem already complicated by weak magnetic forces.

The first Fairchild C-123B *Provider* transport was received during 1958, serving the USCG some fifteen years. This photo shows C-123B 4540 from the USCG Air Detachment based at Naples, Italy, flying over Capri in the Bay of Naples on 11 December 1961. The detachment operated two C-123B transports. (USCG)

A force of approximately fifty scientists represented the US Weather Bureau, the Coast & Geodetic Survey, the Coast Guard, the Geological Survey, the Hydrographic Office, the Naval Research Laboratory, the Naval Ordnance Laboratory, the US Army, the Woods Hole Oceanographic Institute and the Fish & Wild Life Service.

The USCG icebreaker USS *Northwind* carried a USCG Grumman J2F-6 Duck BuNo 33585 plus the only Sikorsky HNS-1 043. One Curtiss SOC Seagull was carried aboard the seaplane tenders USS *Currituck* and *Pine Island*. These aircaft, outmoded for combat use, were selected for the Antarctic expedition because of their sturdy characteristics in rough water and because their rear cockpit provided space for a passenger. The SOCs were also used for reconnaissance, aerial photography and air sea rescue.

Commander Pat Wendt USCG, adequately described the role of the Coast Guard helicopter in Arctic and Antarctic territories in *Naval Aviation News*, May-June 1983:

> The mission of the icebreaker helicopter is to support the icebreakers wherever they may go. And they go, literally, to the ends of the earth. There are generally three operating areas: Arctic East, Arctic West and Antarctica.
>
> Arctic East can loosely be described as the area north of the North Atlantic sea lanes from the eastern Canadian Arctic to northern European coastlines. It includes the North Atlantic Ocean, Denmark Strait, Davis Strait, Baffin Bay and the Arctic Ocean north of Greenland, Iceland and other island groups within the Polar Sea. Greenland, around which most of Arctic East activity takes place, is considered the world's largest island. It is covered with a massive ice cap that is several thousand feet thick. The

pressure of the ice cap over many years has depressed the island's center and created magnificent coastal mountains sliced by forbidding fjords. Glaciers build in the mountains and slowly spill towards Baffin Bay, breaking off in huge chunks the size of battleships and ten times as deep. One such iceberg sank the *Titanic*. In World War II the fjords hid many a landing field that supported the North Atlantic supply route to the Allies. Picturesque Danish villages and stark military installations now dot the coast. The icebreakers are used for resupply, to repair and replenish navigation aids and as a platform for oceanographic and other scientific activity. The helicopters have been used to land glaciologists high on the massive ice formations to measure their progress, mark icebergs, haul personnel and cargo and to locate leads in the ice fields through which the ship can travel. Crews have to be on their toes particularly for rapidly forming fog that reduces visibility to zero zero.

Arctic West comprises that area north of the Aleutians, bordered on the west by USSR territorial waters and on the east by Alaska and the western Canadian Arctic Archipelago. It includes the Bering Sea, Chukchi Sea, Beaufort Sea and the Arctic Ocean. The north slope of Alaska is the land limit of the American western frontier. It's a vast, rugged land rich in resources which, in recent years, has exploded in exploration and fisheries' activities. From the beginning, Coast Guard icebreakers cut barge channels through the ice to build the north slope oil fields and have continued to assist when needed. They primarily serve as platforms for ongoing scientific research into the unspoiled environment to develop means to prevent exploitation and protect its beauty. They service aids to navigation along the coast but have no recurring resupply function for coastal military units, which is the primary mission for Arctic East.

The Antarctic mission, or *Operation Deep Freeze*, is the dream of most icebreaker aviators. The Antarctic area is all the land, sea and ice south of the roaring forties [parallel], that globe-encircling imaginary barrier that can be said to protect the beauty and charm of the land beyond. It's a land over which no country is sovereign and science is king. Its cloud-piercing mountains seem gently subdued by an endless blanket of snow. Yet there are stark contrasts like the Dry Valley areas, for instance, which remain free of snow the year round. The traditional icebreaker mission is to break a channel through the ice pack for the resupply ships to reach McMurdo Station, the largest settlement in Antarctica. From McMurdo, the scientific activities of nearly all US Antarctic stations are managed and resupplied. The icebreakers also serve as platforms for the seemingly endless deciphering of nature's secrets. The Coast Guard helicopters offer access to every nook and cranny of the Antarctic wonderland.

Alaska

When the US acquired Alaska in 1867 it was inhabited by a few hundred Russians and several thousand natives. Although all early census figures are incomplete and unreliable, it would appear that approximately 4,289 whites and 23,531 natives inhabited Alaska in 1890, just before the beginning of the gold rush of 1898. According to the census of 1940 the total population figure had risen to 73,524, or only slightly less than that of Portland, Maine. Of these seventy-odd thousand, only 39,170 were white, about the same number as filled the wartime Pentagon building in Washington. The remainder were natives; the Eskimos of the Arctic and Bering Sea areas, the Athapascan and Tlingit-Haida Indians who respectively occupied the interior and the southern coastal region, and the Aleuts in the Alaskan Peninsular and the Aleutian Islands. The population has expanded greatly since the beginning of the World War II period, being augmented by thousands of military personnel and civilian workers. More recently the oil boom and the Trans-Alaska Pipeline have provided employment for thousands of workers, and aviation has expanded to meet the demand and fit in with modern scientific resources etc.

Juneau is the capital but Ketchikan, as the supply and market center for the fishing and mining area, is the largest city. Skagway, Juneau, Cordova and Seward are the chief ice-free ports in the south. However, Anchorage, ice-bound for half the year, still remains a principal port. Alaska is a land of barren spaces and long distances. As an Organized Territory, including the Aleutian chain, it has an area of 586,400 square miles, of which over 21,000 are in government forest reservations. If superimposed upon the US, this vast region, twice the size of Texas, would cover more than all the land area north of Tennessee and east of the Mississippi River. It lies in the same latitude as the Scandinavian peninsular and has a rather similar climate. Geographically it is divided into six quite well defined regions: The Arctic, Bering Sea coast, south central, south-western, south-eastern and the interior. In both topography and climate, Alaska, like many northern countries, is a land of many contrasts. No general description can characterize so vast a territory. About two-thirds of it lies in the temperate zone, while to the far north remote outposts like Fort Yukon and Point Barrow mark the fringe of Arctic civilization. Mountain ranges, supposedly the northward extension of the American continental chains, roughly divide the interior from the Arctic slope. The waters are inhospitable to all who are not intimately familiar with Alaskan seas. Heavy fogs, excessive rainfall, sudden squalls, icepacks, jagged shorelines, and hidden dangers all combine to render navigation generally hazardous, especially in the Aleutians. In most regions transportation is both difficult and uncertain, particularly in Arctic Alaska. For years the Coast Guard vessels of the Bering Sea Patrol and Arctic Cruise were almost the only contact between southern Alaska and the isolated outposts of the far north.

When the Japanese bombed Dutch Harbor in June 1942, obscure and forgotten Alaska was suddenly in the spotlight of public attention. War-minded Americans searched in their atlases to find Unalaska just as they had looked a few days earlier for strategic Midway. For some fifteen months in 1942 and 1943 war activities in the Aleutians and the Bering Sea area held Alaska in the foreground of popular discussion. Along with the doubts and the fears for the safety of the Pacific coast, it brought to the Territory a long sought recognition. To the average American Alaska was just a yellow coloured section on the map, recently disclosed as an important American outpost in the North Pacific, now threatened by the enemy; the Aleutians were little more than a straggling chain of economically useless islands, the possession of which would put the aggressor in a position to attack our continental shores. During the months of the Aleutian campaign that followed, Alaska was rediscovered and rescued, as it were, from the myth and fantasy of romantic brochures and luring guide books. But lack of definite interest often breeds ignorance. As a people, US citizens were as uninformed of the economic importance of Alaska as they were unaware of its strategic geographical position. Only gradually did they come to learn of the great development that had been taking shape there during the last few decades. In particular, it was soon learned that the military was not caught entirely unprepared. At the beginning of World War II the Coast Guard already had the nucleus of a well established organization operating in Alaska. Soon after

Pearl Harbor the US Navy and Army joined with it and other government agencies in the activation of full defense measures for the Territory, completed as rapidly as construction and military installations were possible. The 17th Naval District soon became the center of feverish war preparations. The Bering Sea and Arctic region had been familiar ground to Coast Guardsmen for many years; it now became a practical theatre of activity for all branches of the military. Alaska constituted the main bulwark of defense for the entire northwest Pacific.

There were those who had almost forgotten that the last frontier of the USA extended to the far Arctic. It was not until the advent of World War II that the Alaskan area was suddenly transformed into an active theatre of defense strategy. Alaska lies approximately in the center of a great world circle around the North Pole, which encompasses part of the three continents of North America, Asia and Europe.

The C-123B served with the Coast Guard in Alaska and 4529 is seen parked at Boeing Field, Seattle during 1966. It carries the identification 'Kodiak', a very active Coast Guard detachment. Other C-123B transports served with the Miami USCG air station. (P. M. Bowers)

The Bering Sea, guarded by the Aleutians which enclose it, is the US' back door entrance to Asia. It is not surprising therefore, that Japan, long cognizant of the strategic position of the Aleutians, should consider them not as outposts but as central keystones in the Pacific war. It is well to remember that Dutch Harbor was nearer to Tokyo than Singapore. In the advantages of geographical position, Alaska is to the Pacific what Newfoundland or Greenland are to the Atlantic. Fairbanks, in the heart of the Interior, is but a two-day polar flight from London, Paris, Berlin or Moscow. Unalaska, where Dutch Harbor was bombed, is only about 2,000 miles from either Honolulu or San Francisco. The US Navy and Coast Guard base at Kodiak is nearer to Tokyo by some 900 miles than Pearl Harbor. Although Attu, the most western American island, is approximately 1,500 miles from Tokyo, it lies only 750 miles north-east of the Kuriles, or the northernmost islands of the Japanese archipelago. After the US recapture of that island American forces were within striking distance of the important Japanese naval base at Paramashiru, less than 800 miles away. The close proximity to Russia is equally significant. The Alaskan peninsular, which terminates in the Aleutian chain, is separated from the Kamchatka peninsular of Siberia by a mere ninety miles of water; Big Diomede Island and Little Diomede Island, respective possessions of the Soviet Union and the US, are but two and a half miles apart.

The US Coast Guard played a vital if unspectacular role in the programme for World War II. As the oldest federal armed force it had been one of the earliest government agencies operating in Alaska. For three quarters of a century Coast Guard vessels had continuously served in Alaskan waters, assisting alike the territory, the national government, and the several federal departments represented there. Each year the Coast Guard's Bering Sea Patrol visited the remote hamlets to bring peace, succor, and safety to the people. It had long been a chief agency of transportation and an avenue of communication through which supplies and news were brought from the outside world. It was natural, therefore, that the US Navy and Army should rely upon the advice and guidance of the Coast Guard in the formation of defense plans for Alaska. The Coast Guard had long been familiar with Japanese activity in the Bering Sea, knew the coastal waters intimately and was anxious to give the complete and invaluable cooperation expected of it.

Rapid expansion of Coast Guard aviation and facilities at Juneau, Ketchikan and elsewhere were inevitable. Coast Guard officials were among the first to make a plea for the extension of transportation facilities, especially aviation, for the improvement of harbors and navigational aids in Alaskan waters and, in general, for defense needs. Coast Guard surface craft, planes and personnel all played a legitimate part in the military operations preceding and during the course of the Aleutian campaign. In short, the story of Coast Guard development in Alaska is typical of that close co-ordination of US military services in other war theatres. Its World War II activities there present a thread of unity by which the major trends of general development can be traced. In a broader sense, the complete history of the USCG in Alaska is a panorama in miniature of the rise and development of the Service. In no other region has it so identified itself with the spirit of achievement and tradition. In its years of operation in Alaska, the Coast Guard has gained its highest record of distinguished service.

After the war a Coast Guard air detachment, Kodiak, was commissioned aboard the US Naval Station during the summer of 1947. Lieutenant Ben B Dameron USCG was the first commanding officer of a group of seven pilots and thirty enlisted men. The initial commissioning was accomplished with a single Consolidated PBY-5A *Catalina* aircraft, a type which had served both the US Navy and the Coast Guard well in the Alaska theatre of operations throughout World War II. A second PBY-5A arrived several weeks later, this being the aircraft complement for several years. The detachment offices and stores occupied one-fourth of Navy Hangar number one. The mission of the air detachment was the traditional Search & Rescue. Other vital tasks included delivery of supplies and material to LORAN station plus delivery and pick-up of mail to remote stations, the latter involving picking up the mail-bag by hook extended from the aircraft.

Coast Guard flight operations in south-east Alaska began on Annette Island during March 1944. Annette Island is twenty-two miles south of Ketchikan. The air detachment consisted of a Lieutenant Commander J J McCue USCG, one other pilot, five enlisted crew members and one aircraft. For the next thirty-three years aircrews from Annette operated a variety of fixed-wing seaplanes including Grumman JRF-*Goose*; Consolidated PBY-5AG *Catalina*; Grumman UF-1G *Albatross* and the later Grumman HU-16E *Albatross*. Both Sikorsky HH-52A *Seaguard* and HH-3F *Pelican* helicopters were used in later years.

On 19 April 1977 flight operations for the three Sikorsky HH-3F helicopters then assigned to Annette were moved to Sitka, 200 miles to the north. Air Station Sitka was commissioned on Alaska Day, 17 October 1977, the day which commemorates the purchase of the Alaska Territory from the Russians. Sitka had been the Russian capital of Alaska — Russian America. Today the Coast Guard air station at Sitka has twenty-one officers, 103 enlisted men, and three civilian employees. The three HH-3F helicopters assigned cover a 500-mile area from Dixon Entrance to Cordova to carry out the many missions of the Coast Guard.

Shortly after World War II, a Coast Guard air facility was established at what was then Naval Air Station, Kaneohe Bay, Hawaii. In 1949 the facility was moved to its present location at NAS Barbers Point and was subsequently commissioned as an air detachment. During the Korean conflict

1950-53 it became the major search and rescue air unit in the 14th Coast Guard District, responsible for deploying aircraft and crews to sustain the primary Search & Rescue effort in the Wake Island SAR Sector. Today, it is the only Coast Guard air unit in the 14th Coast Guard District. It received its designation as an air station in 1965 and is known as *The Guardians of the Pacific*.

During the 1950s a Coast Guard air detachment was established at Naples, Italy, sharing facilities with the US Navy and serving under the Commander, Mediterranean Section. Aircraft assigned included two Fairchild C-123B *Provider* transports which served the unit until the early 1970s and were used on a wide variety of tasks including calibration of navigation aids including LORAN stations. These aircraft were seen as far afield as Luqa, Malta; Wiesbaden, West Germany and occasionally at bases in the United Kingdom. The Fairchild C-123B, although used by the USCG in small numbers, some eight being procured, was a most versatile transport and served the air detachment located at Guam in the Marianas.

Each year, from March to September, USCG Lockheed C-130 *Hercules* are based on TDY (temporary duty) at Gander, Newfoundland on weekly detachments from Elizabeth City, North Carolina, for 'iceberg alley' patrol off the Grand Banks in the North Atlantic. At one time a USCG aircraft was permanently based at Gander during the iceberg season.

During 1975, at the request of the Japanese Government, a Coast Guard strike force trained to fight oil spills flew in a C-130 *Hercules* to the Straits of Malacca near Singapore. A supertanker, *Showa Maru*, had gone aground, spilling more than a million gallons of oil. The strike team helped to siphon off the remaining oil.

Whilst the Coast Guard's primary role is patrolling the US coast line and its 200-mile Exclusive Economic Zone, the service also has a major international role — that of supporting LORAN and Omega navigation stations worldwide.

The first H-model C-130 to arrive in late 1983 at the Clearwater, Florida, Coast Guard air station carried out a 40,000 mile, sixty-day round flight to Asia and Africa as part of the Aids to Navigation mission. The transport was loaded with a special electronics package to monitor Omega radio signals in the Pacific and Indian Oceans.

Omega is a shore-based, very low-frequency radio-navigation system. The signal transmission is reliable over thousands of miles and can provide navigational fixes within a four mile accuracy rate. The all-weather system is available to users of all nations, in the air, on land or water and even on board submersibles.

The purpose of the two month monitoring flight was to check the accuracy of the signal transmitted by the Omega stations in Hawaii, Australia, Liberia, Japan and La Reunion Island near Madagascar.

Always ready to ferry large quantities of equipment and other relief materials to the scene of natural or man-made disasters, Coast Guard C-130s provide regular logistics support to remote USCG radio navigation sites in Alaska and the Pacific. Demonstrating its worldwide capabilities in 1984 USCG C-130s provided Omega navigation system surveys in the South Pacific and Indian Oceans, as well as answering the urgent call to ferry 50,000 lbs of equipment and supplies to Cape St George Island situated sixty-five degrees south, where emergency repairs were effected to a Coast Guard icebreaker which had been trapped against an Antarctic ice-shelf, rupturing the hull.

Being the fifth military air arm of the US, aircraft of the US Coast Guard such as the C-130 may be observed at various foreign air bases during NATO and US Fleet exercises or during deployment of US forces to Europe, for example 'Ocean Safari '87', a large scale NATO amphibious and air exercise off the western coastline of the United Kingdom mounted in 1987.

CHAPTER SEVEN
Coast Guard Alaska — Kodiak and Sitka

Late in the 1930s the US studied closely the defensive and strategic importance of Alaska. The growing significance of air power in modern warfare, plus the concern over Japanese aggression in China, drastically altered America's complacency towards Alaskan defense needs. In December 1938 the Hepburn Board recommended the construction of air bases. In April 1939 US Congress authorized the construction of military facilities on Kodiak Island. After a complete survey of the island, the area at the mouth of the Buskin River was designated as the most suitable. The present site of the Coast Guard Support Centre was initially occupied by the US Navy in August 1939 and the first ground was broken on 23 September of that year.

The air station was established in June 1941 with seven pilots and thirty enlisted men. The initial commissioning was accomplished with one PBY-5A *Catalina* aircraft, a second PBY-5A arriving seven weeks later, this being the total aircraft complement for several years. The detachment offices occupied one-fourth of the US Navy Hangar One. The mission was the traditional Search & Rescue.

Since 1947 the Coast Guard has had units operating out of Kodiak when the first air detachment was established as a tenant command. With the closing of the US Naval station in June 1972, Coast Guard Base Kodiak was established to continue supporting the cutters and aircraft that patrolled in and around Alaskan waters. In December 1974, by order of the Commandant, the name of the base was changed from US

Coast Guard Base Kodiak to US Coast Guard Support Center Kodiak, to better reflect the mission of the base. Today, the Support Center owns some 20,000 acres of land, with a replacement value of approximately $500m.

The air station is currently located in Hangars One and Two. Missions include logistic support for the isolated units in the District Law Enforcement, Fisheries Patrol (ALPAT), and Search & Rescue. The air station once operated a total of eight HC-130H *Hercules,* now reduced to six, four HH-3F *Pelican* helicopters and four HH-52A *Seaguards,* but the latter have been replaced by the new HH-65A *Dolphin.* The varied missions involve flights to practically every part of the state. One of the more unique missions of Coast Guard aviation is the Alaska Patrol (ALPAT), which is an integral part of air station Kodiak. Although utilized when necessary for normal air station missions, the primary function of ALPAT is to provide aviation detachments (AVDETS) for patrolling Coast Guard cutters. The ship helicopter team is tasked with enforcing the Fishery Conservation and Management Act (FCMA), better known as the 200-mile limit. With two to four week deployments, pilots average ninety to 110 days at sea per year and enlisted air crewmen average sixty to eighty days per year afloat.

The Consolidated PBY-5A *Catalina* was the first US Coast Guard aircraft to serve Alaska, two of the type serving for several years after the commissioning of the air station in 1941. This is a Coast Guard PBY-5A seen in take-off sequence on 26 May 1945. (USCG)

In the early days of the air detachment, logistic support required aerial delivery of cargo by parachute to isolated units. Mail air pickups were also made with the pickup hook protruding from the tail hatch. It was always a thrill for the pilots and crew to snatch a bag of mail hanging from a line stretched between two poles. Turbulence and variable winds compounded the problems involved in this unique operation.

Cape Sarichef LORAN station and Scotch Gap light station were also supported by air logistics. The aircraft operated out of the Old Sennat Point landing strip. This strip consisted of smoothed out lava rock with a series of oil drums marking the sides of the strip, a typical Alaska bush pilots operation.

Summer 1952 saw the addition of a third PBY-aircraft to the air detachment along with four more officers and eight enlisted men. Search & Rescue continued to be the major activity with an increase of medical air evacuation from native villages around Kodiak and the Alaskan Peninsular. Such places as Kings Cove, Old Harbor and Chignik Bay were familiar to the pilots and continued to serve as the seadromes of operations for many medical flights.

In the summer of 1953 one PBY and crew were deployed with the US Navy at Point Barrow to work in conjunction with a US Navy PBY. Their mission was ice observation during the DEWLINE support operation. The aircraft patrolled from Barter Island to Icy Cape and an unusually high percentage of scheduled missions was achieved. January 1954 saw the replacement of the ubiquitous Consolidated PBY- by a Grumman UF-1 *Albatross*. Captain Engel picked up the first replacement at the Grumman factory located at Long Island, New York and ferried it back to Kodiak. Mail pickups were continued with the hook protruding from the waist hatch of the UF-1. This operation was later discontinued on command of a succeeding Officer-in-Charge on Cape Saint Flins who was terrified by just watching the maneuver. He felt the operation was too hazardous for the benefit of those concerned.

Those who flew the new Grumman UF-1G, with the short wing and poor de-icing characteristics, will long remember viewing with alarm the ice buildup in the wing slots or the tendency of the carburetor air doors to stick in full open or full closed positions. The carburetor icing problem was soon solved by field change kits, installed locally, so that adequate positive control of carburetor heat was maintained, and so the short wing *Albatross* was enabled to remain in service for several years.

In September 1955 Captain Charles Tighe took command of the air detachment and served during the change of aircraft from the UF-1G to the UF-2G. A most significant change during Captain Tighe's command was the air detachment's assuming all duties of the Kodiak Search & Rescue Coordinator from the US Navy. On 12 January 1956 the detachment received Douglas R4D-5 BuNo 17243 to replace one UF1G aircraft. The 'Gooney Bird' remained at the unit until 23 October when it was transferred to Washington DC.

During one short week in February 1956, Captain Tighe led the Coast Guard US Navy contingent through the rigors of Arctic Survival School and the tunnels of Ladd Air Force base, Fairbanks. They ate moose meat at the home of the trail boss and lived in a nylon teepee during the coldest two days of a two year period. Their 'Peter Polar Bear' certificate says 'Two year record', '56 below zero'. This was the start of the annual winter trek of Coast Guard pilots and crew to Milson Air Force base to attend Arctic Survival School.

In the spring of 1957 the air detachment commenced receiving the UF-2G aircraft with the modified long wing. Lou Donohoe picked up the first UF-2G number 1240 at the Grumman factory and ferried it to Kodiak, arriving on 19 April, Good Friday. UF-2Gs 1241 and 1242 arrived later in May and June. It was in May 1957 that Captain Tighe accepted the duties of Kodiak SAR Coordinator from the Commanding Officer, US Naval Station, Kodiak, which meant an even greater role for the air detachment, for now the control of all Search & Rescue efforts in the Kodiak Sector became their responsibility. With this responsibility also came the operational control of all USCG cutters deployed within the area and several US Navy vessels and aircraft for use in carrying out the Search & Rescue mission. As their Commanding Officer donned two hats, so also did the duty officers who now became Rescue Coordination Centre Controllers as well as Search & Rescue mission pilots.

The capabilities of the Grumman UF-2G increased both rescue and logistics capabilities. The extended wing increased the pay load and the performance under icing conditions. The SAR effort continued to build in hours and missions flown. In 1959, with the Department of Defense requirement for LORAN C, the Alaskan area was surveyed for possible construction sites. With this operation the logistics demand on the air detachment also increased in scope and size. The following year witnessed the construction of the LORAN C stations in Alaska and the addition of a Fairchild C-123B cargo aircraft plus a helicopter to the air detachment complement. By agreement with the US Navy on 15 March

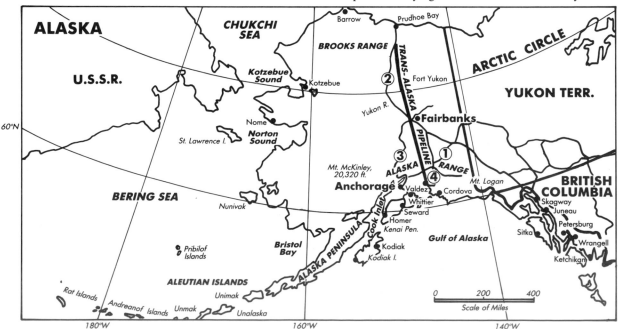

A map showing the location of the Kodiak and Sitka air stations in Alaska.

1960, the Coast Guard was assigned full use of the northeast half of Hangar One. Two Bell HUL-1G helicopters were assigned, primarily for use on icebreakers during the Bering Sea Patrol. These helicopters, although short range, were successfully used around Kodiak Island for many Search & Rescue missions. They had the capability of being transported by the C-123B to isolated areas. In March 1961, a native of Saint George Island in the Pribilofs was reported seriously ill. No landing field existed on the island and there were no means available to transport him over the open water and ice floes to Saint Paul. Captain Richmond had a HUL-1G loaded on board the C-123B and flown to Saint Paul Island and he flew in darkness to Saint George accompanied by a doctor, the island having no nav aids. They returned the patient to Saint Paul and then flew with him to Kodiak for hospitalization. For his outstanding airmanship and courage Captain Chester A Richmond, who was commanding officer of the air detachment, was awarded the Distinguished Flying Cross.

During the summer of 1962/63 the Law Enforcement of fisheries patrols increased tremendously. It was during this period that large scale gear interference first occurred between the Russian fishing fleet and the Kodiak king crab fishermen. The Russian fleet was trawling through the crab fishing areas, tearing up gear and destroying crab pot markers, resulting in a tremendous economic loss to the Alaskan fishermen. During 1964 the situation had improved following agreements between the US and the Russians on fishing areas. However, the intensive Law Enforcement patrol was established and has continued to increase in size to the present date.

Early in 1963, the Kodiak aircraft complement was increased to four Grumman HU-16E *Albatross* aircraft. Under a Department of Defense Directive dated 6 July 1962 all designations allocated to US Navy aircraft types were standardized with those of US Air Force variants, so the UF-2G became HU-16E. This was also the period when the type was experiencing excessive engine failures throughout the Coast Guard. Maximum gross weight logistics loads, coupled with long high power climb-outs only compounded the problem at Kodiak. This period came to a climax when the Commanding Officer, Captain Robert E Hammond lost

an engine on three successive days with three different aircraft while trying to get a load of supplies to Port Clarence. On the third of these aborted flights, although only one engine failed, both engines were found to have a handful of metal in the oil sumps. Shortly after, modified engines were placed in the inventory and the failure rate diminished tremendously.

On 27 March 1964 a destructive earthquake and tidal wave struck Kodiak and many other areas of Alaska. The air detachment hangar was flooded with over four feet of water but despite this six aircraft were moved to high ground and saved from extensive damage and destruction. All ground handling equipment, electronics gear, tools and parts had been either damaged or lost because of the severe shock and salt water immersion. The hangar was without electricity, water, and heat for over a month. The entire area was subjected to snow and additional flooding as a result of high tides and continuous after shocks. In spite of these obstacles and adversities, the air detachment maintained full operational capabilities, answered all Search & Rescue calls, flew survey flights and provided logistics support. For the courageous action of the personnel, their perseverance and collective efforts the air detachment was awarded the Coast Guard Unit Commendation.

On 1 July 1964 the unit was designated Coast Guard Air Station Kodiak. By this time the station had grown from seven officers and thirty men using one-fourth of a hangar in 1947, to twenty-six officers and one hundred men using an entire hangar. In August 1964 Captain Hammond was relieved by Captain Robert E Emerson. Enforcement patrol requirements continued to increase because of increased violations of territorial waters by both Japanese and Russian fishing vessels. The summer of 1965 saw the end of many years supplying Cape Hinchinbrook and Cape Saint Elias by parachute drops. On 7 August Lieutenant Commander Paul Breed and Lieutenants Jim Morton and Jerry Hotchkiss made the last drops to these stations and so ended a colourful and often exciting operation that had commenced in 1947.

The Grumman UF-1G *Albatross* replaced the PBY-5A *Catalina* in January 1954 and served at Kodiak for several years. This early model UF-1G 1279 depicted, had the short wing and poor de-icing characteristics and cost the Coast Guard $521,000 each. (USCG)

The Search & Rescue work at Kodiak continued to increase gradually over the years. In February 1965 Lieutenant Les Rahn performed an outstanding rescue mission for which he was awarded the Distinguished Flying Cross. Lieutenant Rahn and co-pilot Lieutenant Jim Morton departed Kodiak at night in a HU-16E on a medical evacuation at Dutch Harbor. The patient had been seriously injured by an automobile and was not expected to live without immediate medical help. Even for those that know Dutch Harbor, it is a hazardous airport under the best of conditions. Lieutenant Rahn made three radar approaches in a snow storm with low ceiling and poor visibility. The only field lighting was a vehicle and several flares. He successfully made a landing and transported the patient back to Kodiak. This was the only recorded night landing at Dutch Harbor other than during wartime operations.

The USCG cutter *Eastwind* finds the ice of Baffin Bay a formidable foe and her Bell HTL-5 helicopter takes off to scout the area so that a course can be chosen to make passage less difficult. This was part of a US Navy Task Group equipped with US Navy ice-breakers. (USCG)

Preparations were in progress to receive the new Sikorsky turbine powered helicopters at Kodiak. In November 1965 the two H-13 ex HUL-1G helicopters were transported to the new Astoria air station in Oregon. On 19 January 1966 two Sikorsky HH-52A *Seaguard* helicopters arrived in company to again augment the aircraft complement. Since that time these helicopters have served to rescue and assist many persons and vessels in all kinds of weather. In the summer of 1966 another LORAN station at Yakutat was added to the logistics responsibilities of Kodiak. The law enforcement patrols extended from Yakatut to Attu Island, a distance of 1,740 miles, equal to patrolling between Salt Lake City and Washington DC. Twenty to forty thousand pounds of cargo per quarter was being delivered to each of the five LORAN stations serviced. Search & Rescue missions were up to three hundred a year. Lockheed HC-130H aircraft were programmed for Kodiak because of the intensive law enforcement patrols and other operational requirements.

Gradually the complement of Grumman *Albatross* amphibians was increased, the designation changing from UF-2G to HU-16E during 1962. Depicted is HU-16E 7213 flying a law enforcement patrol and making a pass on a Japanese longliner fishing vessel on 2 November 1978. (USCG)

On the morning of 22 March 1967 Lieutenant Commander Bert Potter, aircraft commander of a HU-16E, observed the Russian fishing fleet vessel SRTM-8-457 in violation of Public Law S9-658, fishing within the contiguous fishing zone of the US. The vessel was within six miles of Seal Cape on the south side of the Alaskan Peninsular. This was the first instance of an aircraft detaining a Russian vessel. Continuous aerial surveillance and hot pursuit was maintained by the HU-16E until the USCG cutter *Storis* arrived on the scene some five hours later and placed a boarding party on the Russian ship. These and subsequent seizures of Japanese, Russian and Canadian fishing vessels served to reduce violations of US territorial waters and the nine mile contiguous zone. The realization by these nations that both aircraft and surface vessels could seize violators has significantly reduced illegal operations.

During the first nine months of 1966, the law enforcement patrol was augmented with C-130 *Hercules* aircraft from the air stations at Barbers Point, Hawaii, San Francisco, California, and Elizabeth City, North Carolina. The assistance of these aircraft and crews was highly effective and greatly appreciated by Kodiak, and served to intensify and expand the Coast Guard coverage. In the summer of 1967, LORAN air station Attu was added to the logistic responsibilities of Kodiak. Deterioration of the dock at Attu prevented further supply by USCG cutter from Adak. The deployment of C-130s contributed extensively to the resupply of Attu which was done in conjunction with their patrols in that area.

During 1967 the air station was in the throes of planning and preparing for receipt of their own HC-130H aircraft. Modification of the hangar doors to allow the tail of the C-130 to fit inside was commenced in June and completed in October, at a cost of approximately $200,000. The first aircraft was delivered from Elizabeth City to Kodiak on 2 July 1968 by Lieutenant Commander Jerry Foster, the air station's engineering officer. During the spring of 1969, the air station conducted aerial ice surveillance flights from Alaska's North Slope to Baffin Island in eastern Canada. This surveillance was in preparation for the first purely commercial attempt at the Northwest Passage — the voyage of the Humble oil tanker SS *Manhattan*.

The year 1970 proved a busy one for the air station. Over four hundred Search & Rescue cases were handled by the Rescue Coordination Center. During that year one hundred and sixty eight lives were saved, eight hundred and eighty one persons otherwise assisted and an estimated $39,595,500 worth of property saved. Search & Rescue showed a sixteen per cent increase over 1969. The first half of 1972 was highlighted by numerous violations of fishing treaties and agreements between the US, Russia and Japan. The air station flew many hours maintaining aerial hot pursuit until the violators were arrested.

In June 1972, the air station received three new Sikorsky HH-3F *Pelican* helicopters to replace the older HH-52As. With more than twice the capability of the HH-52A, the HH-3Fs were destined for an ever increasing role in the air station's missions. The US Navy role on Kodiak terminated on 1 July 1972 when the entire complex was transferred to the Coast Guard making Kodiak one of the largest operational units in the entire USCG. One of the new HH-3F helicopters was put to a severe test on 9 August 1972. Piloted by Lieutenant Commander Bob Ashworth, with Lieutenant Bill Wade as co-pilot the helicopter departed Kodiak to hoist a Japanese crewman who was suffering from advanced tetanus from the Japanese fishing vessel *Ryuyo Maru*. The ship was two hundred and fifty miles northwest of Saint Paul Island when the evacuation was requested. After a fuel stop in Cold Bay the HH-3F made the long over-water flight to Saint Paul. On landing, it was refuelled from a waiting C-130 and departed for the rendezvous with the ship. After locating the ship, the ailing seaman was hoisted aboard and brought back to Saint Paul where he was transferred to the waiting C-130 for the flight to the hospital in Anchorage. The entire operation, take-off, hoist and landing back at the island, was conducted in weather that bordered on zero-zero. By the time the helicopter returned to Kodiak 1,566 nautical miles had been flown. This was the longest helicopter rescue by the Coast Guard in Alaskan history. For their outstanding rescue mission in extremely poor weather, the pilots were recommended for the Distinguished Flying Cross.

In March 1973, the fishing vessel *Neptune One,* out of Seattle, sank 110 miles south of Cordova. The five man crew was located by a C-130 and recovered thirty-one hours later by an HH-3F. Admiral C R Bender, Commandant of the Coast Guard, and Rear Admiral Palmer, Command Coast Guard 17th District at Juneau, commended the air crews for 'their professionalism and alertness'. In 1973 increased emphasis was being placed on the enforcement of fisheries laws and treaties. There was a thirty-seven per cent increase in patrol hours flown in the first six months of 1973 compared to the last six months of 1972. On May 2 1973 Sikorsky HH-3F 1495 arrived in Kodiak, bringing the total HH-3F complement there to three.

During June 1973 a C-130 patrol flight from Kodiak detected three Japanese fishing vessels illegally using salmon gill nets. In an effort to escape prosecution the vessels cut away the nets and left them floating free in the salmon run. The cutters *Storis* and *Citrus* were taxed with the arduous task of retrieving the miles of non-biodegradable net. The vessels were apprehended and prosecuted by the Japanese fishing authorities. The vessels' masters were sentenced to one year hard labour, the owners were fined 200,000 yen each and each vessel forfeited a sum of money equal to the value of the catch.

On June 11 a HH-3F from Kodiak evacuated six men stranded on an ice floe near Saint Lawrence Island bringing the total lives saved for Fiscal year 1973 to thirty-eight. Four hundred and fifty-five other persons were assisted that year. The day of 16 September was a busy one. Seventeen persons were recovered from four vessels that were aground or sinking; air crews recovered three people near Dutch Harbor, three near Uganik Island, four in Whale Pass and seven near Seward. In October two C-130s and a HH-3F deployed to Nome to search for the motor vessel *Growler* and its crew.

The motor vessel was located overturned north of Nome. One body was recovered near Tin City. There was no trace of the other crewmen.

On 20 November Lockheed HC-130H 1500 arrived in Kodiak. This marked the beginning of a deployment of C-130 *Hercules* that resulted in B models in Honolulu, older H models in San Francisco and the new H models in Kodiak. The C-130H 1501 arrived on 18 January 1974: earlier model C-130H 1452 departed for San Francisco on 21 February and C-130B 1345 departed for San Francisco on 26 March. C-130H 1502 arrived in Kodiak on 30 April, 1503 arrived on 13 June and older C-130H 1453 departed for San Francisco on 17 June. The fourth Sikorsky HH-3F 1496 arrived in Kodiak on 27 February 1974.

During December 1973 Santa Claus made his first pre-Christmas trip to six isolated villages on Kodiak Island. Santa, who arrived via Coast Guard helicopter, distributed candy and gifts to approximately five hundred children in the villages of Ouxinkie, Old Harbor, Akhiok, Karluk, Larsen Bay and Port Lions. On 21 December a Kodiak C-130 located the bodies from the ill fated motor vessel *Oriental Monarch* which sank 500 miles west of Vancouver Island. Twenty-seven bodies were recovered by the USCG cutter *Boutwell* and the Canadian icebreaker *Vancouver*. The thirteen other crewmen were never located.

On 16 August 1972 Commander George J Roy Jr had taken over command of the air station. During his tenure the unit had flown 2,530 flight hours covering approximately 370,000 miles in the enforcement of fisheries laws and treaties; 209 lives were saved, 1,130 persons were otherwise assisted, more than $180,000 worth of property saved and more than $27m of property assisted. Manpower grew from 128 to 218. When Captain Roy was relieved by Commander Charles A Biondo on 8 July 1974, Captain Roy and the men who had served with him were awarded the Coast Guard Unit Commendation ribbon.

Many Coast Guard cutters and helicopters operated on TDY (temporary duty) in Alaskan waters with the helicopters from wide spread air stations. Seen during 1971 is an HH-52A *Seaguard* helicopter home based at Mobile, Alabama, landing in choppy seas guided by the ship's personnel. (USCG)

The continued emphasis of enforcement of fisheries laws and treaties resulted in apprehension of three vessels in 1975. Their fines totaled $326,000. In January 1975 the *Kikyu Maru* was detected by a C-130 patrol flight in violation of the three mile territorial zone. The vessel was seized by the USCG cutter *Midgett* and taken to Kodiak. The vessel was released later in the month after being assessed fines in excess of $400,000. This was just the beginning. From July 1974 to April 1976 eleven violations were detected and prosecuted with fines totaling more than $3m.

On 7 July 1975 a Kodiak helicopter crew assisted the stork. The helicopter was evacuating a fifteen-year-old native in labour, from Old Harbor when the stork, with the assistance of hospital corpsman Stu Price, delivered a baby girl at 700 feet over Old Woman's Bay. In September 1975 a C-130 was dispatched to Gambeil on St Lawrence Island to aid in the evacuation of twenty-three survivors of the crash of a Wien Airlines F-27 *Friendship*.

During the period 1 June 1975 to 30 April 1978 Kodiak flight crews logged in excess of 20,000 flight hours. Of this total approximately 3,500 hours were devoted to SAR. These hours were directly responsible for a majority of the Kodiak Rescue Coordination Centre's 1,042 cases. During this period over 325 lives were saved with an additional 1,850 persons either directly or indirectly assisted. Increased enforcement of the laws and treaties continued to account for the larger share of the flight time pie. During the period covered over 4,500 flight hours were expended resulting in over 10,000 vessels being sighted during nearly three quarters of a million miles flown. The calendar year 1976 proved an eventful year for the air station. The grounding of the Russian fishing vessel *Samarga,* off Kayak Island, southeast of Cordova provided the start for a busy year. Support efforts were not limited to the *Samarga,* HH-3F helicopters having spent two weeks deployed at Cordova in support of efforts to refloat the ship.

A HH-3F departing Cordova in a snow storm ingested ice into one of its engines, resulting in an unplanned single engine landing and subsequent engine change in the marshes of the Copper River delta.

Throughout the spring and summer, the C-130s remained extremely active in patrolling foreign fishing fleets. With announcement of the approval of the 200 mile limit, it appeared as though foreign interests were making one final big push to catch as many fish as they could. Patrol efforts paid off when they located the *Dong Won* fishing inside the twelve mile limit near Sitka. The USCG cutter *Sedge* took the *Dong Won* into custody and escorted her to Sitka where the owners were assessed fines totaling $530,000.

The programme was bolstered by the addition of HH-52A helicopters which were utilized primarily aboard the USCG cutters. Initially two aircraft, four pilots and the associated crews were assigned to Kodiak in January. Later in the spring an additional aircraft, three pilots and aircrewmen were added. The aid to navigation programme in the 17th Coast Guard District with HQ at Juneau found increasing use for the HH-3F helicopters in support of teams from the various USCG cutters. Spring deployments with teams from the cutter *Ironwood* serviced shore aids from Point Hope in the Bering Straits to Cold Bay on Bristol Bay. A team from the cutter *Citrus* accompanied helicopter crews throughout the year to service aids around Kodiak Island and the south side of the Alaska Peninsular. Additional flights were made in support of the cutters *Sedge* and *Sweetbriar*. The automation of light stations at Cape Hinchenbrook and Cape Saint Elias necessitated additional flights ferrying repair teams.

Search & Rescue activities for the year were highlighted by the drop of emergency supplies to the sailing vessel *Sorcery* a thousand miles south of Kodiak. The *Sorcery* had been demasted and was adrift in fifty-foot seas when she was located by the C-130 crew. The following day, the USCG cutter *Mellon* arrived on the scene and took the vessel in tow. The C-130 *Hercules* were involved in additional searches as far away as San Francisco and Midway Island. The search for

Waco J2W-1, one of three 1936 cabin model EQC-6s procured as J2W-1 for the US Coast Guard V159 on skis, seen at Floyd Bennett Field, Brooklyn, New York. Unfortunately it crashed during October 1939, but all three were capable of being fitted with skis for operations from ice in the Arctic. (USCG)

A sprawling glacier makes a perfect backdrop for the arrival of the first two of three Sikorsky HH-3F *Pelicans* to serve on Alaskan patrols on 17 June 1972. These two, 1483 and 1484, were assigned to Annette air station, their missions to operate in and out of remote native villages, logging camps and fish canneries and to provide SAR as required. (USCG)

the sailing vessel *Spirit* between San Francisco and Honolulu resulted in the rescue of one of the survivors who had been adrift for twelve days in a life raft. In November, C-130 crews were involved in the search for survivors of the sunken Panamanian freighter *Carnelian* north of Midway Island. Thanks to the efforts of both Coast Guard and US Navy search aircraft, fourteen survivors were located and later rescued by surface vessels.

Kodiak helicopter crews were responsible for the evacuation of numerous personnel from sinking vessels throughout the year. Three men were rescued in separate incidents involving small craft near Cordova. Six crewmen from the fishing vessel *Mar Del Oro* were hoisted from a liferaft in the Shelikof Straits less than an hour after the vessel sank. With over fifty-six per cent of the US coastline in Alaska, the implementation of the Fisheries Conservation Management Act on 1 March 1977 provided the air station with one of its greatest challenges. The Act, more commonly referred to as the 200 Mile Limit, provided for tighter control over the foreign fishing industry operating within the confines of the continental shelf. With the staggering volume of fishing activity in Alaskan waters, the only way to successfully provide an accurate assessment of numbers and nationalities of the vessels is by aircraft. When an aircraft returned from its daily patrol, the observer — usually a government agent — files a report listing name, call-sign, type of vessel, position and activity. This information is then fed into a computer and compared with the lists of authorized foreign vessels. Although the vessel may be licensed to fish in US territorial waters, by cross-checking the position it can be determined if it is permitted to fish in the specific area in which it is operating. Through 1977 Kodiak-based C-130 aircraft flew nearly one quarter million miles in 1,200 flight hours, sighting 4,640 vessels.

The year 1977 also marked the second year of operation of Kodiak assigned HH-52A helicopters aboard the Coast Guard cutters on Alaskan patrol. The ship helicopter team has extended the range of the ship, by providing observers with a platform to assess foreign catches while the ship is still a good distance away. Operation of helicopters aboard ships in Alaskan waters could have its pitfalls, however, as was evidenced aboard the USCG cutter *Rush* in October. Caught in a violent storm off the Aleutians, a rotor blade was broken from the embarked helicopter, rendering it unserviceable. Despite incidents such as this, deployed HH-52As flew over three hundred hours, 20,000 patrol miles and sighted more than four hundred vessels. With the dawn of 1978, two additional C-130 aircraft and one HH-52A along with associated crews were assigned to Kodiak, to aid in the enforcement of the Fisheries Conservation Management Act. The additional Sikorsky helicopter was equipped with radar to enhance its navigational capabilities whilst operating aboard USCG cutters.

Search & Rescue cases handled by the air station and other units in the Kodiak SAR Section continued at a steady rate in 1977. In all, 383 aircraft missions were flown, resulting in the saving of 198 lives and assisting 680 additional persons. Property valued in excess of $9m was either saved or assisted by Search & Rescue resources from Kodiak. The year's activity was highlighted by several dramatic rescues. On 1 March the fishing vessel *Viking Rover* was reported disabled and sinking near Cape Sarichef in the Aleutians. A Sikorsky HH-3F from the air station was dispatched to evacuate the vessel's four crewmen. Throughout the 475 mile flight to the scene, the aircraft encountered strong winds, snow, reduced visibility and airframe icing. Prior to its rendezvous with the vessel, *Viking Rover* lost its only life raft over the side leaving its crew in imminent danger. Fortunately the HH-3F arrived on the scene before the vessel sank and successfully hoisted all the crew to safety.

In May a Japanese seaman was evacuated from a fishing vessel near St Paul Island in the Pribilofs. This location,

nearly seven hundred miles west of Kodiak, necessitated the use of the combined HH-3F and C-130 team. The mission required the HH-3F to be flown to Cold Bay, refuelled and then flown to the scene for the evacuation. The C-130 was flown to St Paul Island where it made a rendezvous with the helicopter and provided it with the fuel needed to return to the mainland. Late June found the C-130s and HH-3Fs searching the Bering Sea for the sunken landing craft *Ahaliq*. After three days of searching in dense fog, a C-130 spotted a liferaft with four of the vessel's crew.

As the year came into its final quarter, the winter weather made itself evident. In the space of one week, storms in the Gulf of Alaska sank three fishing vessels and disabled a thirty-six-foot ketch. In near hurricane force winds and twenty to twenty-five-foot seas an air station HH-3F hoisted two crewmen from the disabled sailing vessel *Wind Dance*. It was later learned that one of the vessel's crew was suffering from hypothermia and had she not been evacuated and treated she would have died within a few hours. Two days later a C-130 and HH-3F were launched in response to a distress call from the fishing vessel *Seafarer*. The vessel was reported to be taking on water near the Kennedy entrance to Cook Inlet north of Kodiak. By the time the aircraft arrived on the scene, no trace of the vessel could be found. After searching for approximately forty-five minutes, the HH-3F crew spotted an orange liferaft. In gathering darkness and in spite of sixty- to seventy-knot winds and twenty-five- to thirty-foot seas the *Seafarer*'s four crewmen were hoisted to safety.

Throughout the period air station Kodiak saw its complement increase from 228 for its four C-130 *Hercules* and four HH-3F *Pelicans*, to 357 personnel manning and supporting six C-130s, four HH-3Fs and four HH-52As.

The Support Centre in Alaska is today unique among USCG units in that it is the only overseas support center that supports both air and surface commands. Permanently assigned units include: air station Kodiak, Communications Station Kodiak, Marine Safety Detachment, LORAN station Narrow Cape, and LORMONSTA Kodiak. The floating units home-ported at Kodiak include the USCG cutters *Storis*, *Yocona*, *Firebush* and *Ironwood*. All of these units combine to make Kodiak the largest concentration of Coast Guard forces in Alaska. These operational units are involved in the prosecution of all USCG missions in the Gulf of Alaska, Bristol Bay, the Aleutian Chain, Bering Sea and Arctic coast of Alaska, the primary missions being Search & Rescue, Law enforcement and aids to navigation.

Air Station Sitka, Alaska

Coast Guard flight operations in south-east Alaska began on Annette Island in March 1944. Annette Island is twenty-two miles south of Ketchikan. The air detachment consisted of Lieutenant Commander J J McCue, one other pilot, five enlisted crew members and one aircraft. For the next thirty-three years aircrew from Annette operated a wide variety of fixed-wing seaplanes including the Grumman JF-2 *Duck*, Consolidated PBY-5AG *Catalina*, Grumman UF-1G *Albatross* and the HU-16E *Albatross*. On 11 December 1954 HU-16E 2121 crashed during a water take-off whilst on a rescue mission killing the three crew. On 3 July 1964 HU-16E 7233 crashed into a mountain ridge whilst on an instrument approach to Annette Island killing the five crew. On 15 June 1967 HU-16E 7237 flew into a box canyon and crashed killing the crew of three. In later years Sikorsky HH-52A *Seaguard* and HH-3F *Pelican* helicopters were used.

On 19 April 1977 flight operations for the three HH-3F helicopters then assigned to Annette were moved to Sitka, 200 miles to the north. Air station Sitka was commissioned on Alaska Day 17 October 1977. Today air station Sitka has twenty-one officers, 103 enlisted men and three civilian employees. The three HH-3F helicopters assigned cover a 500-mile area from Dixon Entrance to Cordova to carry out the many vital and important missions of the Coast Guard.

CHAPTER EIGHT
Coast Guard Air Stations

In March 1920 the Coast Guard's first air station was established at Morehead City, North Carolina, when the service took over the abandoned naval air station and borrowed a few Curtiss HS-2L flying-boats and possibly one or two Aeromarine Model 40s from the US Navy. However, funds were not provided to support the operation and the station was closed on 1 July 1921. During 1925 Lieutenant Commander C G Von Paulsen borrowed a Vought UO-1 seaplane from the US Navy and, operating from Squantum, Massachusetts and later Ten Pound Island in Gloucester Harbor, he demonstrated the potential of aviation in combating the smuggling of whisky.

With an appropriation of money by Congress for the purchase of five aircraft — three Loening OL-5 amphibians and two Chance Vought UO-4s — the first to be owned by the service, these were flown from air stations established at Ten Pound Island, Gloucester, Massachusetts and Cape May, New Jersey. By 1936 the Coast Guard had six air stations, two air detachments and forty-two aircraft.

Barbers Point. Grumman UF-2G *Albatross* from the Barbers Point air station seen flying near Oahu, Hawaii, on 27 August 1963. For many years this Grumman amphibian was the workhorse and based at most Coast Guard air stations. (USCG)

During 1935 the Coast Guard had a Vought Sikorsky O2U-2, given by the US Navy, based at a temporary installation located in San Antonio, Texas. The aircraft was used briefly for patrolling the Mexican border for illegal aliens and later moved to the Canadian border to look for rum runners. The aircraft was fabric covered, this being in very poor condition on receipt from the US Navy, so it was stripped and recovered by USCG personnel and their wives.

By 31 December 1941 Coast Guard air stations were established at Biloxi, Mississippi, Brooklyn, New York, Elizabeth City, North Carolina, Miami, Florida, Port Angeles, Washington, St Petersburg, Florida, Salem, Massachusetts, and San Diego and San Francisco, California, plus an Air Patrol Detachment at Traverse City, Michigan. Nearly sixty aircraft of a wide variety of types were on inventory.

In 1943 a USCG Air Sea Rescue Squadron was formed at San Diego, California, and by 1945 Coast Guard ASR was responsible for 165 aircraft and nine air stations. To assist those in distress and to patrol national waters, the Coast Guard today flies some two hundred aircraft from no less than twenty-seven air stations, large and small, throughout the Continental US, Hawaii, Alaska and Puerto Rico.

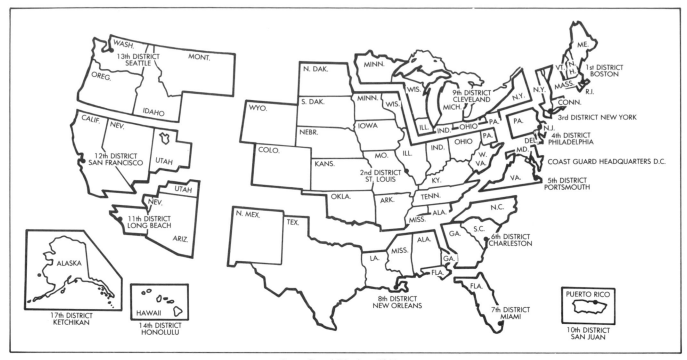

Coast Guard Districts, 1944.

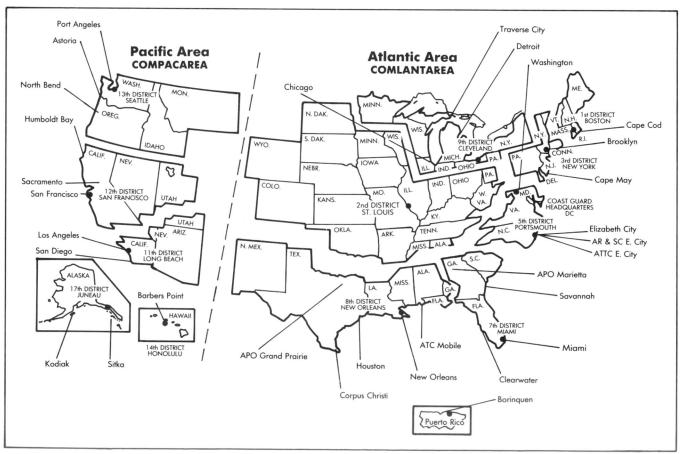

Current US Coast Guard air stations and facilities.

Air Station Astoria, Warrenton, Oregon

The air station at Astoria was established on 14 August 1964 at Tongue Point naval air station with a crew of ten officers and twenty-two enlisted men. Two Sikorsky HH-52A helicopters were operated from that location, staging from the Port of Astoria Airport during periods of inclement weather until the air station was permanently moved to its present location at the airport on 25 February 1966. The HH-52A *Seaguard* helicopters were replaced with three larger Sikorsky HH-3F *Pelican* helicopters in March 1973 to extend the Search & Rescue capability of the air station. The larger helicopters, and plans for assigning two fixed wing jets to the station — HU-25A *Guardian* — for increased surveillance patrols, set the requirements for a larger facility. A $2m construction and modification project commenced in 1974 which resulted in a two-fold expansion of the hangar building and other facilities. To complete the accommodation for the new jets, an additional project, begun in 1983, built the air station into what it is today, including a complete renovation of the hangar complex.

In 1987 Air Station Astoria transitioned to the HH-65A *Dolphin* helicopter, and today operates three *Dolphins* and three HU-25A jets for missions involving Search & Rescue, Enforcement of Laws and Treaties, Marine Environmental Protection and Aids to Navigation. The HH-65A is capable of flying one hundred and fifty miles offshore, hovering for twenty minutes and picking up four persons before returning to base. The HU-25A is capable of flying up to eight hundred miles offshore, delivering a de-watering pump or a raft and returning to base. Combined Search & Rescue operations with an HH-65A and a HU-25A allow an added measure of safety for offshore operations.

Law enforcement patrols cover the coastal fishing grounds and a distance out to two hundred miles between the Canadian border and the California state line. These flights maintain surveillance of the foreign fishing fleets, including the Russian factory ships, and guard against violations of all US laws and treaties. The Marine Environmental Protection mission involves responding to reported oil spills, with particular attention paid to mooring basins, industrial sites and ships in transit. The Aids to Navigation mission includes setting and removing seasonal aids with the helicopter, transporting personnel and equipment for the construction and repair of aids and locating aids reported off station.

The current authorized complement of the Astoria air station is twenty-four officers and sixty-six enlisted personnel. Operations extend from Canada to northern California. Coast Guard Group Astoria is one of five Group Commands within the 13th Coast Guard District which has its HQ in Seattle, and has operational and administrative responsibility for over 350 personnel assigned to five different commands located in the States of Washington and Oregon. These commands include Air Station Astoria, Aids to Navigation Team Astoria, Station Cape Disappointment, Washington, Station Gray's Harbor, Washington and Station Tillamook Bay, Oregon. Group Astoria's area of responsibility extends north to Queets, Washington, and south to Pacific City, Oregon.

Air Station Barbers Point, Oahu, Hawaii

Shortly after World War II a Coast Guard air facility was established at what was then Naval Air Station, Kaneohe Bay. In 1949 the facility was moved to its present location at NAS Barbers Point and subsequently commissioned as an air detachment. During the Korean conflict, it became the major Search & Rescue air unit in the 14th Coast Guard District, responsible for deploying aircraft and crews to sustain the primary Search & Rescue effort in the Wake Island SAR Sector. Today, it is the only Coast Guard air unit within the 14th Coast Guard District with HQ located in Honolulu. It received its designation as an air station in 1965.

The primary mission of the air station is Search & Rescue within the Central Pacific maritime region. Additionally the unit conducts law enforcement and marine environmental protection patrols of the waters surrounding the major and leeward Hawaiian Islands. It provides continuing logistics support of Coast Guard LORAN stations throughout the Central and Western Pacific.

Brooklyn. The hangar inscription identifies the location as Floyd Bennett Field, Brooklyn, New York, with a Douglas RD-2 *Adhara*, ident 129, parked on the apron. (Gordon S. Williams)

Three Lockheed HC-130 *Hercules* turboprop long-range search aircraft and two Sikorsky HH-52A *Seaguard* turbine-powered short-range recovery helicopters perform these missions. The HC-130 is configured primarily as a Search & Rescue aircraft. It can air-drop rescue equipment to survivors at sea and on land and its high speed and endurance are vital to long-range search missions. Because it can take-off and land on short, unprepared airfields, it is an ideal logistics-support aircraft.

The amphibious Sikorsky HH-52A, with a boat hull that permits excellent water-borne maneuverability, is well suited for recovering exhausted swimmers or survivors of maritime accidents. It also delivers personnel and equipment for servicing visual navigation aids to remote sites throughout the islands. Its capability to hoist while hovering has allowed the rescue of many stranded hikers from precipitous Hawaiian peaks.

Modernization of the air station at Barbers Point commenced in 1968 and the combined hangar and administration building was dedicated in August 1970. This building comprises two hangar bays, shops, rooms and offices. Other construction included a ground support equipment shop and a solar-powered hot-water wash system for the aircraft.

Cape Cod. Logistic flights to many offshore towers and oil rigs are a regular chore for US Coast Guard aviators. Crew changes are effected via USCG helio; food, mail and supplies are also delivered. This tower marks the entrance to Buzzards Bay; the helicopter is from Cape Cod air station, Massachusetts, and the date July 1979. (USCG)

A twenty-four-hour vigil of the mid-Pacific is maintained by the 160 officers and crew of USCG Air Station Barbers Point. Night and day an HH-52A helicopter and a HC-130 aircraft crew are ready to respond to any maritime disaster. Every year, countless lives are saved and millions of dollars in property are assisted. The air station's area of operations extends as far west as mainland Japan, as far south as American Samoa, north to Alaska and east to the mainland US.

In addition to Search & Rescue, the air station conducts law enforcement patrols in support of narcotics interdiction and foreign and domestic fisheries patrols in support of fishery conservation. The HC-130 aircraft can air-drop portable pumps, fire-fighting gear and other rescue equipment to distressed boaters and survivors at sea. It can be rigged to carry anything from troops and vehicles to baby incubators. The HH-52A helicopter can be airborne in ten minutes, and the HC-130 in twenty-five minutes. The HH-52As were replaced by HH-65As in the summer of 1987. Whatever the mission or distress call, Barbers Point is always ready.

Corpus Christi. A US Coast Guard HH-52A *Seaguard* helicopter 1374 from Corpus Christi air station, Texas, being clamped down on the deck of a Coast Guard cutter with the helio making the final adjustments. (USCG)

Brooklyn. A Sikorsky HO4S-3G helicopter 1310 seen flying below the New York city skyline on 27 August 1962, an area which can be hazardous when the cloud base is lower than the skyscrapers. (USCG)

Air Station Borinquen, Aquadilla, Puerto Rico

Air station Borinquen takes its name from the Taino Indian name for the island of Puerto Rico. The unit, then Air Station Puerto Rico, was relocated from San Juan in the early 1970s as a tenant activity aboard Ramey Air Force Base. Following the withdrawal of the US Air Force from Ramey in 1973 and an interim assumption of host role by the US Navy, the Coast Guard assumed self-sufficiency and host unit responsibility at Ramey during July 1976. This action was based on the USCG Commandant's decision from alternatives which included the discontinuance of USCG air operations in Puerto Rico, building an air station at Roosevelt Roads or at San Juan International Airport or staying at Ramey.

The air station is under the control of Commander, Greater Antilles Section and is assigned four Aerospatiale HH-65A *Dolphin* helicopters with which to maintain one aircraft in 'Bravo Zero' readiness — thirty minute alert — and three Lockheed HC-130H turboprop *Hercules*. The air station operates within the San Juan Search & Rescue Sector, an area of over one million square miles. The primary mission, Search & Rescue, is but one facet of the multi-mission responsibility. Duties include support for Aids to Navigation, law enforcement, surveillance for illicit drug traffic, environmental protection, oil pollution patrols and patrolling of the 200 mile fisheries conservation zone. In an average year over 2,000 flying hours are flown in support of these requirements. The authorized personnel allowance at Borinquen is 147, and among the nineteen commissioned officers assigned, eighteen are aviators and one is a civil engineering specialist heading the Facilities Engineering Department.

During November 1987 Air Station Borinquen was dedicated as the Coast Guard's newest *Hercules* operating facility. Admiral Clyde Robbins, the Chief of USCG Operations, and Admiral Howard Thorsen, Commander of the USCG 7th District presided. Three HC-130H *Hercules*, 1710, 1711 and 1713, were transferred from Air Station Clearwater, and the three HU-25A *Guardian* jets were moved out. This Air Station in Puerto Rico is now firmly in the front-line of the USCG's battle in the drug war.

Air Station Brooklyn, Brooklyn, New York

Mayor LaGuardia deeded a portion of New York City's only municipal airport at that time, Floyd Bennett Field, to the Coast Guard air arm. Air Station Brooklyn became operational on 23 April 1938 and was one of the Coast Guard's first ten air stations. At that time, such aviation notables as Amelia Ehrhart and Howard Hughes routinely flew in and out of the field. For all practical purposes, rotary wing aviation within the Coast Guard was born at Brooklyn, when Lieutenant Commander Frank Erickson USCG, and Igor Sikorsky designed and developed the Sikorsky XR-4 helicopter. This helicopter was outfitted with a hoist and floats, as Erickson's predictions for the future of the flying lifeboat became reality. While water landings were made in Jamaica Bay, ship landings were made aboard the Coast Guard's first aircraft carrier, the *Governor Cobb*. Erickson went on to train 102 of the US' first helicopter pilots, who were distributed throughout the armed services, and he flew the first helicopter life-saving mission ever from Air Station Brooklyn in 1944.

Innovation has become a watchword of the modern Coast Guard, as increased mission loads are accomplished with already overtaxed resources. However, the ability to accomplish the near-impossible is well-grounded in Brooklyn's aviation history. For example, in September 1946 a Belgian airliner crashed in Gander, Newfoundland. The crash site was inaccessible to all but the newly developed helicopter rescue vehicle. With Air Station Brooklyn over 1,000 miles away, a Sikorsky HNS-1 was disassembled, flown to Gander from Brooklyn in a Douglas C-54 transport, reassembled, flown to rescue eighteen survivors, and the survivors flown to a Coast

Guard PBY- *Catalina* to hospital. The total time from notification to the survivors' arrival at hospital was less than forty-eight hours. This represents only a spattering of the colourful history of Air Station Brooklyn.

Five Aerospatiale HH-65A *Dolphin* helicopters today tackle the diversified flight missions present in the New York Area. The primary mission is familiar to all — Search & Rescue. Two helicopters stand constantly ready to launch on those calls, the majority of which occur during the summer season. Calendar year 1977 saw Brooklyn helicopters fly 602 Search & Rescue sorties, assist 271 persons, and save an additional sixty-four lives. Other missions routinely flown are Port Security and Aids to Navigation, for example the supply of Ambrose Light Tower. Air traffic, weather, and architecture combine forces to make otherwise routine missions quite challenging. The new arrival finds out that the New York buildings and bridges often fly higher than the helicopters. In addition, the Enforcement of Laws and Treaties is accomplished by providing a platform for US Custom agents and other government agencies and by deployment of at least one Brooklyn helicopter approximately eight months of the year

A US Coast Guard Sikorsky HH-3F *Pelican* helicopter 1430 from Brooklyn air station, New York, is seen during July 1969 involved in a rescue drill operation with a 'survivor' being winched aboard in the rescue basket. (USCG)

on temporary duty (TDY). One can encounter an HH-65A in the Caribbean carrying the station name 'Brooklyn', as Coast Guard WMEC's and WHEC's or cutters often carry a Brooklyn based helicopter.

The air station is presently manned by twenty-five officers and 119 enlisted personnel. Although the hangars and support buildings are of 1937 vintage, the rest of the establishment is very modern. Although classic Search & Rescue cases in Brooklyn, as elsewhere, are somewhat seasonal, the air station has aggressively answered a year-round need of the New York City area which hitherto had gone unfulfilled. Commercial air ambulance services are not able to keep up with the emergencies present in a city of nine million with over fifteen well-equipped, but scattered medical facilities. On a not-to-interfere basis, inland MEDEVACS have become routine air operations. Air station Brooklyn, as in the past, has responded to this new mission effectively and has energetically filled the air ambulance gap when necessary.

Air Station Cape Cod, Otis Air National Guard Base, Massachusetts

Coast Guard Air Station Cape Cod was commissioned on 29 August 1970 as one of the many tenants on Otis Air Force

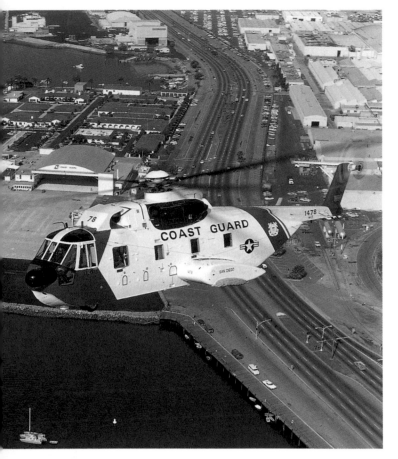

Sikorsky HH-3F *Pelican* 1478 circles over its home air station at San Diego, California. The type entered service in 1968, some forty being ordered by the USCG. Today twenty-nine of the type are in service at eight air stations, including Kodiak and Sitka in Alaska. The *Pelican* has an amphibious capability and can be refuelled at sea. (USCG)

On 31 October 1984 the tanker *Puerto Rican* exploded with a full load of oil just outside the Golden Gate Bridge, San Francisco. Seen here is a Sikorsky HH-52A 1395 from San Francisco air station, with the stricken tanker burning in the background. (USCG)

Right: A USCG Sikorsky HH-52A *Seaguard* helio circles over the fin of a crashed twin-engined Aero Commander on 27 December 1963. Until recovered, the aircraft wreck had to be marked and a warning to shipping issued, all the task of the US Coast Guard. (USCG)

Below: Sikorsky HH-52A *Seaguard* 1367 demonstrates its water-borne amphibious capabilities. This single turbine helio was the first built with a flying boat type hull. Its first flight took place on 22 May 1958 and the type is forecast to be retired in June 1989. Already a number of *Seaguard*s are preserved in US museums. (USCG)

Left: The twin-turbine powered Aerospatiale HH-65A *Dolphin* is the Coast Guard's new short-range recovery helicopter, which has now replaced the ageing Sikorsky *Seaguard* helicopter in the USCG inventory. It has a multi-mission role for use in SAR, law-enforcement, maritime environmental protection and marine science activities. The aircraft can also be deployed aboard Coast Guard cutters. (Aerospatiale Helicopter Corp.)

Below: This photograph, taken in July 1984, shows HH-65A *Dolphin* 4109 undertaking a routine patrol flight. (USCG)

Base. Its primary purpose, then and now, is to provide airborne support along the northeast coast from the Rhode Island/Connecticut border to the Canadian border for the many different Coast Guard responsibilities. These activities include Search & Rescue, Marine Environmental Protection, Maritime Law Enforcement and Aids to Navigation.

Since December 1973, when the US Air Force left, air station Cape Cod has also shared the responsibility of managing the Otis complex with four other agencies. They include the 102nd Fighter Interceptor Wing, Massachusetts Air National Guard, the Massachusetts Army National Guard training site known as Camp Edwards and the Veterans Administration Cemetery.

With approximately 325 military personnel, Air Station Cape Cod has the largest active duty population on Otis. In addition, 150 civilians are employed to help in managing 1,150 acres, 315 buildings, and some twenty-five miles of paved roads. The five HU-25A *Guardian* fan jets based at Cape Cod are used for Search & Rescue, to locate distressed vessels and, if required, to direct the HH-3F helicopter to the scene. The craft is capable of dropping emergency equipment, such as food, water, rafts and dewatering pumps and is also used for medical evacuations to quickly transport seriously ill or injured patients from land-based airports. Other missions are the enforcement of the 200 mile Fisheries Conservation Zone, Marine Environmental Protection Coverage of the offshore area and Drug Smuggling Interdiction Patrols. The 'Guardians of New England' patrol the North Atlantic from the Canadian border to Bermuda. The four Sikorsky HH-3F *Pelican* helicopters at Cape Cod are used primarily for Search & Rescue, but other missions include logistic support of the many offshore lighthouses of New England, Fishery Enforcement and Drug Smuggling Patrols. Missions previously carried out from Air Station Salem are now handled from Cape Cod.

Air Station Cape May, New Jersey

Air Station Cape May, New Jersey, is under the command of Coast Guard Group Cape May, which performs a variety of missions under the control of the Commander, 5th Coast Guard District with HQ in Portsmouth, Virginia. Its area of responsibility extends roughly from just north of Atlantic City, New Jersey, south to the Delaware and Maryland state lines. This area includes the mouth and lower reaches of the Delaware Bay. The primary missions of the units assigned to the group are Search & Rescue and enforcement of laws and treaties. The group enforces regulations dealing with such diverse matters as offshore fisheries to the operation of drawbridges. A significant effort is made to support other law enforcement agencies in the area such as US Customs, National Marine Fisheries plus state and local authorities. The group also has a marine environmental pollution response mission. Support is given to other Federal, state and local agencies in a multitude of ways, such as conducting water fowl inventories.

The Coast Guard Training Center (TRACEN) is located at Cape May, the sole recruit training center for the USCG. Tours are provided for recruits who wish to learn more about Coast Guard aviation. The Air Station Cape May has an allowance of fourteen aviators, one aviation warrant officer, and twenty-five enlisted aviation personnel who operate and maintain three helicopters. Up to 1986 these helicopters were Sikorsky HH-52A *Seaguards*. These were replaced by the new HH-65A *Dolphin,* a unique helicopter which can handle many missions from drug interdiction to polar ice patrols. A unique feature is a computerized flight management system which integrates state-of-the-art communication and navigation equipment. At pilot direction, the system brings the aircraft to a stable hover fifty feet above a selected object, an important safety feature in darkness or inclement weather. Search patterns can automatically be flown, freeing the pilot

and co-pilot to concentrate on sighting the search target. By 1989 the *Dolphin* should have completely replaced the HH-52A.

During the summer months the Cape May group office establishes seasonal Search & Rescue Detachments (SARDETS) who operate boats at Fortescue and Townsend Inlet. A further seasonal SARDET is established at Roosevelt Inlet in Delaware. These detachments are fully supported by the helicopters from Cape May Air Station. In the fiscal year 1984 the air station handled 220 cases, saved ninety-nine lives, assisted 259 persons and saved over $5,000 worth of property. One must not forget that along with Ten Pound Island, Gloucester, Massachusetts, Air Station Cape May was the first to be established by Coast Guard aviation.

Air Station Chicago, Naval Air Station Glenview, Illinois

Commissioned on 1 March 1969 by Coast Guard Commandant Willard J Smith, Air Station Chicago is the primary

Elizabeth City. Hangar scene at the Aircraft Repair & Supply Center at Elizabeth City during 1950 depicting a couple of Boeing PB-1G *Flying Fortresses,* a Grumman JRF- *Goose,* and a Martin PBM-5 *Mariner.* (USCG)

Search & Rescue unit for southern Lake Michigan, responsible for the waters from Milwaukee, Wisconsin, to Muskegon, Michigan, and south to Gary in Indiana. Equipped with two helicopters, the HH-52A *Seaguard* will be replaced with the HH-65A *Dolphin,* the station has eleven officers and thirty-four crew, and is on call twenty-four hours a day for virtually any emergency that may arise.

Being one of the only Coast Guard air stations in the Midwest brings occasional operational deployments as far south as St Louis, Missouri, west to Minneapolis and north to Green Bay, Wisconsin, for such work as flood relief and short range aids to navigation. When the thousands of pleasure craft come out of the water as winter approaches, the station prepares for its frequent ice patrols. The winter of 1978/79 resulted in a record snowfall of almost ninety inches and the complete freezing over of Lake Michigan. However, the twice-weekly pollution patrols along the Chicago Ship Canal to Joliet, Illinois, the weekly patrol north to Milwaukee and the monthly patrol along the Illinois River to Peoria, Illinois, continued. The winter slowdown in Search & Rescue missions provides an excellent opportunity for implementation of Chicago's extensive pilot and aircrewman training. Although AIREVACS are performed throughout the year, they are more frequent during the winter because snow storms and blizzards create road conditions too hazardous for ambulance travel — sometimes even snow-mobiles cannot get through.

Spring brings the boaters out in ever increasing numbers along with the inevitable late night launchers, sinkings, overdues etc. It also heralds almost daily boat and helicopter training flights with nearby USCG boat stations, not to mention a heavy public affairs schedule of helicopter displays and flight demonstrations in support of Coast Guard recruiting. Coming under the command of the 9th District with HQ in Cleveland, Ohio, the primary mission of the air station is to provide Search & Rescue assistance to life and property on southern Lake Michigan. To this end, it has communications links with all Coast Guard units in the area and with the Rescue Coordination Center (RCC) located at 9th District HQ. The air station complex consists of hangar space for the aircraft, quarters for the flight crew on constant alert and normal administrative offices. The air station is a tenant command of the US Naval air station, where it is located.

Air Station Clearwater, Florida

The original air station was commissioned in 1934 at Albert Whited Airport in downtown St Petersburg, and was home base for a wide variety of early Coast Guard aircraft. The addition of four Lockheed HC-130 *Hercules* in 1976 prompted the move to St Petersburg — Clearwater International Airport, hence the name change. Increased responsibilities came with the addition of the C-130 long-range aircraft and personnel strength was boosted to 300 officers and men. A new station motto 'Anytime, Anywhere' was adopted and describes the current operation of the air station. Numerous missions by the *Hercules* in support of Search & Rescue, Law Enforcement, Aids to Navigation, and Marine Environmental Protection are flown on a daily basis. The air station also supports the annual Omega navigation system survey flight which sends C-130 crews on expeditions around the world to collect calibration data necessary to verify the accuracy of this long range navigation system used by civil aviation and maritime operators world-wide. The air station currently has six C-130 transports on inventory, including the new -7 model.

The six Sikorsky HH-3F *Pelican* helicopters, while shore-based, use their long-range capability of 600 nautical miles to support Coast Guard ships on law enforcement patrol, deliver pumps to sinking vessels and evacuate injured crew members

Miami. Historic photo dated 13 April 1935 taken at Miami air station, Florida, depicting Douglas RD-4 *Dolphins* 133 and 135 being serviced near the water's edge. The RD-4 133 was in service at San Francisco at the end of 1941. (USCG)

from vessels far at sea. A yearly average of over three hundred such Search & Rescue cases are handled by the HH-3F along the entire coast of Florida and as far as the Bahamas.

The air station was instrumental in supporting Coast Guard surface units during the massive Cuban boatlift of 1980 and earned both the Humanitarian Service Medal and the Coast Guard Unit Commendation for those efforts. For outstanding performance during the period May to September 1984 the air station received the Coast Guard Meritorious Unit Commendation, plus the Coast Guard Unit Commendation for participation in 'Operation Wagonwheel', an inter-agency, international narcotics interdiction effort which took place from October to December 1984.

Clearwater's flight crews and support personnel are directly responsible for saving over a hundred lives and over $1m of property each year. The air station is justifiably proud of its service to the nation and to the local community. The C-130 can be used as a troop-carrier carrying eight-six passengers, or can easily be converted as an ambulance to carry sixty-six litters. It is capable of take-off and landing on short runways and carries a normal crew of pilot, co-pilot, flight engineer, navigator, radio operator, loadmaster and dropmaster, and will often carry extra people to act as lookouts during long searches.

The HH-3F helicopter was designed by Sikorsky to provide extended range for Search & Rescue operations over the open sea. The normal crew consists of a pilot, co-pilot, navigator and flight mechanic, and will often carry a qualified medical crew member on board during actual Search & Rescue missions. The helicopter also has provision for twenty passengers or nine litters. Capable of landing on the water, it is equipped with a special rescue platform that can be extended from the cabin door for the retrieval of disabled survivors. If seas are too rough to land, the hoist can be used to lower a rescue basket, litter or horse collar to pull out survivors. The hoist is also used to deliver dewatering pumps to sinking ships or small radios in order to communicate with vessels in distress. The helicopter can be rigged for external cargo operations by use of a cargo sling and has an enlarged forward cabin door and windows for better search visibility.

Air Station Corpus Christi, Texas

Air detachment Corpus Christi was established on 20 November 1950 and was later redesignated air station Corpus Christi. Today the air station and the Coast Guard Group Office are located together in Hangar 41 at the US Naval air station located at Corpus Christi, Texas. There are presently thirty-one officers and sixty-six aviation enlisted personnel assigned. The Commander of the USCG Group also serves as Commanding Officer of the air station. Following extensive personnel and equipment changes in the operations department, the Group became fully operational on 15 October 1980. The air station now operates as one of thirteen Coast Guard Group units between Port O'Connor, Texas and the Mexican border. Operations is manned twenty-four hours a day with personnel trained to handle all Coast Guard missions.

Among the many missions handled by the air station, Search & Rescue missions always have the highest priority. It maintains the twenty-four-hour capability to launch quickly an HH-65A *Dolphin* helicopter or a HU-25A *Guardian* fanjet and the station averages over four hundred rescue cases a year. Currently on inventory are three of the Aerospatiale HH-65A helicopters and three HU-25A aircraft. Typical rescue missions include searches for overdue vessels, assisting boats which are on fire, sinking or disabled, and medical evacuations from offshore oil rigs and vessels.

Aircrews frequently fly throughout the Group area on many missions other than Search & Rescue, including Marine Environmental Protection, Federal fisheries law enforcement and drug interdiction. Crews enforce Federal fisheries laws by flying frequent patrols throughout the 200 mile US fisheries conservation zone and close co-ordination is maintained with the air station's resident special agent from the National Marine Fisheries Service. Marine drug interdiction is a joint mission of the air station with other Federal agencies and the vessels assigned to the Group. Aircraft and crews frequently deploy on temporary duty (TDY) outside the South Texas area as far as Florida and the Caribbean to work with other Coast Guard units on law enforcement missions.

Transition from the earlier HH-52A *Seaguard* helicopter to the new HH-65A took place during the spring of 1986. With these impressive new helicopters the air station will be able to accomplish its many missions with greater speed and efficiency.

Air Station Detroit, Selfridge Air National Guard Base, Michigan

The air rescue capabilities of the Great Lakes Coast Guard were expanded in 1965 when $500,000 was appropriated for construction of a second air station at Detroit. Located at the Selfridge US Air Force base in Mount Clemons, Michigan, the new station was to be equipped with three gas-turbine amphibious helicopters. Officially known as the Sikorsky HH-52A *Seaguard,* these helicopters were designed to fly 190 miles, pick up an injured person either by using a rescue hoist or by landing on the water and to return to base with a safe margin of fuel remaining. The air station officially opened on 1 June 1966 under the command of Commander James W Sanson USCG. The original complement for the station was ten officers and twenty-nine enlisted men. During the period from July 1966 to July 1974 air station Detroit was credited with saving 330 lives.

Today air station Detroit is an integral part of the Coast Guard's National Search & Rescue effort. The unit comes under the operational control of the 9th Coast Guard District with HQ in Cleveland, Ohio the 9th being responsible for all Coast Guard activities in the Great Lakes. Manned by fourteen officers and thirty-one enlisted men, the unit maintains a twenty-four-hour Search & Rescue alert readiness posture; the unit's area of responsibility covers Lakes St Clair, Ontario and Erie in their entirety, and Lake Huron south of the 44th parallel. In Search & Rescue emergencies, these boundaries are not recognized and assistance is rendered to any persons in peril, regardless of location.

In addition to Search & Rescue operations, air station Detroit supports the thirty-two Coast Guard units and five major vessels in the Eastern Great Lakes Region. This support consists of ice reconnaissance flights for the winter navigation season, law enforcement patrols, marine environmental flights and logistic support. The air station also co-operates closely with the US and Canadian government agencies on the federal, state or provincial and local levels.

Air Station Elizabeth City, North Carolina

Located on the Pasquotank River in the rural Albermarle region of North Carolina, air station Elizabeth City has provided over forty-eight years of service to both the community and the Coast Guard. Following its commissioning on 15 August 1940, the air station was under US Navy control during World War II and performed Search & Rescue as well as anti-submarine warfare duties. Since World War II the air station has become one of the largest in the service, and boasts the distinction of having the only Airport Control Tower manned by Coast Guard personnel.

Today, aircraft flown by the station include three Sikorsky HH-3F *Pelican* helicopters, five HC-130H *Hercules,* and on VC-4A *Gulfstream* I. Station missions include Search & Rescue, Law enforcement surveillance, marine environmental protection, International ice patrol and Atlantic Strike Team transport. Area coverage ranges from the Eastern Seaboard from Canada to the Caribbean. Elizabeth City also serves as the Coast Guard's primary maintenance and aircrew standardization unit for the Lockheed C-130.

In Fiscal Year 1982 the air station flew 2,260 sorties, logging 5,340 accident free flight hours. As a result the unit was credited with thirty-five lives saved, 265 persons assisted and more than $7,342,000 worth of property protected. In addition, Law enforcement surveillance missions led to the seizure of more than a hundred tons of contraband. In Fiscal Year 1983 the air station's operational capabilities were enhanced by the arrival of the three new HU-25A *Guardian*

Houston. Being a lodger unit with NASA at Ellington Field, Houston, Texas, the US Coast Guard air station aviators are on constant exercise with their astronaut compatriots. With NASA aircraft and vehicles in the background, three Houston based HH-52A helicopters show their skill at formation flying. (USCG)

aircraft, making the unit one of the largest and busiest in Coast Guard aviation.

In 1938 the Coast Guard came to Elizabeth City, the agricultural center of a serene section of Eastern North Carolina. While the station was primarily intended to be a major overhaul center for the eastern seaboard, the location was selected because of its potential strategic importance in regard to possible enemy in time of war. In a sheltered area north of the Albermarle Sound and sixty miles from Cape Hatteras, the station was built on what had been the Old Hollowell Plantation along the sloping banks of the Pasquotank River. When the station was officially opened on 15 August 1940 it had barracks, mess hall, hangar, four runways and a seaplane ramp. The base covered 249 acres.

Remaining under Coast Guard control until World War II, the station developed and expanded its Search & Rescue operations. In 1942 the Coast Guard and its facilities were placed under the command of the US Navy for the war effort. The war years were a time of expansion and renovation for the air station. Additional land was purchased, new buildings erected and one of the four runways was extended. One of the most important additions was the construction of an aircraft modification center by the Consolidated Aircraft Corporation for making modifications to aircraft sold to the United Kingdom for use in World War II. When the war was over, the air station with all its additions was returned to the Coast Guard who wasted no time in putting the station back into operation on a larger scale.

Using the buildings, supplies and aircraft modification center left behind by the US Navy, the Coast Guard established the Aircraft Repair and Supply Center. The responsibilities of this new unit grew to include not only the maintenance and supply of all Coast Guard aviation units and their aircraft but for the training of personnel in almost all aviation related fields. Between 1964 and 1968 the entire complex underwent renovation. A multi-million dollar runway was built and many older buildings were renovated. In 1973 the complex welcomed a fourth unit of command, the Atlantic Strike Force. Elizabeth City was an ideal residence for the fledgling strike force, one of three Coast Guard units forming the basis for the US National Strike Force. Their mission, designated by Congress, is national environmental control. Backed with the support of air transport by the air station, the highly trained specialists of the Atlantic Strike Team can provide on the scene coordination for marine pollution problems and incidents anywhere along America's Atlantic coastline. The Atlantic Strike Team has been consolidated with the Gulf Strike Team at Mobile, Alabama.

The Coast Guard Aviation Technical Training Center was established at Elizabeth City in 1978. The AVTECH TRACEN has consolidated four of the five basic Class A schools for aviation training under one command. The training center also provides Class C school training on numerous types of specialized equipment.

With the closing of the Coast Guard's air stations in Argentia, Newfoundland, and Bermuda in July 1966, the air station at Elizabeth City assumed their duties. This consolidation of facilities, whilst increasing the air station's complement of men by approximately sixty-five and aircraft by two Lockheed C-130s, resulted in an overall saving to the Coast Guard of approximately $14m. The primary mission of the air station is Search & Rescue, with an equal amount of activity in the area of logistics. The Search & Rescue zone of responsibility extends along the Atlantic coast from southern North Carolina to Northern Maryland, well inland and for hundreds of miles out into the ocean.

With the extended range and endurance capabilities of the C-130 aircraft, the air station is often called upon to send an aircraft as far north as Argentia, Newfoundland, south to San Juan, Puerto Rico, or west to Texas. The logistics missions are basically cargo supply and passenger flights, extending from the European countries to Alaska, Hawaii and the Far East. In 1967 the International Ice Patrol aircraft began operating from the air station at Elizabeth City. This patrol, extending from about mid-February through early July, requires the continuous deployment of one of the C-130 aircraft to Argentia, Newfoundland, on a weekly basis. At one time the C-130 and crew plus maintenance personnel were on temporary duty (TDY) to Newfoundland for thirty day periods. In addition to the Ice Patrol in the Atlantic the air station also flew the Bering Sea patrol out of Alaska during the summer of 1967. In January 1967 the old familiar Douglas EC-54 *Skymaster* was replaced by the much improved EC-130 *Hercules* for use in LORAN calibration missions. These flights, several a year, span the entire globe and crew and aircraft are away from home for as much as two months at a time. Other routine patrols requiring many flight hours each month flown by the air station include the fish and wildlife survey flights for the Bureau of Commerical Fisheries and the oil pollution patrols working in conjunction with the Army Corps of Engineers. To accomplish these extraordinarily varied missions requires many well-trained men and readily available aircraft.

The log of the United States Coast Guard Air Station, Elizabeth City, North Carolina, under the temporary command of W B Scheibel, Lieutenant, USCG, Thursday 15 August 1940, reads:

0800: Colors. Officially commissioned station and advised Commander, Norfolk District, by dispatch (151430). Carried out morning routine. Crew engaged in work about station in connection with cleaning and preparing to receive aircraft.

1155: Sea plane V183. Pilot McWilliams, arrived from Cape May Patrol. Detachment under authority of H/L 30 July 1940 (OP-601).

W P SCHEIBEL
Lieutenant

This is an exact copy of the first entry in the official log of Elizabeth City air station. Lieutenant Scheibel was the acting Commanding Officer, and the only officer present for the commissioning. Lieutenant A J DeJoy and Lieutenant (jg) C R Bender arrived later in the day. Two chiefs and fifty enlisted men completed the station complement. Three more aircraft, a Hall PH-2 seaplane, a Grumman J2F amphibian from Cape May and a J2K Fairchild landplane from Charleston arrived later on commissioning day. The first arrival, V183 was a Hall PH-3 seaplane. The following day a second Fairchild J2K was flown up from Charleston and Lieutenant Burke, who was appointed Commanding Officer of the new station, flew in from Cape May in a Hall seaplane.

Coast Guard Aircraft Repair and Supply Center Elizabeth City, North Carolina

In the 1930s, aeronautical supply support for the Coast Guard was achieved by the individual air stations requisitioning from the US Navy or by purchasing direct from aircraft manufacturers. During World War II the air stations continued the pre-war supply support concept with larger reliance on the US Navy, since the Coast Guard was then operating mostly Navy type aircraft such as the OS2U *Kingfisher,* PBM *Mariner* and PBY *Catalina.* With the end of World War II and the subsequent reduction from 150,000 to about 20,000 men, Coast Guard air stations were also reduced, leaving their shelves and storerooms heavily stocked with materials in excess of their needs. The idea of a central aviation supply center for the Coast Guard was first conceived in 1945 and in the following year Elizabeth City was established and today is fully computerized to plan for the future needs of the organization.

Although the idea for a central supply and overhaul unit for Coast Guard was conceived in early 1945, it was not until the end of World War II that locations became available for an activity of this type. Among those available for consideration was the plant on Coast Guard property located at Elizabeth

City, North Carolina, which had been constructed for the Consolidated Vultee Aircraft Corporation by the US Navy. It was designed and used as a modification center for Lend-Lease aircraft being delivered to the Allies and had been closed down as soon as World War II ended. Elizabeth City had been for some time the nerve center of Coast Guard aeronautical activity so the Consolidated plant was selected as the logical location.

In April 1946 a small complement of officers and men were stationed as a sub-unit of the air station for the purpose of establishing the Coast Guard Aircraft Repair and Supply Base. After nine months of concentrated effort, the unit was ready to go into operation. On 3 January 1947 it was placed in commission as a headquarters unit with a complement of ten officers and sixty-three men. Although the supply function of the unit began immediately, it was not until October 1948 that the aircraft overhaul programme first produced results when a re-worked Grumman J4F *Widgeon* was delivered. It was then that the first civilian employees were used to supplement the military personnel.

During May 1964 the Aircraft Repair and Supply Base (ARSB) was re-named Aircraft Repair and Supply Center (ARSC). The fifty-five-acre site includes two large hangars, a workshop and offices, a small hangar used for aircraft maintenance training and several frame buildings. There is a paint hangar and the units which occupy other buildings and hangars include the Repair Division's Industrial Machine Shop, the Support Center Public Works Division, the Warehouse-Management Information Services-Avionics Shop complex and Aviation Repair Division shops.

The overhaul, repair and modification programme at ARSC, also referred to as the rework programme, has included overhaul of fifteen different types of aircraft and modification of about five others. The rework is mainly accomplished by the Aviation Repair Division, with the support of the other divisions within ARSC. In 1973 the modification portion of the programme was placed under the Aviation Engineering Division. From 1948 to 1953 the types of aircraft overhauled included the J4F *Widgeon*, JRF *Goose*, PBY *Catalina*, PBM *Mariner*, OY *Sentinel*, HO3S (S-51), HTL (Bell 47), HO4S (S-55) and UF or HU-16E *Albatross*. By 1954 there had been established a continuing overhaul line for the UF and the HO4S, with occasional overhauls of PBMs continuing. As the number of different types of aircraft in the Coast Guard inventory declined, the types being overhauled were also reduced. In 1955 and early 1956 seven JRFs were overhauled with a decrease in the number of UF and HO4S. During this time, four JRB *Expeditors*, a Douglas R4D, a PB1G *Flying Fortress* and two Martin RM-1Z or VC-3A aircraft were overhauled.

Since late 1958 the programme has consisted almost entirely of Grumman HU-16E *Albatross* and helicopter overhauls, the HU-16E being phased out in August 1979. Other types of aircraft have been overhauled sporadically, specifically the C-123 *Provider* and an RM-1Z during the 1960/61 period. In 1964 the first Sikorsky HH-52A *Seaguard* was inducted and a transition from Sikorsky HO4S or HH-19 to the HH-52A overhaul was made. In 1970 the first Sikorsky HH-3F *Pelican* was inducted, the overhaul programme building up to about fifteen HH-52A and twelve HH-3F overhauls a year. With the phasing out of the HH-52A the emphasis is now on overhauls of the new HU-25A *Guardian* and the HH-65A *Dolphin*. Over the years the drop in maintenance has been conducted on all the aircraft including a Programmed Depot Maintenance (PDM) programme on the Convair HC-131 aircraft which commenced in March 1980.

In addition to aircraft overhaul, a number of electronic modifications and prototype installations have been made. In 1960 the provision of APS-42 radar in the C-123 was accomplished. This included a significant structural modification, as the blunt nose of the C-123 was replaced by the bulbous

Fairchild C-119 *Flying Boxcar* radome. Major modification of the Lockheed EC-130E *Hercules* electronic equipment was also accomplished at Elizabeth City. In addition, other types such as the R5D *Skymaster* have been modified.

Aircraft components as well as aircraft themselves are overhauled. Parts are occasionally manufactured when this is more economical than buying outside or when these parts are difficult to obtain. An example of this is the fabrication of compound curature windows and floorboards for helicopters. Components overhauled include generators, magnetos, and other electrical items, auxilary servos, primary servos, main gear boxes, hand pump selector valves, main rotor heads, instruments of all type and avionics equipment. ARSC also has a complete engine rework and repair facility which ranges from the Allison engines for the C-130 to the General Electric engines for the HH-3F helicopter.

The Aviation Engineering Division comprises about forty highly qualified engineers and technicians who provide technical support for the entire Coast Guard aviation community. A technical services branch reviews all incoming technical data for Coast Guard applicability and provides high priority

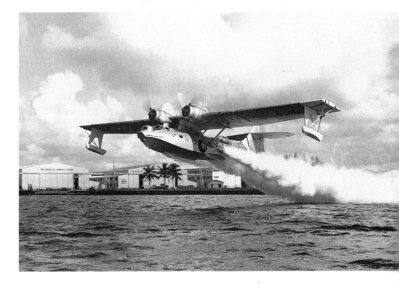

Miami. A Consolidated PBY-5 *Catalina* makes an impressive take-off using JATO bottles for departure from the Miami air station in Florida during September 1949, in answer to an emergency call. First entering Coast Guard service in 1941, the *Catalina* was finally retired in mid-1954, with as many as 114 in service during 1945. (USCG)

technical assistance, particularly to air stations. Services include response to field questions on all aspects of aircraft maintenance, liaison with civilian contractors and government agencies, technical research for maintenance and supply actions, investigating and documenting problems with maintenance and equipment and preparing interim time compliance technical orders (TCTOs) and other urgent information. To assist in these responsibilities, manufacturers' technical representatives for Coast Guard aircraft and engines currently on inventory are assigned to the staff.

A projects branch is a descendant of the prototype branch, which was created in 1957. The branch prepared the prototype design for converting US Air Force SA-16s to Coast Guard UF or HU-16 and has made major changes in the Douglas R5D, Sikorsky HO4s, HH-52A, HH-3F, Lockheed C-130 and the Convair HC-131. It prepares and provides the TCTOs for aircraft modifications. The role was expanded to include preliminary engineering, prototype, kit design, and technical writing for major projects as well as some field team installations.

The support branch provides services concerned mainly with publications and documentation, including technical writing, drafting and photography. It maintains the Master Technical Library, helps to co-ordinate publication changes, generates supplements to major technical orders, provides pre-publication technical reviews for ARSC generated technical documents, and assists in the co-ordination of many projects and investigations. A quality assurance branch has the primary objective assuring that a quality product is put out by ARSC. Its inspectors cover all phases of the ARSC overhaul and repair facility, assigning highly experienced and motivated personnel to keep defects in the finished product to a minimum. Products procured from manufacturers are inspected to assure that manufacturing specifications are met, as are kits designed and assembled by ARSC.

An Aviation Supply Division provides aviation material support for all Coast Guard air stations as well as Comptroller services to all Elizabeth City USCG units. In the 1930s, aeronautical supply support for the Coast Guard was achieved by the individual air stations requisitioning either

Mobile. Sikorsky HH-52A *Seaguard* 1428 from Mobile air station, finished in scarlet, seen parked on the deck of the US Coast Guard cutter *Glacier*, appropriately marked 'GCC Glacier', on operations in either Arctic or Antarctic waters. (USCG)

from the US Navy or by purchasing from aircraft manufacturers and aeronautical equipment vendors. This individual supply effort continued until 1946 when a central aviation supply activity for the USCG was conceived. The latest innovation is the Closed Loop Aeronautical Support System (CLASS) which monitors the location and condition of high value avionics parts on the medium range search (MRS) and short range recovery (SRR) aircraft. An allowance of over a hundred military and civilian personnel provides a prompt, reliable and economic supply support to the expanding Coast Guard aircraft fleet and is accomplished with the most modern equipment and management techniques.

Over the years the engineers and technical experts at ARSC have watched with great interest the evaluation of new types such as the Israeli Westwind, Sabre 75A, Fanjet Falcon, Cessna Citation, the Learjet and the British manufactured Hawker Siddeley HS 125-600 and HS 748. Many types of helicopters were evaluated prior to the HH-65A *Dolphin* being adopted. Looking back they can pride themselves in the many unique conversions completed, such as the conversion of the Grumman HU-16E to Coast Guard requirements, electronics conversions, the Sikorsky HO4S *Tugbird,* which enabled this helicopter to tow ships, and modifications to Coast Guard helicopters for involvement in the huge NASA Gemini Missions for the retrieving of capsules and astronauts from space.

Aviation Technical Training Center, Elizabeth City

The Coast Guard's residential Aviation Technical Training Center opened on 4 August 1978. Beginning with its first

graduates in 1979 through 1980, entry level training was provided through four A schools: Aviation electronics technicians, Aviation electricians' mates, Aviation structural mechanics and Aviation machinists' mates. With the addition in 1981 of an Aviation survivalman A school, the training center reached its full complement of entry level training for the five USCG aviation rates. By its seventh year the center had graduated 2,502 Third Class Petty Officers in these rates. In 1978 Commander George Kriejmeyer and his Executive Officer, Lieutenant Commander F R Tardiff, with a staff of eighty-five introduced the center made up of an administrative division, education specialists, graphic arts division, computer added training, training division officers, Chiefs and military instructors.

This training center is also responsible for developing second generation training for the HH-65A *Dolphin* helicopter and from its inception has provided advanced aviation training through C schools as needed by the Coast Guard. Currently this training covers the ADL-81 LORAN C receiver, various radar units, aviation engineering administration covering logs and records, HU-25A *Guardian* airframe, digital microprocessing, HH-3F *Pelican* automatic flight control and selected electrical maintenance, high reliability soldering, HU-25A avionics and electrical, engine maintenance on the T58-5, T56 and T58-8B engines, to name just a handful of the variety of aviation aspects covered.

Aircraft Program Office, Grand Prairie, Texas

The Coast Guard Aircraft Program Office in Grand Prairie, Texas, was officially established on 17 August 1979 under the operational control of Coast Guard HQ in Washington DC, as a result of the Short Range Recovery helicopter procurement contract for the HH-65A *Dolphin* being awarded to Aerospatiale Helicopter Corporation. The facilities that now house the Coast Guard offices were officially dedicated on 6 September 1980.

This Aircraft Program Office is dedicated to and responsible for the proper administration of this major acquisition contract. The mission primarily requires verification of the contractor's work, testing and acceptance of the ninety-six aircraft ordered, supervision of the maintenance training for Coast Guard personnel and ensuring adequate initial spare parts provisioning to field units. Staffed with nine officers, sixteen enlisted and two civilian personnel, the APO is also responsible for the development and testing of various HH-65A related equipment projects and acts as the HH-65A prime unit, monitoring field maintenance practices.

On 14 November 1984 the first HH-65A *Dolphin* helicopter was accepted by the Coast Guard, and was initially assigned to the APO as a training and support aircraft. The first stations to be equipped included the air stations at Mobile, Alabama, New Orleans, Louisiana, Borinquen, Puerto Rico and Miami, Florida. The plan was to implement sixteen additional Coast Guard air stations by late 1988.

Air Station Houston, Ellington Field, Texas

Located at Ellington Air Force base, some seventeen miles south-east of downtown Houston, air station Houston was commissioned on 23 December 1963 with a complement of seven officers, eighteen enlisted men and initially two Sikorsky HH-52A *Seaguard* helicopters. Right up until its actual opening at Ellington there was a strong possibility that the air station would be located at Scholes Field, Galveston, Texas. The commanding officer was Commander David W Defreest. During 1964 the station assisted the Texas Department of Health in battling an encephalitis epidemic in the Houston area, with the HH-52A helicopters dropping more than 10,000 lbs of insecticide.

Being adjacent the NASA astronauts facility at Ellington, the Gemini astronauts were repeatedly hoisted by Coast Guard helicopters from the station for practice in getting out of the capsule at sea. In September 1965 two helicopters and crews from the air station were deployed to New Orleans in Louisiana to assist in the rescue of victims stranded by Hurricane Betsy.

Two years later, in September 1967, in the south-east Texas region, the two HH-52A helicopters rescued 451 persons from rooftops, treetops and other perilous places during and after Hurricane Beulah. Since 1963 the air station helicopters and crews have been activated more than eight times to rescue people endangered by hurricanes. Locations include Gulfport, Mississippi, in 1969, Brownsville, Texas, in 1978 and Corpus Christi in 1980.

A third HH-52A helicopter was assigned to the air station during 1974. In August 1975 the 734 foot British tanker *Globtik Sun* rammed an unmanned oil rig in the Gulf of Mexico with the result that both caught fire. The Houston helicopters searched for missing crewmen and were involved in pollution patrols, also providing transportation for the injured to hospitals. With increased shipboard deployments for law enforcement the air station received a fourth HH-52A during 1978, with helicopters being deployed for approximately twenty-one weeks annually. During May 1979 the *Ranger 1* drilling platform collapsed twelve miles south of Galveston resulting in the Coast Guard searching for survivors.

Some weeks later, in July 1979, the air station helicopters flew flood relief missions in the Harris and Galveston counties following tropical storm *Claudette*. In November 1979 the tanker *Burmah Agate*, carrying sixteen million gallons of oil, and the freighter *Momosa* collided off Galveston. Houston air station helicopters rescued twenty-seven crewmen from the burning vessels and flew over 115 hours on pollution flights and during the search for thirty-one missing crewmen. The *Burmah Agate* burnt for sixty-nine days. During the huge Cuban refugee exodus in 1980 helicopters and crews were deployed to south Florida to assist other Coast Guard and US government units. USCG personnel assigned to these deployments were awarded the Humanitarian Service Medal.

In August 1983 Hurricane *Alicia* devastated the Galveston and Houston area. Air station Houston weathered the storm with two helicopters hangared and a third deployed to the Coast Guard cutter *Valiant* and half the crew on board. Post storm flights and aids to navigation (ATON) surveys totalled fifty-two flight hours. Station reconstruction after the hurricane extended over several months afterwards.

Unit awards to air station Houston up to 1983 and involving incidents already mentioned included three Coast Guard Meritorious Unit Commendations with Operational Distinguishing Devices.

In Fiscal year 1985 the air station flew over 2,540 hours in support of Search & Rescue, enforcement of laws and treaties, training and other various missions. Whilst maintaining one HH-52A on Bravo Zulu — thirty minutes notice — at all times, the helicopters were launched on 212 Search & Rescue cases, accumulating over 474 hours. The Search & Rescue area covers approximately 200 miles of shoreline from the eastern edge of Matagorda Bay, Texas, to the Calcasieu River in Louisiana. The increase in offshore petroleum and fishing activity, along with the growth in recreational boating, tends to substantiate projections of expansion of the demands that will be placed on the air station and its resources.

Late in 1977 the air station was presented with a new challenge with law enforcement deployments aboard 8th Coast Guard District 210 foot medium endurance cutters. There was an average of eight deployments a year, each being approximately twenty-four days long and involving two pilots and three aircrewmen. The air station also supports aids to navigation (ATON), Port Safety and Security and various other tasks as required.

The air station is situated on just over an acre of land on Ellington air base, with two main buildings comprising a

North Bend. Sikorsky HH-52A *Seaguard* helicopter 1373 from North Bend air station, Oregon, seen on exercise with a locally based US Coast Guard vessel. The beautiful Oregon coastline is wild, with wooded landscape and treacherous inlets feeding into the Pacific. (USCG)

24,000 square foot hangar, constructed in 1942, and an administrative building, constructed in 1943. In the spring of 1987 the air station moved to a new $5m 40,000 square foot new hangar complex. This new facility is located on property purchased by the Coast Guard near the Houston Army Aviation Support Facility, at the north end of Ellington Field. On 1 April 1976 Ellington Air Force base was decommissioned, and on 1 July 1984 Ellington Field reverted to the control of the City of Houston, which is now responsible for essential services such as maintenance and operation of the control tower, runways and related areas, NAVAIDS and crash and fire services.

Air Station Humboldt Bay, McKinleyville, California

Commissioned in June 1977 and with two HH-65A *Dolphin* helicopters now assigned, the mission of air station Humboldt Bay and the US Coast Guard group is to operate shore stations, floating units and aircaft in support of USCG missions and serve as an integral part of the operating forces of the 11th Coast Guard District with HQ in Long Beach. The air station has a primary mission of Search & Rescue, secondary missions including aerial support for aids to navigation, law enforcement and marine environmental protection.

The air station and Group Office are located at the Arcata/Eureka airport in McKinleyville. The cities of Arcata and Eureka lie adjacent to each other on the north and south ends of Humboldt Bay respectively. The cities are located about 250 miles north of San Francisco and about eighty miles south of the Oregon border.

Today at Arcata/Eureka airport in the County of Humboldt, some 217 feet elevation above sea level, stands a memorial to the crew of Sikorsky HH-52A 1363 which crashed on 22 December 1964 whilst attempting to land flood victims at Arcata airport. It happened in that last heroic mission during the storm that deluged all of north-western California and four civilians on board were killed along with the USCG helicopter crew. The pilot was Lieutenant Donald L Prince USCG — the co-pilot was Sub Lieutenant Allen L Alltree of the Canadian Navy who was based with the Coast Guard on an exchange programme. Crewman was Aviation Electrician's Mate AE2 James A Nininger Jr USCG.

The helicopter and crew had flown earlier missions and, guided by radar from the airport at Arcata, had plucked twenty persons from the storm ravaged country and flown them to safety. They took off again, and were returning with four more refugees when the HH-52A disappeared from the radar screens. It was Tuesday before Christmas. The full story of their heroic exploits may never be known because all aboard the helicopter died in the crash, in rugged country twenty miles north of Eureka.

Woodsmen guided from the air by a US Navy helicopter reached the crash scene four days later on 26 December, and reported the helicopter demolished and all aboard dead.

Air Station Los Angeles, California

The Coast Guard air station Los Angeles is located on the south side of the huge Los Angeles International Airport. It was founded in August 1962 through the combined efforts of the Los Angeles Chamber of Commerce and US Congressional leaders. Operations at the air station began in earnest with the arrival of the first Sikorsky HO4S- helicopter on 28 August 1962. With a complement of nine officers and twenty enlisted men, the task of saving lives and property was in full swing by its commissioning on 15 November 1962.

From its beginning in 1962, the air station at Los Angeles has grown to a personal allowance of fifteen officers and thirty-one enlisted men supporting the three Sikorsky HH-52A *Seaguard* helicopters. The new Aerospatiale HH-65A *Dolphin* helicopters have replaced the HH-52As. In this respect the air station has been undergoing modernization in many areas in anticipation of the arrival of the new helicopters.

Search & Rescue is considered the primary mission of the air station. However, this unit supports a myriad of other missions which include Marine Environmental Protection, enforcement of Pacific laws and treaties, general law enforcement, which includes support for other agencies, Aids to Navigation and the training of air station personnel. During the Fiscal year 1983 the unit logged 2,392 total flight hours with 263 Search & Rescue cases.

The southern boundary of the operating area is Dana Point, which is also the northern boundary for air station San Diego for Search & Rescue response. The northern boundary is the Santa Maria River. The islands which lie within the Search & Rescue operations area are San Clemente, Santa Catalina, San Nicolas, Santa Barbara, Anacapa, Santa Cruz, Santa Rosa and San Miguel. The Channel Islands, the last four named, are in Santa Barbara County and Anacapa is a wild life sanctuary. The US Navy controls the islands of San Clemente and San Nicolas. The Pacific Missile Test Centre headquarters is located at the Naval air station at Point Mugu. The test range controls the airspace offshore from Point Mugu and over the Channel Islands. Vandenburg Air Force base, located near the northern operating boundary, controls the airspace offshore from Point Conception and is part of the Pacific Missile Test Centre. It is also the Western US site for the space shuttle launches which commenced in late 1985.

The air station aircraft often deploy on board USCG cutters in support of law enforcement missions. The number of deployments per year varies with an average of between ten and twelve with an average duration of about fourteen days.

It was during August 1969 that I was invited to attend a briefing on the air station at Los Angeles, this being coordinated by Lieutenant T E Omri of the USCG Public Information office attached to the 11th Coast Guard District in Long Beach. After a briefing plus a Sikorsky film, *Flying Lifeboat*, depicting the HH-52A *Seaguard* given by Commander Paul W Tifft, Commanding Officer of the air station, word was received from USCG HQ in Washington DC that authorization for a flight in the HH-52A had been received. A simulated practice take-off for a Search & Rescue mission in HH-52A 1400 soon had the engines heated and we were airborne flying low across the great runway complex of the Los Angeles International Airport. We headed south towards Long Beach harbor with its huge network of bridges, docks, and the US Navy yard. Being mid-week I could not help but notice the thousands of small craft tied up safely in the many marinas, small craft which would be out at sea every weekend, requiring the watchful eye of the patrolling Coast Guard helicopter. An autorotation into Long Beach harbor demonstrated the versatility of the Sikorsky helicopter, and its pilots. As we headed further south the coastline became more distinct, rocky and beautiful, and our destination was the USCG base at Terminal Island.

La Isla de la Culebra de Cascabel, the Island of the Snakes of the Rattle, was so named as a warning to anyone who ventured upon its sandy wastes because it was infested with many reptiles. The Yankees applied the venomous sounding name, Rattlesnake Island. In 1891 the name was changed to Terminal Island and the snakes were exterminated. La Isla de Muerto, or Dead Man's Island, adjacent to but not connecting with Terminal Island, was a sandstone block rising about thirty-five feet above the water. In 1916, Dead Man's Island was transferred to US government ownership. During 1928, in order to widen the main channel, the removal of Dead Man's Island was started and the material deposited along a jetty connecting it with Terminal Island to form Reservation Point.

Reservation Point extends from the north boundaries of the Federal Prison and the present Coast Guard Industrial compound to the south tip of Terminal Island. This area was constructed by the US Army Corps of Engineers in 1930. Its present occupants include the Federal Correctional Institution, the Coast Guard base, Immigration & Naturalization Service offices and a quarantine station. While the land which made the Point was permitted to settle, a lighthouse and the quarters of its keeper were its only occupant. During World War II however, the land was given to the US Navy and a brig, temporary barracks and other buildings were erected. It was after the war that the brig was converted into a medium security Federal Prison and a Coast Guard buoy depot was erected on the site of the present industrial compound. Construction of the boat basin began in 1950 and the present barracks and administrative building were built a year later.

Functions of the USCG base were increased to their present scope in 1956 with the transfer to this site of the Coast Guard moorings formerly located in San Pedro. The base consists of several compounds which includes moorings for the USCG cutters *Heather* and *Morris,* as well as storerooms for these vessels. Coast Guard 82-footers, 40-footers, 64-footers and 95-footers berth at the boat basin. The combined mission of the USCG base is that of a service function supporting the 11th Coast Guard District though logistics, field personnel, construction and repair. It has operational and maintenance responsibility for certain Aids to Navigation in the district. The supply function of the base is in most respects similar to the operational mission of a supply depot. At the time of my visit some fifty-five enlisted men and seven officers were stationed on the base, plus transient personnel and around twenty-three civilians. Lunch in the ward room can be highly recommended.

Air Station Miami, Florida

In June 1932 air station Miami was commissioned at Dinner Key on Biscayne Bay and thus became the first contemporary aviation unit in the Coast Guard. Since then it has evolved into the busiest air sea rescue unit in the world. The unit moved to Opa Locka airport, its present location, during 1965. The new station was commissioned on 20 November 1965 and its location at the airport has afforded needed room for continued growth.

On the sandy shores of south-east Florida lies bustling sun-drenched Miami. In the past few decades Miami has risen in commercial importance to become the Gateway to the Caribbean. Here the lucrative tourist trade offers daily departures to the tropics. The many inter-island shipping lines make regular voyages to the Caribbean laden with supplies to support the native islanders and the inbound tourists. Many major and small airlines are also claiming their share of the business by flying passengers and cargoes to the islands. In addition to the large fleet of fishing boats, Miami also ranks as one of the pleasure boat capitals of the world, with recreational sailing and power boating being a year-round source of enjoyment. Just offshore is the hub of shipping for the West Indies. It is here that the Gulf Stream, the Santaren Channel, the Old Bahama Channel and the Yucatan Channel meet.

With all this activity, both commercial and private, comes a variety of vessel and aircraft mishaps, MEDEVACS, pollution incidents and other predicaments. Also, Miami's close proximity to Latin American countries presents an ever increasing problem of illicit drug traffic. It is no small wonder then that the role of the Coast Guard in Miami has increased in importance. There is a great need for the services of the Coast Guard and it continues to expand to meet this need. Nowhere has this expansion been more evident than at the USCG air station Miami. The original air station was located at Dinner Key in the southeast corner of Coconut Grove. From there the unit competed perilously with the boating traffic in Biscayne Bay operating the HU-16E *Albatross* and the HH-52A *Seaguard* helicopter. Hence the need to move.

Geographically, air station Miami is located fifteen miles northwest of downtown Miami in the northern-most section of Dade County. Like most other USCG air stations it became a tenant on an already-established field. Opa Locka was originally built as a US Naval air station during World War II to be used, among other things, as a blimp base. After World War II the US Navy moved out and left the facilities to the US Marine Corps. The base remained with the USMC until 1957 when it became a US Naval Air Reserve facility. It was then that the airport became Opa Locka under the control of the Dade County Airport Authority. In 1965 the Coast Guard moved in as one of the major tenants. Today, along with the Coast Guard, there are several flying schools, charter services and aircraft maintenance facilities at the airport. Due to increased interest in private flying during the middle-sixties, Opa Locka became the second busiest airport in the USA. Today it is the eighth busiest in the US.

The mission of Opa Locka is much like that of any other USCG air station, primarily Search & Rescue. The station's responsibility stretches west into the Gulf of Mexico, as far east as the outer Bahama Islands and south to Jamaica, Puerto Rico and the Virgin Islands. In fact searches often require aircraft to operate out of the airports at Curacao, Antigua, Martinique and Grenada. Requests for assistance in these areas is normally initiated through US consulates to Commander, Greater Antilles Section. Even though a great deal of time is spent on Search & Rescue there are also routine Marine Environmental Protection patrols which are made almost daily depending on aircraft availability. Local patrols on inland waters, harbors, and coastal waters are made with helicopters, while long-range patrols are made with the HU-25A *Guardian* aircraft. The long-range patrols cover most of the Florida coastline extending from Jacksonville to the Dry Tortugas and up the west coast to St Petersburg.

A third facet of the USCG mission which is claiming an increasing amount of time and resources is that of law enforcement. The air station has a helicopter deployed almost continually on one 7th Coast Guard District cutter or a visiting cutter from the north. Duties include surveillance of US fishing boats operating near Bahamian waters, the location and identification of boats in support of the aggressive Safety and Documentation Boarding Programme and the prevention of illegal drug traffic. The helicopter has frequently assisted in apprehending violators.

The air station aircraft are supported and operated by a complement of approximately sixty officers and between 180 and 200 enlisted men and women. Typical Search & Rescue cases might include the parachute delivery of a dewatering pump to a sinking fishing boat, hoisting survivors of a small aircraft which ditched at sea or performing a medical evacuation (MEDEVAC) of a seriously injured diver from the Bahamas. Miami personnel are justly proud of their participation in over six hundred Search & Rescue cases each year. In 1974 this was accomplished by flying 1,050 missions and compiling 2,641 hours of flight time. In the course of

these sorties the station assisted property valued at $57m, assisted 1,008 persons in distress and saved 110 lives. The great majority of the cases involved assistance to lost, disabled, overdue, overturned or sinking vessels. It is through such efforts that air station Miami has gained the reputation and honor of being the busiest Air-Sea Rescue station in the world. The outstanding performance of personnel has often been recognized. The air station was in the spotlight in December 1972 when it responded to the crash of a Boeing 707 in the Everglades. The assistance provided in this case earned the station a Coast Guard Unit Commendation.

The Bermuda Triangle theory is touted by many in explaining numerous cases of lost vessels and aircraft. In reality, the acts of unskilled and unprepared operators, shoal waters, rapid currents and many violent thunderstorms and cold fronts are more valid explanations for these happenings. In fact a combination of these factors were very evident on one notable Sunday afternoon in January 1975. A cold front

Port Angeles. Daily scene of activity at Port Angeles air station in Washington State during the early 1940s, as Grumman JF-2 *Duck* V148 is beached and washed down after a routine patrol. (Gordon S Williams)

was forecast to pass through Miami early in the afternoon. This was a very active front accompanied by numerous showers ahead and behind and strong winds gusting from thirty to fifty miles per hour veering south-west to north-west The information was forecast and frequently updated by commercial and Coast Guard radio and of course available by telephone through the US National Weather Service, Federal Aviation Administration, etc. Moreover a few minutes of surf

San Diego. Aerial view of the slipway at San Diego US Coast Guard air station, California, on 17 June 1958 showing Martin P5M-2 *Marlin* flying boat 1312 being towed by a tractor after beaching. (USCG)

watching on any Miami area beach should have convinced anyone it was a good day to stay home and watch pro football. Nevertheless, air station Miami quickly became involved in some fourteen cases. They included: a man being swept out to sea whilst swimming in-shore along Miami Beach; a Hobie-cat boat rented from a beach concession capsized a quarter of a mile offshore; a single engine aircraft lost on a flight from Bimini to Fort Lauderdale, which turned up at Key Largo after failing to advise the FAA of change in flight plan; three men stranded in a canoe in Biscayne Bay; nine other disabled or capsized small craft.

At 09.05 on 3 September 1975, the air station was notified that a Cessna 172 aircraft with four persons on board had reported engine failure and was ditching in the Atlantic Ocean with its last reported position approximately twenty-five miles west of Freeport, Bahamas. At that time, a HU-16E and a HH-52A were diverted from training missions to proceed and assist. Fortunately, the cutter *Courageous* with an additional HH-52A embarked was engaged in a law enforcement patrol some fifty miles south of the ditching aircraft. The USCG cutter immediately got under way to assist. By 13.00, units involved in the search for the survivors included three HH-52A helicopters, three HU-16E *Albatross* aircraft, three civilian aircraft, and the cutter *Courageous*. By that time the survivors, if any, would have been in the water approximately four hours and were still unlocated.

At 13.37 Aviation Machinist's Mate Second Class Allen V Neuman was scanning the waters below from his search position in the cabin of Grumman HU-16E 7249. Sighting something different from the countless clumps of Sargassum weed he had observed drifting in the Gulf Stream, he launched a smoke float from the open hatch beside him. Keying his microphone, he told the pilot, 'I believe I see people in the water, 9 o'clock position, one-half mile. Smoke float away'. Petty Officer Neuman had, in fact, located the survivors, three men and a woman, all in their 'fifties. Having no life-raft, they had tied all their life jackets together when they abandoned the aircraft, thus insuring that they would not become separated. They were subsequently recovered by the HH-52A from the cutter *Courageous,* and returned to Freeport for a flight to Opa Locka by HU-16E. All were thoroughly chilled but except for a few cuts and bruises in good condition.

Another case, whilst not so dramatic, was equally vital in the saving of a life. At 15.50 on 10 October 1975, the Operations Duty Officer at air station Miami was notified by the Rescue Co-ordination Center (RCC) that the motor vessel *Bolero* had a passenger on board who had suffered a heart attack and was having difficulty breathing. The vessel was located in the Old Bahama Channel near Cuba, some four hundred miles from Miami. Special medications, oxygen and a respirator were urgently needed. A Sikorsky HH-52A was launched immediately to pick up the needed medications from downtown Miami and extra oxygen bottles and a respirator from Homestead Air Force base. Simultaneously, a Sikorsky HH-3F *Pelican* helicopter from air station St Petersburg was launched with still more medical oxygen on board for delivery to the *Bolero*. At 17.10, HU-16E 7228 departed Miami with medicines and oxygen equipment on board for parachute delivery to the motor vessel. The night parachute drop was successfully completed to the medical personnel waiting below. With the subsequent delivery of additional oxygen cylinders by the St Petersburg helicopter, sufficient medical supplies were on hand to preserve the patient's life until the ship's arrival in port.

These two cases illustrate and emphasise the need for close co-ordination with other units and agencies and illustrate the varied nature of aid furnished by air station Miami.

A second area of concentration at Miami is Marine Environmental Protection. During calendar year 1975 the station flew seventy MEP missions with the HU-16E and sixty-four missions with the HH-52A for a combined total of 255 hours. During these pollution patrols the station's aircraft crews spotted fifty-six oil spills on the territorial waters. More importantly, the combination of routine patrols and successful prosecution of violators is an effective deterrent to would be polluters. Probably the most notable pollution case was the major oil spill which occurred in the Florida Keys in July 1975. This spill, which stretched from the Marquesas Islands to Marathon is now a landmark case in Coast Guard MEP history. Through oil sample analysis by the USCG Research & Development Center at Groton, Connecticut, the offending tanker was apprehended four months later after tracking him down. Air station Miami flew numerous sorties during the period of this spill in surveilling its extent as well as flying specialists and equipment to the area.

The other major area of operations centers around law enforcement, a demanding mission which continues to grow in importance in Miami as throughout most USCG air units. In 1973, Rear Admiral Austin C Wagner, the 7th Coast Guard District Commander, began to lay the foundation for a more aggressive and effective law enforcement campaign, especially to inhibit the very lucrative contraband drug commerce. As part of the campaign the air station provided a helicopter for generally one week of a three week cutter patrol. Since its inception the programme has continued to escalate in both duration and area of patrol. Now ships on patrol in the 7th District, which has its HQ in Miami, have a helicopter embarked almost continually as a matter of routine. The major part of the support comes from air station Miami. In 1975 Miami flew 478 law enforcement missions for a total of 1,028 hours. Of these flights, 344 totaling 472 hours were flown from deployed cutters on multi-unit law enforcement patrol (MULEPAT) and surface law enforcement patrol (SURLEPAT).

A noteworthy example of law enforcement took place on 22 July 1975. Sikorsky HH-52A 1466 was operating from the USCG cutter *Diligence* on a routine surveillance flight south-west of San Juan. The pilot, Lieutenant Pennington, located a boat on a south-easterly course seventy-five miles south-west of San Juan. He commenced a normal approach to hover astern the sailing vessel *Double Eagle*. As the helicopter approached, her crew saw people on board the *Double Eagle* throwing several bundles overboard. The helicopter recovered many of these which were later identified as marijuana. The cutter *Diligence,* commanded by Commander S W Geletka, effected a rendezvous and sent a boarding party for inspection. The boat, licensed for pleasure only, was also carrying large quantities of coffee and sugar. The boarding officer arrested the seven persons on board on charges of conspiracy to import controlled substances and carrying contraband. The crew were found guilty and sent to a prison in Puerto Rico to await sentence.

The air station at Miami at Opa Locka is one of several that I have visited over the years. The commanding officer at the time was Captain Arthur E Ladley Jr and the unit was equipped with seven HU-16E aircraft and five HH-52A helicopters. Excluding the Coast Guard aviation training center at Mobile, Alabama, Miami is the largest of the air stations. At the time of my visit the personnel included forty-five officers, forty aviators, 190 enlisted men and approximately a hundred civilians. The air station encompassses twenty-nine acres in the center of the airport, Hangar 103 being the largest building on the station and the center of activity. It serves as an aircraft repair and service area and as an administration complex. The Operations Center includes the Search & Rescue console, the radio room and flight planning with office space adjacent for the majority of the operations department plus numerous helicopter and fixed wing maintenance shops. On the upper level are located the Commanding and Executive Officer's offices and the normal administration, personnel and engineering department offices. The station is very proud of its medical section with one doctor, who is also a flight surgeon, and six hospital corpsmen. This fine medical and dental clinic is always a hive of activity with the needs of assigned personnel and dependents as well as those of the large retired community in the area.

During 1976 both the HU-16E and the HH-52A were showing the need for increased maintenance due to their age and usage. Also, each suffered peculiar problems concerning procurement of many replacement parts. The HU-16E faced a mandatory retirement at the 11,000 hour mark. The HH-52A required a greater effort in corrosion control due to the overall increase in shipboard deployment time. Despite these difficulties Miami's aggressive and effective maintenance programme enabled assigned aircraft to more than meet the demanding operational commitments of the 7th Coast Guard District HQ.

On Thursday 14 July 1977, the air stations seven twenty-six year old HU-16E *Albatross* aircraft bade farewell to their home base by flying in formation over the air station at Opa Locka, the first time they had all been airborne at one time. In their lifetime they had logged over 10,000 hours each, had flown 13,800 Search & Rescue missions and given aid to 108,000 people. During the 1960s when hordes of Cubans fled the Castro regime in small boats and rafts, it was the 'Goat' (as the HU-16E was known by the Coast Guard) crews that spotted them and organized the surface vessels to pluck them from the ocean. Due to corrosion they had not been permitted to land on water for at least five years. The fate of the veteran seven had already been decided. In August 1977 one was assigned to air station Cape Cod in Maine, one was destined to be overhauled at Elizabeth City, North Carolina for future use there, another was to go somewhere in the midwest and the remaining four were to be disposed of as scrap.

The interim replacement was the Convair HC-131, a twin engined medium range transport, which was faster, quieter and more comfortable than the *Albatross*. At this time the

new Medium Range Search (MRS) jet, the HH-25A *Guardian* was in the early stages of procurement. A computerized, on-going maintenance programme for the HH-52A helicopter was in inception at Miami, Detroit and Corpus Christi which enabled greater availability by eliminating the time consuming mandatory check period.

As testimony to the efforts of the air station, the Coast Guard Meritorious Unit Commendation for 'outstanding resourcefulness, initiative and ingenuity' in maintaining a level of operational readiness well in excess of normal requirements was awarded for the period 1 July 1973 to 31 March 1975.

One of the Grumman HU-16E aircraft based at Miami at this time was unique. It was HU-16E 7246 carrying the symbol and name *Seaveyor* and was minus the wing floats. Equipment carried by the *Albatross* included the latest sideways looking radar fitted on the starboard side (SLAR), infra-red and ultra violet sensors. At the time it was the only ARSS equipped aircraft in the Coast Guard inventory, and was transferred to air station San Francisco where its capability of detecting pollutants could be more effectively used.

In 1980 the air station at Miami served as a primary response center for the humanitarian Coast Guard efforts in the Cuban refugee sea lift. The combination of new aircraft and new procedures together with well-trained and dedicated aircrews will continue to respond to the many challenges at Miami Air Station — Where the Action is.

San Francisco. Today restricted to helicopter operations only, here is the US Coast Guard air station at San Francisco seen from the air on 6 November 1970. Parked on the apron are two Lockheed HC-130 *Hercules,* two Grumman HU-16E *Albatross* amphibians, and a visiting Fairchild C-123B *Provider* transport. (USCG)

Coast Guard Aviation Training Center, Mobile, Alabama

Since the birth of Coast Guard aviation in 1920 when Lieutenant Elmer Stone was designated the first USCG aviator, there has been a need for professional training for Coast Guard pilots and aircrewmen. From the beginning, most Coast Guard pilots received their initial training from the US Navy. This training, widely recognized as the best in the world, provided the Coast Guard with pilots who were well trained in basic airmanship and aeronautical skills but who, in most instances, were unfamiliar with the techniques, equipment, and procedures used by the USCG to accomplish its many missions. This basic operational training was initially conducted by the individual air stations at which the new pilots were assigned. This system had many long-recognized disadvantages which grew more severe as aircraft became more complex and the Coast Guard missions more diverse.

In 1965 the Coast Guard initiated action to solve what was fast becoming a critical problem. Headquarters formulated plans for an aviation training center and began an investigation of locations with good year-round flying conditions and suitable facilities. Mobile, Alabama, received careful attention, as did many other locations throughout the US. In early 1966 the Coast Guard made its decision to locate the training center in Mobile and took steps to acquire the 232-acre former US Air Force Reserve facility at the municipal airport. This location not only met the weather and size requirements, but also offered plenty of good housing for several hundred military personnel and their families in a community that was receptive to their presence.

The new facility was commissioned as air station Mobile on 17 December 1966. The station was under the operational control of the Commander, 8th Coast Guard District in New Orleans, and provided training for all newly-designated aviators as well as fixed-wing Search & Rescue coverage for the middle and eastern Gulf of Mexico. In July 1969 air station Mobile was renamed the United States Coast Guard Aviation Training Center and was designated a headquarters unit. This placed the training center under the direct control of the Commandant of the Coast Guard, a move which streamlined the logistics and administrative procedures necessary for coordinating the movement of several hundred pilots in and out of Mobile each year.

San Francisco. A full volume could be written on the various liveries adopted by US Coast Guard aviation over the years. Seen here is a Martin PBM-3C *Mariner* BuNo 6566 carrying the radio call-sign 'Frisco — D for Dog'. (USCG)

The missions performed at the aviation training center are three-fold: training, Search & Rescue and polar operations. In the area of training, the center provides instruction in the HH-3F *Pelican*, the HH-52A *Seaguard* and the HH-65A *Dolphin* helicopters, plus the HU-25A *Guardian* jet. The Training Division instructs aviators that fall into three categories: newly designated aviators from the US Naval Air Training Command School at Pensacola, Florida, helicopter pilots who return to Mobile annually for a week of intensive review in the flight simulators and experienced Coast Guard pilots who are learning how to fly a different aircraft.

The center is an innovator in the use of flight simulators for operational training. The simulator complex was completed in 1972 and has been studied by the air forces of many allied nations. These devices are used extensively in the initial and recurrent training programmes. They have significantly increased training effectiveness and safety while substantially reducing operating costs. Two new simulators were installed for the HU-25A *Guardian* and the HH-65 *Dolphin*. Both feature a full-motion platform with audio and visual cues that result in a truly realistic training environment.

Search & Rescue, the second mission, has historically been performed at the training center with fixed-wing aircraft. First the HU-16E *Albatross,* then the HC-131 *Samaritan* and finally the HU-25A *Guardian* assumed the responsibility for providing twenty-four-hour fixed-wing coverage for the area. With the increased emphasis on the Coast Guard's law enforcement mission in recent years, the fixed-wing aircraft of the Search & Rescue Division are seeing more and more usage in this capacity. Several significant drug seizures can be credited to this division.

The third mission at the center is polar operations. In 1969 the requirements for Coast Guard aviation support of polar icebreakers were established and the Polar Operations Division was formed. One must remember that the Coast Guard and its aviators have a great history of activities in both Arctic and Antarctic regions. It supported Admiral Byrd on his return to Antarctica with Operation High Jump in 1947 and since then has played vital support tasks in the US Navy's Operation Deep Freeze programmes to the Antarctic. The need existed for a central location which would allow access to both coasts, and Mobile proved to be the ideal spot. Not only did it provide the central location: it also allowed the training division access to the extra helicopters available when detachments were in port. In this way, helicopters assigned to both divisions are used with maximum efficiency.

Polar Operations mission detachments include scientific research in support of the US National Science Foundation, re-supply of remote stations in the Arctic and Antarctic, general air logistics support, ice observations, Search & Rescue and enforcement of laws and treaties.

The Aviation Engineering Division has the responsibility of keeping the center's complement of twenty-seven varieties of aircraft ready for flight. The men and women are all specialists in aircraft maintenance and have had formal training in increasingly complex aircraft systems. To support these missions and the ninety-seven officers and 333 enlisted personnel aboard the Aviation Training Center, there is a full service medical dispensary which is staffed by two doctors, two dentists and a pharmacist, plus a complete staff of hospital corpsmen.

Air Station New Orleans, Louisiana

The Coast Guard air station was commissioned in July 1955 and was located at the US Naval Aviation air station, New Orleans, which was located on Lake Pontchartrain at that time. The initial unit consisted of four pilots and seven enlisted men operating two Sikorsky HO3S- helicopters. In December 1957 the air station moved with the US Navy to Alvin Callender Field, and shared a hangar with the US Navy and US Marine Corps Air Reserve.

Today, located on US Naval air station New Orleans, the air station is under the operational control of the 8th Coast Guard District with HQ in New Orleans. The primary mission of the air station is Search & Rescue coverage in the Gulf of Mexico from Apalachicola, Florida, to the Texas-Louisiana border. Unit aircraft are on twenty-four-hour call to assist persons or vessels in distress. Typical assistance cases consist of medical evacuations, delivery of dewatering pumps for foundering vessels, and locating lost, disabled or otherwise overdue vessels. In addition, the unit's helicopters are often employed in maritime law enforcement, survey flights in support of pollution control and co-operative efforts with local and Federal agencies.

COAST GUARD AIR STATIONS 105

The present hangar facilities were opened and dedicated in September 1968. Designed and built by the Coast Guard, the building provides maintenance facilities, administrative offices and supply spaces for the twenty-eight officers and ninety enlisted personnel of the unit assigned in December 1985. Quarters for the ready flight crews and an Operations Center for controlling the various station missions are also located in the hangar. In the summer of 1986 a new building to house administration, medical, and operations department was completed.

Many milestones have been achieved at the station. On 1 April 1969 air station New Orleans was the first operational unit to operate the new Sikorsky HH-3F *Pelican* twin-engine helicopter, which had the most sophisticated electronics package installed on a helicopter at that time. On 24 March 1980 rescue efforts resulted in the 1500th life saved by air station personnel. In June 1980 Sikorsky HH-52A *Seaguard* short range, single engine helicopters returned to the air station inventory. During August 1985 New Orleans became the first Coast Guard air station to operate the new Aero-spatiale HH-65A *Dolphin* helicopter, becoming fully operational on the type on 11 September 1985. The HH-65A has the most advanced electronics package available installed and the computerized navigation system allows the helicopter to 'fly itself', freeing pilots to spend more time in searching. The *Dolphin* is able to cruise at 142 knots, with a top speed of 165 knots, and can carry three survivors in addition to its three crew members. In October 1985, during Hurricane Juan, the air station recorded its 2,000th life saved. Lasting from 27 to 30 October 1985 the hurricane kept the air station busy with over 150 rescues accomplished.

With over five hundred Search & Rescue cases annually, air station New Orleans is the busiest all-helicopter air station in the Coast Guard. It is equipped with two HH-3F and three HH-65A helicopters. The air station has received three Coast Guard Unit Commendations, in addition to outstanding ratings in district inspections. July 1985 marked the thirtieth year of rescue services provided to the New Orleans Gulf coast area by Coast Guard air station New Orleans.

Air Facility, Norfolk Naval Air Station, Virginia

In an effort to stop the flow of illegal drugs into the US, the Coast Guard is using two Grumman E-2C *Hawkeye* surveillance aircraft. These aircraft have a key role in the Coast Guard's new mission of air interdiction. The E-2C allows the Coast Guard to survey nearly three million cubic miles of surrounding air space at sea, while monitoring 150,000 square miles of ocean surface. As an example, an E-2C flying over New York City can monitor all the air traffic in the congested Boston to Washington corridor while maintaining a watch over vessels in that same ocean area.

Designed and constructed by the Grumman Corporation, the current E-2C is the result of over twenty years of progressive engineering. Changes to the airframe, propulsion, and related aircraft systems have enhanced the performance of the aircraft, enabling it to use short runways, have low search speeds and long mission time. On loan from the US Navy, the unique feature of the E-2C is a twenty-four-foot diameter rotating radar dome on top of the aircraft. Also, for better storage capability, the wings of the E-2C fold up.

The air facility at Norfolk, Virginia, was formed on 22 January 1987, initially operating out of the US Navy CCAEWW-12 headquarters building — Commander, Carrier Airborne Early Warning Wing 12 — and as the unit is home based at a US Naval air station it has become necessary to attach a designator which fits into the US Navy operating procedures. That designator is CGAW-1, which means Coast Guard Airborne Warning Squadron One, the 1 being symbolic of the first squadron.

Carrying the Coast Guard serials 3501 and 3502 the E-2C aircraft are interesting in that 3501 is the 45th production aircraft and had the US Navy BuNo 160698, while 3502 is the

23rd production aircraft with US Navy BuNo 159497. The aircraft are not yet in Coast Guard livery, but still retain their US Navy finish, 3502 retaining 9497 on the outer fins.

The introduction of the Grumman E-2C *Hawkeye* aircraft has produced a new aviation task and a new insignia, these being the Coast Guard Flight Officer (CGFO) holding rank as commissioned officers and in the new unit operating the radar systems. Their insignia is identical to the US Navy Flight Officer's wings, and CGAW-1 is the only Coast Guard unit that has flight officers. In addition to the CGFOs, the unit has also enlisted radio operators called Flight Technicians (FLT TECHS). These are Avionics Technician (AT), who have gone through specialized training and are qualified to operate the radar equipment in the E-2C. They wear the aircrew insignia which all of the Coast Guard's enlisted aircrew wear. Flight crews for the Grumman E-2C are made up of two pilots and three radar operators. There is at least one CGFO on board who is in charge of the radar operations. The commanding officer of this new and unique unit is Commander Norman V Scurria Jr.

Fort Point, San Francisco. A two-year experiment with two Bell SK-5 hovercraft was held in 1970 at Fort Point, San Francisco. This was the US Coast Guard's first introduction to this air cushion vehicle, which proved too expensive to operate. Seen here is one of the unit's Surface Effect Rescue Vehicle (SERV) with a forty-four-foot USCG motor lifeboat at Fort Point. (USCG via Bell Aerospace)

The Anti-Drug Abuse Act of 1986 established a Coast Guard role in the interdiction of air smuggling. This legislation increased the resources available to the Coast Guard to help stop illegal substances destined for the US via the air routes over the maritime region. The legislation included authorization for the US Navy to loan the USCG two E-2C *Hawkeye* aircraft for use in combating drugs being brought into the country by aircraft.

San Francisco. Consolidated PBY-5 *Catalina* with its radio call-sign 'Frisco — F for Freddy' on the mainplane, based at San Francisco Coast Guard air station, California, seen on 28 April 1945, about to alight on the calm waters of San Francisco Bay. (USCG)

Operating from the US Naval Air station at Norfolk, Virginia, these aircraft will deploy to the Caribbean, Gulf of Mexico and off the Atlantic coast to participate in detecting suspect aircraft. In addition to the E-2Cs, the Coast Guard has modified some of its HU-25A *Guardian* medium range search (MRS) aircraft to provide day and night interceptor capability. This twin engined, turbofan powered aircraft built by the Falcon Jet Corporation of Teterboro, New Jersey, is presently used by the USCG for law enforcement and Search & Rescue missions. Until modified, HU-25s presently located on the southeast of the US are concentrating on day-time intercepts.

Air Station North Bend, Oregon

The Coast Guard Group and Air Station was built in 1974 for $2.4m and actually houses two USCG units with a complement of twenty officers and eighty enlisted men. Coast Guard Group North Bend is the senior of the two. It has operational and administrative control over all the lifeboat stations on the southern Oregon coast from Depoe Bay to the California border, covering 220 miles of picturesque coastline. The Group provides the majority of the support functions for its eight units in everything from paperwork to money matters. It also has a team of experts for the maintenance and repair of the equipment of these stations, including everything from sewer lines in the housing unit to the electronics and engines in the motor lifeboats.

As well as lifeboat stations, USCG Group North Bend also co-ordinates the efforts of an Aid to Navigation team, a telephone teletype repair station and the air station. The Group Commander is also the Commanding Officer of air station North Bend. In fact, many of the fourteen pilots assigned to the air station have additional duties in the Group. Commissioned on 28 September 1974, the air station was the result of an increase in the amount of Search & Rescue activity on the Oregon coast during the late 'sixties and 'seventies. Three Sikorsky HH-52A *Seaguard* helicopters were assigned, these being initially 1369, 1373 and 1439. Commander Lewis was the first Commanding Officer, and US government officials attending the commissioning included Congressman Dellenbach and Senator Hatfield.

The primary mission of the air station over the past decade has been Search & Rescue and a close mutually supportive relationship is maintained with the six Coast Guard lifeboat stations that protect the ports along this stretch of the coast. The first life saving by a North Bend HH-52A helicopter occurred on 6 December 1974 when a light aircraft crashed into Coos Bay near the Coos Bay–North Bend airport. Since that day the air station has been credited with saving many lives, not only those in peril on the sea, such as loggers injured in areas inaccessible by ambulance and victims of dune buggy three wheeler accidents, which account for a significant percentage of the total.

Now being replaced by the new HH-65A *Dolphin* helicopter, the Sikorsky HH-52A is fully amphibious thanks to its boat hull. It has a cruising speed of eighty-five knots and a maximum speed of 109 knots. It can carry 325 gallons of fuel and when burning sixty gallons per hour this will last over five hours. With one and a half hours fuel, it is capable of carrying eight people. The normal crew is two pilots and one crewman/hoist operator. It is a fully instrument rated aircraft with excellent radio coverage and homing capabilities. Its hydraulic winch has 120 feet of cable and a 600 lb capacity.

As I discovered on a visit to air station North Bend in August 1978, during an interview with the Commanding Officer, Commander Thomas P Keane, the station's involvement in the community is not limited to long searches and dramatic rescues. The air station planned and hosted the first annual North Bend airshow back in 1981, an event which helps out a sometimes sluggish bay area economy as well as providing entertainment. The airshow can attract crowds estimated at 15,000 people to the area for the weekend, and although the air station has gradually turned the show over to a mostly civilian committee, USCG personnel still actively participate in the planning and execution of the growing event.

Air Station Port Angeles, Washington

Coast Guard air station Port Angeles, Washington, was commissioned.in ceremonies by the Commanding Officer, Lieutenant Carl G Bowman, on 1 June 1935. Located on Ediz Hook, a level sand spit extending from the mainland northward and eastward into the Strait of Juan De Fuca, it became the first Coast Guard air station on the Pacific coast.

Its location at the tip of Ediz Hook was originally chosen for its strategic position in the coastal defenses of the north-east. At the time of commissioning, the only buildings on the spit were the Ediz Hook lighthouse, the hangar, which had been dedicated on 27 April 1935, a wharf and a private club house operated by a local fishing club. Resources attached to the air station were three seventy-five-foot patrol boats and four picket boats.

The first aircraft, a Douglas RD-4 *Dolphin* amphibian, was flown to the air station by Lieutenant Bowman on the evening of 11 June 1935. Dubbed the 'Deneb', it flew the air station's first mercy-hop on 9 August 1935. During World War II the air station was expanded by the addition of numerous temporary buildings, a few of which remain today. A gunnery school was established to train aerial gunners and local defense forces. By the summer of 1942, most of the aircraft assigned to Port Angeles were employed investigating reports of enemy submarines in the Strait of Juan De Fuca and offshore waters and for convoy escort duty.

The Port Angeles inventory as of 31 December 1941 consisted of three Grumman aircraft — a JF-2 *Duck,* JRF-2 *Goose* and J4F-1 *Widgeon*. These carried USCG serials V148, V176 and V203 respectively.

In the spring of 1943 the station's runways were expanded to include a short runway for field carrier landing practice by the US Navy. By this time the air station had responsibility for all USCG anti-submarine operations down to the Californian border, with detachments of aircraft and boats at Neah Bay, Quillayute, Astoria, and North Bend in Oregon. By the spring of 1944 the station was also operating five sub-units including the air station, the commissary warehouse, the Pilot station, the Ediz Hook light station, and the Dungeness light station. In addition it served as headquarters for the Straits patrol and for an independent US Naval Intelligence Unit temporarily attached to the station. On 15 March 1944 the Air-Sea Rescue system was organized for the Northwest Sea Frontier area. The Commanding Officer of the air station at Port Angeles was designated to head this new organization. By 28 February 1943 the air station had eight aircraft assigned which included JRF-2 V175 and V176, J4F-1 V203, V206, V207 and V221, J2F-4 1667 and J2F-5 BuNo 00796 the latter two aircraft being ex US Navy. The Commanding Officer of the air station at this time was Lieutenant Commander Donald B MacDiarmid. On 3 September 1943 Lieutenant Commander W E Sinton took over command.

On 24 September 1943 a US Army Air Force Lockheed B-34 bomber No AJ405 from Paine Field crashed and burned on take-off with a loss of five Army personnel, two seriously burned and two with minor injuries and burns. The air station and US Navy section, plus local fire departments responded promptly and the injured were cared for by air station surgeons at the US Navy infirmary. Runway 09 transformer and runway floodlights were demolished by impact and fire. An Army Board of Investigation was held by the USAAF. On 26 September a submarine was reported off Tatoosh. The air station aircraft on evening 'Plan Victor' patrol was on the scene and investigated with negative results. On 28 September a Grumman F6F *Hellcat* squadron number L2 from Fighting Ten squadron had an engine failure after a 'wave off' whilst practising carrier landings. The aircraft immediately sank approximately 150 yards offshore north of the spit in about twenty-five fathoms of water. The US Navy pilot suffered only minor cuts and was rescued by a skiff launched from the north beach by USCG air station personnel.

A US Navy Consolidated PBY-5A *Catalina* BuNo 33999 crashed and burned in Latitude 48-14-30 N, Longitude 124-10-30 W, which is about three and a half miles south-east of Slip Point. There were eight dead and two injured in the crash. A second US Navy PBY-5A BuNo 33975 landed on the water and was later beached with severe damage to the hull. Trucks and USCG personnel were dispatched. Weather conditions prevented aircraft operations until late afternoon when a message block was dropped at the scene of the incident with instructions from the US Naval Air station located at Whidbey Island. The beached *Catalina* was later salvaged by the US Navy.

On 7 October 1943 a submarine was reported sighted off Angeles Point in Latitude 48-12 N, Longitude 123-33 W. Upon receipt of the information three aircraft were dispatched with depth charges. Search was continued until dark with negative results and went on throughout the night by surface craft. Bad weather prevented further air search the following day. On 15 October at 1025, Coast Guard Curtiss SO3C-1 *Seamew* aircraft BuNo 4813, piloted by James E Nesmith, aviation pilot, first class, crashed on landing at the air station. It was the pilot's first flight in this model and the crash occurred on his second landing. As the SO3C-1 had no dual controls no flight instruction can be given and undoubtedly some accidents of this nature can be expected. The aircraft was severely damaged. A board of investigation and trouble board were convened and both recommended that the *Seamew* be stricken, all usable parts salvaged and retained for spares, and the engine turned in for inspection and repair or salvage.

The following message was intercepted on 500 kcs on 17 October 1943, 'SSSS DE KCXF THINK WE HAVE SIGHTED SUB 12820 WEST 4915 NORTH'. Although the vessel was 150 miles off Tatoosh Island and a Grumman JRF-5's range is extremely limited the Commanding Officer got airborne with two depth charges and contacted the vessel which was underway and undamaged. The vicinity was searched for twenty minutes with negative results at which time the diminishing fuel supply necessitated a return to base. If PBYs had been available air coverage could have been given to this vessel until she reached the Straits.

The following are direct extracts from the air station's War Diary:

Orders have been received from Coast Guard Headquarters to send six commissioned aviators to US Naval Air station, Banana River, Florida, for a six weeks' operational training course in Martin PBM-3 *Mariner* aircraft. The officer crews report on 16 December 1943 and the enlisted crews about two weeks earlier. Headquarters indicates that when crews are trained three PBM-3 seaplanes will be assigned to the station for operations and training of additional pilots and crews. During this training period at Banana River the air station will be somewhat short-handed but present operations and training of new pilots will be continued. From information available the PBM-3S fully loaded weighs 52,000 lbs and our present ramp will not carry such a load. However ramp strengthening and enlarging project will be started the first week in November. It is imperative that this programme be expedited in order not to delay delivery of the PBM-3S aircraft the first part of February 1944. The acquisition of these planes should increase the effectiveness of this station several times over.

Curtiss SO3C-1 BuNo 4762 aircraft was received at the air station on 31 October and after a thorough inspection will be used to complete the training of all pilots in this type which was interrupted by the crash of SO3C-1 BuNo 4813. A Grumman JRF-5 *Goose* with a crew from the air station has been reported missing since 19 November 1943. This plane was on special duty in Alaska. Grumman JRF-2 V175 departed the air station on 27 December for a major overhaul at San Diego, California. It will be replaced by another JRF-2.

In September 1944 the air station became officially known as Coast Guard Group, Port Angeles, which, together with its neighbouring sub-units, operated as an Air-Sea Task unit for the north-western sector of the Sea Frontier Region. The air station had 29 aircraft assigned by the end of 1944 — its all time high.

The early post-war years brought new and innovative technology to the Search & Rescue arena. In 1946 the first helicopter, a Sikorsky HO3S-1G, arrived, still in its experimental stages. This was replaced in 1951 with the arrival of the Sikorsky HO4S helicopter dubbed the 'eggbeater'. In 1953 the Grumman HU-16E *Albatross* made its debut at the air station. Affectionately called the 'Goat', it was said that the only reason it took off was because it scared the ground with all its noise. Retired in 1973, the HU-16E was the last fixed-wing aircraft stationed at Port Angeles. The air station became a helicopter only station utilizing the Sikorsky HH-52A *Seaguard* helicopter first acquired in 1965 as a modern replacement for the earlier HO4S. The HH-52A is now replaced by the HH-65A *Dolphin*. The future looks exciting as the air station continues to provide invaluable service in the north-west and most particularly the community of Port Angeles.

With the lighthouse in the background, a peaceful early post-war scene at Salem US Coast Guard air station, Massachusetts, on 21 May 1947, with two Martin PBM-5G *Mariners* BuNo 84732 and 84686 parked. The aircraft have yellow fuselage bands, wing tips, floats and a panel on the mainplane carrying the word 'RESCUE'. (USCG)

Air Station Sacramento, California

Coast Guard air station Sacramento was commissioned on 5 September 1978, on the McClellan Air Force base facility and is one of the USCG's newest operational aviation units. It was established as an outgrowth of air station San Francisco, where ramp space and an increase in the number of aircraft required that the fixed-wing contingent be relocated. With a complement of more than two hundred officers and enlisted personnel operating four Lockheed HC-130 *Hercules* aircraft, Sacramento is an asset of the US Department of Transportation under the operational control of the Commander, Pacific Area located in Alameda. The move from air station San Francisco was initiated in March 1978 and involved a number of Grumman HU-16E *Albatross* aircraft, which are now retired.

Air station Sacramento participates in a wide variety and range of Coast Guard missions. Primary among them but perhaps not widely known is Search & Rescue. The air station maintains a twenty-four-hour, immediate response capability, with a ready Search & Rescue crew on duty at all times. Coverage is provided for the Eastern Pacific Ocean, the entire west coast of the US, areas west of Canada and south along the Baja California coast. It conducts numerous patrols year-round, which are often co-ordinated with USCG cutters. The aircraft extends the eyes of the ship while patrolling not only coastal waters, but also shipping lanes and fishing grounds miles out to sea. Should a violation be detected, the ship or cutter provides the boarding capability.

Other missions of the air station are Marine Environmental Protection and US Federal law enforcement. These efforts include fisheries patrols in support of the Fisheries Conservation and Management Act of 1976 and law enforcement patrols aimed at enforcing the 200-mile limit and combating the ever-increasing problem of drug smuggling. Another major responsibility of the air station is that of providing transportation for the Pacific Strike Team, the Coast Guard's oil and hazardous materials spill prevention and containment team on the west coast. Located at Hamilton Field, California not too far distant, the Strike team is immediately alerted in the event of a spill, responding to provide expert assistance in containment and clean-up of environmentally damaged areas.

The Sacramento aircrews constantly conduct training flights to maintain proficiency in basic airmanship and Search & Rescue techniques that so often result in the saving of lives and property at sea. Training flights include approaches and landings at many of the airports located in the Sacramento area, especially those airports with a hospital adjacent, where it may be necessary to land night or day to deliver survivors from an incident.

Four Lockheed HC-130H *Hercules* are operated by air station Sacramento, this being recognized as one of the most versatile aircraft in the world today. Four powerful Allison turboprop engines enable short field take-offs and landings as well as a respectable cruise speed of 290 knots. The HC-130's fuel capacity allows for covering long distances as well as extended on-scene endurance in the event of long searches or emergencies at sea. Visibility, an extremely important factor in any search, is excellent. The aircraft's high maximum weight allowance and large cargo compartment permit handling of a wide variety of cargoes. An aft ramp and door may be opened in flight, allowing aerial delivery of cargo or emergency equipment. Overall, the Herky Bird is an extremely versatile and reliable aircraft, well suited to the multiple mission needs of Coast Guard aviation.

Port Angeles. The aircrew and ground personnel attend a Curtiss SOC-4 *Seagull* V173 resting in the water off the ramp at Port Angeles US Coast Guard air station. In 1941 and 1942 it was assigned to Miami air station, Florida. (Gordon S. Williams)

Air Station San Diego, California

The birth of Coast Guard air station San Diego began on 4 May 1934 when Lieutenant Luke Christopher USCG arrived in San Diego bearing a letter from the Commandant of the Coast Guard authorizing the establishment of a USCG air patrol detachment. The primary duty of the detachment was the prevention of smuggling, but as more and more missions were diverted to lifesaving efforts offshore, the unit's primary

reason for existence changed. On 21 May 1935, command of the detachment was assumed by Commander Elmer F Stone, one of Coast Guard Aviation's most colourful figures, best known for his actions as pilot of the NC-4, the first aircraft to cross the Atlantic in May/June 1919. It was under his able hand that the detachment began to grow into an air station.

In June 1936 construction began at the air station's present location across Harbor Drive from Lindbergh Field. On 1 April 1937 the detachment was commissioned as an air station. The outbreak of World War II added personnel and the Consolidated PBY-5A *Catalina* to the station, and it was during this period that it was officially charged with the protection of lives and property offshore.

On 31 December 1941 the air station had the following aircraft assigned: Hall Aluminium PH-2 V166, Hall Aluminium PH-3 V178, Douglas RD-4 *Dolphin* V127 and Grumman JF-2 *Duck* V139. By 30 November 1942 the complement of aircraft had been increased to five and included Hall Aluminium PH-3 V178, Grumman J4F-1 *Widgeon* V204, V219 and V220, plus Douglas RD-4 *Dolphin* V127. On 28 February 1943 the same five aircraft remained at the air station.

Since those early days all operational units from the Mexican Border northward to Oceanside have been consolidated under one Command. Coast Guard Group San Diego is made up of Point Loma light, USCG cutters *Point Brower* and *Point Stuart,* both berthed at Ballast Point, USCG cutter *Point Hobart* at Oceanside and the air station, with its three helicopters and several small boats. The Group is completed by an electronic repair facility and Aids to Navigation team whose responsibility it is to ensure the proper operation of all the Aids to Navigation and radio beacons in the area, as well as the well-being of the Group surface units. Missions include Search & Rescue, enforcement of laws and treaties, Marine Environmental Protection, Aids to Navigation, military readiness and other support activities. A tenant command on the air station, the Coast Guard Marine Safety Office combines the functions of the previously separate Captain of the Port and Marine Inspection Office. Today the air station has a complement of four Aerospatiale HH-65A *Dolphin* helicopters and three HU-25A *Guardian* fan jets.

One of the many Commanding Officers of air station San Diego was Captain David L Andrews. A native of Baldwin, New York, he graduated from the Coast Guard Academy in 1963. His first tour of duty was aboard a buoy tender, the USCG cutter *Heather,* home ported in Long Beach, California. After one year on the cutter he was assigned to the US Naval Flight Training Command at Pensacola, Florida, where he received basic and rotary wing flight training and his USCG wings in 1965. Operational aviation tours followed at the air stations located at St Petersburg, Kodiak and San Diego. In 1975 Captain Andrews was assigned to Coast Guard Headquarters in Washington DC as the aviator detailer in charge of aviator assignments. He then returned to an operational aviation assignment as Deputy Group Commander, Astoria, Oregon. This was followed in 1981 by assignment as Commanding Officer at the air station located at San Francisco. Captain Andrews spent the next year at the Air War College, Maxwell Air Force base, Montgomery, Alabama where he also received a Masters Degree in Business Administration from Auburn University. Prior to his transfer to San Diego, he was assigned as the USCG Liaison Officer for Personnel to the Office of the Secretary of Defense in the Pentagon.

Captain Andrews is qualified in both fixed and rotary wing aircraft. He has been awarded the Distinguished Flying Cross, the Air Medal, two Unit Commendation Awards, the Meritorious Unit Commendation, the National Defense Service Medal and the Expert Rifle and Pistol medals. He also wears the American Legion Aviation Valor Award and was chosen pilot of the US Navy Helicopter Society Search and Rescue Crew of the Year in 1974.

Air Station San Francisco, California

The Coast Guard air station at San Francisco was established at Mills Field, California, close to the airport on 15 February 1941 and was built at a cost of $600,000 with barracks for sixteen officers and 100 enlisted men. The first commanding officer of the air station was Lieutenant George H Bowerman and by August 1941 the station was operating a Consolidated PBY-5 *Catalina* V189 and two Douglas RD-4 *Dolphins* V126 and V128. Since those early days Mills Field has seen numerous changes in its physical plant, crew, aircraft, missions and assignments.

Shortly after the air station was established, its aircraft and personnel were placed under the operational control of the US Navy and conducted maritime air and sea rescue and coast patrol missions throughout World War II. At the end of the war, the air station was released from the US Navy and continued as a USCG Search & Rescue unit.

Since its commissioning, a wide variety of fixed wing aircraft and helicopters have been based at the air station. These include the Boeing PB-1G *Flying Fortress,* Douglas C-54 *Skymaster,* Consolidated PBY- *Catalina,* Martin P5M-1G *Mariner,* Consolidated P4Y-2G *Marlin,* Douglas R4D-(DC-3), Hall PH-3 and a wide variety of Grumman built aircraft including the *Duck, Goose, Widgeon* and later the *Albatross.* A wide variety of Sikorsky helicopters have also operated from San Francisco, these including the HO3S-, HO4S- and more recently the HH-52A *Seaguard* and HH-3F *Pelican.* After thirty-seven years at the air station the fixed wing element including the HC-130 and HU-16E aircraft moved out to McClellan Air Force base, Sacramento during March 1978, leaving the short-range helicopters behind, which have been replaced by the twin engine HH-3F *Pelican.*

Over the years I have received invitations to visit the air station at San Francisco, the initial visit being when Captain Charles E Larkin was Commanding Officer, now retired as Vice Admiral and residing in Seattle. During the visit on 8 August 1975 the Commanding Officer was Captain Robert C Branham and present on the ramp was the unique HU-16E *Albatross* 7246 carrying the symbol and name 'Seaveyor' and heavily modified with equipment for detecting oil spills. It was fitted with sideways looking radar (SLAR) fitted to the starboard side and infra-red and ultra violet sensors, all this equipment being evaluated for future installation in USCG aircraft such as the HU-25A *Guardian.* The wing floats of the HU-16E had been removed.

Sikorsky H04S-3 1304 doing a winch demonstration at San Francisco US Coast Guard air station in California on 28 August 1954. The huge range of the Sikorsky family of rescue helicopters has remained close to the USCG for more than a decade. (William T. Larkins)

Left: Sikorsky HH-52A *Seaguard* helicopter 1373 based at the Houston, Texas, air station of the US Coast Guard seen on exercise with NASA astronauts, also based at Houston, with an Apollo type capsule in the water and an astronaut being winched into the USCG helicopter. (NASA S-66-58526)

A US Coast Guard Sikorsky HH-52A Seaguard 1419 helicopter based at San Juan air detachment, Puerto Rico, rescues a man stranded in the surf from an outboard motor boat beached on the rocks on 1 September 1970. (USCG)

Grumman HU-16E *Albatross* 7234 in early post-war markings, an attempt to
introduce high visibility markings for all weathers and theatres of operations.
This particular aircraft is from ex US Air Force stock and in USCG service the
type was more than a workhorse. (USCG)

Left: Today the USCG operates a fleet of twenty-three Lockheed HC-130H transports, serving at air stations located at Kodiak, Alaska; Barbers Point, Hawaii; Borinquen, Puerto Rico; Clearwater, Florida; and Elizabeth City, North Carolina. Shown here is 1340, an early HC-130B model now retired. (USCG)

This Lockheed HC-130B 1344 was one of an order of twelve Model 282-2B aircraft and was delivered to the US Coast Guard on 25 January 1961. It spent its entire USCG life based at Elizabeth City air station in North Carolina. It was retired in April 1986. (Lockheed RL 9296-C)

The primary mission of air station San Francisco has remained the same over the decades: the air station is responsible for maritime rescue along 300 miles of coastline from Point Conception to Point Arena, California. In addition, helicopters respond to missions in the bays and rivers, as well as inland, when other resources are not immediately available. In a typical year the air station responds to over 250 rescue cases, saves 100 lives, provides assistance to 200 others, and saves property valued at $5m.

In addition to SAR, it is regularly tasked with a variety of maritime law enforcement and fisheries missions. The helicopters also provide logistic flights for Aids to Navigation such as offshore lighthouses and aerial surveillance for marine environmental protection. In support of all these missions, the crew and aircraft average over 2,500 flight hours per year. To accomplish these missions, the air station is staffed with a complement of approximately seventy highly qualified officers, petty officers and non-rated personnel. These include fifteen pilots, thirty-five aircraft maintenance crew and twenty general service personnel.

The men and women of the USCG air station at San Francisco are proud to be of service to the citizens of northern California, a statement that was demonstrated one Sunday in the spring of 1987 when I attended a demonstration of emergency services at Concord, California. Forty emergency vehicles, three helicopters (including USCG HH-3F 1484) and an array of modern communications equipment were brought together at the Fire College of the Consolidated Fire District. The display was designed to bring emergency workers together and get them to learn how other agencies work, sponsored by a club that aims to improve disaster readiness and emergency communications, all very vital in any disaster.

During the early 1970s the Coast Guard found that Air Cushion Vehicles were a versatile and cost effective addition to the traditional shoreline rescue station. The first and only USCG Air Cushion Vehicle Unit operated from Fort Point

Station located beneath the south end of San Francisco's Golden Gate bridge and was commanded by Lieutenant William R Waller. The unit operated two amphibious SK-5 Surface Effect Rescue Vehicles (SERV) provided by Textron's Bell Aerospace Division at Buffalo, New York. In addition the unit operated two forty-four-foot Motor Life Boats (MLBs).

In a report comparing the two types of craft in the second half of 1972, the Coast Guard stated that probably no area of study surprised the USCG personnel more than the close operational and maintenance costs figures comparison between the MLB and the SERV. The tabulations clearly indicated that the SERV and small boat station could be very cost effective if both types of surface craft were used for their designed characteristics. Maintenance man hours required for the two types of craft for the period were 3.8 man hours per operating hour for the MLBs, and 4.2 man hours per operating hour for the SERV. 1973 was the third year of the USCG operating with the SK-5.

In the six months covered by the study, the station at San Francisco responded to 270 Search & Rescue missions. Other duties were servicing of Aids to Navigation, aiding in law enforcement, and assistance to other US government agencies. In addition, the SERVs were tested at Oakland International Airport for use as Air Crash Rescue platforms. The ten ton SK-5s are craft originally delivered by Bell Aerospace to the US Navy in 1966 for service in Vietnam, where they logged more than 4,500 hours of combat duty before assignment to the Coast Guard in 1970. The amphibious craft are thirty-eight feet long and twenty-three feet wide. They ride on a four foot thick cushion of air produced by a fan turned by the same engine that propels the SERV.

Mobile. The US Coast Guard co-operates with the activities of NASA and its astronauts, and this unique photo shows the space shuttle Eagle on its Boeing 747 mount landing at New Orleans for a week-long visit during the Louisiana World Exposition. A US Coast Guard HH-3F 1492 is seen parked, with the crew taking great interest in the shuttle's arrival. (USCG)

Air Station Savannah, Georgia

Air station Savannah was commissioned on 16 June 1963. In 1965 USCG aviation's original Sikorsky HH-52A *Seaguard* basic operational training unit (BOTU) was established at Savannah, the forerunner of the Coast Guard's specialized aviator training programme which has evolved into the USCG aviation training centre (AVTRACEN) at Mobile, Alabama. The air station provides Savannah and the coastal empire with round the clock Search & Rescue coverage of its coastal areas. It also flies law enforcement patrols from the North Carolina–South Carolina state line to Melbourne, Florida and throughout the Caribbean and Gulf of Mexico. As a result the air station's sixteen officers and thirty-seven enlisted men have become more than familiar with ship helicopter operations aboard 7th Coast Guard District cutters.

Law enforcement has become one of the air station's most frequently flown missions, second only to Search & Rescue. Georgia's maze of waterways and uninhabited islands make it a prime target for illegal drug operations. Coast Guard air station Savannah, located on Hunter Army airfield, has seen the field change hands from the US Air Force to US Army, from being a training base for helicopter pilots to being placed in a caretaker status, to being reopened with one of the US Army's major divisions. Hunter Field may see even more changes in the future, but the USCG air station has become as much a part of Savannah's heritage as its old homes and historic riverfront.

Today air station Savannah continues its many missions, having made the change over the past few years from its complement of three Sikorsky HH-52A *Seaguard* helicopters to a similar strength with the new HH-65A *Dolphin* helicopter.

Elizabeth City. A Beechcraft JRB-4 *Expeditor* BuNo 90564 seen parked at Elizabeth City US Coast Guard air station on 16 January 1955. This aircraft was used mainly for administrative flights, a total of seven being used by the service, all ex US Navy transports. (USCG)

Air Station Traverse City, Michigan

From 1938 to 1943 the Coast Guard maintained a one aircraft Air Detachment at Traverse City airport on a seasonal basis. On 21 August 1941 this was a Grumman JRF *Goose* V192, and by the end of 1941 a J4F *Widgeon* V204 had been added. Today, located at the Cherry Capitol Airport, the air station provides a central location from which USCG aircraft conduct their multi-purpose missions over the Great Lakes. The air station was originally formed in 1938 to provide summer assistance to mariners. It became a full air station in 1946 occupying an old US Navy hangar. From that time until the present day the unit has operated on a round the clock basis under the control of Commander, 9th Coast Guard District, Cleveland, Ohio.

Until September 1978 the air station operated two Sikorsky HH-52A *Seaguard* helicopters and three Grumman HU-16E *Albatross* fixed wing aircraft. In September 1978 the aging HU-16s were replaced by three Convair HC-131 *Samaritan* aircraft, these remaining in service until October 1980 when budget cuts forced their retirement. In June 1983 two HU-25A *Guardian* fan jets were assigned and supported USCG missions in the Great Lakes as well as the Atlantic east coast. In 1986 three HH-3F *Pelicans* replaced the HU-25A *Guardian* and HH-52A *Seaguard* aircraft.

At the end of World War II the US Naval Air Facility at Traverse City was made available to the Coast Guard, and in January 1946 the USCG air station Traverse City came into being. In 1949 the USCG returned the previously leased ten acres and previously deeded ten acres to Traverse City, leaving the USCG with seventy-eight acres. Until the late 1960s the air station retained this acreage, although many of the US Navy buildings were removed as excess to air station needs. With the expansion of the Cherry Capitol Airport additional land was returned to the city for construction of the new 10-28 instrument runway.

Today the air station retains about forty acres. On this area are eleven buildings which include a large hangar with associated ramps and two aviation fuel farms, an aviation metal and welding shop, a radio transmitter building and an administrative building. Much of the physical plant is twenty-nine years old, although it was constructed by the US Navy to last only ten years. However, Traverse City provides a central location from which USCG aircraft and helicopters can conduct their multi-purpose missions over all the Great Lakes, known in planning circles as the Fourth Sea Coast of the US.

Traditionally, Search & Rescue is at the top of the list of priority missions. Once the USCG had only one air station on the Great Lakes, today it has three: Detroit, Chicago and Traverse City. The helicopters make good short range search and rescue vehicles but when it comes to large scale searches of the waters of a lake, perhaps 150 miles long and fifty miles wide, the HH-52A was not adequate. These missions were left to the larger fixed wing types. Search & Rescue on the Great Lakes is normally controlled by the Rescue Coordination Center (RCC) at the 9th Coast Guard District HQ at Cleveland, Ohio.

To give some idea of the size of the Search & Rescue area, the Great Lakes themselves have a surface area of about 90,000 square miles and a shore line of more than 8,000 miles. From Messina, New York — the first city of any size on the St Lawrence River — to Duluth, Minnesota, by ship is 1,300 statute miles and to Chicago, Illinois, 1,200 statute miles. A HU-16E had to fly 150 miles to reach central Lake Huron, 250 miles to central Lake Erie and 450 miles to reach eastern Lake Ontario. At 150 knots in the HU-16E or ninety knots in the HH-52A, these distances translate into considerable flight time.

Today the Search & Rescue customers are the common types found elsewhere: small pleasure craft estimated to number around 2,000,000, lake vessels (numbering about four hundred), sea going vessels visiting the lakes through the St Lawrence Seaway (about three hundred vessels from fifty-seven companies), numerous aircraft, duck hunters and the usual special situations such as flare sightings. The size of the Traverse City SAR clientele is not surprising if one considers the fact that roughly one-fifth of the population of the US lives in the Great Lakes drainage basin and that over forty per cent of the gross national product is generated in the same area. Fortunately about sixty Coast Guard stations with small boats and a number of large cutters are located on the Lakes and rivers to share the Search & Rescue burden. The case load runs to approximately 150 to 200 cases per year at present.

The current National Ecological Revolution really is involved in the Great Lakes basin. Thousands of currently polluted rivers and streams empty into the Great Lakes.

Large lake dry bulk carriers, 650 feet or more in length, lake tankers ocean going vessels, harbor tugs and, of course, the million or more small craft are all potential pollutors. The more stringent laws now coming from the US Congress to stop future pollution and to clean up existing pollution will involve Traverse City air station in their enforcement.

Grumman HU-16E aircraft used to fly frequent combination pollution and Search & Rescue patrols on all the Great Lakes. Small marker flags pinned to a wall chart covering the Great Lakes area in the Operations Room bear testimony to pollution incidents surveyed and in some cases initially reported by USCG air crews. Marine pollution potential lessens when the regular navigation season ends about 15 December with the coming of the ice season. Each year, however, the plan is to extend the navigation season. At some future time, pollution surveillance may extend to twelve months a year.

Although the need for pollution patrols decreases in December and January, the need for ice surveillance patrols increases. Assisting the Coast Guard icebreakers, and the iron ore and cement carrier 'Lakers' in safe navigation of the growing ice fields becomes, at times, a daily task for both helicopters and fixed wing aircraft. A miscalculation in capability of one of these vessels could result in a wintering over in an ice field or worse, the crushing of a ship's hull. Most vessels have only one compartment which means that if a hole in that compartment admits water at a faster rate than the vessel's pumps can handle, the vessel is likely to sink.

Educating the public is just one of the tasks of the Community Relations department of the US Coast Guard, each air station having its own officer, often a rated pilot. Here the author is briefed on the Sikorsky HH-52A helicopter by the resident Community Relations Officer during a visit to San Francisco on 13 September 1972. (USCG)

In the spring, as the ice breakup nears, it is necessary for the proper analysis of ice conditions to send out either men on foot or in helicopters to drill out ice cores in critical channels. The HH-52A was used for this task. The same vessel support which was provided in the fall as the Great Lakes froze must be again provided in the spring as the ice thaws. In the winter of 1972-73 Coast Guard icebreakers and bulk carriers operated from Lake Superior ports to Lake Michigan and Lake Erie port up until 8 February, a 53 day extension of the regular season. Between 1955 and 1970, the latest closing date for navigation in the St Marys River, which connects Lake Superior to Lake Huron, was 22 December. In the two months of relative quiet during the shutdown of the navigation season in critical lake-to-lake channels, helicopters and fixed wing Coast Guard machines fly regular ice patrols in support of inter-lake tankers which operate twelve months a year to nearby lake ports.

A mission of growing importance is that of Aids to Navigation, which has long been a major USCG mission, but only recently has the use of aircraft, specifically helicopters, seriously been considered. Within the northern hundred-mile diameter semi-circle centered on Traverse City are nearly 150 buoys, lights, fog signals and radio beacons. The manned offshore aids during severe weather can only be reached by helicopter, this applying to an emergency at one of these stations or a requirement for urgent supplies or parts. Some years ago air station Traverse City assisted in the installation of a LASAR range in the St Marys River. During one extended ice season HH-52A helicopters supported the air compressor station on Lime Island. The station's compressors supplied compressed air to a bubbler pipe system in the Lime Island channel of the St Marys River complex to soften the ice.

The Coast Guard assists many other US government agencies. Two examples are taken from the history book of Traverse City air station. Bomb threats against two neighbouring US Air Force bases necessitated the transportation of an FBI agent and a bomb squad in a HU-16E *Albatross* to these bases in the middle of the night. Several hundred pounds of bombs were detected and removed. One summer, 500,000 fingerling salmon were released five to eight miles off the Michigan west shoreline for the Michigan Department of Natural Resources. Truly unique, this latter operation made use of a US Forest Service fire fighting bucket suspended from the HH-52A cargo sling to transport and release the fish.

A great deal of time, effort and money has gone into maintaining a facility to support Coast Guard aviation operations and each year the cost goes up. Until the passing of more stringent pollution legislation and increased pressure on the USCG to extend the Great Lakes navigation season there was serious doubt whether operational justification in fact existed to keep the air station in being at Traverse City. Strong general operational justifications now exist. The situation now indicates that the air station will be rebuilt in the near future — in fact a new 25,000 square foot hangar was commissioned in March 1980, and two of the World War II buildings were refurbished during the summer of 1982.

External to the unit's ongoing operations were some factors which culminated in a number of administrative changes. For example, in mid-1964 the unit was redesignated as a USCG air station, in conjunction with a service wide changeover of naming self-supporting aviation units as air stations. Subsequently, in February 1974 the unit's name was changed to USCG air station Washington, in recognition of its location at Washington National Airport, as well as the fact that the passengers being serviced were primarily from Washington DC. In February 1984 the unit was moved to share a facility with the Federal Aviation Administration in Hangar 6.

In recognition of superior performance, the unit was awarded the USCG unit commendation in 1971. In 1976 the unit was recognized by the award of the USCG unit commendation for exceptionally meritorious service. In February 1982 the unit was awarded the USCG meritorious unit commendation awarded for participation in rescue and recovery operations at the crash site of the Air Florida airliner Flight 90.

With an authorized complement of four aviators, one warrant officer and seven enlisted personnel, the unit is

Port Angeles. Seen at Port Angeles US Coast Guard air station completing preflight checks is a land-plane version of the float-plane Curtiss SO3C- *Seamew*, of which some forty-eight served with the USCG during World War II. (Gordon S. Williams)

Air Station Washington, District of Columbia

The origin of the unit was marked by the official commissioning ceremonies at Washington National Airport on 20 February 1952, when Lieutenant L V Perry assumed his duties as the first Commanding Officer of Coast Guard Air Detachment Arlington. With the subsequent acquisition of two Martin 404 VIP transport aircraft, the unit became fully operational later that year and carried out its assigned mission of providing transportation to senior Coast Guard and Treasury Department officials.

In 1963 a new aircraft, the Grumman VC-4A, also known as the *Gulfstream I* was acquired. This modern aircraft soon proved to be ideally suited for the air transportation mission and gained immediate acceptance by crew and passengers alike. Later, increasing worldwide travel requirements on the part of the Secretary of Transportation, as well as the Coast Guard Commandant, provided ample justification for the acquisition of a new high speed executive jet transport. Accordingly, in February 1969 the Grumman VC-11A *Gulfstream* with Coast Guard No 01 allocated, entered service as the 'Queen of the Fleet'. In September 1983 the earlier Grumman VC-4A was reassigned to the air station at Elizabeth City, North Carolina.

always ready to carry out its assigned mission of providing air transportation for the Secretary of Transportation and certain members of his staff, the Coast Guard Commandant and members of his staff and such other personnel as may be authorized by the Commandant.

The Grumman VC-11A Gulfstream II acquired in 1969 is powered by two Rolls-Royce Spey turbojet engines. The aircraft can fly at speeds up to 511 knots and operate at altitudes up to 43,000 feet. Maximum take-off weight is 62,000 pounds and maximum range is 3,000 miles. Precision navigation to any point in the world without outside input is possible through the use of the aircraft's Inertial Navigation System (INS). The aircraft is manned by a crew of four and can carry a maximum of twelve passengers.

Finally, the Coast Guard maintains an Aircraft Programme Office (APO) located at the Lockheed Aircraft company factory, Marietta, Georgia, which provides integrated logistic support development for future Coast Guard procurement of the HC-130H *Hercules*. Whilst researching this book with personnel from Coast Guard HQ in Washington DC, I met the Commanding Officer of this small but essential cog in the huge wheel of Coast Guard Aviation, Commander Michael Billingsley USCG. The APO was closed in June 1988 after the last Coast Guard-procured HC-130 was delivered.

CHAPTER NINE
Search & Rescue

It was a quiet day as dawn broke over the air station at Miami, Florida, on 5 May 1983. As planned, the day for the duty section began with an early HU-25A *Guardian* launch. The aircraft piloted by Lieutenant Paul Redwine and Lieutenant (jg) Gary Tabony, departed the airfield on a routine three hour patrol at 06.38. Lieutenant Commander Bill Spitler, the senior duty officer, and the ready HH-52A *Seaguard* helicopter aircraft commander, manned the operations desk. By 07.30 the remainder of the air station mustered to begin what was scheduled to be a training day. The only other planned morning launch involved a HH-52A piloted by Lieutenants John Murray and Eric Fagerholm. Their mission was an administrative flight to Bimini in the Bahamas. They departed on the two hour flight at 09.06.

All was quiet on the operational desk until 09.25 when LCDR Spitler overheard a conversation between the local air traffic control center and the 7th Coast Guard District Rescue Co-ordination Center (RCC). The air controller reported that an Eastern Air Lines Lockheed L-1011 had shut down one of three engines after receiving low oil pressure indications. The airliner crew had elected to turn back from Nassau in the Bahamas and return to Miami. At that point LCDR Spitler elected to divert the airborne HU-25A to intercept and escort the jumbo jet as a precautionary measure. Several minutes later at 09.30 the airliner reported a second engine loss. At that instant LCDR Spitler sounded the ready helicopter alarm and made a station public address announcement on the situation. Within seconds the station went to the nautical equivalent of general quarters.

The crew of a US Coast Guard HH-52A *Seaguard* helicopter sprint across the apron at Miami air station on a scramble which could be practice or real. By the time they reach the helicopter the ground crew will have done vital checks with the turbine already turning. (USCG)

The first rescue helicopter was pushed out, manned, started and airborne by 09.37. Simultaneously, the previously airborne HH-52A was diverted. The situation with the airliner continued to deteriorate. The crew reported the loss of the third engine. Ditching was now imminent. At 09.39 the second helicopter piloted by Lieutenants Seidal and Lord departed the field. Four additional aircraft, two helicopters and two *Guardians,* were being pushed out and loaded with extra dropable liferafts.

By approximately 09.40 the diverted HU-25A had intercepted the crippled airliner descending through 4,000 feet twenty miles east of Miami. At that point the crew was able to restart one engine. With one engine now on line a decision was made to attempt the approach to Miami airport. As the L-1011 approached the shoreline the helicopter piloted by LCDR Spitler and Lieutenant (jg) Turk joined in the escort. Eastern Air Lines Flight 855, flanked by a Coast Guard HU-25A and a HH-52A completed a successful touchdown at 09.46.

This case clearly documents the response capabilities of Coast Guard aviation. In nineteen minutes the record shows that air station Miami was able to rendezvous one fixed wing and one helicopter with the stricken airliner. Two other helicopters were airborne and en route. Additionally, two *Guardians* and two *Seaguards* were turned up and being loaded with sufficient liferafts to accommodate over two hundred people. In essence, eight rescue aircraft would have been on the scene within minutes had the Lockheed L-1011 jet ditched. The USCG personnel at the air station met the challenge of a near disaster that could have resulted in an aircraft ditching at sea involving 178 people.

Events of the evening, 24 December 1983

During the night of 24 December 1983 air station Miami received a distress call at 21.50 requesting a HU-25A *Guardian* to launch and deliver a liferaft to a twenty-eight-foot Openfisherman reported as sinking approximately twenty nautical miles southwest of Marathon, Florida. The Rescue Co-ordination Center (RCC) at Miami also decided to send a HH-52A helicopter to assist as necessary.

At 22.12 HH-52A 1421 initially launched but aborted due to a faulty fuel pump. At 22.14 the HU-25A 2214 was launched, soon followed by HH-52A 1379, airborne at 22.41. The *Guardian* 2214 located the subject vessel at 22.58 in position 24-21.5 N, 080-49.7 W — approximately twenty nautical miles from Marathon, Florida. The subject vessel was taking on water, and was adrift due to engine malfunction. All four persons on board were requesting to be removed from the sinking boat.

Early Coast Guard aircraft, such as the Douglas RD-2 *Adhara* depicted, were often involved in rescue work. When two seamen were severely injured in a ship's boiler explosion in 1933, a Cape May FLB-52 of the Coast Guard saved their lives, picking them up at sea and transporting them to a Philadelphia hospital in less than two hours. (Douglas Aircraft Co.)

On scene weather was particularly foul due to the passage of a winter cold front resulting in a temperature reduction of 45° in less than twelve hours; the winds were from the north west at thirty knots, gusting to fifty knots; ceiling was approximately 400 feet broken to overcast, visibility five nautical miles below cloud layer and outside rain squalls. The seas had increased from calm at noon to ten to twelve feet high at the time of the incident. All personnel on the subject vessel were dressed for summer, wearing shorts and T-shirts, obviously not prepared for the onslaught of a major winter storm. Surface assistance would be delayed due to the severity of the weather conditions.

Helicopter 1379 arrived on scene at 23.40. The HU-25A *Guardian* maintained an overhead orbit at 300 feet while the HH-52A attempted to DF-home with VHF-FM on channel 16, along with vectors from the HU-25A overhead. The subject boat fired a red flare which enabled the helicopter to locate it from a Mk 25 smoke flare. The helicopter then set up to perform a 'Beep to a hover' pattern. This maneuver was particularly difficult due to the severity of the wind.

After successfully arriving in a hover near the subject, a second smoke flare was deployed. This additional flare added more visibility to the scene, aided in determining the wind direction, and provided an additional reference in the event of a 'no reference hoist'.

The following is the statement from Lieutenant (jg) Donald S McNeil, pilot of HH-52A 1379.

> Once I was established in a hover near the sinking boat, I instructed my crewman, AD2 Wood, to rig for a basket hoist with a trail line. While he was preparing for the hoist, I had Lieutenant (jg) Tabony advise the boat of hoisting procedures. I also utilized the loud hailer to make sure that the persons aboard were positive about being removed, and aware of the necessary pro-

cedures for that removal. I noticed that the boat, while adrift was riding abeam to the seas, resulting in the vessel taking quite a pounding by wave action and chop. Waves were breaking over the gunwale of the 28 foot boat. All persons were wet and eager to leave the boat, previously refusing a dewatering pump.

After briefing the hoist with AD2 Wood, I maneuvered the aircraft over the drifting boat. With gusty conditions, and choppy seas, we were immediately in a 'no reference', 'lost target situation'. My aircrewman directed the helicopter with precise commands that minimized the lost target situation. AD2 Wood delivered the trail line, and prepared to lower the basket to the boat. We were encountering a multitude of problems that were weather induced. The 28 ft Openfisherman was 90 degrees to the windline, leaving the pilot in a no reference situation — a very uncomfortable feeling for pilots. The boat was 'surfing' or 'sleigh-riding' down the swells, away from the hovering aircraft. The gust spread resulted in some very discomforting attitudes for the aircraft in maintaining a safe relative position from the drifting boat. We were able to place the rescue basket aboard the sinker.

During the recovery of the first person, the vessel began 'surfing' away from us. After a second attempt to lift the basket we encountered a strong gust effect that resulted in the aircraft moving forward, while the boat again slid down the back of a wave. Under these hazardous conditions, AD2 Wood paid out all of the available slack cable. The rescue hook was later found to have been bent during this evolution. AD2 Wood called for 'shear', because the man in the rescue basket was in danger. I immediately flew the aircraft in a closing movement relative to the boat. This allowed for slack to develop in the cable, my aircrewman was able to direct me back in to a visual position with the boat. The 'shear' command was cancelled.

We now discussed the possibility of hoisting the people from the water, thus minimizing the no reference situation. We were able to extract all four persons from the vessel safely and expeditiously. After all persons were secured, we departed scene at 00.10 25 December 1983. At 00.41, rescued persons were debarked at Marathon Airport to await relatives. Aircraft and crew returned to air station Miami.

At 15.40 on 2 March 1971 the US Navy ship USS *Mt Whitney* advised that they had an acute appendicitis case on board who required air evacuation to a hospital. The *Mt Whitney* was then 130 miles east of Charleston, South Carolina. At 16.20 a USCG helicopter from Savannah left to make the evacuation. Bad weather and mechanical difficulties forced the Sikorsky HH-52A *Seaguard* helicopter to land at Charleston Air Force base. The bad weather persisted until about 20.00. A second helicopter then left to make the evacuation. It landed and refuelled at Charleston Air Force base and at 21.37 the second helicopter, HH-52A 1389, left Charleston under the escort of a US Air Force Lockheed C-5A *Galaxy* transport. The helicopter landed aboard the *Mt Whitney* at 22.18 which was then sixty miles east of Charleston. At 23.08 the helicopter delivered the patient to Charleston Air Force base for transfer to the hospital.

The crew of the USCG rescue helicopter were Lieutenant Commander Bob Miller, Lieutenant Jim Marcotte, and AE2 Craig Harris, all from the air station at Savannah, Georgia.

The patient, RD1 V L Seabolt, USN of Norfolk, Virginia, was operated on at Charleston Naval Hospital for a ruptured appendix. His condition was reported as satisfactory. The evacuation took place in spite of bad weather, darkness and the distance offshore.

The Coast Guard Base at Charleston maintained communications with the *Mt Whitney,* and the US Air Force 437th Military Airlift Wing at Charleston Air Force base provided the huge C-5A, the world's largest aircraft, to escort the USCG helicopter offshore.

Commander R C Powell, Commanding Officer of USCG air station, Savannah praised the flight crew for their skill and perseverence; and also commented that the assistance from Coast Guard Charleston and Charleston Air Force base was a vital factor in the success of the mission.

The Lockheed C-5A *Galaxy* aircraft involved was US Air Force 68-0213 from the 437th Military Airlift Wing of Military Airlift Command.

Of all emergency procedures with which the over-ocean pilot must be familiar, none is so important as communications. It is the means by which the Search & Rescue organization is alerted and put into action. It enables the numerous and varied facilities to function as a team. International distress frequencies are allocated for use in any emergency, these being 243.0 MHz on UHF, and 121.5 MHz on VHF, plus 500 KHz, 2182 KHz, 8364 KHz.

The pilot of the distressed aircraft is a vital member of the Search & Rescue team. From the inception of distress, the pilot can guide and assist the Search & Rescue organization in its efforts to help him. If he cannot, or does not, announce his predicament at the earliest possible moment, his chance of survival may be greatly reduced. It is imperative that the pilot of the aircraft in distress start the distress procedure when doubt exists as to the safety of his aircraft. The pilot, as commander of the aircraft has the responsibility of deciding when an emergency exists or when a forced landing or bailout may be necessary. It is a grave responsibility. Some pilots are reluctant to declare an emergency even when the situation requires it. Wise pilots do not hesitate to call for assistance when confronted with the remotest possibility of a forced landing at sea. It is far better to start the distress procedure, and then not to need assistance, than to delay it until it is too late. The Search & Rescue organization is always ready to respond immediately and render timely assistance which may well prevent the development of a full emergency.

When a decision is made that an emergency situation exists, the pilot should at once start the appropriate emergency procedure.

The following two aircraft in distress emergencies, involving two US airliners, which crashed in the Pacific Ocean during January 1969, both had lost radio communications with the Air Traffic Control agency controlling their flight. In both these cases it was the ATC agency who initiated the Search & Rescue. It is unique that only five days elapsed between the two emergencies, involving exactly the same Search & Rescue facilities and the same USCG air station.

At 19.27 on 13 January 1969 the Rescue Co-ordination Center (RCC) advised USCG air station Los Angeles that Los Angeles International Airport Approach Control had lost radio and radar contact with an inbound Scandinavian Airlines System (SAS) Douglas DC-8 airliner.

19.28 — Los Angeles ARTC advised RCC they had the same report and indicated that an incident had occurred three miles west of Los Angeles International.

19.30 — RCC directed USCG cutter *Point Judith,* USCG cutter *Pendant* and USCG air station Los Angeles to proceed and assist, and notified Los Angeles County Lifeguard vessel *Bywatch.*

19.32 — USCG cutter *Pendant* underway to assist.

19.35 — RCC directed USCG cutter *Morris* to proceed and assist.

19.40 — RCC directed USCG cutter *Point Bridge* to proceed and assist.

19.43 — HH-52A 1390 airborne from USCG air station Los Angeles. 1390 was vectored to last known position by LAX (Los Angeles) Approach Control.

19.45 — Los Angeles Approach Control advised contact was lost 250 and one and a quarter miles from Marina del Rey.

19.49 — 1390 arrived at datum and commenced search. On scene weather, ceiling 700 feet, visibility three miles in rain and fog, wind 060 magnetic 12 knots, seas 200M three feet.

19.50 — RCC directed USCG air station San Diego to launch a HU-16E with flares for illumination. USCG cutter *Point Judith* underway to scene.

19.53 — RCC requested airspace reservation of three miles radius and 2,500 feet altitude. Los Angeles ARTC was initially reluctant to grant this reservation as it would necessitate closing Los Angeles International to landings. This request was subsequently granted without delay.

20.05 — HH-52A 1355 airborne from air station Los Angeles. 1355 was vectored to datum by LAX Approach Control.

20.08 — 1355 arrived at datum. 1355 and 1390 commenced expanding sector search.

20.10 — HU-16E 2126 airborne from air station San Diego with 48 flares aboard.

Scene at the US Coast Guard Rescue Control Centre (RCC) in New York on 3 March 1953 as Captain Theodore J Harris, on the right, and Lieutenant George A Gyland plot the position of a US Navy Lockheed P2V- *Neptune* which ditched in the Atlantic on 27 February. (USCG)

20.18 — US Marine Corps Air Station, El Toro, advised RCC they would be unable to assist. Their rescue helicopters were engaged in a crashed F-4 Phantom case. Los Angeles Approach Control advised 1355 and 1390 that they were searching out of the area. Control advised 1355 he was five miles west of datum, 1390 was 2 miles north of datum. 1390 reversed course to datum. 1355 continued to search westward to investigate a light sighted by the crewman.

20.23 — 1355 located the floating forward section of a DC-8 with survivors in liferafts and standing on the wing. LAX Approach Control advised 1355's position was 250° magnetic eight miles from LAX VORTAC. 1390 proceeded to this position.

20.24 — 1390 was directed to assist vectoring USCG cutter *Point Judith* to this position.

20.25 — USCG cutter *Morris* underway to scene.

20.26 — 1355 lowered a PRC-63 radio to the survivors on the wing. A man, who identified himself as the pilot, advised 1355 that the passengers were safe and one woman might be missing. This man also stated he would advise if helicopter evacuation was necessary for the injured passengers. 1355 advised the survivors that surface assistance would be on scene in approximately 10 minutes.

Crew members respond to a scramble as a Martin P5M-1G *Marlin* 1284 is called out on a search and rescue (SAR) mission from the USCG air station at Elizabeth City, North Carolina, on 2 January 1954. A distress signal has been received from a sinking ship off the Carolina coast. (USCG)

20.30 — USCG cutter *Point Judith* designated On-Scene Commander. 1390 continued to vector *Point Judith* to scene.

20.33 — Fleet Air Control and Surveillance Facility San Diego (FACSFAC) advised they had helicopters on immediate standby for assistance if necessary.

20.35 — USCG cutter *Point Bridge* underway to scene.

20.37 — FACSFAC advised they had a naval vessel 130 miles from datum and would assist if necessary. RCC advised FACS-FAC their services would not be required. Scandinavian Airlines System at Seattle reported that there were 34 passengers and 7 crew aboard. This was in conflict with the report of 36 passengers and 9 crew received from the airline in Los Angeles. It was subsequently determined that the Los Angeles report was correct.

20.39 — 1355 reported that numerous private surface vessels were arriving on scene.

20.41 — *Point Judith* arrived on scene and commenced recovering survivors in vicinity of fuselage. 1355 and 1390 on scene providing illuminations with landing, flood and hover lights.

20.50 — FACSFAC reported their helicopters were on 30 minutes standby.

20.53 — 1355 reported private vessels were departing the scene with survivors on board. Vessels enroute Marina del Rey.

20.55 — HU-16E 2126 on scene holding. No illumination utilized due to low ceiling and aircraft fuel on water.

20.59 — RCC confirmed with Marina del Rey Harbor Department that they could handle all survivors.

21.03 — *Point Judith* departed scene with 12 survivors on board enroute Marina del Rey.

21.10 — *Point Bridge* on scene, relieved *Point Judith* on On Scene Command (OSC). Cutter circled the fuselage searching for possible survivors. Results of this search were negative. *Point Bridge* commenced a visual search three-quarter mile radius around datum.

21.12 — 1355 remained on scene searching. 1390 vectored approximately 30 private vessels to scene.

21.24 — 1355 departed scene to refuel and replace landing light.

21.25 — RCC requested and received revised airspace reservation to three mile radius 300 feet around datum. Reservation requirements reduced as no illumination was being used. Marina del Rey Harbor Dept reported ambulance standing by at Marina del Rey.

21.30 — Chevron Oil Tender *Lawrence Redondo* reported five survivors aboard.

21.35 — RCC released HU-16E 2126 to return to San Diego.

21.36 — 1355 arrived air station Los Angeles.

21.40 — RCC directed USCG air station San Diego to launch an HH-52A to augment air station Los Angeles forces.

21.50 — *Point Judith* arrived Marina del Rey and debarked 12 survivors. Marina del Rey Harbor Dept reported County Lifeguard vessel *Baywatch III* had eight survivors, Marina del Rey Patrol vessel *BRAVO I* had three survivors. Tug *Lawrence Redondo* had five survivors.

21.53 — HH-52A 1386 airborne from air station San Diego to scene. HH-52A 1355 airborne from air station Los Angeles to search.

22.00 — 1355 on scene commenced searching. *Point Judith* underway from Marina del Rey to search.

22.03 — 1390 departed scene.

22.06 — 1355 reported no survivors could be seen in the fuselage or water surrounding fuselage.

22.09 — USCG cutter *Pendant* arrived on scene, chopped OSC with *Point Bridge* and commenced SE search around datum.

22.11 — 1390 arrived air station Los Angeles.

22.23 — 2126 arrived air station San Diego. RCC directed cutter *Morris* to assume OSC when on scene.

22.24 — 1390 airborne from air station Los Angeles to search.

22.28 — 1390 on scene searching. *Morris* relieved *Point Bridge* of OSC.

22.29 — 1355 and 1390 searching a three mile radius around datum. 1355 controlling altitude separation for aircraft.

22.30 — *Point Judith* on scene, commenced searching.

22.31 — Tug *El Segundo* reported recovering three bodies.

22.32 — *Morris* on scene. Datum position 251° true eight miles from Marina del Rey.

22.33 — 1355 reported on scene weather was deteriorating and recommended 1386 be diverted to air station Los Angeles. Weather made three aircraft search impracticable.

22.40 — RCC issued local broadcast notice to mariners requesting all vessels with survivors on board report to Coast Guard Radio Station Long Beach.

22.52 — RCC directed USCG cutter *Morris* to put a man aboard fuselage if practicable and check for survivors.

22.55 — Santa Monica Lifeguard boat Rescue 2 reported one body on board.

23.00 — A private vessel was reported to be placing four divers in the fuselage.

23.11 — Divers report no survivors or bodies in the fuselage.

23.30 — USCG aircraft and surface vessels continued to search in vicinity of the fuselage to a radius of four miles for survivors or bodies.

14 January 1969

00.00 — 1355 departed scene for gyro repairs. USCG cutter *Point Bridge* commenced three-quarter mile radius SE search around datum.

00.14 — HH-52A 1386 arrived from air station Los Angeles.

00.16 — 1355 arrived air station Los Angeles.

00.35 — USCG cutter *Point Judith* recovered the three bodies aboard the tug *El Segundo*.

00.45 — 1390 departed search area. Single helicopter to be used balance of night hours due to deteriorating weather.

01.00 — 1355 airborne from air station Los Angeles to search.

01.06 — 1390 arrived air station Los Angeles.

01.15 — 1355 on scene searching.

01.20 — USCG cutter *Pendant* secured from night search by On Scene Commander, enroute Marina del Rey. *Pendant* located no survivors or bodies. General debris recovered.

02.15 — USCG cutter *Point Judith* secured from night search by OSC, enroute to Marina del Rey with three bodies on board.

02.29 — 1355 reported on scene weather deteriorating to ceiling 150 ft, visibility 1 mile. OSC with RCC concurrence suspended aircraft night search.

02.31 — USCG cutter *Point Bridge* secured from night search by OSC. *Point Bridge* search results were negative. Cutter enroute to Marina del Rey.

02.35 — 1355 dropped a datum marker buoy and departed the scene.

02.59 — 1355 arrived at air station Los Angeles.

03.00 — USCG cutter *Pendant* moored Marina del Rey. *Pendant* released recovered debris to Harbormaster.

03.05 — USCG cutter *Point Judith* moored Marina del Rey and released three bodies to coroner.

03.28 — USCG cutter *Point Bridge* moored Marina del Rey.

06.05 — USCG cutter *Point Bridge* underway to search.

06.09 — 1355 airborne to search.

06.15 — 1355 on scene datum 174° true 5.25 miles from Malibu Point. 1355 commenced searching 5 mile radius northern semi-circle about datum. New datum established on predicted survivor in water drift. (Area designation B-1).

06.18 — USCG cutter *Morris* reported on scene weather wind 080 true 1.9 knots, seas 065 true 3 feet, visibility 15 miles.

06.20 — USCG cutter *Pendant* underway enroute to forward section of fuselage.

06.22 — USCG cutter *Point Judith* underway to search. 1386 airborne to search.

06.28 — 1386 on scene, commenced searching 8 miles radius southern semi-circle about datum. Area B-1.

06.40 — USCG cutter *Point Bridge* on scene, commenced searching and recovering debris.

07.00 — USCG cutter *Point Judith* on scene, commenced searching and recovering debris.

07.35 — *Pendant* on scene commenced searching and recovering debris.

07.45 — RCC was advised one male survivor previously unaccounted for had come ashore and gone home during the night. Count of passengers was 30 survivors, four bodies, and 11 missing, total POB 45.

08.57 — 1355 departed after completing assigned search B-1.

A US Coast Guard Sikorsky HO4S-2 helicopter from Port Angeles air station hovers over a miscellany of USCG surface craft. The event was the 1957 Gold Cup Regatta held at Seattle in Washington State. (USCG)

09.00 — *Pendant* directed by OSC to determine if operator of salvage vessel *Que Paso* required any assistance in towing nose section of fuselage.

09.04 — 1386 departed after completing assigned search B-1. 1355 and 1386 marked numerous pieces of debris with smoke floats for vessel recovery. Helicopters also made water landings to recover debris.

09.07 — 1390 airborne from air station Los Angeles to search.

09.14 — 1390 on scene commenced eight miles radius visual search, northern half area B-2. Datum 170 true three and a quarter miles Malibu Point.

09.20 — 1355 arrived air station Los Angeles.

09.30 — *Pendant* relieved *Que Paso* of DC-8 tow after *Que Paso* indicated he was unable to tow subject.

09.31 — 1386 arrived air station Los Angeles and was released from search. 1386 RON (remained overnight) Losa due to weather at San Diego.

09.43 — 1355 airborne to search.

09.45 — 1355 on scene commenced eight mile radius visual search southern half area B-2.

11.25 — 1390 completed assigned search and departed. Search results were negative.

11.36 — 1390 arrive air station Los Angeles.

Coast Guard vessels and a Sikorsky HH-52A 1352 fight flames and smoke which erupted on impact after a collision between the 6,722 ton Norwegian freighter *Fernview* and the 3,100 ton American coastal tanker *Dynafuel,* on 14 November 1963 at Buzzards Bay, Massachusetts. The helicopter brought foam, pumps and other equipment from the shore. All forty crewmen on the freighter and twenty-two on the tanker were saved. The Coast Guard completed more than 130 hoists. (Sikorsky)

12.08 — 1390 airborne from air station Los Angeles to search.

12.25 — 1390 on scene, commenced eight mile radius visual search. Researching southern half area B-1.

12.30 — *Pendant* intentionally grounded the nose section of the fuselage 210° magnetic 1300 yards from Malibu Point in 60 foot of water.

12.55 — 1355 departed search area, having completed assigned search: results negative.

13.11 — 1355 arrived air station Los Angeles.

13.58 — 1355 airborne to search.

14.11 — 1355 on scene researching northern half area B-1.

14.30 — *Morris* departed scene to pick up National Transportation Safety Board (NTSB) members.

14.48 — 1390 completed assigned search, enroute air station Los Angeles. Results negative.

15.02 — *Morris* embarked NTSB passengers to inspect wreckage of nose section.

15.03 — 1390 arrived air station Los Angeles. *Pendant* reported nose section sank in position of previous grounding.

15.35 — *Point Judith* released from search by OSC.

15.51 — *Pendant* marked position of nose section and was released from search by OSC vessel. *Que Paso* stood by wreckage during the night.

16.45 — *Morris* debarked NTSB passengers.

17.00 — *Point Bridge* released from search by OSC.

17.01 — *Morris* enroute to assist COMMINEPAC. (US Navy) units in locating sunken tail section of DC-8. 1355 complete assigned search with negative results and departed enroute air station Los Angeles.

17.15 — 1355 arrived air station Los Angeles.

18.13 — *Morris* on scene crash position in company with USS *Conflict* and USS *Reaper* to search for tail section.

15 January 1969

06.10 — *Morris* reported USNS *Gear* on scene to assist in search for tail section.

08.00 — *Morris* advised sonar search of crash area yielded negative results.

10.54 — 1355 airborne to mark datum for NSTB.

11.00 — 1355 on scene marked datum by vectors by Los Angeles Approach Control. New radar datum of tail section 33-35.0N, 118-34.7W.

11.39 — 1355 arrived Losa.

12.32 — 1355 airborne to search.

12.47 — 1355 on scene conducting shoreline search from King Harbor to Point Dume to two miles offshore.

14.21 — 1355 completed search, and recovered one pillow and one arctic survival kit.

14.47 — 1355 arrived air station Los Angeles.

17.35 — *Morris* released from search as US Navy vessels had secured.

18.54 — USCG District II (SMC) suspended active search pending further developments.

From 16 to 28 January Coast Guard units continued to support the National Transportation Safety Board (NTSB) in their investigation of the crash and search for the missing tail section. Coast Guard participation consisted of HH-52A helicopter flights to located debris and USCG vessels to investigate sonar contacts and control spectators around salvage operations.

The forward section of the DC-8 was salvaged on 19 January 1969. The tail section was subsequently located by the Lockheed Submersible *Deep Quest* and the flight recorder was recovered.

Deep Quest reported at least 2 bodies were on the ocean floor alongside the tail section.

A final accounting of the 45 persons aboard the DC-8 shows 30 survivors, four known dead, and 11 missing.

30 January 1969: Case closed.

G. F. THOMETZ Jr.
By direction.

At 1826 on 18 January 1969 USCG air station Los Angeles reported they had been advised by Los Angeles International Airport that the tower had lost communications and radar contact with United Air Lines Flight 266, a Boeing 727, three miles southeast of Bay Intersection after departing LAX.

18.27 — Rescue Co-ordination Center (RCC) directed air station Los Angeles to launch two HH-52A helicopters. Directed USCG cutter *Point Bridge,* currently underway, to proceed to a point 270° true 6-7 miles from Marina del Rey. RCC commenced contacting all available units including city and county lifeguards and Coast Guard Auxiliary.

18.29 — Los Angeles Center confirmed that Los Angeles Departure Control had lost communications and radar contact with United 266. United 266 had previously reported a fire warning light in number one engine and stated he was returning to Los Angeles.

18.35 — Directed USCG cutters *Bollard* and *Point Judith* to proceed and assist.

18.40 — Directed air station San Diego to launch a HU-16E to provide illumination.

18.45 — POB (persons on board) UAL 266 reported as 36.

18.50 — Los Angeles Center watch supervisor advised last radar position of United 266 was 263° true six and a half miles from Marina del Rey. Subject was on a west-bound heading and starting a left turn when lost from radar. Information passed to all units.

18.54 — Directed USCG cutter *Walnut* to proceed and wait. Designated *Point Bridge* On Scene Commander. *Point Bridge* on scene datum.

19.00 — HH-52A 1355 airborne air station Los Angeles. HU-16E 7236 airborne from air station San Diego with parachute flares. Directed USCG cutter *Morris* to proceed and assist.

19.05 — *Bollard* underway, enroute to scene.

19.06 — HH-52A 1355 on scene, chopped to *Point Bridge,* and commenced a five mile radius visual search, search altitude 300 feet, on scene weather, ceiling 400 feet, overcast, visibility 10 miles, wind 115° true at seven knots, seas 215° true at one foot.

19.13 — HH-52A 1390 airborne from air station Los Angeles.

19.29 — HH-52A 1390 chopped to On Scene Commander *Point Bridge*. 1390 and 1355 commenced CM search, search altitude 200 feet, track spacing half a mile. USCG cutter *Venturous* under-way.

19.30 — *Point Judith* underway enroute to scene. Numerous civilian surface craft, including Coast Guard Auxilary and lifeguards reported either on scene or enroute.

19.40 — Directed USCG cutter *Point Evans* to proceed and assist.

19.44 — Directed USCG cutter *Cape Hatteras* to proceed and assist.

19.45 — Directed USCG cutter *Point Divide* to proceed and assist.

19.48 — HU-16E 7236 arrived on scene and commenced illumination.

19.50 — *Point Evans* underway, enroute to scene.

19.54 — US Naval Air station Los Alamitos reported three Navy Grumman S2F air-craft were enroute for possible search-light search of area.

19.55 — HH-52A 1386 airborne from air station San Diego to augment forces at air station Los Angeles.

20.51 — Lifeguard vessel *Baywatch III* reported to *Point Bridge* that they had found aircraft debris and a partial body in approximate position 33-57N, 118-37W. RCC diverted all search units to this position. Aircraft searches conducted to this time were ineffective and in-complete due to the aircraft being diverted to investigate sightings reported to RCC and on-scene weather con-ditions.

21.00 — RCC directed air station San Diego to provide additional aircraft for continu-ation of illumination.

A dramatic scene on 22 July 1971 as a San Francisco air station based HH 52A *Seaguard* 1386 airlifts a survivor near treacherous rocks on the Californian coast. Coast Guard aircrewmen are specialists: qualified medics, skin divers, etc. in order to meet all eventualities. (USCG)

21.05 — US Navy S2Fs secured. Weather and other on-scene aircraft prevented utilization.

21.12 — HH-52A 1400 airborne to relieve 1355.

21.14 — *Point Bridge* on scene with *Baywatch III*. Position 33-57.5N, 118-39W. Established as new datum.

21.20 — HH-52A 1400 on scene, chopped to *Point Bridge* HH-52A 1355.

21.25 — *Bollard* on scene. Departed scene, HU-16E 7236 departed scene after expending all flares.

21.40 — HH-52A 1386 on scene, 1386 and 1400 searching two mile visual search. Vessels in the area around datum recovering debris and body parts. Debris is small and badly fragmented. Debris found included mail sack with current date.

21.42 — RCC issued an urgent marine broadcast requesting all vessels with no assigned rescue responsibility to remain clear of the area.

A Sikorsky HH-52A *Seaguard* helicopter 1382 from San Francisco air station answered a distress call after a small vessel caught fire. The vessel is seen beached, as the helio searches the water for any survivors. (US Navy)

22.05 — RCC direct *Cape Hatteras* to secure and assume Santa Barbara Search & Rescue responsibility.

22.10 — HU-16E 2126 airborne from San Diego to provide illumination on scene.

22.15 — RCC directed maintain but one helicopter on scene due to deteriorating weather. HH-52A 1386 remaining on scene. *Point Bridge* commenced a PM search with USNS *Gear* and civilian vessels in the area about datum.

22.45 — *Point Divide* on scene.

22.55 — Cutter *Morris* on scene. Relieved *Point Bridge* as On Scene Commander. HU-16E 2126 arrived on scene and commenced illumination. Search units on scene when *Morris* assumed OSC consisted of HH-52A 1386, HU-16E 2123, USCG cutters *Walnut, Point Judith, Point Bridge, Point Divide,* and *Bollard. Morris* commenced PM search utilizing Coast Guard vessels. Upon locating area of heaviest debris two miles west of datum, units were directed to commence individual search and recovery operations.

23.38 — HH-52A 1400 airborne to relieve 1386.

23.45 — *Point Evans* on scene.

23.47 — 1400 arrived on scene, chopped to *Morris*. 1386 departed scene.

19 January 1969

00.29 — RCC directed *Morris* to secure aircraft search due to weather. HH-52A 1400 departed scene. Vessels in the area continued recovery operations. Recoveries consisted of small debris and partial body parts.

01.05 — HU-16E 2126 departed area.

02.35 — Cutter *Venturous* arrived on scene and assumed On-Scene Commander from *Morris. Venturous* utilized all USCG vessels on scene for PP search in area of heaviest debris. The debris at this time was drifting NW. RCC continued to calculate drift based on a man in the water. These drift calculations were checked against actual drift of debris.

03.15 — Directed air station Los Angeles to provide two HH-52A helicopters for first light visual searches from 33-37.5N 118-37.2W and 34-00.1N 118-47.3W utilizing five mile radius and five mile track spacing. Helicopters directed to chop to *Venturous* on arrival.

03.16 — *Point Evans* released from search to fulfill previous operational commitments. Searching shore line to Marina del Rey enroute.

05.10 — *Point Evans* arrived Marina del Rey. Results of shoreline search negative.

06.47 — HH-52A 1400 airborne from air station Los Angeles to search.

06.50 — HH-52A 1390 airborne from air station Los Angeles to search.

07.00 — OSC on USCG cutter *Venturous* reported that human remains and general debris was recovered by most Coast Guard units during the night search. No sightings of survivors were made.

07.04 — HH-52As 1390 and 1400 on scene, chopped to *Venturous,* commenced assigned visual searches.

07.07 — On scene weather reported as ceiling 500 feet overcast, visibility two miles, seas 210° true three to four feet.

08.10 — United Air Lines confirmed 38 POB aboard Flight 266. 29 adults and three children as passengers, six crew members.

09.08 — HH-52A 1355 airborne to relieve 1390.

09.17 — HH-52A 1386 airborne to relieve 1400.

10.25 — HH-52A 1355 diverted to Search & Rescue case at Catalina Island.

10.38 — Helicopters completed visual searches with negative sightings except for general debris.

11.12 — HH-52A 1400 airborne to search.

11.26 — 1400 chopped to *Venturous. Venturous* commenced CMCS search with 1400 and 1386. Coast Guard vessels continued CS searches from Point Dume to Point Mugu. Debris continued west and northwesterly drift.

12.00 — RCC secured helicopters due to deteriorating weather.

14.55 — RCC directed OSC to release all units at sunset with the exception of cutters *Venturous* and *Morris*.

15.35 — HH-52A 1390 airborne to search coastline from Point Dume to Point Mugu. Weather in area improved to 500 feet ceiling.

15.49 — 1390 on scene chopped to OSC and commenced search.

16.27 — 1390 directed to another Search & Rescue case.

17.13 — OSC on *Venturous* released Coast Guard units as directed. *Venturous* advised CS and CM searches during the day by USCG units yielded 80 per cent POD. Area searched was from Point Dume to Point Mugu to six miles offshore. USCG units continued to pick up general debris during the day.

19.15 — *Morris* secured from search for the night, enroute Marina del Rey.

20 January 1969

01.10 — *Venturous* reported on scene weather ceiling zero feet, wind 072° true 25 knots, visibility four miles in rain.

07.20 — HH-52A 1355 airborne from air station Los Angeles for search.

07.37 — 1355 on scene, chopped to OSC.

07.55 — USCG cutter *Morris* on scene; weather ceiling 1,000 feet, wind 075° true 21 knots, visibility 10-12 miles. *Morris* and 1355 commenced search of areas from Point Dume to Point Mugu to four miles offshore.

09.55 — HH-52A 1400 airborne to relieve 1355.

10.13 — HH-52A 1400 relieved 1355.

10.52 — RCC directed *Venturous* to have *Morris* and HH-52A 1400 search the area NW of Point Mugu for debris.

11.25 — Units on scene NW of Point Mugu for assigned search.

11.55 — HH-52A 1400 secured from search due to poor weather. 300-400 feet ceiling, visibility one and a half miles, wind 250° at 30 knots. *Morris* and *Venturous* continued surface search.

12.55 — *Venturous* and *Morris* completed assigned search with negative sightings.

13.23 — RCC cancelled UMIB.

13.49 — RCC directed Coast Guard Station Point Hueneme to make beach search Hueneme to Point Mugu.

17.00 — RCC suspended active Coast Guard vessel search.

18.00 — Point Hueneme reported beach search negative.

21 January 1969

07.21 — HH-52A 1390 airborne from Los Angeles for shoreline search from Point Dume to Santa Barbara.

10.29 — 1390 completed assigned search with negative sightings.

19.10 — Active search suspended pending further developments.

17 February 1969

11.00 — Case closed.

The chronological summaries of these two airline disasters were supplied by the Public Information Officer, 11th Coast Guard District located in Long Beach, California. The investigation into the two accidents was conducted by the Accident Inquiry Branch of the National Transportation Safety Board (NTSB). The summaries have been reproduced *in toto,* except for minor translation in parts.

From the open sea to a Marine Hospital on Staten Island, New York, a radio message flashed at 8 am on 15 July 1939. It was from the ketch *Atlantis,* the floating laboratory used by the US Oceanographic Institution at Woods Hole, Massachusetts. For several months her crew had been measuring area and currents of the Gulf Stream. Now one of them was seriously ill with pneumonia. The *Atlantis* lay 150 miles south west of New York. At top speed it would take the ketch eighteen hours to reach a port.

Back to the *Atlantis* from the Marine Hospital flashed instructions: 'Force liquids . . . administer aspirin . . . put man ashore as soon as possible'. At 10.05 am the Coast Guard Hall Aluminium PH-2 V164 took off from Floyd Bennett air station with a crew of seven to pick up the sick sailor. Shortly before noon pilot William L Clemmer reported he had sighted the ketch and was preparing to land. The weather was dangerous — 'thunder squalls and a cross swell'. But the PH-2 landed safely and quickly took aboard the ailing passenger who had been rowed out by boat from the *Atlantis*. Then, taxiing over the swells into wind, the flying ambulance rose slightly, levelled off, and mysteriously, with motors roaring wide, dived headlong into the sea. Both pilots and the sick man drowned, trapped in the forward cabin. Five others were rescued by the *Atlantis.*

A Sikorsky HH-3F *Pelican* helicopter 1484 from New Orleans air station hovers to pick up a stranded injured victim from the roof of some burning elevators at the Continental Grainery at Westwego, near New Orleans. After an explosion, the containers were a twisted hot mass of metal. Date was 22 December 1977. (USCG)

Two days later an official board of inquiry began piecing together the narrative fragments of the crash. From many a conflicting and vague detail they deduced that the PH-2 V164 had struck a long swell on the instant of leaving the water, had lost speed and nosed into the waves, its throttles open. Most provocative testimony offered was that of Lieutenant Watson A Burton, commander of the Coast Guard base at Floyd Bennett Field, who deplored the unnecessary hazards to planes and men involved in the department's famed aerial ambulance service:

In the majority of cases it is discovered later that the patient is not as sick as reported. Also there are many cases that are sick as reported who would survive in spite of delay . . . . Many times the information as to the ailment comes from the master of the ship, who is not qualified to make a sound analysis.

The day of 26 May 1954 started out calmly at the USCG air station at Salem, Massachusetts. Then, at 08.33 the station was alerted. The US Navy aircraft carrier *Bennington* had been rocked by an explosion off the coast of Rhode Island and air evacuation was critically needed. Within minutes the air station's two Sikorsky HO4S- helicopters were in the air heading for the scene of the disaster. Almost as quickly, two Grumman UF-1G Albatrossses and a large Martin P5M-Mariner were launched from the station's seaplane ramp.

The Coast Guard helicopters joined with US Navy helicopters in evacuating the badly-burned *Bennington* officers and crewmen. The seaplanes from the Salem air station flew escort for the helicopters between the stricken carrier and the hospital at Quonset Point.

Admiral John Hoskins, commandant of the Quonset Naval Air Station, commended the rescue work done by both Coast Guard and US Navy helicopters.

> Without any doubt the helicopters were responsible for saving the lives of dozens of the seriously burned crewmen by speeding them to the medical facility.

For the Coast Guard it was another chapter in the growing saga of rescue work that had gained momentum in the postwar period. It was also an outstanding example of the Coast Guard's willingness to tackle any task. Before the *Bennington* evacuation the USCG helicopter pilots had never before landed on a carrier deck at sea.

Careful planning is necessary when an SAR mission places the man and machine on both range and endurance limits. This is overcome by refuelling at sea, be it from a USCG or US Navy facility, or even an oil platform or rig. Seen here is a refuelling at sea by a Cape Cod air station based HH-3F *Pelican* 1484. (USCG)

At the little all-water air station located at the site of historic Fort Pickering in Salem, Massachusetts, every call to action is treated as an emergency. Within minutes after a Search & Rescue operation is flashed from the Coast Guard's nerve-center in Boston, aircraft are ready to go. The aircraft ordered out may be a helicopter — the base has two Sikorsky HO4S-'s — a Martin P5M- *Mariner,* or one of the four Grumman UF-1G amphibians. Most of the assignments are routine, many of them fruitless. But each one is handled as if human lives were at stake — as often they are.

Lieutenant Dave Young, a Coast Guard pilot, typifies the attitude of the pilots at the station.

> Like the others here, I've spent a lot of flying hours squinting down at the water looking for a reported capsized boat only to find it's another dead whale floating around. But no matter how many goose chases you have, it only takes one where you are able to save some lives to keep you squinting even harder.

Many times the search and rescue missions are not cases of squinting down at the sea from an airplane. For instance, a freighter floundering off the coast was able to radio its position. The position was picked up by the monitoring Coast Guard radio and in less than an hour the Martin *Mariner* was circling overhead.

During the summer pleasure boating season, the air station experiences some of its most unusual distress calls. Many times the inexperience of the occasional boatman, off with his family in the outboard, causes trouble. 'You have to admire the amateur's seafaring spirit sometimes,' says Commander Ray Tuttle, the air station's executive officer, 'even if his carelessness is disconcerting. Some of the voyages undertaken by amateur sailors with families on a Sunday afternoon are something to contemplate. Five kids and mom in a rowboat with an eggbeater slapping the water and they are off on a shakedown that would test an eighteen-footer.'

Tuttle recalls one instance where such a pleasure party bobbing about off Marblehead, Massachusetts, in a tiny boat, without power, was reported in distress. After being spotted by helicopter which radioed for surface craft assistance, the party rebuffed offers of assistance until they had carefully repacked their lunch basket.

The Coast Guard is the smallest military service of the US government. The present overall complement of the service is only slightly more than 30,000 officers and men. As a comparatively small unit, with a broad and diverse assignment, the service demands maximum versatility from its men. At Salem where 119 officers and men operate seven airplanes and three boats, the number of hats worn by individual heads is amazing. Commander Frederick G Wild, commander of the Salem air station, is a veteran Coast Guard airman.

There is no such thing as a typical day at the Coast Guard Air Station. As Lieutenant Commander John Natwig, operations officer, states, 'When you are a lifeguard some days you get a tan and some days you get wet.' The commander's logbook for a recent day disclosed a variety of activity within a twelve hour period. First came a report of unidentified wreckage floating several miles off the coast. Next, in an entirely different area, an oil slick was reported. From Boston harbor came word of an empty sport fishing boat about two miles at sea. Three fishing vessels overdue from Gloucester comprised the next report. Presently, a light aircraft flying from Cape Cod to New Jersey was reported missing.

As each of the calls came through, Natwig called his pilots into the operation shack for briefing. On each call an airplane was dispatched. As it happened, happily, the wreckage was part of a destroyed pier and the oil slick had made its way to sea from an industrial plant. However, the empty sport fishing boat was the remaining evidence of a Sunday fishing party tragedy in which one of two sportsmen was drowned; the fishermen reported overdue were just late. Unfortunately, the light plane had crashed due to bad weather and was not found until three days later with all occupants dead. The air search for this plane had involved six aircraft, eleven sorties and fifty-two search hours flown by aircraft and helicopters from the Salem air station.

(The above item was published in the *Sikorsky News* magazine of summer 1954.) On 29 August 1970 a new USCG air station was commissioned at Cape Cod which took over the Search & Rescue missions previously carried out from the air station at Salem.

Unfortunately, Coast Guard Aviation suffered its losses to both men and machine through accidents. On 18 May 1957 a Grumman UF-1G *Albatross* 1278 crashed whilst demonstrating a JATO (Jet Assisted Take-Off) at Salem, Massachusetts, killing the two crew. On 22 August 1959 a Grumman UF-1G 1259 from Brooklyn air station, New York crashed during a post maintenance test flight after suffering control problems and four were killed. On 7 August 1967, a Grumman HU-16E from San Francisco (2128) crashed into a mountain whilst on a search mission, killing the crew of three. In Alaska, on 18

December 1967, a HU-16E 1271 crashed whilst attempting a water landing in rough seas off St Paul Island. One of the crew was killed. On 21 September 1973 a Grumman HU-16E 2123 from Corpus Christi air station, Texas, crashed into the Gulf of Mexico after a flare ignited inside the fuselage during flare dropping on a rescue mission. The crew of six were killed.

During the night of 8 November 1979 men from the LORAN Station St Paul, Alaska, performed a daring sea rescue with one of the oldest methods used by the Coast Guard, a ship to shore lifeline. The Japanese fishing factory ship *Ryuyo Maru Nr 2* had run aground seventy-five yards off St Paul Island in the Bering Sea. The seas were running ten to twenty feet and it was impossible to reach the vessel with the boats available. The vessel was holed and was being smashed by the rough seas. It was imperative that the eighty-one people on board be evacuated.

Using their snow cat vehicles, crew members from the LORAN station were able to reach the remote area where the ship was aground. Steep cliffs prevented their reaching the beach and they were forced to find a more accessible spot. After discovering a route to the beach, the rescuers made their way back along the two miles of rocks to the *Ryuyo Maru*. A line was passed from the ship to the men on the shore. They secured the line to a large rock and fashioned a bos'n chair, reminiscent of a breeches buoy, and began bringing the crew to shore one at a time. After a half dozen of the Japanese had been pulled over the rough seas, a second chair was rigged to speed the operation.

Even though darkness, tricky seas and high winds hampered the rescue, the entire crew and National Marine Fisheries agent were brought ashore without injury. After reaching the beach, small groups of the crew were guided back over the rocks to the waiting vehicles. Working against time as the tide crept in, the last group of people made it through the rocks being splashed by the incoming sea.

Hall Aluminium PH-2 V164 seen beached at its home base of Floyd Bennett air station, New York. Unfortunately this flying boat was lost with all on board during a rescue from the ketch *Atlantis* on 15 July 1939, when it struck a long swell on take-off. (Fred E. Bamberger via Gordon S. Williams collection)

Members of the Pacific Strike Team and Marine Safety Office, Anchorage personnel who arrived later reversed the breeches buoy and used it to gain access to the vehicle. They reported that the ship had ruptured nine of its twelve oil tanks, dumping some 66,000 gallons of oil into the surrounding waters. A Sikorsky HH-52A *Seaguard* helicopter 1462 from the USCG cutter *Munro* assisted the clean-up effort by lifting heavy oil removal equipment onto the ship and made checks of the beach for oil pollution. Personnel and equipment from the Pacific Strike Team and Marine Safety Office in Anchorage joined with Crowley Environmental Services to clean up the spill and prevent further spillage and pollution.

Vice Admiral Scarborough, then acting Commandant, sent the following message to LORAN Station St Paul:

> I note with pride and pleasure the professionalism, competence and ingenuity shown by the crew of Coast Guard LORAN Station St Paul in the rescue of 81 persons from the grounded Japanese factory vessel *Ryuyo Maru Nr 2*. In this modern day of sophisticated helicopters and small boats, it is heartening to see that Coast Guardsmen can still improvise when the chips are down to answer the call for help. Rigging an improvised breeches buoy to rescue the 81 Japanese seamen is proof that the Coast Guard motto 'Semper Paratus' is not just words on the pages of history. Please convey my sincere appreciation for a job well done.

The following item appeared in *US Naval Aviation News* for May-June 1983:

> Around USCG air station Barbers Point, Hawaii, Lieutenant Commander Tony Meader is known as *SAR Man*. It is a nickname pinned on him by his fellow Coast Guard personnel who have come to admire his skills, leadership, dedication to duty and courage.
>
> In a recent 13-month period, Meader and his HH-52A crew rescued 34 persons. Meader isn't

keeping count. To him, each case is a total crew effort. 'I only did what I was supposed to do', he says. Meader is engineering officer at Barbers Point and has over 3,700 combined hours in the HH-52A helicopter, and Convair HC-131 and HU-16E fixed wing aircraft.

While he has had his share of heroic rescues, Meader has especially vivid memories of the first person he saved. 'I can work for 20 years just on those feelings alone', he says. Just out of flight school, nearly 14 years ago, then Lieutenant (jg) Meader was assigned as a copilot at USCG air station Port Angeles, Washington. A fishing boat, located across the Strait of Juan de Fuca, was taking on water and sinking with four people on board.

Within 15 minutes, Meader, his pilot and crew were on the scene in their HH-52A. One of the men was safe in a small boat. But when they hoisted the others, two were dead and the third, a woman, was barely alive. Meader and a crew member immediately administered first aid. 'I can still remember her face, her expression. She looked up at both of us and said thank you', he recalls. That experience had a lasting impact on his life, just as it has had on many others involved in lifesaving.

Since arriving at Barbers Point nearly two years ago, the soft-spoken Meader has lived up to his reputation as a superb aviator. In one Search & Rescue case, he and his crew rescued 13 survivors from a sailboat that went aground at the entrance of the Ala Wai Boat Harbor Canal in Waikiki.

But his most challenging rescue was last October. A young woman was stranded on a ledge at the base of a cliff on the north shore of the Island of Kauai. A previous attempt to help was made by a man who had been swimming in the area, which resulted in his becoming trapped also on the ledge.

Local firemen were first called to the scene. On the beach nearby they were unable to reach the two because of the pounding surf below the ledge, so they notified the Joint Rescue Co-ordination Center in Honolulu.

Within minutes, USCG HH-52A helicopter 1462 was launched with LCDR Meader as aircraft commander. When he and his crew arrived at the scene, it was already dark. The night was cloudy and moonless and the wind was from the northeast at 10 knots, with gusts and tremendous downdrafts around the cliffs in the area. The surf was rough and averaging around four feet along the jagged coastline.

From radio contact with the firemen, the crew of 1462 learned that this particular ledge was at the base of a cliff with an overhang of 75 to 100 feet. The overhang formed a shallow cave around the ledge where the two people were stranded.

Meader, using a high intensity searchlight, surveyed the area around the ledge to get a better perspective of the situation and the hazards involved. It was obvious that the overhang would prevent any attempt to hoist the two from the ledge directly. Swimming was out of the question with the high surf.

Meader landed HH-52A 1462 at the nearby beach where the firemen were waiting. The landing was not easy since the beach was steeply inclined and very narrow, and there was little available light. The firemen provided information about the local weather and sea conditions, and the previous rescue attempts. They agreed on a plan of action and the firemen gave the helicopter crew 300 feet of line.

Meader knew that the only way to get the two off the ledge was to float a raft to the couple and tow them to calmer waters. Once clear, they would then be hoisted aboard. It seemed very logical and clear-cut, but it was dark and windy and the surf was pounding on the rocks below.

In the cabin of the helicopter, the copilot Lieutenant Andrew Moynahan and aircrewman Charles Warren prepared three rafts. They remained aft in the aircraft making rescue preparations while Meader maneuvered the HH-52A as close as possible to the overhanging cliff. He kept the helicopter in position while his two crewmen prepared to lower the first raft. During this phase, the downdrafts from the cliffs threatened the hovering helicopter. Meader was able to use only the small light on the nose of his aircraft to illuminate what few references were available.

Moynahan and Warren deployed the first raft, only to see it destroyed by the angry surf. Undaunted, they lowered a second raft, making sure the lines were taut and doubled. This time they successfully let the surf carry it to the couple. 'I don't know what we would have done had we lost the rafts', recalled Moynahan later, 'and I'm glad we didn't have time to think about it'.

This time the two stranded people were able to grab hold of the raft, after which Meader slowly maneuvered his helicopter away from the cliffs to open water while pulling the raft away from the ledge.

Each time a wave approached the raft, Meader had to pause while the crew took the slack out of the trail lines. Every time a wave hit the raft, however, the two victims were swamped and submerged. In order to advance at all, the helicopter had to maneuver between wave intervals, and only after the raft and the victims had surfaced. Needless to say, they only moved ahead 10 to 15 feet between waves, and sometimes lost double that amount when the raft and victims were hit by a particularly large wave.

Nearly an hour passed after the first raft was dropped, when finally they were far enough offshore to begin hoisting the victims free of the water. As the woman was being lifted from the choppy waves she became entangled in the trail line of the raft. Warren cut the line which freed her legs and dropped the raft down to the man in the water. The man was then quickly hoisted on board.

With the rescue complete, the survivors were flown to a nearby hospital for treatment and the crew returned to Barbers Point. The success of that night's rescue can be attributed to Meader's ingenuity, skill and courage. But he sees it as 'just doing my job' — a job he thoroughly enjoys.

Meader's accomplishments as a pilot have earned him many awards. But to him these aren't the real reward. He says, 'There is so much more than just the ribbon and medals. If you have ever helped save a life, that justifies everything else'.

Author's note: This story was written by Lieutenant Deborah A Dombeck, USCG Public Affairs Officer.

During July 1976 the oil drilling platform *Canmar Explorer II* had departed Galveston, Texas, under tow of a tug and was enroute to Halifax, Nova Scotia. On 31 July a distress call was received at the USCG air station Elizabeth City indicating the platform had a critically ill seaman on board. A Lockheed HC-130 *Hercules* from the air station located the tug and drilling platform 35 miles southeast of Cape Hatteras. A Sikorsky HH-52A *Seaguard* helicopter 1400 from air station Elizabeth City, North Carolina landed on the platform and evacuated the ill crewman, flying him to hospital.

The pleasure voyage of the chartered yacht *Hattie D,* a converted World War II 105-foot US Navy vessel, began in Seattle, Washington, on 24 January 1964. During a terrific storm whilst abeam Cape Mendocino, California, the yacht lost its rudder after collision with a floating object during the storm. Her distress call was received at the 12th Coast Guard District Rescue Coordination Center in San Francisco on Wednesday 5 February, whereupon USCG rescue units were dispatched to assist the vessel. Aircraft from the air station San Francisco, the USCG eighty-two-foot patrol cutter *Point Ledge* from Noyo, and the USCG cutter *Avoyal* from Fields Landing sped to the scene. A Lockheed HC-130B *Hercules* and a Grumman HU-16E *Albatross* fixed wing aircraft alternated turns in communicating the position of the yacht, now twenty miles below Cape Mendocino, until the arrival of the HH-52A helicopter which performed the rescue a few hours later on Thursday 6 February.

An attempt was made by aircraft to drop a pump to the yacht but the strong wings carried it away. The helicopter executed the rescue in two trips, hoisting six persons on the first round and discharging them on a beach, one and a half miles north of Loleta on Copenhagen Road in care of the Humboldt sheriff. On the return trip to the sinking yacht, the helicopter picked up the remaining five persons, then flew the survivors to Arcata airport. The converted World War II vessel sank shortly afterwards.

Above: Artist's impression of the heavily modified version of the Rockwell Sabra 75A executive jet which was submitted to the US Coast Guard during April 1975. It had two choices of engine, but was not adopted as a suitable type for the USCG. (USCG)

Below: Today the US Coast Guard fleet includes a single Grumman VC-4A *Gulfstream I* and a VC-11A *Gulfstream II* which have been in service since 1965. Both are powered by Rolls-Royce engines, and the *Gulfstream I* 01 is based at National Airport, Washington DC, for use by the USCG Commandant and his executives. (Grumman)

On 30 May 1988 the USCG commenced operations with the first of eight HU-25C *Interceptor* aircraft fitted with long-range radar and a forward looking infra-red sensor to detect and track suspected drug smugglers at sea or in the air. The aircraft are based at Miami, Florida, and Mobile, Alabama. (Aerospatiale)

Left: US Coast Guard HU-25A *Guardian* 2107, a type which replaced the HU-16E *Albatross*. Designed with multi-mission capabilities, it is used for SAR, law enforcement patrol of US territorial waters and the 200-mile Fishery Conservation Zone, and oil pollution surveillance. It is currently in use in the massive drug interdiction operation. (USCG)

Right: With a view to the future, the USCG monitor the progress of such advanced types as the Bell XV-15 tilt-wing research aircraft with interest. Seen here is the first of two being tested by NASA at Ames, California. Financial involvement by the US Army and US Navy would assist USCG procurement from any Department of Defense contracted. It has already completed shipboard trials. (AP Photo Library)

An artist's conception of the new Bell JVX tiltrotor engaged in a US Coast Guard Search & Rescue (SAR) Operation. Known as the V-22 *Osprey*, it has been developed by a Bell-Boeing tiltrotor team at Ford Worth, Texas, and the first delivery to the US Armed Forces is expected in late 1991. (Bell-Boeing)

Left: Described as a miniature AWACS, two USCG Grumman E-2C *Hawkeye* are currently part of the forward front line equipment assisting in the drugs war. Their home station is Norfolk, Virginia, but deployments are as required. The huge radar dish is evident in this photo which shows 3502. Powered by two Allison turbo prop engines, the airborne early-warning picket will enhance the capability of the USCG. (USCG)

Below: E-2C *Hawkeye* 3501 from the unit CGAW-1 formed at Norfolk, Virginia. (Grumman)

One US Air Force, one US Navy, and four US Coast Guard aircraft carried out a wide search on 6 April 1965 after a Douglas DC-3 transport aircraft was reported overdue since 21.00 on 5 April, on a four hour flight from Haiti to Fort Lauderdale, Florida, with eight persons on board.

Around 14.30 the US Air Force aircraft first spotted the ditched DC-3 with six persons standing on the wing. It was in three feet of water off Andros Island in the Bahamas. The US Air Force removed the six persons, whilst a Sikorsky HH-52A Seaguard helicopter 1384 from air station Miami located the remaining two persons who had waded ashore to get help. All were reported in good condition on their safe arrival at Miami.

The sixty-five-foot training ship Aquanaut II owned by the National Youth Science Foundation of Portland, Maine, had completed a chartered mission in the Casco Bay area off Massachusetts and was enroute southward when her pilot, who was alone on board, discovered a blaze erupting from an oil burner in the engine room. Smoke from the burning vessel was first sighted by a Coast Guardsman from a window of the Merrimac River, Newburyport, Massachusetts, USCG Station. A telephone call to the Group Commander at Gloucester soon brought Coast Guard units to the rescue. The weather was clear with a brisk 49° temperature, eighteen miles per hour winds, and four foot seas.

The position of the burning vessel was two miles east of the Merrimac Jetty, Plum Island, Massachusetts and the date 2 November 1964. Two thirty-foot utility boats from Coast Guard stations at Merrimac River and Hampton Beach, New Hampshire, were soon on their way to help combat the fire. A Sikorsky HH-52A helicopter 1362 from the air station at Salem, Massachusetts, was also called in to assist.

A forty-foot boat from the Coast Guard Merrimac River Station helped tow the burning vessel to the station boathouse where the blaze was completely squelched and the vessel dewatered.

It was a dark and stormy night when the tanker Puerto Rican, with 29 people on board, left its mooring just after midnight on 31 October 1984 on a journey that was scheduled to take it from San Francisco Bay, California, to the Panama Canal.

A Lockheed HC-130H Hercules from air station Sacramento, California, was searching for a missing fishing boat when at 03.30 the crew witnessed a giant explosion and fire on board the tanker. They immediately called in on the distress frequency. Boats and crews from the USCG station at Fort Point at the entrance to San Francisco Bay, located beneath the south end of the Golden Gate Bridge, responded and were at the scene of the disaster 40 minutes after the explosion. They were joined by a HH-52A Seaguard helicopter 1395 from the air station San Francisco.

Already at the scene was the San Francisco pilot boat that had been preparing to take the departing harbor pilot from the Puerto Rican when the explosion occurred. The force of the explosion threw the pilot and a crew member into the sea. The crew from the pilot boat rescued both men. Both men were alive but injured. The pilot suffered second degree burns over 40 per cent of his body, plus broken bones. The crewman also received burns. As soon as the HH-52A helicopter arrived on the scene the two injured men were hoisted and flown to a nearby hospital.

A passing commercial tugboat, Harry M, also assisted in the rescue by maneuvering close to the burning ship and taking most of the remaining crew to safety. The USCG cutters Point Heyer and Cape Cross and a US Navy tug were the next units to arrive. Firefighters from both cutters were put on board the burning tanker. They used foam to combat the flames while the tug cooled the hull with a steady stream of water.

At 09.30, six hours after the explosion, the fire was still burning out of control. A commercial tug, hired by the owner of the burning tanker, towed the ship away from the harbor entrance. The tug stayed with Puerto Rican for the next four days.

On 31 July 1976 an HH-52A helicopter 1400 from Elizabeth City air station landed on board the drilling platform Canmar Explorer II thirty-five miles south-east of Cape Hatteras, to evacuate a critically ill crewman. A USCG HC-130 Hercules located the tug and platform which were en route from Galveston, Texas, to Halifax, Nova Scotia. (USCG)

Media interest in the case was extremely high. Questions about the incident started before dawn and continued throughout the first two days of the case. The 12th Coast Guard District Public Affairs staff in San Francisco answered thousands of telephone calls and questions from international, national and local news media.

The fire raged throughout Wednesday and half of Thursday until it was finally extinguished by a combined Coast Guard and US Navy assault.

The next worry was of an approaching storm that raised the seas 20 feet and carried winds up to 40 knots. Marine safety experts were afraid that with the ship in such a weakened state, the sea conditions could break it in two. But the ship was tough. For two days, the seas battered the tanker, until 12.15 on Saturday, when the ship could take no more. For four hours, three parts of the ship floated close together. Then, with a belch of bunker oil, the rear quarter of Puerto Rican sank.

The tug still had the forward three-quarters of the ship in tow and headed to the southwest. One of the large internal tanks, where it appears the original explosion occurred, floated free and took three days to lasso. It was later towed into port where Coast Guard and Federal Bureau of Investigation (FBI) investigators checked for signs of sabotage.

Author's note: The above story appeared in the USCG Commandant's Bulletin dated 7 December 1984 and was written by PAC John Hollis, USCG 12th Coast Guard District Public Affairs Office in San Francisco.

Prior to the outbreak of World War II the main function of Coast Guard Aviation was that of patrol in the interests of safety at sea and law enforcement. During World War II it managed to continue rescues whilst at the same time fighting the war. One of the centers for rescue operations was the air station at Elizabeth City, North Carolina, commanded in 1943 by Lieutenant Commander R C Burke USCG. Two enlisted men there perfected the food bomb which was dropped to survivors of torpedoed vessels in much the same way of the Coast Guard dropped storm warnings to fishermen who lacked radio communication facilities with shore. The food bomb resembled a depth charge having a soft concrete cap which disintegrated on contact with water. Its contents include seven cans of water, a first aid kit, a pint of whisky, two food rations and several packs of cigarettes and matches. AMM First Class Harold V Booth and AMM Third Class Frederick J Denio were officially commended for this invention.

A HH-52A *Seaguard* helio 1375 from Miami air station alights on the water in the Straights of Florida on 20 September 1966 to pick up thirteen Cuban refugees from two crudely hand-made craft. They were spotted sixty-seven miles south-west of Key West and were transferred to the US Coast Guard cutter *Diliuerce* for transfer to the authorities. (USCG)

Aviation Machinist Mate First Class A M Cupples, an aviation pilot, particularly distinguished himself in the rescue of the crew of the *Sturtevant*. Immediately upon sighting the survivors, he attempted to communicate with shore. However, since he had no radioman aboard, he returned full throttle to a US Navy base where he made his report so accurately that a rescue boat was immediately dispatched to the scene. He then refuelled, took aboard a radioman and flew back to the scene of the sinking. He saw that the one rescue boat was inadequate to pick up the survivors and sent for another rescue ship.

The team work of a US Coast Guard HH-52A helio 1384 and a forty-foot patrol boat save seven Cuban refugees at sea on 28 January 1968. The HH-52A is seen hoisting Jesus Palaez with an infected foot from the USCG boat. The refugees were spotted ten miles east of Elliot Key by the Liberian freighter *Arcturus* which notified the Coast Guard. (USCG)

During my visit to the USCG air station Los Angeles during 1969 I was naturally interested in the various containers which were available to be dropped to survivors. A dewatering pump is dropped to vessels that are flooding, a fully equipped liferaft where many survivors are in the water, plus other individual items including an oxygen resuscitator. Commander Paul W Tifft, Commanding Officer of the air station, kindly gave me a breakdown of the items.

Dewatering Pump Manufacturer, OHLER Machinery Co., PO Box 820, Waterloo, Iowa 50704. Model, 6320 AC, powered by a Briggs and Stratton four cycle air cooled three hp motor. The pump has a capacity of 8,000 gallons per hour and employs a fifteen-foot, two-inch diameter suction line.

Mark 20 Air Droppable Raft Capacity twenty men, neoprene coated nylon. The contents include: pyrotechnic distress signals; radar reflector; sponge; sea dye marker; towline; first aid kit; flashlight; sunburn ointments; sea anchor; heaving line; sea water distillation kits; survival rations; signal mirror; compass; bailing bucket.

Oxygen Resuscitator Elder Model 32-102. Oxygen duration of two hours and fifteen minutes as a resuscitator, three hours as a demand valve. Weight thirty-three pounds complete. Manufactured by Elder Oxygen Co Inc, 4047 8th Avenue, San Diego, California 92103.

Additional individual SAR items
(a) 'Space' Rescue Blanket 56 x 84 inches unfolded, wallet size folded, weight approximately four ounces. Manufactured by National Research Corporation, 37 East Street, Winchester, Massachusetts 01890.
(b) Mk 25 smoke float marker, burns fifteen minutes.
(c) Mk 58 smoke float marker, burns forty-five minutes.
(d) AN/PRC-63, survival radio, frequency 243.0 MHz.

A different type of Search & Rescue operation, but equally as important, was carried out by the Coast Guard Border Patrol Detachment based at El Paso, Texas, in 1939. An exciting panorama can be easily conjured up by the name Border Patrol. Kaleidoscope pictures of bandits, sombreroed cattle rustlers, smugglers, border raids, scenes belonging to the heroic past, all become suddenly alive merely at the mention of the term. In the southern boundary area of the US, the grim war between the forces of law and order and those on the opposite side of the fence continued as relentless as ever in the past. It was primarily for this reason that the Coast Guard undertook the maintenance of a permanent air patrol detachment on the international boundary line.

Using El Paso as a central base of operations, the small but extremely efficient unit carried out the truly herculean programme of patrolling 1,400 miles of border line and covering a territory which included the States of Texas, New Mexico and Arizona. An idea of the immensity of this offensive against smuggling and other law-evading activities can be gained by the detachment's report for the fiscal year of 1937 which shows an area of close to 400,000 square miles searched, and 38,000 miles cruised in less than 200 flights.

Although law and enforcement was the Border Patrol detachment's chief duty, assistance to life and property was always a most important consideration. The air patrol detachment found itself constantly called upon to perform rescue and assistance missions inland, in much the same manner as the coastal air stations performed at sea.

> Rescue tasks were varied. A request to transport a badly injured person from a mining camp to a hospital hundreds of miles away, a child taken dangerously ill or some serious ailment demanding immediate attention of a physician, or it may be that an epidemic was spreading throughout some mountain community, serums needed quickly to check its murderous progress. A call for help brought a Coast Guard Waco biplane to the scene as fast as the engine will carry it — often to make a risky landing upon rough and dangerous terrain, or in a clear spot the size of a handkerchief.

The flat wastelands of Texas are deceptively smooth when viewed from the air, but a forced landing on the part of a pilot may often spell disaster. A washed-out landing gear, or the biplane on its nose, propeller damaged, is a comparatively fortunate experience. Unable to land and pick up the pilot and passengers, the USCG Border Patrol drops a cargo parachute laden with food and water; then radioed the location to his home base. In a few hours or so an automobile rescue party was on the scene.

Tourist and inexperienced exploring parties were often the victims of the desert; attempting trips without bothering to take on a good supply of water or food, or sufficient tools to be used in case of breakdown. Once, two women driving a brand-new car got a flat tyre, only to find they had no jack. Aside from keeping a watchful lookout for any such cases while out on regular patrol, the Border Patrol aircraft often went out on a search at the request of anxious relatives or friends.

It was not always a simple matter, however. In one instance, a party of three motorists were reported almost two days overdue on a trip that ordinarily would have taken perhaps six hours. Residents of the eastern US, they had travelled at night to avoid the scorching heat, turned off the main road to some little-used track, and finally wound up in the desert with a broken fan belt, overheating the automobile's engine. Foolishly, although they had sufficient food and a quantity of water, they attempted to walk their way toward help, after spending a fairly comfortable night in the car, when the proper tactics would have been to have waited at least half a day to see whether anyone would come along. Several hours of tramping under a boiling sun soon had its effect. Extreme dizziness and nausea caused by going bareheaded weakened their resistence. A fitful night spent in the open on hard ground somewhat recuperated their strength, but left the three wanderers with practically no water and not the faintest idea of where they were.

Waco J2W-1 V159 took off at 07.00 for the search, and some fifty minutes later began a methodical crisscross circuit of the area in which the lost party was thought to be. Like the whitecaps encountered over the ocean, the mesquite bushes of the flat wastelands make observation extremely difficult, although in clear spots it was possible to discern tracks and automobile tyre marks, and so trace them onward. Cruising at 110 miles per hour, at altitudes of between 400 and 700 feet above the ground, almost four hours elapsed, fuel supply meanwhile growing steadily lower, before the Coast Guard pilot was able to catch a glimpse of brightly coloured cloth which led to the lost party.

After swooping down low in a deafening dive which scared the unhappy three out of their wits, an already prepared cargo parachute containing emergency supplies was dropped. They were evidently as yet physically strong and able, as well as enthusiastic over the prospect of food, water and rescue, if the speed at which they raced to the life-saving 'chute was any evidence. A message dropped with the supplies informed them that help would soon be on its way — and that they should stay put instead of wandering away. Enthusiastic waving of arms acknowledged this word from the skies, and the Waco biplane waggled its wings in farewell as the Coast Guard radioman tapped out their location. That evening they were safe in El Paso, undaunted by their experience. However, they were fortunate, for the saga of the desert has woven far grimmer tales of people who disappeared into the unknown and were lost forever. For this is stilll a land that has never been conquered by man, and still wages constant battle with him.

Hovering over the sixty-five-foot burning training ship *Aquanaut II,* two miles east of the Mirrimac Jetty, Plum Island, Massachusetts, on 2 November 1964, is a Sikorsky HH-52A helicopter 1362 from Salem air station. The helicopter carried foam for the USCG thirty-foot utility boats to fight the fire with. (USCG)

Major disasters provided the hardest work. Whenever a serious flood was imminent, or a hurricane expected, the aircraft were sent out to warn the inhabitants of farms and isolated communities of their approach. Preventive measures like these have been instrumental in the saving of countless lives. During the summer and fall seasons, the air patrol detachment remained always on the alert for the dreaded hurricane calls. When one of these terrible storms threatened the area around the Gulf of Mexico, it was up to the Coast Guard to give warning as quickly as possible. The detachment spent their winter months preparing, whenever spare time allowed, by making up hundreds of small wooden containers to which were attached long white or yellow streamers bearing the terse message 'Hurricane Warning'. A hollow space inside of the blocks provided room for a more detailed measure as to the course of the storm and the possible time it was expected to strike — and reiterated the warning to move to higher ground, if near a river, and to safe and stronger quarters, if away from immediate water.

A US Coast Guard HH-52A helio 1405 scoops up a stranded man from the roof of a house during Hurricane 'Betsy' near Dalacroix, Louisiana, during September 1965. This HH-52A, based at New Orleans air station, was one of eleven USCG helicopters that evacuated 1,144 people, transported twenty-two medics and flew 140 sorties during the devastating storm. (USCG)

After a storm or flood had struck, the Coast Guard aircraft were employed in surveying and charting inundated areas, searching out marooned persons and directing rescue parties to their aid. The result of one USCG flight alone was instrumental in rescuing eight persons stranded in treetops barely sticking out of the flood water. After the actual rescue work had been completed, the aircraft acted as aerial ferries for transportation of serums and other medicinal supplies to those engaged in the inevitable struggle against disease that follows every major disaster of nature.

This unique Coast Guard Border Patrol Detachment earned itself, without any fanfare of publicity and limelight, the inevitable reputation of being one of the US Government's military forces. The citizens of the farflung area covered by the Coast Guard's winged watchers took equal pride in the manner in which this tiny unit of the US peacetime army carried out the best traditions of a service that has always been a credit to the country — the Coast Guard itself.

Author's note: This item was extracted from an article which appeared in *Air Trails* for August 1939 written by Lieutenant Perry S Lyons USCG who commanded the Border Patrol Detachment.

In 1938 the Coast Guard base at Salem, Massachusetts, was one of the newest and best equipped. In addition to a large hangar capable of housing two or three Douglas RD-*Dolphins* plus one or two Grumman amphibians there were barracks for the enlisted personnel and one of the country's finest seaplane ramps. One wintry afternoon one of the USCG air station's *Dolphins* arrived back with so much ice on her wings that one wondered if she would ever fly again or not. In command of the Douglas RD- was Lieutenant Perry S Lyons who had spent the entire night rendering assistance to a crippled vessel which had drifted ashore in the tempest of a sweeping snow storm. Unshaven, cold and hungry, Lieutenant Lyons' only comment was that the trip had been rather unusual — a moment typical of the men of steel who manned the flying equipment of the Coast Guard.

A mid-ocean landing was not unusual for any Coast Guard pilot — yet how many pilots in other branches of US Government service had even attempted such a thing intentionally? The following are the first hand comments by a survivor of an aircraft that had crashed in the sea, Norman Foster: 'We were standing on the deck of a small freighter — inbound from Lisbon. We were listed on the ship's log as castaways, having been picked up a few hours before by a lifeboat from this vessel. We had been in an airplane accident and had crashed at sea. Darkness fell shortly after we did. Perhaps an hour elapsed before the purr of two Wasp engines pierced the otherwise quiet of dusk. Even though this freighter was still a hundred miles from shore, a Coast Guard *Dolphin* had found her. The captain of the freighter — a gallant Swede — stopped his vessel while Lieutenant Lyons circled a few times and then squared away far astern of us for a landing. At the suggestion of a member of our little group of castaways, the boat had been headed into the wind as a guide for Lieutenant Lyons. But he needed none. In a few seconds the *Dolphin* skimmed across the water, bounced a few times and settled peacefully on the ocean. A lifeboat was put over and a member of Lieutenant Lyons' crew came aside to inquire the extent of our injuries.

'Eight of us had survived the accident — one of our group we had planned to rush back to shore with Lieutenant Lyons to receive hospital care but he had passed away a little while before. Even though the *Dolphin* took off again without any passengers aboard, my heart went out to the Coast Guard air service that night. Without thought of his own well-being, Lieutenant Lyons had pointed his ship into the inky blackness of the unforgiving Atlantic to relieve suffering'.

Apparently, on countless occasions before this Lieutenant Lyons' daring and courage had saved many lives. Even on his brief vacations from the service he had been occupied by flying. In the 1930s he was a member of a flying team that manned a Northrop monoplane in the annual Bendix Trophy race. His assignment after Salem was at El Paso, Texas, where he commanded the Border Patrol Detachment.

At this time one of the most adventurous flying tales ever heard used to be told at hangar flying sessions at any Coast Guard air station. Heroes of the escape were Lieutenant Richard L Burke and the late Commander William L Foley — and the scene was off the Florida coast. They received word one night that a small boat with two boys aboard had been caught in the teeth of a hurricane. With scarcely a moment's consideration Burke and Foley set the course of a Coast Guard flying boat for the open sea. After flying about for some time they sighted the crippled vessel. In landing on the raging seas, a main spar on the monoplane wing was shattered, rendering the plane unflyable. However, the crew of the skiff were taken aboard the now crippled plane. Both motors were running and Burke and Foley put the plane about in an attempt to taxi it ashore.

After taxying all night long, with the motors idling to conserve precious gasoline the plane finally reached a small cove, shattered by a fierce battle with the sea — but its mission complete and two more lives saved by the Coast Guard air service.

Landings in the open sea are not uncommon to Coast Guard airmen. Nor is it unusual for a sick member of a vessel's crew to be taken ashore for hospital treatment in a Coast Guard plane. Way back in the mid-1930s a feverish wireless report came from a small vessel, telling that a nude man had been picked up in the water. Apparently he had leapt from a passenger carrying boat. Further apparent was the fact that he had been in the water for many hours. He was raging mad when taken from the water. A radio message was dispatched to the Coast Guard air station at Salem and a plane was sent to the scene.

With the famous Alcatraz Island in the background and the Golden Gate Bridge just visible in the mist, a San Francisco air station based *Seaguard* helicopter approaches to land on the deck of a US Coast Guard cutter in San Francisco Bay on 3 July 1968. (USCG)

After considerable difficulty a landing was made at sea and the insane man was transferred to the plane. He rebelled against his aerial rescue and was quite a problem for the boat crew, but no problem to the Coast Guard enlisted men. They quietened him down during the flight to Boston Airport. He was taken to the US Marine Hospital nearby and completely recovered a few weeks later. Prime mystery — from what boat had this man jumped? He didn't know and neither did the Coast Guard.

Author's note: Extracts from *Popular Aviation* for March 1938.

Commander John Lewis USCG, Chief, Search & Rescue Divison, ATC Mobile, Alabama, has provided the following interesting story.

Trivia buffs may find it fascinating that there is only one point in the US where four states meet. In the desolate high elevations west of the San Juan mountain range and east of the Grand Canyon lie the 'Four Corners' region of Arizona, Utah, Colorado and New Mexico. This vast area of arroyos, mesas, dry river beds and towering rocky escarpments would seem an unlikely setting for a Coast Guard search and rescue case.

The new 210-foot Reliance class US Coast Guard cutter seen on 22 August 1966, with a Sikorsky HH-52A *Seaguard* helicopter 1371 making an approach to land despite the cutter being on the move. (USCG)

On 10 January 1983 the pilot of a single engine Cessna was struggling against strong winds as he attempted to navigate his craft from Grand Junction to Cortez, Colorado. He was blown off course and carried far beyond his destination. Disorientated and with only an hour of fuel remaining, he called on the VHF distress frequency for assistance. The control tower at Farmington, New Mexico, and the flight service station at Gallup attempted, without success, to fix his location.

Meanwhile, far above, a Coast Guard crew from Aviation Training Center, Mobile, was enjoying the rugged vistas as they ferried HU-25A *Guardian* 2104 to Long Beach, California. The *Guardian's* automatic direction finding equipment had already established a line of position on the distressed aircraft's transmissions, and the chance to assist was readily accepted. A change of course, a burst of speed, and the HU-25A was soon established over the Cessna.

The *Guardian's* RNAV computer immediately provided the course and assistance to Cortez Airport, and the errant Cessna was escorted by 2104 to destination, landing safely with only ten minutes of fuel remaining.

On 4 October 1980, the Holland cruise liner *Prinsedam* on a scheduled month long voyage from Vancouver, Canada, to Singapore was abandoned by 320 passengers and approximately 200 crew members after a fire roared out of control whilst it was in the Gulf of Alaska. All the passengers and crew clambered into lifeboats leaving the liner drifting. It sank eight days later.

Three Coast Guard cutters and the 1,000 ft US Supertanker *Williamsburgh* went to the aid of the *Prinsedam*. It was enroute from Valdez, Alaska to Texas. Coast Guard HH-3F *Pelican* helicopters from Kodiak air station dropped two pumps aboard the liner to help fight the blaze that began in the engine room and spread below decks. Preliminary accounts indicated that a fuel line may have broken, causing diesel oil to spurt on hot pipes and burst into flames. The fire knocked out the electrical system, shutting down the fire-fighting pumps. Crewmen sprayed carbon dioxide from hand held extinguishers but could not keep the fire from spreading to other parts of the ship.

Despite stormy seas the passengers and crew were picked up from lifeboats by Coast Guard Sikorsky HH-3F *Pelican* helicopters. All the passengers were elderly retirees. It was the biggest ever rescue at sea without loss of life. The HH-3F had a lot to do with that. The co-pilot watched the torque, the pilot did the hoist maneuvering, the crewman pulled them up. The Coast Guard filled the helicopter, flew them to the shore, then came back and did it again, and again.

October 25, 1983

Commanding Officer
Coast Guard Air Station
Opa Locka Airport
Opa Locka, Florida 20593

Dear Sir,

We were rescued by your group after ditching an aircraft in the ocean off Andros Island in the Bahamas, Sunday October 23. I would especially like to thank and commend the pilot and crew of the Coast Guard jet that was over us from the beginning. He was 40 miles away when he first heard our Mayday and homed in on us and was overhead within 14 minutes just as we went into the water. Under the most difficult conditions he stayed overhead searching for us until he located our position and dropped a life raft within 50 feet of me and my wife so we had no difficulty in reaching it. He showed the greatest professionalism and skill and I would like to nominate him for the highest award possible for him to receive. He stayed with us until we were picked up by a helicopter. A US Navy helicopter from Autec at Andros picked us up and took us to Andros. A Coast Guard helicopter then returned us to Opa Locka.

The crew of the helicopter and the team at Opa Locka showed us the utmost courtesy and care and I would like each one to be thanked personally. I am not able to remember names and did not get a list but my wife and I will always remember them in our thoughts and prayers. They were very kind to us and provided me with shoes and both of us a meal. They provided comfort at a very important time.

Thanks again and may God bless each one of you.

Yours with love

Charles H Smart Jr
RCA, GBI
PO Box 4308
Patrick AFB, FL 32925

The above letter was supplied by Commander R L Murphy, USCG, Assistant Operations Officer at air station Miami in August 1984.

Seen on 10 September 1965 is a US Coast Guard victim of the devastating Hurricane 'Betsy'. The wreck of a Sikorsky HH-52A *Seaguard* helicopter 1397 awaits recovery. The small 'd' after the serial indicates the modification state. (USCG)

Close-up of a US Coast Guard Sikorsky HH-52A *Seaguard* helicopter with a rescue basket and survivor being winched to safety. This photo taken in 1967 during a basket hoist rescue drill, part of each air station's training programme. (USCG)

CHAPTER TEN
Lockheed Hercules

According to Greek mythology, Hercules achieved twelve labours imposed on him by Eurystheus, king of Tiryns.
Lockheed-Georgia Company Press release dated 11.00 31 May 1983.

The US Coast Guard took delivery here today of the first of five new Lockheed HC-130H-7 *Hercules* patrol aircraft now under contract, launching the modernization of the service's long range patrol fleet. Rear Admiral Donald C Thompson, Coast Guard Seventh District Commander, from Miami, accepted the aircraft from Lockheed-Georgia Company in ceremonies at the Clearwater Coast Guard Air Station's flight ramp.

In his acceptance remarks, Admiral Thompson declared:

'We in the Coast Guard welcome this first in the 1700 series to our fleet of long range C-130s. This HC-130 and the ones to follow — carrying numerous state-of-the-art improvements over our older B models — will give us greatly increased capabilities to carry out our expanding work load in the enforcement of laws and treaties, Search & Rescue and the interdiction of drug traffic and illegal immigrants.'

Admiral Thompson turned the symbolic key over to the Commanding Officer of the Clearwater station, Captain Kenneth Gard. Representing the manufacturer of the aircraft at the delivery event was A II Lorch, executive vice-president of the Lockheed-Georgia Company, Marietta, Georgia.

The new aircraft — designated HC-130H-7 by the Coast Guard and painted in the service's red and white colours — was ferried here by a crew headed by Commander William H Rollins, who is Commanding Officer, USCG Aircraft Programme Office, Marietta, Georgia. Prior to delivery here, the aircraft received special Coast Guard modification work at Elizabeth City, North Carolina.

Four of the new HC-130s will be based at Clearwater, replacing the station's current inventory of four older 1959 vintage B-model Hercules transports that are being phased out.

The new HC-130H-7s feature numerous improvements over the Coast Guard's earlier B model airframes, as well as modern state-of-the-art avionics and numerous systems and structural updates.

A Russian factory ship at anchor somewhere in the Pacific, with a trawler alongside, is given a close inspection by a Coast Guard Lockheed HC-130B 1344. In Alaskan waters the fishing fleets from Japan, Russia and Canada come under close scrutiny from Coast Guard rotary and fixed wing aircraft. (USCG)

The Coast Guard's new acquisition resulted from its decision to retain the C-130 as its prime long-range patrol aircraft through this century. Officials felt a fleet modernization was essential since its patrol missions typically involved low level, long duration flights over saltwater, resulting in widespread corrosion and steady deterioration. Its B-version C-130s have been in service more than 23 years.

While obtaining brand new airframes and systems, the Coast Guard is utilizing Dash 7 propjet engines from the older aircraft that are being phased out.

'The USCG modernization programme could involve the acquisition of up to sixteen new C-130s', the Coast Guard said. 'The Fiscal year 1984 budget, now being considered by Congress, contains requested funds for five HC-130H-7s for delivery to the Coast Guard in 1984.'

The USCG utilizes its long range C-130 fleet on a wide range of missions, operating out of stations on the Atlantic and Pacific Coasts, on the Gulf of Mexico and in the Caribbean, Alaska and Hawaii. USCG C-130 missions include Search & Rescue; enforcement of laws and treaties, embracing the growing role of illegal drug traffic interdiction; Marine Environmental Protection and many other missions, such as North Atlantic iceberg patrols and cargo/personnel transport.

A major reason for the C-130's surveillance effectiveness, according to Coast Guard officials, is the plane's low altitude long range, which can exceed 2,600 nautical miles and its mission endurance, which can reach up to 16-18 hours, depending on mission radius.

Thanks to its low speed controllability, the propjet can fly 'low and slow' over target areas. To conserve fuel and increase time-on-station, crews have the option of shutting down two of the propjet's four engines.

While equipped especially for long range surveillance, the HC-130 can be converted quickly for use as a cargo and/or personnel transport, including the handling of oversize equipment.

The US Coast Guard chief of aviation, Captain L H Seeger, discusses the first Lockheed *Hercules* for the service with Captain A E Harned, commanding officer of Elizabeth City air station to which the new aircraft, 1339, is to be delivered. This 'Herky Bird' was to be the first of many. (Lockheed)

The US Coast Guard is one of the largest operators of the surveillance/patrol version of the Hercules transport. Other operators of C-130 patrol versions include the US Air Force and several nations overseas.

It was during 1957 that the choice of the Lockheed C-130 *Hercules* to equip the Coast Guard was first confirmed, the basis of the selection being of the aircraft's long-range capability at low altitude, its mission endurance and its ability to conserve fuel and increase time-on-station by shutting down two engines. Early USCG evaluation trials confirmed and demonstrated the C-130's excellent low-speed handling qualities when required to fly low and slow over target areas.

In 1958 four aircraft were ordered by the Coast Guard under the US Navy designation R8V-1G receiving the USCG numbers 1339 to 1342 and having the US Air Force serials 58-5396/7 and 58-6973/4. During December 1959, 1339 was delivered to Elizabeth City, North Carolina, and 1340 was delivered to Barbers Point, Hawaii. In January 1960, 1341 was delivered to San Francisco, California. By this time the designation had been changed to SC-130B, a derivative of the US Air Force C-130B model. All were powered by Allison T56A-7 engines. Two identical aircraft were ordered after authorization in 1960, USCG 1344 and 1345 both being assigned to Elizabeth City initially. All six aircraft at that time were redesignated HC-130G.

The next three C-130s were delivered in 1962, 1346 going to San Francisco in March, 1347 going to Elizabeth City, North Carolina, (assigned to Ice Patrol duty out of Argentia, Newfoundland) in the same month, followed by 1348 in April, also going to Elizabeth City, but temporarily deployed to Argentia for work in the North Atlantic including the International Ice Patrol (IIP) mission. Later 1347 moved to Elizabeth City and during 1979 it was equipped with sideways looking radar (SLAR) pods on the main undercarriage housing and under-wing sensor pods.

Three more C-130B aircraft, USCG 1349 to 1351 were delivered during the winter of 1962/3, the first going to Elizabeth City in December 1962, the others to San Francisco during January and February 1963 respectively. These completed the initial Coast Guard procurement and all twelve aircraft remained in service for over twenty years. The latter three aircraft were later redesignated HC-130B.

In the early days of the *Hercules* it was customary to maintain two aircraft at each station on rotation with two aircraft which have been periodically subject to re-engineering, corrosion and fatigue inspection and control. As was to be expected, they have had to operate in some of the most testing of all operating conditions, being based at coastal air stations and flying in turbulent air at low level as well as in constant salt air. The spacious internal accommodation provides room for an extra radio operator, search equipment operators and between twenty-two and forty-four passengers as the need requires. The rear paratroop doors incorporate large clear vision panels for visual search.

A special aircraft, a Lockheed Model 382-4B EC-130E USCG 1414, was delivered from the factory at Marietta, Georgia to Elizabeth City for equipment installation on 23 August 1966. This Coast Guard EC-130E, employed to calibrate LORAN long-range navigation equipment, was based at Elizabeth City but often employed on temporary duty (TDY) at other air stations in the US or overseas.

Soon after the first C-130H *Hercules* had been delivered as the extended-range HC-130H to the US Air Force Aerospace Rescue & Recovery Service (ARRS), the US Navy gained appropriation authority on behalf of the Coast Guard for three of these new T56A-15 powered aircraft. They were CG 1452 to 1454, the first two being delivered initially to San Francisco in March and May 1968, with 1454 going to Kodiak, Alaska, in May. It was joined by the earlier two at a later date. Mention must be made that 1453 was the 1,000th *Hercules* built. Five Lockheed Model 382C-27D HC-130H aircraft followed in 1973/4 these completing the second 10 year procurement by the Coast Guard. These were USCG 1500 to 1504, the first three going to Kodiak in August, September and October 1973 respectively. The last two were delivered to San Francisco in March and April 1974. Unlike the US Air Force HC-130Hs the USCG aircraft possessed no provision for the Fulton ground-air recovery system.

With a further procurement due for ratification in the late 1970s, purchase orders were divided between four Lockheed Model 382C-70D HC-130Hs; USCG 1600 to 1603 were delivered to Kodiak during the last three months of 1977, and five Lockheed Model 382C-37E HC-130H-7 aircraft, USCG 1700 to 1704, in 1983. All were delivered initially to Elizabeth City for the installation of equipment before assignment to air station Clearwater, Florida, during mid-1983. Unfortunately, 1600 crashed during a visual landing in bad weather at Attu in the Aleutians on 30 July 1982.

One out-of-sequence HC-130H-7, 1790, was delivered in July 1983 to Kodiak, a Lockheed Model 382C-22E, the number signifying the date when the US Coast Guard was established. Five more Lockheed Model 382C-50E aircraft, USCG 1705 to 1709, were delivered to Kodiak between June and December 1984, whilst six more HC-130H-15s went to Clearwater. Model 382C-57E 1710 was delivered in March 1985, three Model 382C-61Es, 1711 to 1713, between August and October 1985, a Model 382C-57E 1714 in October and a Model 382C-64E 1715 in November 1985. A Model 382C-76E registered with the Lockheed company as N73235 became USCG 1716 and was delivered in December 1986, whilst three Model 382C-79Es became 1717 to 1719 and were delivered in November and December 1987. There is no doubt at all that the Coast Guard intends to retain and continue flying its latest model of ubiquitous *Hercules,* at least until, and probably well beyond, the end of the century.

New features on the new HC-130H aircraft include an improved Omega interial navigation system, a ground proximity warning system and an improved weather tracking display. The aircraft has a new center and outer wing, has been modified to take external fuel tanks for a thirty per cent increase in fuel capacity and the gross weight has been increased from 135,000 to 155,000 lbs. The modernization programme could involve the acquisition of an undisclosed number of new C-130s. The Fiscal 1984 budget had a funding request for five new HC-130H *Hercules.*

The delivery of these five brought the total number of new and replacement aircraft received by the service in recent years to twenty-three, and increases the USCG fleet to thirty-one HC-130H *Hercules.*

Historically, the Coast Guard has been a seagoing agency, relying on ships and aircraft to carry out maritime missions such as enforcement of laws and treaties and Search & Rescue on the high seas. These priorities continue, but today's US Coast Guard has responsibility for thirteen other missions including radio-navigation, marine environmental response and bridge administration. Recent years have seen continued expansion of Coast Guard responsibilities.

Oil spill surveillance

Today the USCG mission of Marine Environmental Protection (MEP) is focused on its National Strike Force, a select sixty-man group that is specially trained to fight oil spills. Divided into two teams, the units fly to the scenes of oil contamination in their C-130s. The Pacific team is based at Hamilton Air Force Base, not too far from the air station at Sacramento, California, as is the C-130 which will fly them to the area required. The Atlantic team is based in Mobile, Alabama.

Since the creation of the strike force in 1973, the men and their *Hercules* have flown to hundreds of spills, taking along their sophisticated equipment. As mentioned earlier, in 1975, at the request of the Japanese Government, a strike force flew to the Straits of Malacca near Singapore. A supertanker, *Showa Maru,* had gone aground, spilling more than a million gallons of oil. The strike team helped to siphon off the remaining oil.

The Atlantic team, based in Mobile, owns some unusual equipment, including a thirty-two-foot motor home which functions as a mobile command post and which can be rolled right into the C-130 and transported by air to the disaster scene. The team also has an Air Deliverable Anti Pollution Transfer System (ADAPTS) that can pump 1,800 gallons of oil a minute. Another unit, the High Seas Oil Containing System, is packed like an accordion. When put into service, it unfolds onto the water like a snake and inflates to surround and keep the oil confined. Six hundred feet long, the boom can survive twenty knot winds and five foot seas.

To help combat the illegal spills problem, the Coast Guard has developed an airborne detector that photographically records oil in the water with such precision that the images can be used in court as evidence. After an oil discharge is spotted, a second method called 'oil finger printing' is used. Samples are taken from the oil slick and also from all vessels known to have been in the area. Laboratory analysis enables the Coast Guard to match the ship that discharged the oil.

Unfortunately, detailed cockpit photos have never been considered very important. The spacious layout of the 'front office' of the first Coast Guard *Hercules* 1339, initially designated R8V-1G, later SC-130B, is evident in this photo. Captain A E Harned from Elizabeth City is seen giving the many panels and dials the once over. (Lockheed)

Search & Rescue

The most important continuing responsibility of the Coast Guard is Search & Rescue, known by its acronym, SAR. In one year, the USCG responded to more than 80,000 calls for assistance by surface vessels, launched more than 93,000 aircraft sorties, saved almost 7,000 lives and salvaged over $2bn worth of property. Throughout America's inland waters and along her coastal borders, the USCG maintains rescue stations manned around the clock, ready to respond within minutes of a distress call, ready to lend search assistance or to perform rescues when surface vessel rescue is not possible.

The ability to undertake a Search & Rescue mission, the unexpected mission of greatest demand, is the common denominator of all Coast Guard aircraft. A mixture of both fixed and rotary wing aircraft is employed to support the basic search and recovery requirements. Fixed wing aircraft such as the Lockheed C-130, due to their speed and endurance advantage, efficiently resolve uncertainties by searching wide areas, but are inherently limited to aerial delivery of supplies and equipment in the saving of life and property.

Hercules 1414 was the only EC-130E model delivered to the Coast Guard, leaving the factory in Georgia on 23 August 1966. It was employed by Elizabeth City on calibration duties until retired in April 1986 and was appropriately nicknamed 'Pasquotank Roadrunners'. (Military Aircraft Photo)

The emergency call came at 09.20 on 14 March 1987. QMCS Bradley Greuling at Coast Guard Third District Operations Center, New York, reported that a Russian freighter with thirty-nine persons aboard was listing twenty-six degrees in heavy seas at 38-15N, 70-19W. Could the USCG support a rescue if required? Three Sikorsky HH-3F helicopters were launched from air station Cape Cod, Massachusetts, and HC-130H 1501 was flown to the scene as on-scene commander from its base at Elizabeth City, North Carolina. It was later relieved by HC-130H 1502 and 1501 escorted HH-3F 1472 to Atlantic City with Russian survivors on board. Co-ordination between two air stations, three HH-3F helicopters and two C-130s had resulted in the safe rescue of thirty-seven people 200 miles offshore.

Based at Argentia, Newfoundland, this Lockheed HC-130B 1348 is seen about to take on board a mobile communications unit. The spacious cargo compartment enables a large variety of specialized equipment to be carried, the rear ramp even allowing vehicles to be carried. (USCG)

Drug interdiction

While the USCG and its fleet of C-130s have become famous for their role in patrolling America's coastal waters, the red and white turboprops are today pressed into duty chasing down illegal drug smugglers. Sometimes the *Hercules* swoop down to fifty feet above the water to identify suspected ships and in some cases scare them into tossing their contraband overboard. 'The Coast Guard C-130s are very valuable to us,' said Drug Enforcement Agency's Tony Acri of Miami, 'They do a remarkable job in helping us seize illegal drug vessels.'

The only loss by accident to the Coast Guard fleet of *Hercules* aircraft involved this HC-130H 1600 based at Kodiak air station in Alaska, which crashed on 30 July 1982 at Attu in the Aleutian Islands. (USCG)

Their role in joint operations with the DEA and US Customs has been very effective.' Lieutenant Jeff Steuer, an intelligence officer with the USCG 7th District in Miami, said the C-130 'sometimes seem to be kissing the water', when they drop down on the deck to photograph the name and home port of suspected vessels. This information is then fed into DEA's computer in Miami.

On such law enforcement patrols, the C-130 usually fly at 500 feet, but drop down to fifty feet, sometimes lower, to make a positive identification. The lettering on the stern of a forty-foot boat, for instance, is usually only twelve inches deep. *Hercules* crewmen use gyro-stabilized binoculars to help verify identification. High-quality automatic data recording camera equipment is also used to officially record information necessary for legal requirements.

While drug patrolling often is combined with the Coast Guard's ongoing mission of offshore patrol and search and rescue, sometimes the C-130s are used strictly for a drug mission. Recently a C-130 operating alone was credited with a 'seizure' when the crew spotted what appeared to be a drug-laden ship. The *Hercules* swooped low down and buzzed the vessel. The ship's terrified crewmen shoved their cargo overboard — brown bales of marijuana.

International Ice Patrol

The Coast Guard depends on its long range HC-130s for its ice patrol reconnaissance. Each year, a C-130 from Elizabeth City, North Carolina, is deployed on ice patrol approximately every two weeks. A crew of eleven, along with three ice observers from the International Ice Patrol, Groton, Connecticut, deploy with the aircraft. The task is to provide long range reconnaisance over the Grand Banks region south-east of Newfoundland, Canada. The crews search the area both visually and with a new side looking airborne radar (SLAR). The new SLAR equipment enables the C-130 to cover twenty-seven miles on each side, up to eighty miles, of poorer resolution, of the aircraft's flight path, making it possible to cover vast areas of water in a single flight.

Lieutenant Commander A D Summy stated, 'This combination of visual and electronic reconnaissance of the area provides us with thorough coverage. At the end of each flight the data is relayed to Groton, Connecticut, where it is put into our computer files. Twice a day, the computerized positions of all known icebergs are then broadcast to ships in the area.

'We normally fly at 8,000-foot altitude. We can fly six hours and never see the surface of the ocean and yet 'paint' a number of SLAR targets.'

A normal C-130 ice patrol mission lasts from five to seven hours, covering between 1,200 and 1,600 miles. Information coming via the SLAR unit is recorded on film giving the icebergs' position in latitude and longitude, the time, speed and approximate size. Later, specialists can make an overlay of the photos and determine the direction and speed of selected icebergs.

Commander Mont Smith, chief of operations of the USCG air station Elizabeth City, said the Ice Patrol crewmen are very pleased with the Lockheed C-130: 'It's a real crowd pleaser with us. It's rugged and has lots of loiter time. We can go out and do missions in all types of weather. The C-130 will be with us well beyond the year 2000.'

During the week of 11 July 1983, with only a day and a half of weather clear enough for visual sighting during six days' flying, the Ice Patrol C-130 crew charted seventy-six icebergs ranging from twenty-foot 'growlers' to multi-billion pound icebergs the size of an aircraft carrier. The arrival of the new high technology sensing equipment, built by Motorola and installed on either side of the C-130 fuselage over the landing gear, couldn't have come at a more appropriate time. The year 1983 will go down as the second biggest year for icebergs since the sinking of the *Titanic,* with almost 2,000 icebergs sighted.

Another technology advance has helped to turn the International Ice Patrol (IPP) exercise into a real science: the computer. 'Our computer is accurate within a five-mile radius,' said Lieutenant Iain Anderson, the senior observer from IPP headquarters. He cited a June 1982 ship and iceberg collision, 'We checked our charts and found the iceberg the ship hit was within a few feet of where our records said it would be. We weren't happy that the ship struck the iceberg, but were glad our computer forecasts were confirmed'. The information on that particular iceberg and others had been broadcast by radio to ships in the area.

A Lockheed HC-130 *Hercules* from San Francisco air station circles over a boat of shipwrecked mariners after dropping a life raft of supplies to them. The rear ramp of the HC-130 remains open, ready to drop any further requirements. (USCG)

Coast Guard officials say that eventually satellites may take over the job. But that is a long way off. Meanwhile, the USCG and their SLAR equipped C-130s provide near perfect coverage in accuracy and dependability. 'Sure the missions are demanding and the hours long,' stated a C-130 crewman, 'but we all feel good in realizing that we are performing a real service for mankind and saving lives.'

Fisheries Patrol

Patrolling America's valuable fishing zones is one of the USCG's vital missions and has received even greater emphasis with the nation's incorporation of the 200-mile off-shore Exclusive Economic Zone (EEZ). While USCG aircraft and high-speed cutters patrol Atlantic and Pacific fishing regions, including the WOC zone — Washington-Oregon-California — the most important fisheries surveillance takes place off the state of Alaska. There, the service operates a fleet of six long-range HC-130H Hercules, along with cutters and cutter-borne helicopters. Daily eight and a half hour C-130 patrols are flown at low levels on special tracks ranging from Kodiak to Attu on the western end of the Aleutian chain of islands. Lockheed C-130 crews seek to identify each fishing boat, along with its position and activity. Cutters are brought in to board the boats and verify their compliance with US fishing regulations. Certain species such as salmon, halibut, herring and crab are off limits to non-US ships with the exception of those from Japan, which can fish for salmon.

Lieutenant Commander Steven Bagts recalls his duty as an HC-130 pilot assigned to air station Kodiak, Alaska. 'Flying up there is quite a challenge', he noted, 'mainly due to the weather. Operations are seldom boring.' He noted that the HC-130s also fly Search & Rescue and logistic missions in addition to carrying out EEZ surveillance. Another USCG pilot, Commander Jim Keller, has logged 5,000 hours in the C-130, including many hours out of Kodiak, Alaska. 'For my money', he said, 'the C-130 is the best airplane ever built. It's a very reliable machine. I feel like being at home in it.'

Lieutenant Commander William Schleich, who has also flown over 5,000 hours in the Hercules, said the USCG, in buying a new fleet of advanced model HC-130Hs 'is looking to flying 'em into the 21st century. I've heard it said that the C-130 is the modern day DC-3 Gooney Bird. That's absolutely true. That airplane . . . she has really been good to me. I think I've probably done everything wrong in one and she's pulled me out every time.'

'About the trickiest C-130 landing', Schleich recalled, 'was going into French Frigate Shoals, a LORAN station 400 miles west of Honolulu. It's a man-made reef . . . looks like an aircraft carrier . . . about 2,500 feet long. It's coral. On one side of it are some buildings. It's closed now. We used to supply the station with the C-130. I went in there three times. I don't ever care to go again.'

Commander Schleich noted that while he has had some thrilling moments in the C-130, he also has had a few embarrassing ones. He remembered an incident while flying a Hercules equipped with the Airborne Oil Surveillance System (AOSS). He was flying a patrol near Miami. 'It was about midnight. We were zipping along . . . it was a beautiful night and someone said on the intercom, "There's a ship dumping oil down there." We went down and looked him over. I called out a small boat from Miami and orbited overhead for about an hour.' The cutter went over but was unable to spot the oil. 'It's right there', Schleich radioed, 'just off his starboard bow.' The cutter took a sample and radioed their finding back to the C-130 pilot. 'It was a party fishing boat,' Commander Schleich said with a grin. 'They had been cleaning fish. It was the oil from the scraps that we had detected. The AOSS was just a little too sophisticated in that case.'

Not all routine patrols are exciting. The HU-25A Guardian twin-jet and the lumbering HC-130 fly reconnaissance patrols across the Caribbean involved in the drug interdiction campaign, looking for anything that moves. One Lockheed C-130 pilot described law-enforcement patrols as 'hours and hours of complete boredom interrupted by a box lunch'.

Two AN/TRC-168 Transportable Communications Central (TCC) units are stationed at USCG air station Sacramento and are under the operational control of the Coast Guard's Pacific Area Commander in Alameda, California. TCC is a transportable communications station that provides complete facilities for point-to-point, air-to-ground and ship-to-shore communications. It consists of an air conditioned electronics shelter-trailer with installed communications equipment and a portable gasoline generator.

Deployment of a TCC unit can normally be made in six hours or less from the time of initial notification. Transportation of a TCC can be accomplished via cargo aircraft, helicopter or towing vehicle. A Lockheed HC-130 Hercules aircraft will provide transportation if mission response time is critical or the deployment area is located 300 miles or more from air station Sacramento. It will be accompanied by its Dodge B-300 towing vehicle van with camper package.

Once a TCC unit is on scene, communications can be provided in the high frequency (HF), very high frequency (VHF), FM and AM and ultra high frequency (UHF) radio bands. The entire system is designed to provide continuous service under all adverse operating conditions that are encountered during floods, storms or other disasters which would require deployment of the TCC.

Small island rescue

Even with his experience of landing Lockheed C-130s on isolated islands in Alaska, the short grassy strip on Fanning Island looked inaccessible to Commander John Barnstein. He and the C-130 flight crew from air station Barbers Point, Hawaii, knew the 3,200 foot strip was not ideal for an aircraft as large as the Hercules. But it was enough to land — a life depended on it.

During the morning of 9 August 1986, two aircrews headed for the small island 1,200 nautical miles south of Honolulu to evacuate a young woman with stab wounds in her stomach. The doctor on Fanning requested the Coast Guard's help and also asked that a physician be on the flight. A doctor, nurse and corpsman from the Tripler Army Medical Center went on the HC-130 1602 with HS1 William Munsey to prepare the patient for the flight back.

The US Army and Coast Guard medical team stabilized the woman's condition and made her as comfortable as possible during the four-hour flight back. 'We kept in constant communication with Honolulu. The message that she was in serious but stable condition helped prepare the ambulance and medical people waiting for her,' said AT2 Hall Rose, a member of the aircrew.

Upon landing back in Hawaii, the C-130 crew transferred the injured woman to an ambulance at Honolulu International Airport. Two aircrew had been assigned to the flight in case the C-130 could not land on the small island and the woman patient had to be taken to Christmas Island by boat or small aircraft, increasing the Hercules flying time.

A well known UK historian, Francis K Mason, introduced his book on the Lockheed Hercules, published in 1984, with the following words:

> Some 30 years ago, at a time when the world was still struggling to find its feet after the most devastating war in history, there was born in California an aeroplane which, despite its military raison d'être, was to become one of the most remarkable tools of world reconstruction and development, an aircraft so powerful and robust, and capable of moving such great loads, that it could bear but one name — Hercules.

CHAPTER ELEVEN
Past, Present and Future

Intent on continuing its superiority in aerial surveillance, the US Coast Guard's Office of Research & Development is always actively investigating the use of modern state-of-the-art equipment to improve its capabilities. Over the past ten years this department has been responsible for the evaluation and introduction of major projects such as the development of an all-weather, day/night, multisensor system for the HU-25A *Guardian* medium-range search aircraft, development of a forward-looking infra-red (FLIR) sensor for the new HH-65A *Dolphin* helicopter, and looking ahead, investigation of a satellite-aided Search & Rescue system. Together, these three systems have the potential for dramatic improvements in locating vessels in distress.

Management responsibility for the Coast Guard rests with the Commandant. He carries out this responsibility through the Chief of Staff, who co-ordinates the efforts of the Programme Directors. The responsibilities of the Commandant and Chief of Staff involve the overall objectives of the USCG while those of the Programme Directors involve the component parts, called Programmes, which are the means of achieving these objectives. The USCG has twenty-five programmes, each representing a specific operating mission area, such as Search & Rescue, or a support function, such as personnel.

The initial document in the planning process is the Commandant's Long Range View, where the Commandant sets forth his view of the environment in which the Coast Guard will be operating over the next twenty-five years. Based on these projections, specific policy guidance is provided. The Long Range View is a policy document which provides a common foundation for all planning at Headquarters and in the field.

History has proved that Coast Guard aviators are great improvisors, and over the years have flown and evaluated many unique aircraft types, with the *Flying Lifeboat* as the ultimate target to aim for. When the Sikorsky HH-3F *Pelican* helicopter is eventually retired from service, the USCG will have no amphibious aircraft facility. A Rescue Swimmer Programme is supposed to take up some of the inevitable slack in the missions, because there are certainly times when there is no substitute for reaching out and grabbing a survivor by the scruff of the neck from a helicopter in the water. That operation will be more than difficult to do from a low hover.

An artist's impression of the ultimate 'Flying Lifeboat' design for the US Coast Guard. It would be capable of being towed and dropped in the ocean, then it would taxi under its own power, carrying survivors to safety. Many such designs and drawings originated from 'doodles' on an engineer's desk. (USCG)

During 1944 came the first of a unique and interesting series of engineering
design proposals which were submitted by McDonnell Aircraft. Even though
appropriate designations were allocated by the company, research has failed to
unearth these in detail. The last McDonnell project appears to be the XHJH-1
Whirlaway, the company having acquired control of the Platt LePage Aircraft
Co of Eddystone, Pennsylvania, in June 1944.

Peter Wells '88

The Curtiss R-6 seaplane was used to train Coast Guard aviators in World War I, and was later used by them on the cruiser *Huntington*. The cruiser also carried Gallaudet and Martin hydroplanes, but records do not indicate whether the two Coast Guard pilots on the *Huntington* flew them. A Vought U0-1 operated from Base 7 in Gloucester, Massachusetts in 1925 and 1926. Curtiss HS-2L and MF flying boats were taken over from the US Navy at Morehead City after the end of hostilities. The National Archives indicate that four HS-2Ls, one MF, and one U0-1 were returned to the US Navy in 1925. Whether the HS and MF received at Morehead City were the aircraft returned to the US Navy, whether they had long since deteriorated leaving only a book-keeping transaction, or whether there was an entirely separate transaction, is not known. During World War I, Coast Guard pilots commanded or served at US Naval Air Stations which operated the French DD, the Curtiss HS-1, and N-9 among others. As already related, one of the pilots of the famous NC-4 was a Coast Guard officer. In the narratives, an Aeromarine Model 40 with an OXX engine is mentioned among Morehead City aircraft, but no verification has been found in the historical archives.

Between the wars and during World War II, the Coast Guard was at first an interested observer but later became very active in helicopter development. Some unusual designs evolved during that period. Most of them never progressed beyond the proposal stage, but their influence on the trend of helicopter design is more than evident.

During World War II, the Coast Guard again operated US Navy aircraft, most being later turned back to the Navy, but some were scattered among the Mutual Defense Assistance Programme (MDAP), US Air Force, War Assets Administration, Civil Aeronautics Administration, the US Fish & Wildlife Service and the National Advisory Committee for Aeronautics (NACA). A few were retained by the Coast Guard, to be replaced eventually by modern aircraft.

Early Coast Guard aviators commanded or served at US Naval air stations abroad and in the USA during World War I. They are shown here operating the Curtiss HS-1L pusher flying boat powered by a 360 hp Liberty engine. (Peter M. Bowers)

Many unique ideas, originating as doodles on a desk, were discussed at Coast Guard headquarters during 1942. Suggestions were submitted by a Captain Kossler USCG and drawings were made by Henry Cocklin, a civilian aeronautical engineer, dean of the Technical Section of the Aeronautical Engineering Division. At the time the drawing was made, the only helicopter flying in the US was the Platt-LePage XR-1 powered by a 440 hp R-985-21 engine driving two three-bladed rotors mounted on lateral outriggers. The drawing by the Coast Guard introduced the idea of fore-and-aft twin rotors, rumour having it that this idea was seen and picked up by a young designer who eventually made it into one of the prominent helicopter types in the world.

During 1944 came the first of a series of design proposals submitted by McDonnell Aircraft and designated H-1A. The Coast Guard suggested that the wings be removed from the Douglas RD-4 amphibian, and a set of Platt-LePage XR-1 rotors fitted. Rotor diameters of forty feet eight inches, with 117 square feet of blade area and 227 square feet of pylon area, were planned. Weight empty was to be 7,300 lbs, full weight 10,000 lbs. Top speed of 128 mph, sea level climb of 1,000 feet per minute and 15,000 feet service ceiling were projected. Engines were to be R-985-AN-1, providing a range of 450 miles with 200 gallons of fuel.

Second design proposal from McDonnell in 1944 was the H-1B to utilize hulls from Coast Guard Grumman JRF-2 *Goose* aircraft, fitted with Platt-LePage XR1 rotors. Empty weight was to be 7,000 lbs, gross weight of 10,000 lbs. R-985-AN-1 engines were to give a top speed of 148 mph, a range of 540 miles, and a 1,000 feet per minute climb from sea level. A disadvantage of the side-by-side rotor arrangement was lack of stiffness in the pylon structure.

Third of the McDonnell 1944 proposals was the amphibian H-1C. A completely new hull was proposed, with the Platt-LePage XR-1 rotor system. Empty weight was to be 6,700 lbs, with a gross weight of 9,700 lbs. With a Wasp Junior R-985-AN-1 engine this model proposed 160 mph, a range of 570 miles, a climb of 1,240 feet per minute from sea level and a service ceiling of 15,000 feet.

Last of the 1944 proposals by McDonnell was the H-1D which eventually became the US Navy XHJD-1. With a rotor diameter of forty feet driven by a R-985-AN-1 engine, it proposed 127 mph at 9,320 lbs gross weight, a range of 590 miles at 85 mph with a fuel load of 195 gallons, twenty gallons of oil and a climb from sea level of 1,100 feet per minute. One model of the US Navy XHJH-1 ex XHJD-1 was built with BuNo 44318.

Commencing in 1945, experiments were carried out on the design of a glider borne lifeboat which could be launched from water or land, and towed by powered aircraft to survivors of airline crashes and maritime casualties, by the Coast Guard and Stevens Institute of Technology. Possibilities for the efficient use of this airborne lifeboat were visualized especially where accidents occurred in frigid waters and time of exposure became a critical factor in the victims' survival.

It was developed by Aero Affiliates Inc under a Coast Guard contract Tcg 37120. Wings, struts and empennage of Waco CG-4A *Hadrian* gliders were to be used. Using a specially designed hull it could be towed by a powerful aircraft to the scene of the disaster. Upon reaching the scene the gliderboat was released from the tow plane and glided to the surface of the water. When waterborne, wing and tail are jettisoned clear of the boat. A small engine and propeller serve to maneuver the boat in the water so that all survivors over a rather wide area can be removed. This boat could be hoisted aboard rescue ships arriving on the scene, returned to any USCG air unit, fitted with new wings and tail surfaces, and so once again be ready for flight.

Hull models of this glider borne lifeboat were built and towing tank tests for resistance, take-off and landings were completed. Wind tunnels were in progress in March 1947, after which the entire project was suspended on 2 April 1947, in view of economies being directed by Congress at that time. Other developments that suffered the same fate due to lack of proper funds included further research and developments in the field of helicopter aviation.

The Aeromarine 40 is mentioned as one of the early Coast Guard aircraft operated from Morehead City, North Carolina. It was powered by an OXX engine. (Peter M. Bowers)

The model which completed wind tunnel tests at New York University had a thirty-six foot long dual hull with a ten foot beam. Full scale dimensions were: span 86 feet 7 inches, length 52 feet 6 inches, height 18 feet 7 inches and a wing area of 882 square feet. Hull weight was 4,900 lbs, glider weight 6,050 lbs empty. Weight full was 7,000 lbs. It had a crew of two. Stall speed was 48 mph. Take-off was to be from a dolly. Wings were to be jettisoned by a JATO bottle upon landing. Several engines were envisaged, from 25 hp to 125 hp.

Two designs were considered for this glider borne lifeboat. The second had a single tail boom, and water skis under each wing.

A further consideration by the Coast Guard was a helicopter glider. In a press release dated 2 August 1947 it revealed that the design was intended to be towed behind a search plane, to be landed vertically when needed. The rotors were to revolve oppositely, and fold or be jettisoned upon landing. Take-off was to be from water or from a jettisonable carriage, aided by a 600 hp engine in the helicopter glider. The engine could be clutched in to the water propeller. Proposed crew was to be a pilot, co-pilot and a doctor. No action was ever taken on this proposal.

Between the years 1956 to 1962 a great deal of research was conducted in the US on aircraft and vehicles with vertical take-off and landing (VTOL) — these including Hiller and the VZ-1 one-man flying platform; Vertol with the VZ-2 tilt-wing research aircraft; Ryan Vertiplane with the VZ-3 VTOL research aircraft; Doak VZ-4, a flying platform; Fairchild with the VZ-5 VTOL research aircraft; Chrysler built the VZ-6 a VTOL ducted-fan test vehicle. Curtiss-Wright built two models of the VZ-7 for the US Army, and Piasecki built two Model 59K VTOL research aircraft also for the US Army. In Canada Avro built a VZ-9 'flying saucer', back in the US Lockheed the VZ-10 *Hummingbird* and Ryan built the VZ-11. The British Hawker-Siddeley *Kestrel* became the VZ-12. Unfortunately no details are available, but it appears that the Coast Guard evaluated one of the two Piasecki Model 59K VTOL research aircraft built for the US Army. Power was by a Turbomeca Artouste IIB driving two ducted rotors. It was a cushion or hovercraft type vehicle.

A very unusual photo taken on 8 April 1977 depicting a US Coast Guard Lockheed HC-130B *Hercules* 1414 when it was based at St Petersburg air station in Florida. This aircraft was delivered on 23 August 1966 and was retired gracefully during April 1986. (USCG)

A close-up of Lockheed HC-130B 1340 taken while based at St Petersburg, Florida. It was delivered to the USCG in December 1959, initially going to Hawaii. During April 1986 this aircraft was retired from the USCG inventory and the fuselage/wings stored at Davis-Monthan, Arizona. (USCG)

Opposite: A USCG HH-65A *Dolphin* prepares for a night sortie from the air station located at New Orleans, Louisiana. It is the only type operated today by this facility, but they are fitted with the latest all-weather navigation equipment, plus sensors for involvement in the drug war. (George Hall)

Left: Seen awaiting a night sortie during November 1987 is a HU-25A *Guardian* at the USCG Aviation Training Centre, Mobile, Alabama, a unique air station which operates all types with the exception of the HC-130. On 1 April 1988 the station had on inventory three HH-3Fs, six HH-65As, ten HH-52As and six HU-25s, which today include the 'A' and 'C' models. (John Gaffney USCG)

Below: The USCG can claim a long record of achievement with its fleet of Lockheed HC-130 *Hercules*. Since 1959 they have operated no less than forty-eight of the type, with twenty-three in front-line service today. The profile of this ubiquitous Lockheed transport is now recognized world-wide. (USCG)

The forty-eighth and latest Lockheed HC-130H *Hercules* was delivered to the
USCG during May 1988. The tasks for this transport are numerous and Coast
Guard aviators have traversed the globe many times in the type. It was custom
built by Lockheed for the force, and the profile of this ubiquitous aircraft is
emphasized in this excellent photo. (USCG)

Medium Range Search Aircraft Evaluation

On 7 January 1977 the US Coast Guard awarded a $200m multiyear contract to the Falcon Jet Corporation for the purchase of forty-one Medium Range Surveillance (MRS) Falcon 20G aircraft. This twin-engined modified executive jet was the replacement for the HU-16E *Albatross* amphibian.

The origin of this MRS procurement can be traced back to 1966 when the USCG elected to participate jointly with the US Navy, US Air Force and the Royal Canadian Air Force, in a full-scale wing fatigue test of the Grumman HU-16E — in fact, the USCG provided the airframe to the Naval Air Development Center at Warminster, Pennsylvania, for the testing. The object of the test was to determine whether major wing repair or replacement of the wing would be required. Testing commenced on 24 January 1968 and, after a myriad of systems and funding problems, terminated on 31 October 1968 with the failure of the starboard wing. Subsequent engineering calculations resulted in the establishment of a wing service life of 11,000 flight hours for the USCG HU-16E fleet. When the wing fatigue testing was initiated, the fleet numbered seventy-six aircraft, down three from the 1963 high of seventy-nine.

In 1967, while the wing fatigue test programme was in process, the Coast Guard began exploring possible replacement aircraft options for the aging *Albatross* fleet. This exploration resulted in the publication of the Coast Guard's Aviation Issue Paper in September 1967, which recommended procurement of a mixed fleet of Sikorsky HH-3F *Pelican* helicopters and Lockheed C-130 *Hercules*. Any ornithologist worth his salt would immediately have challenged the premise that Herky Birds and Pelicans, in any combination, were suitable substitutes for the crafty old Goat. Some two years later, as HH-3F helicopters joined the C-130 fleet, the USCG similarly concluded that the mix of aircraft was not a viable operational or financial alternative.

In July 1971 the Coast Guard Aircraft Characteristics Board was convened to develop operating characteristics and performance requirements for the ultimate HU-16E replacement. Over the next two years, the board evaluated in excess of thirty aircraft and in April 1972 developed some broad MRS characteristics and requirements. Concurrently, a planning board was tasked with determining MRS fleet size and geographical distribution. This effort led to the development of the USCG's first Aviation Plan which established a requirement for forty-one MRS aircraft.

During April 1972, the Aircraft Characteristics Board recommended the leasing of one representative multi engine aircraft for mission evaluation in each of the following three classes: turboprop, turbofan (high or medium by-pass) and turbojet. A Request for Proposal (RFP) issued to industry in November 1972 culminated in the leasing of a Cessna Model C-500 *Citation* fan jet and an Israeli Commodore Jet 1123 *Westwind* turbojet. As the RFP failed to ellicit a timely response from any turboprop manufacturer in the USA, the Coast Guard's Grumman Gulfstream I turboprop aircraft (VC-4A) was dispatched to an operating unit for trial employment as a multimission vehicle.

Between 1 April and 30 September 1973 a detailed operational and technical evaluation of the two candidate aircraft — *Citation* and *Westwind* — was conducted at a home base of Coast Guard air station AVTRACEN located at Mobile, Alabama. However during the evaluation they deployed throughout the USA introducing the aircraft to and evaluating it under different climes and conditions. The MRS Task organisation consisted of Captain P A Hogue, programme director, Commander B Harrington, project manager, Commander H J Harris Jr, flight evaluation, Lieutenant Commander W C Donnell, engineering evaluation, Captain A J Soreng, support activity ATC Mobile, Commander J C Arney, operations section and Lieutenant G D Sickafoose, engineering section.

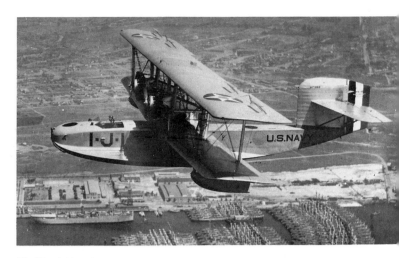

The Naval Aircraft Factory PN-12 patrol flying boat was one of the many types evaluated by the US Coast Guard over the years. This type was in service with the US Navy during the 1920s, had a crew of five and was powered by two 525 hp Wright R-1750D engines. (Peter M. Bowers)

The operational evaluation of the three aircraft focused on ascertaining suitability of each class of aircraft for the range of USCG operational missions and on establishing a weight and volume baseline for the MRS specification. The evaluation did establish the viability of turbofan technology in multimission applications. Additionally, it was concluded that the turbofan offered significant potential for life cycle cost benefits, over recips and turboprops, such as improved reliability, maintenance, overhaul, reduced level of spares, and elimination of the propeller system.

Perhaps the most significant item of knowledge gained from this evaluation concerned the issue of aircraft size. The *Citation* was, by consensus of the evaluators, grossly inadequate in size and consequently incapable of performing the USCG missions. The *Westwind,* although slightly larger, was also found space restrictive and not deemed capable of accommodating mission related equipment and personnel. After reviewing the interim and final reports, the Aircraft Characteristics Board issued a revised specification for the MRS characteristics requiring as a minimum, that the aircraft weigh no less than 20,000 lbs gross weight, be powered by fanjet engines, have a combined cockpit and cabin interior volume of 600 cubic feet, have aerial delivery capability, accommodate a radar antenna with twenty-seven inch sweep diameter and accommodate a 3,185 lbs payload.

The prototype Platt-LePage XR-1A 42-6581 was powered by two 450 hp R-985-AN-1 engines driving two three-bladed rotors mounted on lateral out riggers, and carried a crew of two in tandem. It provided the basic idea on which the McDonnell projects for the US Coast Guard 'Flying Lifeboats' were designed. (USAF Museum via David E. Manard)

Commander Richard D Schmidtman, USCG, later Rear Admiral, seen holding a model of a glider-borne lifeboat design which for over a year in April 1947 was under development by the US Coast Guard and Stevens Institute of Technology. (USCG)

Three minimum size candidate aircraft identified as potential contenders under these revised requirements were the Rockwell Sabre 75A, the French Avions Marcel Dassault Falcon 20 and the United Kingdom's Hawker-Siddeley HS125. However, the HS125 was later reassessed as not fully compliant since it was powered by turbo jets which in low altitude loiter missions would impose severe and unacceptable fuel consumption penalties. In the view of those USCG officers who had surveyed the market, the probable competitors appeared to be the Falcon 20 and the Sabre 75A. Apparently the two aircraft had just completed a head-on Federal Aviation Administration (FAA) procurement competition. Rockwell's offering significantly under-priced that of the Falcon Jet Corporation, even without application of Buy American pricing penalties.

The decision was made to proceed with the issuance of a Military Interservice Procurement Request (MIPR) to the US Navy for the purchase of the Sabre 75A. The Sabre was of US origin and the type either were, or soon would be, in the Department of Defense and FAA inventories. On 9 October 1973 approval was obtained from the Deputy Secretary of the Department of Transportation to move forward with this sole source procurement and preliminary discussions were held with the US Naval Air Systems Command, the purchasing agent for the USCG procurement. Some concern was expressed by the Coast Guard as to the adequacy of the endurance of the Sabre 75A at low altitudes. In an effort to enhance this aspect of performance the feasibility of re-engining the Sabre 75A was explored.

The Research & Development department of the Coast Guard has a never ending task in planning the future of the vital service. This rare photo depicts 58-5510, a Piasecki Model VZ-8P type of cushion or hovercraft vehicle undergoing Coast Guard evaluation. Where and when? (Peter M. Bowers)

The decision to proceed with a non-competitive procurement drew some criticism from both industry and Congress in May 1974. Not intending to circumvent procurement regulations, and not anticipating that such a viable competitive market existed for MRS aircraft, the Coast Guard was quite unprepared for this reaction. After reappraising the situation, the Commandant directed the cancellation of the MIPR and the initiation of a competitive two-step, formally advertised, procurement. In January 1975 a Request for Technical Proposals (RFTP) was issued to industry. Although the technical description was lengthy and detailed, the more salient characteristics which served to initially screen the competitive range were 20,000 to 65,000 lb gross weight, 5,000 foot critical field length, 375 knot dash speed, capability for aerial delivery of equipment, minimum of 600 cubic feet combined cockpit and cabin interior volume, ability to perform a specific search mission profile (equating to a range of approximately 1,050 miles), 3,185 lbs payload and accommodate Coast Guard modified APS 115 radar with a twenty-seven inch sweep width antenna.

In April 1975 proposals were received from Rockwell International plus VFW Fokker, the latter a German, Dutch, French and British consortium. Rockwell offered the Sabre 75C and Fokker the VFW-614. The Rockwell offering was an extensively modified version of its 75A Executive jet. Modifications included a supercritical wing, five-foot fuselage plug, raised horizontal stabilizer and new Lycoming ALF 502 high bypass turbofan engines. This represented quite a technical stride forward for the Sabre production line, and there was understandable corporate concern as to whether the degree of technical and financial risk imposed by a fixed price, multi-year contract was acceptable. The VFW-614 was a wide body, short haul commuter fanjet with density seating for forty passengers. It was unique in having over the wing mounted Rolls Royce M45H turbofan engines.

As October 1975 was drawing to a close, and with both contending aircraft having been found technically acceptable, Rockwell International announced their intent not to bid a fixed price contract, forcing the USCG to find the company non-responsive. Rather than enter into negotiations with the surviving competitor, a second RFTP was issued on 19 January 1976 and the specifications modified slightly. These involved the power plants and spare parts.

Five US manufacturers responded to this second solicitation. Most responded with two or more proposals. In mid-July 1976 the technical evaluation which was step one was completed and at least one proposal from each company was found acceptable. The competitors were Grumman American with a re-engined Gulfstream II, Lockheed Marietta with the Jetstar 2, Rockwell International with a re-engined Sabre 75A and the Falcon Jet Corporation with the Falcon 20G.

Prior to the August 1976 initiation of the second step of price bids, Grumman withdrew from the competition. At the bid opening on 28 October 1976, bids were received from Lockheed, the Falcon Jet Corporation and VFW Fokker. Rockwell declined to bid. With its bid price of $4,996,251 per aircraft, the Falcon Jet Corporation was the apparent lowest bidder. The next and final action prior to any award was the execution of a pre-award survey by the Coast Guard to determine if the Falcon Jet Corporation and its major subcontractors were financially sound and had the technical and manufacturing capability to meet the terms of the contract. The survey was completed and it was recommended that the Falcon Jet Corporation be awarded the contract.

During the six weeks that elapsed until the contract award, there was a resurgence of pressure by some US aerospace manufacturers of small executive jets to force a reopening of the competition. It was their contention that the cockpit and cabin interior volume of 600 cubic feet was excess to the USCG needs. The new aircraft after all was replacing the HU-16E which had in excess of 1100 cubic feet, indicating the MRS size requirements had been understated.

Despite this final flurry of challenges from a segment of the US aviation industry, Secretary of Transportation Coleman, after very careful deliberation, approved the award to Falcon Jet Corporation and the new HU-25A *Guardian* was born.

The initial Coast Guard programme extended over a seventy-one-month period with the first aircraft scheduled for delivery in July 1979, thirty months after the award of contract. Subsequent deliveries to be scheduled at the rate of one per month for forty-one months, this including a multi-year procurement with funded lots of fourteen, twelve, twelve and three aircraft. The aircraft was fabricated at various facilities in France, final assembly taking place at Merignac near Bordeaux. The aircraft were then crated in a partially disassembled state and flown by stretched Lockheed C-130 *Hercules* to Little Rock, Arkansas, for assembly. Final assembly included the fitting of Garrett ATF 3-6 engines, an integrated Collins avionics navigation and communication package, a Texas Instruments APS-127 radar, LORAN-C receiver, other comm-nav equipment, interior panels and furnishings, hard points and console to accommodate and manage a wide variety of surveillance sensor systems, a drop hatch for air delivery of equipment to distressed vessels and cabin search windows.

In terms of dollars the HU-25A procurement is the largest ever undertaken by the Coast Guard. Because of its 0.85 mach speed capability, the aircraft can quickly be moved between Coast Guard districts in response to urgent Search & Rescue, law enforcement (ELT) or any other missions. This rapid response capability permitted the procurement of a minimal number of aircraft. The fuel efficient turbofan engine provides ample loiter capability in the low altitude, slow flight mode and quick turn around service times, and reliability requirements should provide for optimal utilization. Included in the aircraft price was a requirement for continued technical support over the guaranteed 30,000 hour life of the aircraft.

Short range recovery helicopter

The Coast Guard received ninety-nine of the Sikorsky HH-52A *Seaguard* helicopter between 1962 and 1969. During 1977 an acquisition programme was launched to give the USCG a short-range recovery helicopter by late 1979 or early 1980. Proposal response from helicopter manufacturers was required by December 1977 (it was issued in September) with a Coast Guard decision on the new machine planned for mid-August 1978. The short programme cycle was due to the USCG, in consultation with the US Navy, in requiring all candidates to be able to receive a Federal Aviation Administration (FAA) derivative type certificate or a military equivalent in the acquisition time frame.

The requirements for the Coast Guard's prime mission, Search & Rescue, stated that the short-range recovery candidate must take off, cruise outbound at 1,000 feet in excess of 100 knots, travel 150 nautical miles from base, hover for thirty minutes and then pick up three 170 lb survivors, return to base and have ten per cent of the available fuel, or twenty minutes of fuel remaining, whichever is greater, as reserve fuel at shutdown.

Helicopter manufacturers who competed for the Coast Guard request requirements included Bell Helicopter Textron with a utility version of its Model 222, Sikorsky with a version of its S-76 and Aerospatiale with a modified version of its SA365.

Bell's entrant was basically a Model 222 stripped down to a utility version, but with the following modifications. The sponsons were to be extended by eighteen inches to accommodate a fifteen gallon fuel tank to meet the necessary fuel reserve requirements. The interior would be changed to accommodate a hoist operator using modified McDonnell Douglas DC-10 seats for comfort on long-range flights. The rear bulkhead would be removed to allow access to the rear storage area, and three of the four doors would be removed, with cabin windows enlarged, and bubble windows installed

One of the two Grumman E2-C *Hawkeye* aircraft, 3501, of CGAW-1 based at Norfolk, Virginia, parked alongside a HC-130 *Hercules*, 1501, based at Elizabeth City, North Carolina, on 2 March 1987. The Anti-Drug Abuse Act of 1986 established a Coast Guard role in the interdiction of air smuggling. The legislation included loan of two E2-C aircraft from the US Navy. (USCG)

in the cockpit for better visibility whilst hovering. Gross weight was estimated between 7,000 and 7,500 lbs. Its two blade rotor system would not need to be folded when stored on USCG cutters.

Sikorsky anticipated very little modification from the commercial S-76 as the folding rotor blades, hoist crew seat and auxilary flotation gear that the Coast Guard required were all options on the commercial S-76. The proposed navigation, communication and sensor package would be changed from the commercial version. The S-76 was reputed to be able to pick up six 200 lb survivors and satisfy the Coast Guard rescue profile requirements.

Aerospatiale conducted studies to see if the SA365 would be a viable candidate for the programme. It was estimated it would have to install a pressure refuelling system and adapt the nose to accommodate a radar. The main change to the SA365 was to be replacement of the two Turbomeca Ariel engines to conform with the Buy American Act. A version of the helicopter had flown with US manufactured Lycoming LTS 101 engines. They proposed to enrol US vendors for the avionics, auxilary power unit (APU) and the environmental controls. Aerospatiale emphasised the single pilot instrument flight rules ability, the hover stability and the fan-in-fin as attributes to the SA365.

On 13 November 1984 in a news release the US Department of Transportation announced that the US Coast Guard had announced plans for conditional acceptance of HH-65A

During 1987 the US Navy awarded the UK based Airship Industries Limited a huge £106 million contract for a fleet of airships, from which it was hoped the US Coast Guard could make a procurement. The contract involved the huge US Westinghouse avionics company. This artist's impression depicts a USCG airship 8301 in flight over the San Francisco city skyline. (USCG)

Dolphin helicopters from the Aerospatiale Helicopter Corporation. The first of ninety-six helicopters ordered was to be delivered from the Aerospatiale assembly plant in Grand Prairie, Texas. Acceptance of the aircraft had been delayed by snow ingestion problems. Under certain conditions ingestion of snow caused the engine to surge and to risk a snow or ice build up which could damage the engine compressor. Tests were conducted in the climatic chamber at Eglin Air Force base in Florida and were successful.

The twin-engine *Dolphin* has a range of 400 nautical miles, and is replacing the ageing single-engine Sikorsky HH-52A *Seaguard* as the Coast Guard's short range helicopter. It can be carried aboard the USCG medium and high endurance cutters, and is being used in law enforcement and ice surveillance as well as Search & Rescue.

The HH-65A is constructed of high strength corrosion resistant composite structural materials. It is powered by Avco Lycoming LTS 101 turboshaft engines and features a shrouded tail rotor. It also has a state-of-the-art communications and navigation equipment fully integrated into a computerized flight management system.

The first six aircraft went to the Coast Guard Training Center located at Mobile, Alabama, for training USCG aviators with the first operational helicopter assigned to air station New Orleans, Louisiana. The initial delivery schedule called for one aircraft a month for the first six months, two a month for the next sixteen months, and three per month until final delivery. The average cost of the ninety-six HH-65A

Dolphin helicopters is $3.2m. As of 1 October 1988 a total of eighty-three had been accepted and placed in service.

New medium range recovery helicopter

Today the US Coast Guard is currently in the stages of acquiring a new medium range recovery (MRR) helicopter to replace the aging Sikorsky HH-3F *Pelican* helicopters. These HH-3F aircraft will reach the end of their economic service life by the end of the decade unless some extraordinary service life extension programme is developed. It is not expected to be in the Coast Guard inventory until the early 1990s.

On 30 September 1986 a news release from United Technologies Sikorsky Aircraft at Stratford, Connecticut revealed that the Department of the US Navy had announced the awarding of an $84.5m contract to Sikorsky Aircraft for an initial production of five Combat Search & Rescue-Special Warfare Support (HCS) helicopters for the US Navy, and two Medium Range Recovery (MRR) helicopters for the US Coast Guard.

The new helicopter is a close derivative of the Sikorsky SH-60F *Seahawk* and builds on the $1.3bn invested in the development of the H-60 series. It combines the best of combat attributes, seaworthiness integrated systems, supportability and helicopter performance to provide the Coast Guard with the optimum MRR solution. The total number of aircraft expected to be produced is fifty, with eighteen going to the US Navy and thirty-two to the Coast Guard where it will be known as the HH-60J.

Sikorsky Aircraft's proposed SRR helicopter for the US Coast Guard in 1977 was the utility version of its twin-turbine powered S-76 *Spirit*. On 20 July 1978 a mock-up was unveiled, and this photo dated April 1977 shows the proposed helicopter in USCG livery with the appropriate equipment. (Sikorsky)

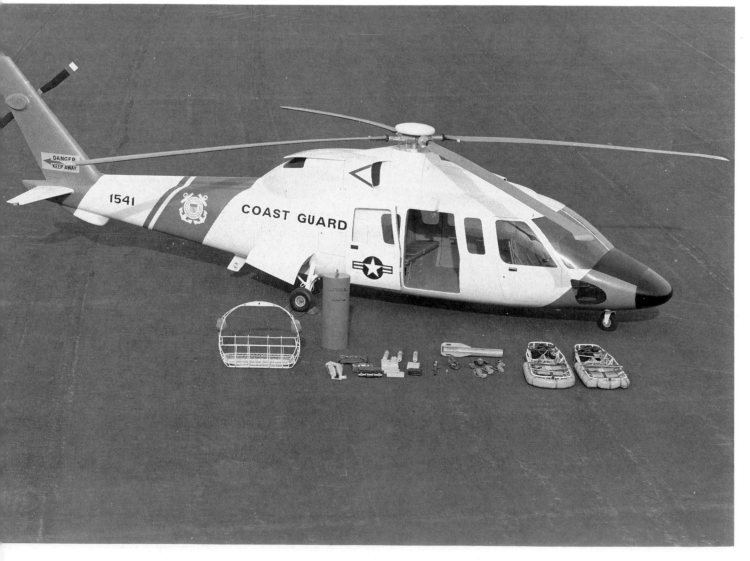

CHAPTER 12
Semper Paratus — always ready

It has flown over every continent and on every ocean in the world. It has fluttered in every conflict in which the US has been involved, ranging from the quasi-war with France in the late eighteenth century to the conflict in Vietnam. In nearly 190 years of existence, it has steeled Coast Guard personnel against every hardship they have been called upon to face. Smugglers and pirates have cursed it, but countless shipwreck victims have prayed for a glimpse of it.

Its concept is truly unique among US Military Services. It is the Coast Guard ensign and 1989 marks the 190th anniversary of its origin.

The US Coast Guard ensign was born in 1799, when Secretary of the Treasury Oliver Wolcott stipulated to his Collectors of Customs 'that the cutters and other vessels employed in the service of the Revenue are hereafter to be distinguished from other vessels by an ensign'. He ordered that the design of the ensign would consist 'of sixteen perpendicular stripes [one for each state in the Union at that time], alternate red and white, the Union of the ensign to be, the Arms of the United States in dark blue on a white field'. The authority for this innovative ensign was based in the '102d Section of the Act of March 2, 1799, entitled An Act to regulate the Collection of Duties on Imports and Tonnage', which ordered the Collectors of Customs to provide 'such flags' to Revenue cutters and to then inform the masters of all merchant ships of their existence.

Initially, USCG aircraft after World War II maintained an overall metal finish with yellow ident stripes as on USAF Rescue aircraft. Seen here is a Grumman UF-1G 1276 showing the distinctive yellow fuselage band. (via Peter M. Bowers)

During the early years of the Revenue Marine, as the Coast Guard was known at the time of this directive, many men were gaining infamous reputations as pirates. Masters of merchant ships soon became suspicious of any ship trying to overtake their vessels and would sooner shoot someone trying to board than ask what his business was. Definite proof of honorable intentions was needed. A Revenue Marine officer, therefore, needed an easily recognizable badge of authority to enable him to accomplish his job without receiving an eye full of musket shot as he poked his head over the gunwale of another man's ship. The Treasury Department at last recognized this need and, following Secretary Wolcott's directive of 1 August 1799, began equipping their cutters with the ensign.

There existed, of course, the possibility than an enterprising pirate would duplicate the distinctive design of the ensign to facilitate the overtaking of another vessel. To discourage this, and other unprincipled uses of the ensign, the Act of 2 March 1799 which authorized the ensign, addressed this problem explicitly: 'If any ship, vessel or boat, not employed in the service of the revenue, shall, within the jurisdiction of the United States, carry or hoist any pendant or ensign prescribed for a vessel in the service . . . . . . the master or commander of the ship or vessel so offending shall forfeit and pay one hundred dollars.' The fine seems almost frivolous when one considers that an apprehended offender, more often than not, would be a pirate who consequently would be hanged.

As the years wore on, the number of ships heeding the orders of a vessel flying the ensign grew, as did the Serviceman's pride in it. Authorized strictly as a seagoing symbol of authority, it began to be used more and more as another kind of symbol. During the scientific exploration of the newly acquired Alaskan territory by the Revenue steamer *Lincoln* in 1867, for example, First Lieutenant D B Hodgedon hoisted and left the ensign on the highest pinnacle of the Makuskin Mountain near Unalaska. In a separate report to the Secretary, Lieutenant Hodgedon told of 'placing the ensign of our Service on the lee side of a huge lava rock and securing it well against the heavy squalls of wind abounding at this height'. The height was determined by barometic measurement to be 5,691 feet, an accepted record for that time and for many years to come.

The air station at San Francisco adopted the system of the station ident on the inside of the wing floats of their HU-16E *Albatross* amphibians so that any Press photos could be accurately credited. The author took this picture on one of many visits to the air station. (AP Publications)

As the ensign continued to grow in esteem and popularity within the Service, so, too, did the practice of flying the ensign over Custom Houses. This practice was formalized in 1874, when Secretary of the Treasury Benjamin Bristow signed an order making the ensign the official badge of the entire Custom Service, to fly over all custom houses and custom boats as well as cutters.

President William Howard Taft recognized the importance of having a distinctive symbol for the Revenue cutters and, on 7 June 1910, issued an Executive Order directing 'the distinguishing flag now used by vessels of the Revenue Cutter Service be marked by the distinctive emblem of the service in blue and white'. The placement of the emblem, as defined by President Taft, was on a line with the lower edge of the Union, over the center of the seventh perpendicular stripe from the mast and covering a horizontal space of three stripes.

There existed one drawback to the President's order — there was no set design for the emblem. This precipitated numerous variations of the emblem and, subsequently, of the ensign. The ensign, however, retained its distinctive visual identity largely because the variations of the emblem were not readily noticeable to persons on a ship viewing a cutter several thousand yards away through binoculars.

These discrepancies, however, proved to be an annoyance to the members of the Service. Thus on 26 February 1927 Secretary of the Treasury Andrew S Mellon officially designated the familiar shield with thirteen stripes, within two concentric circles, superimposed upon two old fashioned anchors, as the 'Distinctive seal and emblem of the United States Coast Guard'. Contained within the concentric circles were the words 'United States Coast Guard' and the founding date 1790. Separated above and below the shield was the Service's motto, *Semper Paratus* (Always Ready).

The ensign maintained this design for several decades. During prohibition, the ensign fluttered over the cutters as they fought to stem the illegal flow of alcohol into the country. This action, for understandable reasons, marked a low point in the popularity of the Coast Guard with a large portion of the public. The Service endured however and regained the public's esteem, particularly during World War II when the ensign saw action in every combat theatre in the world.

In 1951, the ensign received a minor face lift. The thirteen stars previously arched over the eagle's head were transformed into a cluster. In all probability this change occurred to make the union conform to the Arms of the US, as earlier ordered in Secretary Wolcott's directive of 1799.

Six years later, in 1957, President Dwight D Eisenhower signed an Executive Order that required a more detailed drawing of the emblem than the Secretary Mellon version.

When the US Coast Guard was transferred from the Treasury Department to the Department of Transportation in 1967, the change to the emblem affected the ensign. The words *Semper Paratus* were dropped from the emblem. This change, although minor, was necessary to obtain harmony between the distinctive symbols of the Coast Guard and to implement the new Coast Guard Visual Identification Programme that has given the Coast Guard its now famous slash.

Despite the numerous changes that have taken place in the Coast Guard ensign, eighteenth century cuttermen would have no difficulty in recognizing it as the ensign they served under.

During 1958 Norman N Rubin, US Government aeronautical engineer employed in Coast Guard headquarters, was involved in studies which led to the adoption of the slash. Two disparate problems converged on his desk that year.

The first was the 'see and be seen' campaign being waged by the US Department of Defense in the aftermath of a series of mid-air collisions and near misses with airliners. Emphasis upon increased flying discipline was only part of the answer. Because of the widespread use of bare aluminium as the skin of aircraft, the most alert crews could be caught by surprise. Silver colour makes a good camouflage, except in the unusual case of sunlight glinting off it. Several complex lighting systems were proposed to provide instant information, none of which achieved widespread acceptance.

Drug interdiction

As early as February 1983 it was revealed that the US Navy would like to drop its role in drug interdiction, which required operation of Grumman E-2C *Hawkeye* surveillance aircraft, and proposed transferring to the Coast Guard some twenty year old Lockheed P-3A *Orion* aircraft that were scheduled to be placed in desert storage at Davis-Monthan, Arizona. Senator Mark Andrews, chairman of the US Senate Appropriations transportation sub-committee, thought he had a better idea and directed US Transportation Secretary Elizabeth Dole to suggest alternative ways that her department (USCG) could finance the purchase of five E-2C aircraft. They would be used for military preparedness, drug interdiction plus Search & Rescue. With effect from January 1987, two Grumman E-2C *Hawkeye* aircraft on loan from the US Navy now operate from Naval Air Station, Norfolk, Virginia. These will deploy to the Caribbean, the Gulf of Mexico and off the Atlantic Coast to participate in detecting suspect aircraft.

Because of the horrendous lead time, the Coast Guard is already looking ahead at potential candidates for its fleet of the twenty-first century. One vehicle generating interest is the Bell-Boeing JVX *Tiltrotor* which is currently under development for the US Department of Defense. Combining the range and speed of a fixed-wing aircraft with the hovering capability of a helicopter, such a concept presents the attractive possibility of replacing several types in the Coast Guard inventory with a single all-purpose vehicle.

The Bell-Boeing V-22 *Osprey* is involved in a joint service programme involving the US Navy, Marine Corps Army and Air Force with some 1,213 aircraft needed. First flight was due in August 1988. The US Marine Corps requirement is for 552 to replace aging CH-46 helicopters; the US Navy would require some 320 to replace Lockheed S-3 *Viking* ASW aircraft. The US Air Force plans to purchase eighty *Ospreys*. It is envisaged the Coast Guard will follow the evaluation of this unique craft with great interest.

Admiral Thompson, when Chief of Staff with the US Coast Guard, wrote:

> 'Poopy-bag pilots' [lighter-than-air] can take heart, we haven't written off that technology. In fact we are testing concepts using state-of-the-art airships to explore solutions for our extended surveillance requirements. Next time you see a blimp overhead, check it, it might have the familiar Coast Guard red and blue 'racing stripes!'

The US Navy and Coast Guard have been conducting flights from a leased airship from Andrews Naval Air Facility, Maryland, which were followed by extensive performance trials and maritime mission demonstrations at the Patuxent River, Maryland, Naval Air Station and the USCG air station at Elizabeth City, North Carolina. The tests were conducted with a state-of-the-art blimp, known as the SKS-500 under lease from Airship Industries Limited from the United Kingdom.

These performance trials were a follow-on to numerous analytical studies of lighter-than-air vehicles conducted by the Naval Air Development Center, Warminster, Pennsylvania. The center managed the lease contract for the US Naval Air Systems Command and the US Coast Guard Office of Research & Development. The test vehicle involved was built in the United Kingdom and assembled in Toronto, Canada, before flying to Maryland for evaluation.

The SKS-500 is 164 feet in length, and was used as a proof-of-concept vehicle in assessing real potential for maritime roles requiring much larger airships. It incorporated modern technology with features such as tilting, ducted fans for vertical take-offs and landings, and extensive use of composite, non-metallic materials. For the trials the airship was equipped with a MEI Marec 2 surveillance radar, a Marconi thermal imager infra-red device, a search and rescue winch and an inflatable four-man boat with outboard motor capable of deployment and recovery.

The Coast Guard evaluated the airship's potential for surveillance in missions such as anti-smuggling and fisheries patrols, and water pollution detection, as well as its use in Search & Rescue.

In 1987 a 106 million pound contract was awarded to Airship Industries from the US Navy with the US company Westinghouse involved.

Fluorescent paints were becoming available and offered promise. It seemed wise to limit use of fluorescents to small areas of the aircraft and to attempt to avoid a dazzle effect. Several schemes were considered, and finally Norman Rubin evolved an arrowhead design over the nose of the aircraft in an attempt to give indication of direction of motion. It was necessary, of course, to keep the markings within the framework of national and international usages for state-owned law enforcement and Search & Rescue aircraft. The geometry of the Grumman UF-1 *Albatross* aircraft (later HU-16E), a Coast Guard mainstay of the period, made the application of an arrowhead awkward, and it became a slash, leaning forward at the top. Sometime later, a small stripe was added for cosmetic effect.

The second problem was offered by the Coast Guard's Public Information personnel. Their need was to so mark the Coast Guard aircraft that their identity could not be missed in

Sikorsky HOS-1G *Hoverfly* BuNo 15594 seen at Floyd Bennett Field, Brooklyn, New York, during 1946. It is the same type as that which John Greathouse bailed out of over the city of Philadelphia on 25 September 1945. (via William T. Larkins)

press photos. Of course the legend 'US Coast Guard' appeared in letters two feet high on both sides of fuselages and hulls, but the public information people showed Norman Rubin a photo depicting a helicopter rescue operation in which the Coast Guard legend had been painstakingly retouched to identify the helicopter as belonging to another service.

A statistical study of photos of people deplaning after search and rescue missions indicated that the highest probability of a legend appearing in such photos was offered by locating the words either at left or above the cabin exit. The smallest letters legible in typical newspaper halftones would be three inches high. This size and location were adopted. For long-range photos, the fluorescent orange bow bordered by a black slash, coupled with a bold legend and a Coast Guard insignia of good size, made the aircraft uniquely recognizable as Coast Guard. As a final touch, the overall colour of white was adopted, both for uniqueness and to satisfy service demands for solar heat reflection to keep down cabin temperatures in the summer sun.

There were exceptions to the rule and additional means of identification. Helicopters which were seconded to US Coast Guard cutters in the Arctic and Antarctic regions were given a deep red overall finish for ease of identification in snow and ice regions. The USCG air station ident or name now appears on all aircraft and while the HU-16E *Albatross* was in service the air station ident was painted on the inner side of the wing floats so that photos taken from the fuselage hatch included automatically the wing float and name.

When the current US Coast Guard 'slash' livery was adopted, it naturally took time to have the fleet repainted. This historic photo taken at San Francisco air station on 18 May 1968 depicts two HH-52A helios, 1388 in the old marks and 1477 in the new. An interesting comparison for the modeller. (William T. Larkins)

Coast Guard Aviator No 1

He was decorated by a President and received a medal from royalty. He was a Coast Guard and Naval Aviator pioneer who established a world speed record for amphibious aircraft and made history as one of the pilots of the first aircraft to fly across the Atlantic. He was a quiet hero.

His name was Commander Elmer Fowler Stone, the first US Coast Guard aviator, who was enshrined in the US Naval Aviation Museum's Hall of Honor, Pensacola, Florida, on 12 May 1983.

Elmer F Stone, 1887–1936. He was the very first US Coast Guard aviator and a pioneer in the use of aircraft for both rescue and patrol work. He is buried in Arlington National Cemetery. (USCG)

As a man of vision and great courage, Elmer Stone is best known for his role as one of the pilots who flew the first transatlantic flight aboard the US Navy's NC-4 Curtiss seaplane. The NC-4, in May 1919, was one of three US Navy flying boats that took off for Plymouth, England, via the Azores from a starting point at Rockaway Beach, New York. Stone was the only non-US Navy member of the three NC crews.

Eight years before Charles Lindbergh flew his epic solo flight aboard the *Spirit of St Louis,* the NC-4 proved the feasibility of trans-ocean flight, contrary to the beliefs of many sceptics at the time. The fifty-two-hour trip, flown mostly through mist and drizzle, also demonstrated the potential of the US Navy's 2,800 lb flying boats which later became the mainstay of the US Coast Guard for Search & Rescue missions.

'CDR Stone always spoke of the flight as being rough and bumpy,' said Alvin Fisher, Stone's friend and aircraft captain while Stone was commanding officer of the USCG air station at Cape May from 1932 to 1934. Fisher said Stone knew everything about the NC-4 and contributed significantly to the success of its missions.

Clarence F Edge, a retired USCG commander agreed with Fisher. 'He was one of the key men of the flight,' said Edge, a twenty-two-year Coast Guard veteran and a close friend who served with Stone during three tours of duty. The history making crossing was not without problems, however. Edge explained that Stone, US Navy Chief Machinist's Mate Eugene 'Smokey' Rhoads and US Navy Lieutenant James Breese were responsible for repairing two of the NC-4's Liberty engines, which had forced the aircraft down near Chatham, Massachusetts. At the time, the NC-4 was enroute to Trepassey Bay, Newfoundland, the flight's final stopover point before making the big jump across the Atlantic.

The NC-1 and NC-3 were forced down by weather conditions and landed in stormy seas before reaching their destination, the Azores. The NC-1 sank while under tow by a ship that came to its aid. The NC-3 crewmen landed safely and drifted to the Azores, 205 miles away, and later taxied into the harbor under their own power. The NC-4 made it all the way to Ponta Delgada in the Azores and then went on to Lisbon, Portugal and finally Plymouth, England.

Prior to and for many years after the NC-4 flight, Elmer Stone energetically supported the use of aircraft in the Coast Guard, especially for rescue and patrol work. Stone believed 'flying machines' could locate vessels in distress, as well as derelicts which might be a hazard to shipping, faster than the dwindling number of Coast Guard cutters. But new ideas are slow to be accepted and Coast Guard Aviation was not officially established until 1926.

Clarence Edge said that Stone, whom he called Archie, was one of three founders of Coast Guard Aviation, the others being Captain Norman B Hall and Captain Carl C von Paulsen. 'We called them the triumvirate', he said, 'all of them contributed greatly to the effort, but Stone was the driving force.'

Elmer Stone was born 22 January 1887 in Livonia, New York. He joined the Revenue Cutter Service, later the US Coast Guard, in 1910 and graduated from the Coast Guard Academy three years later.

Stone's first shipboard duty assignment was aboard the cutter *Onondaga.* Later, during a tour aboard the cutter *Itasca,* Stone supervised the rescue of seven seamen from the lumber laden schooner *CC Wehrum,* which was shipwrecked in gale force winds off False Cape, Virginia. He was commended by then Assistant Secretary of the US Navy Franklin D Roosevelt for his skill and judgment during the incident.

In April 1916 Stone reported to Naval Air Station Pensacola, Florida, for aviation training. He earned his Wings of Gold in April of the following year and became Seaplane Aviator No 38 on the US Navy's roster. Then, in 1920, he was designated Coast Guard Aviator No 1.

After flight training and a short tour aboard US Navy cruiser *Huntington* during World War I, Stone was ordered to Naval Air Station Rockaway, New York, a move that was to etch his name in history. It was here that he began his transatlantic flight aboard the NC-4, in company with Lieutenant Commander Albert C Read, aircraft commander, Lieutenant (jg) Walter Hinton, pilot, Lieutenant James L Breese, engineer, Ensign H C Rodd, radio operator, and Chief Machinist's Mate E C 'Smokey' Rhoads, mechanic.

Stone was assigned test pilot duty with the US Navy Department's Bureau of Aeronautics in 1920 for six years and flew everything from aircraft to dirigibles and balloons. Said Alvin Fisher with a laugh, 'CDR Stone always said he served more years in the Navy than he served in the Coast Guard.'

'The Navy hung onto Stone because he was a brilliant aviator and engineer,' Clarence Edge said. 'They knew he knew what he was talking about whenever he said that something was right or wrong with an airplane.'

At one point, according to Edge, the US Navy offered Stone the chance to transfer from the Coast Guard and accept a Navy commission. It never happened, largely because of his dedication to the concept of Coast Guard Aviation and his desire to see it become a respected branch of his service.

During his duty as a test pilot with the US Navy, Stone did considerable work developing aircraft arresting gear and catapults for the aircraft carriers *Lexington* and *Saratoga.* On 27 February 1926 Stone piloted a powder-catapulted amphibious aircraft from a barge anchored in the Potomac River. The powder catapult, which Stone helped develop, received its power from the discharge of a three-inch blank shell. His flight marked the first time an aircraft was catapulted using powder, rather than air pressure. Years later, the US Navy Department commended Stone for his 'valuable' services and involvment in carrier development.

On 20 December 1934 Stone established a world speed record for amphibious aircraft when he piloted a USCG Grumman amphibian at a speed of 191.734 miles per hour over a three-kilometre test course at Buckroe Beach, Virginia. Alvin Fisher was his plane captain.

Prior to this, Stone served as a senior member of the trial board for new Coast Guard aircraft that were being built at the General Aviation Manufacturing Corporation in Baltimore, Maryland.

There was more to Elmer Stone than his technical expertise. His ability as a leader is attested to by the way his subordinates remember him. 'He was the best skipper I ever know,' said Alvin Fisher, a first class petty officer at the time, who later earned a Coast Guard commission. 'I was in the Coast Guard thirty-two years and I never met a commanding officer who cared so much for his men. He treated us like a father.'

Fisher had many memories of him and recalls vividly how Stone grilled Coast Guard student pilots assigned for flight training at Pensacola, Florida. He wanted to make sure they measured up to his standards and would make a good impression for Coast Guard Aviation. At the time, Stone was commanding officer of the USCG air station at Cape May, New Jersey.

'All the Coast Guard officers who were headed for Pensacola had to go to Cape May first,' Fisher said. 'When they got there, Stone would give them ten hours of preliminary flight training and then evaluate them. He was hard with them, but sincere, and he had their complete respect. He, in turn, respected the men under him and his fellow officers.'

Elmer Stone received numerous awards during his career, including a special Congressional Medal presented to him by President Herbert Hoover for his participation in the NC-4 flight. Although Stone received other decorations, including the World War I Victory Medal with Aviation Clasp and the US Navy Cross, he was a modest individual who did not feel comfortable with public recognition of his achievements.

Stone had become acquainted with the Prince of Wales following his NC-4 flight, and Edge remembers that the Prince, while on a visit to the US, was to give Stone a British medal for his participation in the historic event. Stone reportedly sent a letter to the Prince thanking him for the honor but asking him to mail the medal parcel post. According to Edge, the letter wound up in the British ambassador's hands, who passed it on to the Prince of Wales. Weeks later, Stone received a package stamped with the Royal Seal. Appreciating Stone's feelings, the Prince of Wales had forwarded the medal and an accompanying letter which read, 'Dear Archie, I hope you like it. — Wales.'

On 20 May 1936, while observing a new type of flying boat patrol plane that was undergoing US Navy trials at Naval Air Station San Diego, California, Stone, aged forty-nine, suffered a fatal heart attack. Clarence Edge was with him at the time.

Commander Elmer F Stone is buried at Arlington National Cemetery. But, his legacy of personal achievements and his dedication to the highest professional standards live on for fellow Coast Guard and Naval Aviators who follow him.

The awards given to Commander Elmer Stone included the following:

> Portuguese Knight of the Order of the Tower and Sword.
> US Navy Cross.
> British Air Force Cross.
> Victory Medal with Aviation Clasp.
> Congressional Medal (for NC-4 flight).
> Certificate of Record for establishing an international amphibian speed record.

On 26 January 1983 the USCG Group and air station new multipurpose building, housing Facilities Maintenance and Coast Guard Reserve at San Diego, was dedicated to the memory of Commander Elmer F Stone. Stone was commander of the unit's predecessor, the Coast Guard Air Patrol Detachment in San Diego, from May 1935 until his death one year later.

The Ancient Albatross

When he was a seaman, Master Chief Petty Officer John P Greathouse learned to fly and became a Naval Aviation Pilot First Class. After thirty-seven years of active duty, he retired in January 1979 as the US Coast Guard's last Naval Aviation Pilot (NAP). During his years as a World War II era enlisted Naval Aviator he logged more than 15,000 hours in the air and was one of the first Coast Guard Aviators to reach the 10,000 flight hour mark. A native of Wills Point, Texas, Greathouse entered the Coast Guard in October 1941 and reported to his first assignment at Fort Point Lifeboat Station, California. He entered flight training as a seaman and became one of approximately 200 enlisted men designated NAPs in the Coast Guard.

The US Coast Guard has always kept a close link with the US Navy in many ways, including flying training, exchange of aircraft and equipment, plus procurement of types from US Navy appropriation funds. Seen here is a Naval Aircraft Factory N3N-3 V196; four of these trainers were acquired by the US Coast Guard in exchange for four Grumman JF-2s with the US Navy during World War II. The addition of the N3N-3s accelerated the pilot training programme in the Coast Guard. (Gordon S. Williams)

He received his wings on 6 August 1943 and was designated Aviation Pilot No 134. During his thirty-four years as a pilot, John flew almost every aircraft that existed in the Coast Guard history. He logged more than 15,000 hours in the air, over 10,000 of those logged in the Grumman HU-16E *Albatross*.

Although he was the last enlisted pilot, Chief Greathouse was once a commissioned officer, in fact, twice. He was commissioned as an Ensign on 1 October 1944 and redesignated Coast Guard Aviator No 334 on 26 October. During World War II, he flew anti-submarine patrols and Search & Rescue missions from San Francisco air station. In 1946 he was transferred to Mayport, Florida and reverted back to Chief Aviation Pilot. Again in 1947 he was commissioned having completed officer training at the Coast Guard Academy in New London, Connecticut, but in September was reverted back to Chief for budgetary reasons.

Fortunately there are one or two retired US Coast Guard aircraft preserved in flying condition, including this Fairchild J2K-1 V160, registered N81234 and owned by Carl Sirckley. The USCG acquired two J2K-1 Model 24R three-seat high-wing cabin monoplanes in 1936, numbered V160/161. (Peter M. Bowers)

On 25 September 1945 John accomplished a feat that even Evel Knievel has not tried, becoming the first pilot to successfully bail out of a helicopter in flight. Chief Greathouse was on temporary duty (TDY) to Floyd Bennett Field air station when, on 24 September 1945 the Operations Officer assigned him the task of flying a HOS-1G *Hoverfly* single-rotor Sikorsky helicopter. His mission was to fly over a US Navy battleship in Philadelphia Harbor at 5,000 feet so they could calibrate the radar on their anti-aircraft guns. Since the flight was to be at high altitude for a helicopter, John had his mechanic AD3 John Smith put parachutes on board although they were not required by USCG regulations.

They flew to Philadelphia that night and began the calibration flight the next morning. After take-off, Greathouse noticed that convection currents were developing and the *Hoverfly* was bouncing about badly. Once on the scene, he notified the ship, 'Dove chaser, this is number two. I'm in position at this time.' 'Roger number two, we have you on the scope. Try to stay there while we tweak up this sector.' 'Roger,' replied John, 'but I've got a pretty stiff wind out of the south and it's hard to keep this thing hovering in one place at this altitude.'

Cumulus clouds were starting to form and the turbulence wasn't getting any better. The only redeeming feature of the flight was the beauty of the autumn scenery in the surrounding area. 'Number two this is Dove chaser. Move to a position two miles north of the ship.' 'This is number two, Roger.' John directed the helicopter to a position just north of the ship's bow. This placed him over the edge of town. While he was looking out of the side window, the HOS-1G was tossed quickly up and then down. A loud snap sent a quick dose of adrenalin shooting through both men's hearts. The helicopter nosed over quickly. John gave a yank on the cyclic, but nothing happened. John looked over at AD3 Smith and yelled, 'Bailout.'

It was a simple matter to lift the emergency escape latch on the large side window and roll out. John was thrown aft by the rotor wash and Smith was thrown forward. Seconds later John pulled the ripcord and the sudden jerk assured him that the chute was opened. He looked around trying to get orientated and see where he was going. He saw Smith's chute and was relieved to know that he had made it out OK. John looked up and saw the complete rotor assembly whirling its way past him. The rotor seemed so stable that John felt if he could grab it he could safely ride it to the ground. He watched the rotor for a few more seconds then began to think about where he was going to land.

The southerly wind was drifting the two men back over the city where there were a lot of buildings and wires. John tugged at the risers and was able to start maneuvering toward an open street. The closer he got to the ground the faster it seemed to rush up at him. A million thoughts were running through his mind and he didn't have time to grasp many of them. He landed right in the middle of the intersection at Broad and Bigler Street, where the parachute blew against a tree and collapsed.

John collected his thoughts as he lay on the ground. He could move all his limbs and only had a few scratches on his knuckles. He quickly removed the parachute and stood up. A station wagon pulled up beside him and a gentleman opened the door and said, 'Hop in and I'll take you over to the other guy. He landed a few blocks away.' John placed the chute in the back of the car and they drove off to pick up Smith. The incident astonished many downtown Philadelphia shoppers. John never flew another helicopter.

The Ancient Albatross Award, presented to the Coast Guard aviator on active duty holding the earliest designation in recognition of a clear defiance of the private realm of the Albatross and all its seabird kin while in the pursuit of time-honored Coast Guard duties.

John Pershing Greathouse is truly a legend in Coast Guard Aviation and it is altogether fitting that, when Rear Admiral Chester Richmond retired on 30 June 1977 John Greathouse succeeded him as the Ancient Albatross. He is not, however, very forthcoming about the decorations which adorn the left breast of his uniform. Via news releases one can learn that Greathouse located a lost ship out of Port Angeles, Washington, in 1962 and effected rescue operations. For this heroic action he was awarded the Coast Guard Commendation Medal. John has a collection of eight Air Medals. As for the rest of the 'fruit salad' that supports his 'Wings of Gold' the Chief will only say, 'They came with the uniform.'

Coast Guard aviation history

Visitors to the US Naval Aviation Museum located at Pensacola, Florida, can now trace the history of Coast Guard Aviation starting with the USCG support at Kitty Hawk in 1903 and leading up to present day missions and aircraft. The Naval Aviation Museum provides a proper setting for displaying artifacts associated with this element of aviation history. A Coast Guard advisory group has been working hard to identify historical material and memorabilia, equipment and aircraft that are suitable for the Coast Guard exhibit.

Acquisitions include a Sikorsky HO3S-1G helicopter, and the Grumman JRF-2 *Goose* V175 credited with sinking a German U-boat in the Gulf of Mexico during World War II has been located, plus Grumman J4F-1 *Widgeon* V212. A Grumman HU-16E 7236 is on display at the museum. A brief preview of the Coast Guard exhibits finds the story unfolding into a chronological sequence of historical periods commencing with the assistance given at Kitty Hawk. The final panels on display at the museum update the missions and aircraft of the 1970s and 1980s. They include a roster of distinguished Coast Guard Aviation personnel and an art exhibit depicting current aviation activities.

The first major milestone was the opening of the Coast Guard Aviation exhibit on 11 May 1983 and Commander Elmer F Stone's induction into the Naval Aviation Hall of Honor.

However, the task is not finished. Many exciting additions are in store for this fascinating and important part of the saga of Coast Guard Aviation in the Naval Aviation Museum. The exhibits express the goals and missions of the Coast Guard and how aviation supports them. To visit the museum is to savor eight decades of Coast Guard history as seen from the vantage point of a special breed of Naval Aviator.

When the aircraft carrier USS *Intrepid* commenced her second career as a historical exhibit in New York City, Coast Guard Aviation jumped at the opportunity to place a Grumman HU-16E *Albatross* aboard. The problem was that the amphibian 7216, much loved by so many USCG aviators, had been sitting outside for ten years and needed a major rework, inside and out.

The Coast Guard Auxiliary from the 3rd Northern District, with full backing of the Third District Coast Guard regulars, went to work, starting in April 1983. After more than a year and a half of hard work, the airplane was completed and hoisted aboard. The restoration project was headed by Lieutenant Ed Ward of the Coast Guard Auxiliary, who holds both the FAA Airline Transport and the Airframe and Powerplant Mechanics ratings. Volunteers came from the Coast Guard air station in Brooklyn and the Coast Guard Auxiliary in the Third District. The HU-16E, says the Coast Guardsmen, is now an intrepid bird in her *Intrepid* home.

The last operational Grumman HU-16E *Albatross* 7250 made its final flight on 10 March 1983 at USCG air station Cape Cod, Massachusetts. The crew consisted of Commander Eric J Stout, pilot, Lieutenant David E Elliott co-pilot, ADCM John E Bloom, CWO Dean A Long and CWO Stephen P Marvin, crewmen. Commander Stout had logged over 2,800 hours in the HU-16E. At the farewell ceremony, Rear Admiral Louis L Zumstein, Commander First Coast Guard District, said, 'I've flown forty-six HU-16s in my career and they have brought me home when the odds were stacked against me several times.' For more than one-half million flight hours, it performed a variety of Coast Guard missions. The *Albatross* was used extensively during the Cuban boat exodus in the 1960s and again in the 1980s. Thousands of Cuban refugees owe their lives to the men who flew the 'Goats', patrolling the waters between Cuba and Florida.

It is safe to say that many of those present at the retirement ceremony experienced lumps in their throats as 7250 heaved itself into the air, made a short farewell flight and then came down to rest for the last time. On display at air station Cape Cod, it will be a monument to Coast Guard Aviation and to those who flew the *Albatross*.

Located at 1519 Alaskan Way South, Seattle, WA 98134 at Pier 36 on Seattle's waterfront is the Coast Guard Museum Northwest, one of several activities located at the USCG Support Center, home of the US' two largest Polar icebreakers, *Polar Star* and *Polar Sea*, and of two high endurance cutters, *Munro* and *Boutwell*. The museum was established to collect, preserve and exhibit objects which illustrate the scope of the history of the US Coast Guard in the Pacific Northwest and Alaska, and informs the general public of USCG activities in the area. The museum is a non-profit corporation registered in the State of Washington and depends on the services of volunteers and membership fees for its operation. The current curator is Captain Gene Davis USCG (Rtd) who is assisted by a small team of able bodied volunteers.

US Coast Guard Pterodactyls

The Ancient Order of the Pterodactyls has nothing to do with paleontology. It is a non-profit, fraternal and semi-professional organization established to promote interest in and support of Coast Guard Aviation. It also encourages fellowship and *esprit de corps* among its members, who are mainly active duty and retired Coast Guard Aviators.

But why pterodactyls? It was decided at the founding of the Order in the spring of 1977 that, because of the nature of the Coast Guard Aviation experience, the uniqueness of the pterodactyl made it an appropriate symbol of the organization. It is perhaps not as recognized for its accomplishments as it could be, but it is highly respected by all who may be fortunate enough to see it in action and benefit from its services.

The Order itself, despite its short history, was deemed 'ancient' because of the Coast Guard's participation in the birth of aviation, when personnel from the nearby lifeboat station helped the Wright brothers make their memorable first flight a success. Roots that reach down into the very beginning of powered flight impart to the fraternal order the mystique of antiquity, without reflecting in any way on the age of members or aircraft.

The Grumman JRF- *Goose* was a real workhorse with the US Coast Guard between 1939 and 1948, being utilized for every kind of duty. They carried depth charges, bombs, passengers and mail, ditched pilots and stranded mariners and even USO troupes. Seen here is JRF-2 V175, the *Goose* flown by Lieutenant Commander R L Burke USCG who damaged a German U-boat off Virginia Beach in the Atlantic on 27 January 1942 while flying to answer a distress call from the tanker *Frances E Powell*. (Gordon S Williams)

Rare photograph of a Beech JRB-4 BuNo 44605 of the US Coast Guard Reserve taken at Opa Locka, Florida, on 5 June 1969. The type was used primarily for administrative flights; seven JRB-4s were in service with the USCG from the war years through to the 1960s. (William T. Larkins)

The Ancient Order of the Pterodactyl was organized by a group of retired Coast Guard Aviators at their first meeting in Long Beach, California. Membership is open to all persons who are serving or who have served honorably as pilots in Coast Guard aircraft, including those of other military services and foreign governments involved in exchange programmes with the Coast Guard. Associate memberships are tendered to individuals who have served in other capacities in Coast Guard aircraft, such as aircrewmen, flight surgeons, or personnel otherwise under official flight orders. Regular membership includes pilots in the US Navy, and in the US, Canadian and British air forces. To keep members and interested parties informed, the Pterodactyls publish a newsletter called *Sitrep*. Regional chapters are established wherever there is sufficient interest, whilst an annual gathering across the US is a highlight of the programme for members. The Ancient Order of the Pterodactyl fully supports the fund-raising drive to support the establishment of the USCG Aviation exhibit in the Naval Aviation Museum at Pensacola, Florida. Headquarters are located at PO Box 3133, Seal Beach, California 90740.

St Patrick's Day — 17 March 1987

We were escorted into the Rose Garden after reporting to the White House. We were briefed by the White House aide, CDR Vivien Crea. Shortly after that the Russian crew showed up. It was time to form up. Things happened rather quickly after that. Secretary of Transportation Elizabeth H Dole arrived, escorted by VADM James C Irwin, our Vice-Commandant. Then there was a hush and I picked up this movement out of the corner of my right eye. A bright green tie and that smile came into view. The next thing I knew I was shaking hands with the President, the Commander-in-Chief.

He addressed the gathering, as did Soviet Charge d'Affaires Sokolov. LT Cromer presented *Kirgir II*'s master with a model of the HH-3F. The President then passed out medals. The last man to receive one was ASM3 Joe Rock. Joe then presented the President with an air station Cape Cod ball cap. The President put it on and saluted us. A very happy St Patrick's Day.

Later we had a chance to meet Admiral Yost, our Commandant. He reflected how the co-ordination between two air stations, three districts, three HH-3Fs, two C-130s and the safe rescue of thirty-seven people 200 miles offshore was remarkable, and he was proud of us. We then left and flew back to Cape Cod on a C-130. What a day!

LCDR Gary G Poll USCG.

In recent years there have been many changes in Coast Guard Aviation. But the sea is still the sea, and until that changes, Coast Guardsmen will continue to risk their lives going out to save others. A veteran of US Coast Guard Aviation once reminded me that 'the rules say we have to go — but there is no rule that says we have to come back'. He was repeating a time-honored Coast Guard adage.

Coast Guard aircraft and helicopters are now preserved in museums and parks throughout the USA. Seen here is Grumman HU-16E 2129, very well preserved in the USS *Alabama* Memorial Park in Alabama. Later this year a Sikorsky HH-52A *Seaguard* helicopter will be added to the Museum of Flight in Seattle. (AP Publications)

APPENDIX ONE

UNITED STATES COAST GUARD AIRCRAFT 1915-1990

Manufacturer Designation/Name		Service Years	No.	Procurement Agency	Contract	Price $	Remarks
Curtiss F Boat		1915-1918	1	US Navy			Borrowed from Curtiss
Curtiss H-10		1916	1	US Navy			Borrowed from US Navy
Curtiss R6		1917-1918	?	US Navy			Flown by USCG in WW 1
Curtiss HS-2L		1920-1926	4	US Navy			Borrowed from US Navy
Curtiss MF Boat		1920-1926	?	US Navy			Borrowed from US Navy
Chance-Vought UO-1		1925-1926	1	US Navy			Borrowed from US Navy
Chance-Vought UO-4		1926-1934	2	USCG	Tcg.		
Loening OL-5		1926-1935	3	USCG	Tcg.		
Sikorsky S-39		1930-1935	2	USCG			ex US Customs Service
Viking Boat Company 00-1		1931-1941	6	USCG	Tcg.	6,500	
Douglas RD	Sinbad	1931-1939	1	USCG	Tcg. 12608	31,500	
Douglas O-38C		1931-1934	1	USCG	AC-4553	17,900	Army Air Corps contract
Douglas RD-2	Dolphin	1932-1937	1	USCG	AC-4921	43,350	Army Air Corps contract
Douglas RD-1	Dolphin	1932-1939	1	USCG	AC-4460	36,500	Army Air Corps contract
Consolidated N4Y-1		1932-1941	1	USCG	AC-4625	8,000	Army Air Corps contract
Fokker PJ-1	Flying Lifeboat	1932-1941	5	USCG	Tcg. 12154	73,343	
Fokker PJ-2	Flying Lifeboat	1932-1941	1	USCG	Tcg.		
New Standard NT-2		1934-1935	2	USCG		12,000	ex US Customs Service
Vought O2U-2	Corsair	1934-1940	6	US Navy			Procured for USCG
Grumman JF-2	Duck	1934-1941	14	USCG	Tcg. 33862	45,000	
Stinson R3Q-1	Reliant	1934-1941	1	USCG	Tcg. 23248	11,370	
Douglas RD-4	Dolphin	1934-1943	10	USCG	Tcg. 34223	60,000	
Northrop RT-1	Delta	1935-1940	1	USCG	Tcg. 23391	45,000	
Lockheed R30-1	Electra	1936-1942	1	USCG	Tcg. 44920	65,000	
Waco J2W-1		1937-1939	3	USCG	Tcg. 26677	12,054	
Fairchild J2K-1		1937-1941	2	USCG	Tcg. 26669	6,466	
Fairchild J2K-2		1937-1941	2	USCG	Tcg. 26669	7,123	
Curtiss SOC-4	Seagull	1938-1941	3	USCG	Tcg. 27787	48,603	Second source says $18,603
Hall PH-2		1938-1944	7	USCG	Tcg. 26491	116,104	Also Tcg. 26810
Grumman JRF-2/3	Goose	1939-1948	10	USCG	Tcg. 29648	79,526	
Hall PH-3		1940-1944	7	USCG	Tcg. 29347	170,000	
Lockheed R50-1	Lodestar	1940-1941	1	USCG	Tcg.	185,000	
Consolidated PBY-5	Catalina	1941-1943	1	USCG	Tcg.		
Naval Aircraft Factory N3N-3		1941-1945	4	US Navy		20,868	
Grumman J4F-1	Widgeon	1941-1948	12	USCG	Tcg. 33459	75,526	
Vought OS2U-3	Kingfisher	1942-1944	53	US Navy			Some were OS2N-1
Vultee SNV-1 (BT-13A)	Valiant	1942-1945	2	USCG	Tcg.	75,413	
Grumman J2F-5/6	Duck	1942-1948	10	US Navy			
Lockheed R50-4/5	Lodestar	1942-1953	4	US Navy			
Consolidated PBY-5A/6A	Catalina	1942-1954	120+	US Navy			
Martin PBM-3	Mariner	1943-1956	27	US Navy			
Martin PBM-5	Mariner	1943-1956	36+	US Navy			
Curtiss SO3C-1/3	Seamew	1943-1944	48	US Navy			
Stearman N3S-3	Kaydet	1943-1947	11	US Navy			
Sikorsky HNS-1	Hoverfly	1943-1948	21	USCG	Tcg.	43,940	
North American SNJ-5/6	Texan	1943-1948	15	US Navy			
Curtiss R5C-1	Commando	1943-1950	10	US Navy			
Grumman JRF-5/6	Goose	1943-1954	6	USCG	Tcg.	70,950	Second source says $79,526
Grumman JRF-5/6	Goose	1943-1954	30+	US Navy			
Beech JRB-4/5	Expeditor	1943-1958	7	US Navy			
Douglas R4D-5	Skytrain	1943-1958	8	US Navy			
Howard GH-2	Nightingale	1944-1945	3	USCG			
Consolidated PB2Y-3/5	Coronado	1944-1946	4	US Navy			
North American B-25J	Mitchell	1945	1	USAAF			On loan
Consolidated P4Y-1	Liberator	1944-1951	5	US Navy			
Curtiss SB2C-4	Helldiver	1945-1947	2	US Navy			
Sikorsky HOS-1G		1945-1949	27	USCG	Tcg.		Built by Nash Kelvinator
Boeing PB-1g	Flying Fortress	1945-1957	17	USAAF			
Convair P4Y-2G	Privateer	1945-1959	9	US Navy			
Douglas R5D-3/4 C-54	Skymaster	1945-1962	6	US Navy			Also ex USAAF models
Sikorsky HO2S-1G		1946-1950	2	USCG	Tcg.	86,000	
Sikorsky HO3S-1G		1946-1957	9	USCG	Tcg.	91,977	
Bell HTL-1		1947-1955	2	USCG	Tcg.	49,290	
Piasecki HRP-1	Flying Banana	1948-1952	3	USCG	Tcg.	256,912	
Stinson OY-1/2	Sentinel	1948-1962	5	USAF			
Kaman HK-1	Mixmaster	1950-1954	1	USCG	Tcg.	37,684	
Grumman UF-1G	Albatross	1951-1959	30	USCG	Tcg.	521,000	
Sikorsky HO4S-2G/3G		1951-1966	14	USCG	Tcg.	177,530	
Sikorsky HO5S-1G		1952-1955	8	USCG	Tcg. 15513	82,928	
Bell HTL-5		1952-1960	3	USCG	Tcg. 19087	49,290	
Martin VC-3A (RM-1Z)		1952-1969	2	USCG	Tcg. 38422	647,140	
Grumman HU-16E (UF-2G)	Albatross	1955-1977	77	USAF			
Martin P5M-1G	Marlin	1956-1961	7	USCG	Tcg.		Built for USCG
Martin P5M-2G	Marlin	1956-1961	4	USCG	Tcg.		Traded to DoD for HU-16E's
Lockheed HC-130B-E-H	Hercules	1957-Present	48	USCG	Tcg.		Airframe $2m to $6m
Sikorsky HUS-1G		1959-1962	6	USCG	Tcg.		
Bell HUL-1G (HH-13Q)		1959-1967	2	USCG	Tcg.		
Bell HTL-7 (HH-13N)		1959-1967	2	US Navy			
Fairchild C-123B	Provider	1960-1972	8	USAF			
Grumman VC-4A	Gulfstream I	1963-Present	1	USCG	Tcg.		
Sikorsky HH-52A (HU2S-1G)	Seaguard	1963-Present	97	USCG	Tcg.		Airframe $1/4m to $1/2m
Sikorsky HH-3F	Pelican	1968-Present	40	USCG	Tcg.		Airframe $900,000
Grumman VC-11A	Gulfstream II	1969-Present	1	USCG	Tcg.		
Israeli Commodore Jet 1123	Westwind	1973	1	USCG	Tcg.		6 months evaluation
Cessna Model C-500	Citation	1973	1	USCG	Tcg.		6 months evaluation
Convair HC-131A	Samaritan	1976-1983	17	USAF			
Falcon Jet HU-25A	Guardian	1982-Present	41	USCG	Tcg.		
Aerospatiale HH-65A	Dolphin	1984-Present	96	USCG	Tcg.		
Grumman E-2C	Hawkeye	1987-Present	2	US Navy			On loan for drug interdiction

APPENDIX TWO

LOCKHEED C-130 HERCULES (See Chapter 10)

USCG	c/n	Model	Desig.	USAF	Del Date	Station	Remarks
1339	3529	282-2B	HC-130B	58-5396	31 Dec 59	Elizabeth City	Retired Apr 1986
1340	3533	282-2B	HC-130B	58-5397	31 Dec 59	Barbers Point	Retired Apr 1986
1341	3542	282-2B	HC-130B	58-6973	31 Jan 60	San Francisco	Retired Apr 1986
1342	3548	282-2B	HC-130B	58-6974	24 Mar 60	St Petersburg	Retired Apr 1986
1344	3594	282-2B	HC-130B	60-0311	25 Jan 61	Elizabeth City	Retired Apr 1986
1345	3595	282-2B	HC-130B	60-0312	09 Mar 61	Elizabeth City	Retired Apr 1986
1346	3638	282-2B	HC-130B	61-2081	23 Mar 62	San Francisco	Loadmaster trained at Cherry Point, South Carolina
1347	3641	282-2B	HC-130B	61-2082	01 Mar 62	Argentia	Retired Apr 1986
1348	3650	282-2B	HC-130B	61-2083	19 Apr 62	Argentia	Retired Apr.1986
1349	3745	282-2B	HC-130B	62-3753	14 Dec 62	Elizabeth City	Retired Apr 1986
1350	3763	282-2B	HC-130B	62-3754	31 Jan 63	San Francisco	Retired Apr 1986
1351	3773	282-2B	HC-130B	62-3755	22 Feb 63	San Francisco	Retired Apr 1986. Back to USCG Jan 1987
1414	4158	382-4B	EC-130E	66-4299	23 Aug 66	Elizabeth City	Retired Apr 1986. "Pasquotank Road Runners"
1452	4255	382-12B	HC-130H	67-7183	Mar 68	San Francisco	Retired Apr 1986
1453	4260	382-12B	HC-130H	67-7184	01 May 68	San Francisco	Retired Apr 1986. 1,000th production C-130
1454	4265	382-12B	HC-130H	67-7185	May 68	Kodiak	Retired Apr 1986
1500	4501	382C-27D	HC-130H	72-1300	Aug 73	Kodiak	
1501	4507	382C-27D	HC-130H	72-1301	Sep 73	Kodiak	
1502	4513	382C-27D	HC-130H	72-1302	Oct 73	Kodiak	
1503	4528	382C-27D	HC-130H	72-0844	Mar 74	San Francisco	
1504	4529	382C-27D	HC-130H	72-0845	Apr 74	San Francisco	
1600	4757	382C-70D	HC-130H	77-0317	26 Oct 77	Kodiak	Crashed 30 Jul 82 Attu, Aleutian Islands
1601	4760	382C-70D	HC-130H	77-0318	01 Nov 77	Kodiak	
1602	4762	382C-70D	HC-130H	77-0319	15 Nov 77	Kodiak	
1603	4764	382C-60D	HC-130H	77-0320	07 Dec 77	Kodiak	
1700	4947	382C-37E	HC-130H-7	82-0081	31 May 83	Clearwater	
1701	4958	382C-37E	HC-130H-7	82-0082	01 Apr 84	Clearwater	
1702	4966	382C-37E	HC-130H-7	82-0083	20 Jun 84	Clearwater	
1703	4967	382C-37E	HC-130H-7	82-0084	29 Jun 84	Clearwater	
1704	4969	382C-37E	HC-130H-7	82-0085	20 Jul 84	Clearwater	
1705	4993	382C-37E	HC-130H-7		29 Jun 84	Kodiak	
1706	4996	382C-50E	HC-130H	83-0505	20 Aug 84	Kodiak	
1707	4999	382C-50E	HC-130H	83-0506	18 Sep 84	Kodiak	
1708	5002	382C-50E	HC-130H	83-0507	18 Oct 84	Kodiak	
1709	5005	382C-50E	HC-130H	83-0508	10 Dec 84	Kodiak	
1710	5028	382C-57E	HC-130H		16 Aug 85	Clearwater	Transferred to Borinquen during November 1987
1711	5031	382C-61E	HC-130H		16 Sep 85	Clearwater	Transferred to Borinquen during November 1987
1712	5033	382C-61E	HC-130H		07 Oct 85	Clearwater	
1713	5034	382C-61E	HC-130H		16 Oct 85	Clearwater	Transferred to Borinquen during November 1987
1714	5035	382C-57E	HC-130H		29 Oct 85	Clearwater	
1715	5037	382C-64E	HC-130H		15 Nov 85	Clearwater	
1716	5023	382C-76E	HC-130H		Dec 86	Clearwater	ex GELAC N73235
1717	5104	382C-79E	HC-130H	86-0420	03 Nov 87	Clearwater	
1718	5106	382C-79E	HC-130H	86-0421	25 Nov 87	Elizabeth City	Temporary assignment, will go to Clearwater
1719	5107	382C-79E	HC-130H	86-0422	09 Dec 87	Elizabeth City	Temporary assignment, will go to Clearwater
1790	4931	382C-22E	HC-130H		23 Jul 83	Kodiak	Out of sequence USCG number; year the USCG was formed
1720	5120	382C-84E	HC-130H		Apr 88	Clearwater	
1721	5121	382C-84E	HC-130H		May 88	Clearwater	

APPENDIX THREE

EARLY US COAST GUARD AVIATION SERIALS – THE 'V' SERIES 1936-1945

Serial	Type	c/n	Period	Contract No.	Cost	Remarks
V101	Loening OL-5		1926-1935		$32,710	Crashed
V102	Loening OL-5					Withdrawn April 1935
V103	Loening OL-5					Crashed
V104	Vought UO-4		1926-1934			Direct Purchase
V105	Vought UO-4					
V106	Douglas RD	703	1931-1939		$31,500	Ex-X145Y. Originally amphibian, converted to seaplane
V107	FBA 17HT4 (Schreck)					Commissioned Dec 1931. Destroyed by fire Mar 1934 Imported from France
V108	Douglas O-38C	1120	1931-1934	AC-4553	$17,900	Ex-Army Air Corps 32-394. Commissioned 11 Dec 1931
V109	Douglas RD-1	1000	1932-1939	AC-4460	$36,500	Ex-USN XRD-1 BuNo A-8876
V110	Consolidated N4Y-1		1932-1941	AC-4625		Commissioned Aug 1932
V111	Douglas RD-2	1122	1932-1937	AC-4921	$43,500	Could take off in 594ft with nil wind. Crashed Mar 1937
V112	General Aviation PJ-1		1932-1941	Tcg. 12154	$73,343	FLB-52
V113	General Aviation PJ-1					FLB-53
V114	General Aviation PJ-1					FLB-54
V115	General Aviation PJ-1					FLB-55
V116	General Aviation PJ-2					FLB-51. Modified with tractor engines 1933
V117	Vought O2U-2		1934-1940			Purchased by US Navy. All but V118 disposed of in 1937
V118	Vought O2U-2					V118 disposed of in 1940
V119	Vought O2U-2					
V120	Vought O2U-2					
V121	Vought O2U-2					
V122	Vought O2U-2					
V123	New Standard NT-2		1934-1935			
V124	New Standard NT-2					
V125	Douglas RD-4	1268	1934-1943	USN-34223	$60,000	
V126	Douglas RD-4	1269				Crashed in ocean off San Francisco Sept 1941
V127	Douglas RD-4	1270				
V128	Douglas RD-4	1271				
V129	Douglas RD-4	1272				
V130	Douglas RD-4	1273				
V131	Douglas RD-4	1274				
V132	Douglas RD-4	1275				
V133	Douglas RD-4	1276				
V134	Douglas RD-4	1277				
V135	Grumman JF-2	188	1934-1941	USN-33862	$45,000	To US Navy 1941 as BuNo 0266
V136	Grumman JF-2	189				
V137	Grumman JF-2	190				
V138	Grumman JF-2	191				
V139	Grumman JF-2	192				
V140	Grumman JF-2	193				
V141	Grumman JF-2	194				To US Navy as BuNo 00371
V142	Grumman JF-2	195				
V143	Grumman JF-2	196				
V144	Grumman JF-2	263				To US Navy 25 Sept 1941 as BuNo 01647
V145	Grumman JF-2	264				Crashed St Petersburg, Fla 29 Sept 1940 on night training flight
V146	Grumman JF-2	265				To US Navy 1941
V147	Grumman JF-2	266				
V148	Grumman JF-2	267				
V149	Stinson R3Q-1	74	1934-1941		$41,909	Delivered 20 Feb 1935. Sold for $1,400
V150	Northrop RT-1	74	1935-1940	Tcg 23391	$45,000	Sold surplus as NC28663
V151	Lockheed R3O-1	1053	1936-1942	44920	$65,000	VIP aircraft. Delivered Mar 1936. Model 10B Electra
V152	OO-1 Viking		1931-1941		$6,500	Crashed Mar 1939
V153	OO-1 Viking					
V154	OO-1 Viking					
V155	OO-1 Viking					
V156	OO-1 Viking					
V157	Waco J2W-1	4545	1937-1939	Tcg 26677	$12,054	Crashed Jan 1939
V158	Waco J2W-1	4546				Crashed Apr 1939
V159	Waco J2W-1	4547				Crashed Oct 1939
V160	Fairchild J2K-1		1937-1941	Tcg 26669	$6,466	Crashed Aug 1940
V161	Fairchild J2K-1					
V162	Fairchild J2K-2		1937-1941	Tcg 26669	$7,123	Crashed May 1941
V163	Fairchild J2K-2					Crashed Aug 1939
V164	Hall Aluminium PH-2		1938-1944	Tcg 26491	$116,104	
V165	Hall Aluminium PH-2			Tcg 26810		
V166	Hall Aluminium PH-2					
V167	Hall Aluminium PH-2					
V168	Hall Aluminium PH-2					
V169	Hall Aluminium PH-2					
V170	Hall Aluminium PH-2					
V171	Curtiss SOC-4 Seagull		1938-1941	Tcg 27787	$48,603	To US Navy 1941 as BuNo 48243
V172	Curtiss SOC-4 Seagull					To US Navy 1942 as BuNo 48244
V173	Curtiss SOC-4 Seagull					To US Navy 1942 as BuNo 48245
V174	Grumman JRF-2 Goose	1063	1939-1948	Tcg 29648	$79,526	Sold as surplus Feb 1947
V175	Grumman JRF-2 Goose	1064				To US Navy as BuNo 0266. Traded for Lockheed XR3O-1
V176	Grumman JRF-2 Goose	1065				
V177	Hall Aluminium PH-3		1940-1944	Tcg 29347	$170,000	

Serial	Type	c/n	Period	Contract No.	Cost	Remarks
V178	Hall Aluminium PH-3					
V179	Hall Aluminium PH-3					
V180	Hall Aluminium PH-3					
V181	Hall Aluminium PH-3					
V182	Hall Aluminium PH-3					
V183	Hall Aluminium PH-3					
V184	Grumman JRF-2 Goose	1076	1939-1948	Tcg 29648	$79,526	
V185	Grumman JRF-2 Goose	1077				
V186	Grumman JRF-2 Goose	1078				
V187	Grumman JRF-2 Goose	1079				
V188	Lockheed R5O-1	2008	1940-1946		$185,000	L-18-40 Model 18 Lodestar. Sold as ZS-BAJ, Transocean Airlines N54549
V189	Consolidated PBY-5		1941-1943			Ex-US Navy BuNo 2290
V190	Grumman JRF-3 Goose	1085	1939-1948	Tcg 29648	$79,526	
V191	Grumman JRF-3 Goose	1086				
V192	Grumman JRF-3 Goose	1087				
V193	Naval Aircraft Factory N3N-3		1941-1945			
V194	Naval Aircraft Factory N3N-3					
V195	Naval Aircraft Factory N3N-3					
V196	Naval Aircraft Factory N3N-3					
V197	Grumman J4F-1 Widgeon	1222	1941-1948	Tcg 33459	$75,526	Crashed
V198	Grumman J4F-1 Widgeon	1223				
V199	Grumman J4F-1 Widgeon	1224				Crashed
V200	Grumman J4F-1 Widgeon	1225				
V201	Grumman J4F-1 Widgeon	1226				
V202	Grumman J4F-1 Widgeon	1227				
V203	Grumman J4F-1 Widgeon	1228				
V204	Grumman J4F-1 Widgeon	1229				
V205	Grumman J4F-1 Widgeon	1253				
V206	Grumman J4F-1 Widgeon	1254				
V207	Grumman J4F-1 Widgeon	1255				
V208	Grumman J4F-1 Widgeon	1256				
V209	Grumman J4F-1 Widgeon	1257				
V210	Grumman J4F-1 Widgeon	1258				
V211	Grumman J4F-1 Widgeon	1259				
V212	Grumman J4F-1 Widgeon	1260				To Dept of Interior
V213	Grumman J4F-1 Widgeon	1261				
V214	Grumman J4F-1 Widgeon	1262				
V215	Grumman J4F-1 Widgeon	1263				
V216	Grumman J4F-1 Widgeon	1264				
V217	Grumman J4F-1 Widgeon	1265				
V218	Grumman J4F-1 Widgeon	1266				To Dept of Interior
V219	Grumman J4F-1 Widgeon	1267				Sold as surplus Feb 1947 at Concord, California
V220	Grumman J4F-1 Widgeon	1268				Sold as surplus Feb 1947 at Concord, California
V221	Grumman J4F-2 Widgeon	1269				To US Navy as BuNo 34585
V222	Vultee SNV-1 Valiant		1942-1945		$75,413	
V223	Vultee SNV-1 Valiant					
V224	Grumman JRF-5G Goose		1943-1954		$70,950	Ex-US Navy BuNo 34079
V225	Grumman JRF-5G Goose					Ex-US Navy BuNo 34082
V226	Grumman JRF-5G Goose					Ex-US Navy BuNo 34087
V227	Grumman JRF-5G Goose					Ex-US Navy BuNo 34090
V228	Grumman JRF-5G Goose					Ex-US Navy BuNo 37772
V229	Grumman JRF-5G Goose					Ex-US Navy BuNo 37773

THE EARLY US COAST GUARD SERIAL SYSTEM
INDIVIDUAL AIRCRAFT NAMES

The US Coast Guard in the thirties was able to make use of one of those fascinating peacetime luxuries that are normally limited to small organisations — the naming of individual aircraft. This practice was so common that many official Coast Guard communications, and nearly all press releases and newspaper stories, referred only to the name of the aircraft. These names appeared on each side of the nose and serve as an accurate means of identification of the individual aircraft. In photographs where the serial number is not visible, it is often the only means of positive identification.

Name	Type	3-Digit Serial
Acamar	General Aviation PJ-1	254
Acrux	General Aviation PJ-1	253
Adhara	Douglas RD-2	129
Aldebaran	Douglas RD-4	135
Alioth	Douglas RD-4	132
Altair	General Aviation PJ-1	252
Antares	General Aviation PJ-2	251
Arcturus	General Aviation PJ-1	255
Bellatrix	Douglas RD-4	138
Canopus	Douglas RD-4	139
Capella	Douglas RD-4	137
Deneb	Douglas RD-4	134
Mizar	Douglas RD-4	131
Procyon	Douglas RD	227
Rigel	Douglas RD-4	136
Sirius	Douglas RD-1	128
Spica	Douglas RD-4	130
Vega	Douglas RD-4	133

Index

COAST GUARD AIR STATION NEW ORLEANS · FIRST OPERATIONAL HH65 SAR UNIT 1985

U.S. COAST GUARD AIR STATION ASTORIA, OREGON · GUARDIAN OF THE SUNSET EMPIRE

US COAST GUARD · BUREAU de AVION PROJET · GRAND PRAIRIE TEXAS

UNITED STATES COAST GUARD · AIR STATION MIAMI, FLORIDA

SAR

STILL THE BEST · OVER 50 YEARS · 1935 · OF SERVICE · AIR STATION PORT ANGELES

CGAW-1 U.S. COAST GUARD AIRFAC NORFOLK · JAN. 22, 1987

COAST GUARD AIR STATION · ANYWHERE · ANYTIME · CLEARWATER FLORIDA

USCG PTERODACTYLS

COAST GUARD AIR STATION TRAVERSE CITY, MI · GREAT LAKES GUARDIAN

USCG AIR STATION DETROIT · GREAT LAKES REGION · MOTOR CITY SAR

COAST GUARD AIR STATION CHICAGO

A R & S C · ELIZ. CITY